Dodger Dogs
to
Fenway Franks

Dodger Dogs *to* Fenway Franks

...AND ALL THE WIENERS
IN BETWEEN

BOB WOOD

McGRAW-HILL BOOK COMPANY
New York   St. Louis   San Francisco   Auckland
Bogotá   Hamburg   London   Madrid   Mexico   Milan   Montreal
New Delhi   Panama   Paris   São Paulo   Singapore   Sydney   Tokyo   Toronto

3 4 5 6 7 8 9 DOC DOC 8 9 2 1 0 9 8

ISBN 0-07-071696-X

LIBRARY OF CONGRESS CATALOGING-IN-PUBLICATION DATA

Wood, Bob, 1957–
  Dodger dogs to Fenway franks.

  1. Baseball fields—United States—Evaluation.
1. Title.
GV879.5.W66   1988   796.357'06'80973   88-750
ISBN 0-07-071696-X

Book design by Eve Kirch

To my Dad, the best baseball coach I ever played for.
To my Mom, the most dedicated fan that ever watched me play.

CONTENTS

ACKNOWLEDGMENTS

When a junior high school teacher with a list of publications that you could fit inside a thimble gets a book published, there's gotta be a lot of folks around helping out. There were! To the following people a special thanks.

To my agent, David Black, the most significant person in making *Dodger Dogs* a reality. Your eternal optimism and enthusiasm, writes and rewrites through the Sox–Mets Series, even when Schiraldi was getting shelled and Billy Buc was checking behind him in right, kept me pumped. It's amazing what you put up with. Thanks!

To my editor, Tom Miller, who saw enough in this thing to take the chance on a junior high school teacher with a list of publications that you could fit inside a thimble... and then went and made it better.

To Margery Luhrs, also at McGraw-Hill, for letting me keep my odd-ball vocabulary, but mostly for being a nice person.

To Bob Weathers at Seattle Pacific University for helping me out of the starting blocks and convincing me that the idea really had potential.

To the South Kitsap School District in Port Orchard, Washington, for allowing me leave time to add the final touches. If you all were closer to the Midwest and Big Ten football, and if the sun came out a little more often, I'd have probably been a lifer.

To Bill and Mary Jo Abbe for renting me the quietest office on the face of the earth... then letting the monthly rent checks pile up until something actually came in instead of out.

To Ruth Reed and Jana Saunders for words of encouragement at times when I really needed some encouraging.

To Mark, Patty, Zach, and Puget for being good friends.

To Bob Matyas for all the road trips. And for converting me to the Bosox. (Come to think of it, life before the Sox was a lot less frustrating...maybe I shouldn't be thanking you.)

To Murph, a Pirate fan, whose self-proclaimed greatest memory in life is Mazeroski's shot. Thanks for wading through the rough drafts. And not being bored by all my "You think they'll really publish it?" questions.

And to Hendy, who along with Murph was the only person I could find in Seattle dedicated enough to brave the desolate horrors of the Kingdome with me on a regular basis. Thanks for the Hoody's and the Kingbeers.

To Mr. Francis Sinatra for your music and Mr. Bruce Williams for your friendly talk show. For getting me through those empty highways in between the ballparks...especially in Texas.

To Mr. Ernie Harwell for your thoughtfulness. Also for those nights when I was a kid and tuned in to you and Ray Lane doing the Tigers from the corner of Michigan and Trumbull. Baseball's lucky to have such an ambassador.

To Jack Moss at the *Kalamazoo Gazette*. Thanks for the ink!

To my family. My folks, Bob and Connie. My sister, Amy, the Cubbies fan in Wrigleyville, and my brother, Drew, another Bosox backer. I love you all.

Finally to baseball fans across America. It's you that provide baseball its finest asset. Ball players are blessed with God's greatest occupation—loyalty may or may not come with the package. Sportswriters cruise the parks each season; they get a paycheck to sit and watch and write. I guess you could say they have it made too. But it's you fans that really make it happen...whether it be the crazies in South Side Chicago that sing along with Nancy till the final out, the trillions that flood into Dodger Stadium each and every season, everybody who makes sure to wear just the right amount of Cardinal red to Busch, Sox and Cubbie faithfuls who seem to wait forever and ever and ever, or those few that sneak inside the dreary Kingdome....It's your dedication, your loyalty, your love of the game that makes baseball so very special.

FOREWORD

In 41 years of big-league baseball broadcasting I've heard a lot of questions. The one I hear the most is: "What is your biggest lifetime thrill?" My answer: "Walking into a big-league park."

There's something about entering a big-league park that touches every one of us. Sure, it evokes the memories of childhood, but it reminds us, too, that we've all grown up, and in the process we've all loved to learn about our favorite game. Bob Wood has touched me the same way with this book. He has brought that feeling of walking once again into a big-league park.

Each of us is moved by this event in a different way. And Bob has pointed out to me many facets of a ballpark that previously have not concerned me. I haven't bought a ticket to a baseball game since I was 13 years old. (I was always a peanut vendor, batboy, sportswriter, or broadcaster.) But after reading this book I can understand how important ticket prices, scoreboards, parking, concessions, and rest rooms might be. (We freeloaders aren't bothered by many of these problems.)

Bob Wood's journey through the big-league parks is unique. I like the way he describes his own personal reaction to each park, although I disagree with some of his observations and also with some of the grades he gives my favorite and un-favorite parks.

But he approaches each park in a dual role—as a fan and as a school-teacher. The fan part of him tells us his reaction. His schoolteacher role demands that he grade each park. To me, the grading is most fascinating. A park I dislike, Oakland Coliseum, receives a high grade. My personal (and prejudiced) favorite, Tiger Stadium, is midway down the list. I agree with Bob's low rankings of the domes; but he surprises me by putting Jack Murphy Stadium high on his list. However, different opinions make the world go 'round and add a little spice to our conversational life.

Anyway you look at it, Bob Wood deserves an "A" on his own report card for the glimpse he has given us into the big-league baseball parks of America.

—Ernie Harwell

INTRODUCTION

"Such a sojourn is a fantasy that exists somewhere in the
minds of all baseball fans. . . ."

That's how the Chicago White Sox put it after I wrote and told them what I
planned on doing. I'd like to think that they were right. My ultimate dream,
all the major league ballparks in one summer, had to be something that crossed
the minds of a lot of normal folks. I'm just a normal guy with a semi-normal
brain, and I had thought of it a lot. Drizzly, dreary Februarys all over the
civilized world must be filled with dreams of this kind of stuff. It's ideas like
these that get people through 22 straight days of rain, snow, and wet slushy
sidewalks. Without them, ordinary brains would warp and winter bridge-
jumping statistics would, no doubt, soar.

Just wanting to go is not enough. To lounge in Dodger Stadium on a sunny
Sunday afternoon and wolf down Dodger Dogs, to catch a Brewers game in
the company of cold beer and bratwurst in Milwaukee, then roll into Fenway
for a weekend series under blue Boston skies, all in the span of two months,
takes one of two necessities—big bucks or lots of free time.

Well, my relatives who have passed away have done so quietly and poor.
I do, however, have the time—lots of it. For three months each and every
year I can do whatever I please. If I want to turn to mold on the sofa, sip
lemonade, and watch the *Beverly Hillbillies* for 72 straight days I can. If I
want to spend the time driving 535 miles in 24 hours just to see the Rangers
play in 98-degree heat, I can do that too. I even get a paycheck in the process.
Such privileges, however, come at great cost. You see, the rest of the time I
teach ninth-grade history. For nine months out of the year, seven hours a
day, I live with 35 kids all going through puberty at the same time. Three
months of driving all over the continent following baseball or endless hours of
daytime TV and summer couch snoozing are about the only things that keep
my mind from changing into a totally abnormal state. Although the ballpark

1

journey, to most regular nine-to-five guys with real-life responsibilities, will always have to remain a fantasy, for me it was a necessary pilgrimage.

The seed to take such a trip was planted in my mind in 1977, when I was 20 years old. We drove over from my hometown, Kalamazoo, Michigan, to see the Red Sox play the White Sox at Comiskey Park. "We" were Bob Matyas and myself. Back then summers were the Bosox. And every Midwest ballpark that welcomed the Sox lured us as well.

"A most memorable night" could have no finer setting than Comiskey. A true gem in the rough, it isn't convenient, like the newer, more sophisticated stadiums. In fact, it's kept up no better than the dirty broken streets surrounding it. It's not unique in its peculiarities, as is Fenway with the "Green Monster" or, to the north, Wrigley with its precious ivy. While it's the game's oldest, nobody ever says so. The number of World Series played in it rivals Cleveland rather than the Yankees. Nevertheless, the ancient stadium has a certain sincerity about it. Arising out of a seemingly unending highway of slums in South Side Chicago, propped up by decaying walls and creaking iron gates, it's an oasis of green grass, brown dirt, and blue skies. The essence of an urban park, it's a garden submerged in the filth of the city. Gracious in the heart, hard and stubborn on the outside, as charming as the atmosphere is, Comiskey never yields that tough-side-of-town character.

The evening in question was typically Midwestern for August. The day had been beastly muggy. Bob and I sweltered in our three-hour drive over from Kazoo. A cold six-pack and a couple of large economy-size bags of Nacho Cheese Doritos tried to help us forget the weather and prepare us for the game. By the time we got to town the sun had already been scared off by huge, threatening thunder boomers (Midwestern storm clouds). The sky had turned purplish black, and the temperature had plummeted. It looked like we'd be washed away. I was sure we'd be gypped out of not only the ticket cost and a two-way split on the gas but the Red Sox and the White Sox as well—plus Tiant was pitching. Still, the Doritos were eaten and the tickets already paid for, so we went on in.

At some point in the game three people sat down behind us. I can't recall what the trio looked like or what their names were. I do remember that they consisted of two girls and a bearded fellow. All knew, and were talking, baseball. While the Sox were changing pitchers—which Sox it didn't matter since each has a legacy of doing so so often—the three began to talk of ballparks and traveling. I turned around and listened. Since I already was eavesdropping, I figured it wasn't as rude. Plus I could ask legitimate questions and make impressionable comments.

The fellow rather nonchalantly revealed that he had been to all 26 ballparks. That he had seen a game in every major league stadium. At the request of us all, like a sage offering up his wisdom, he gave his opinions of all the stadiums, explained the intricacies of the various parks, and how they flavored the game within. His travels were amazing, his stories grand. For a while I sat silently, almost mesmerized by them. Finally I couldn't wait any longer.

"Which one's best?" I blurted out.

I felt so simple even bringing it up. As if you could just slap a grade on each. But I was in love with Fenway. I'd heard from many folks, especially those in Boston, that it was the majors' best. I merely wanted my belief confirmed, an expert to tell me what I'd already decided. He agreed that Boston's classic ballyard was indeed beautiful. It, along with Wrigley, was definitely one of the two finest. Yankee Stadium also impressed him. I could tell by his manner that he was a Yankee fan. Too bad!

I'll never forget, though, the one he said was his favorite.

"It has character," he told us, "lots of character. Baseball inside it is better than at anyplace else. I know," he reminded us. "I've seen 'em all." He led us on, making us more intent on the precious information he was about to disclose.

"Which is it?" I had to know.

Not too many people would have guessed. But realizing just how important loyalty is in the game, I should have figured it out. It was there in the second level of the Chicago ballpark overlooking another Red Sox–White Sox hit-a-thon that I was told by a real expert just what was the major leagues' most magnificent stadium. The best home for baseball in both leagues, according to this world traveler, was... Comiskey Park. Broken-down, beat-up Comiskey, bordering on the South Side Chicago ghetto, was his MVP (Most Valuable Park). It was his home field. How could I disagree? He was an expert. I wasn't. It was at that moment that I knew someday I, too, would see them all. That I, too, would go to all 26. That I would also become a prophet and enlighten others. While it was just a dream, it had taken root. Somehow, someway, I figured, I'd do it.

In 1985, it had been eight years since that memorable evening in Chicago. On many occasions I had thought about taking the sojourn to all 26. Deep down, unbeknownst to me, it probably affected my decision to become a teacher. I'd hate to think there wasn't some deep-down force like baseball that lured me back into junior high. Anyhow, having taught three years full-time, June of '85 would begin my third summer off. A return to two and a half months of one continual, frustrating round of golf, daily visits with Andy Griffith and the Munsters, and a large amount of front-porch hammock swinging. And since I'd nearly gone loony with boredom during those first couple of summer vacations, my brain was jogged to recall why I'd gone into teaching in the first place—to see the ballparks in one year. It was time; destiny had arrived. I could do it, write my memoirs, retire, then get back to working on my slice and catching up on the Munsters.

So in mid-January I started getting mentally prepared. Sick of pro football playoffs and of the NBA, beginning to mold from Seattle's winter monsoons, I began envisioning springtime. I started thinking of those warm spring days without pro football, when NBA playoffs would be in their third and final month, and Seattle's winter monsoons would be drizzling into springtime showers. Most of all, though, I thought of baseball. ESPN (Entertainment Sports Network) and *Sports Illustrated* and their hints of spring training were getting my brain in the right perspective. It was my incentive; I began my pretrip preparation.

A trip like the one I was dreaming of is as much mental as physical. A journey where you leave the comforts of civilization for two months, dispense with a permanent mailing address, go from a refrigerator to an ice chest, and the only television available is subject to the channel selection of the man behind the bar takes enormous amounts of mental preparation. Ball-game dates are fixed. Stadiums don't move. If a schedule can be set up, it will be. Yet to prepare yourself mentally is a much more complex process. It takes many beers, deep discussions at the tavern, and thorough self-convincing.

As I labored through January and February, Sunday after Sunday of NBA game of the week, I seesawed the idea in my brain. Each night that I went to the local tav for a beer and bounced it off of anybody who would listen, the idea seemed brilliant—especially on the eve of spring training. Each morning I'd wake up to the realities of my situation. My car had 112,000 miles on it. Where would I sleep? What would I eat? Scheduling was sure to be impossible. And that was if it didn't rain.

Lifelong dreams, however, have a way of overcoming such problems. And in April I decided that I'd at least lay the groundwork. By sitting down with both league schedules and drawing up an itinerary, the expedition would be taken out of my hands. Since scheduling couldn't be adjusted, I figured my journey'd be impossible. I wouldn't be able to go and would be off the hook. But something happened when I picked up the schedules. The excitement that grabbed me on that August night in Comiskey eight years before rekindled. The mysterious reason that lured me into teaching revitalized. And with renewed interest the planning began. I decided I'd map out the West Coast swing first. Starting in Seattle, I'd work my way down the coast to Oakland and San Francisco. Then I'd hit L.A., Anaheim, and San Diego. If I couldn't make the West Coast run in a two-week span after school got out, the trip would be impossible.

Sitting in the Apogee Tavern, the place where my slow-pitch softball team hangs out, I ordered up a draft and went to work. I laid out all the necessary items—a Rand McNally map of the United States, both leagues' season schedules, a couple of number two pencils, and the *Sporting News* spring-training issue. I felt like a mad scientist on the brink of some ludicrous discovery. On the back side of a daily menu I sketched a copy of the West Coast. Stars were placed where California's five ballparks stood. I matched dates with home schedules, listed, shuffled, and crossed my fingers. Like some magical formula, it all fell perfectly into place. I shivered and laughed a sinister mad-scientist-type laugh. People at the bar stared at me. The die had been cast. With the West Coast swing falling into place, my plans were on. I'd open June 16 at the Kingdome in Seattle. Three days later I'd be in the Bay Area, first the Giants then the A's. Both were at home. A day off would get me comfortably down to L.A. for two more games. Another day off would allow a leisurely drive to San Diego. California scheduling not only worked, it did so at a pleasant pace. I'd even have time to go to Disneyland in between ball games. It'd be a teacher's dream, a vacation within a vacation.

The following night I planned out the rest of the trip. The West Coast swing had been a piece of cake. Now if it got scrubbed, it'd only be because I'd weenied out. Phase two would be America's heartland—right up the gut. Texas on Independence Day. The Rangers and Astros could be reached easily in four days from San Diego and were together at opposite ends of a home stand. If I didn't evaporate in the heat along the way, both were possible. The same was true of Kansas City and St. Louis. Even the Cubbies were in on time. The White Sox were out, but I could catch them on the return trip. I was making my way back to Kalamazoo anyway.

Eleven ballparks and over 5,000 miles of the good old U.S.A. covered, I figured I'd be tired. Well, major league baseball had a break. Why not me? A week in Michigan with the folks is always good for the soul and tummy. So a week and a half at All-Star time was scheduled. The All-Star game was being played in Minneapolis. It wasn't far from Kazoo—what the heck, I'd go to it. I just hoped that the ticket scalpers would take Visa.

Halfway through the journey things had fallen neatly into place... at least on paper. As for the second half, I wasn't so sure. While problems with that long Western haul would deal with 600 miles a day on the road, in "frying an egg on the sidewalk" temperatures, the Eastern swing would feature added roadblocks. There, other issues would haunt me—mainly where to sleep. And how to survive the sleep. Lodging in Detroit, New York, and Philadelphia was bound to be life-threatening. Scheduling ball games was priority number one though getting there alive would just be gravy. So I mapped out my Eastern tour... the heartland of the majors. Again perfection. Despite a four-in-a-row shot at the end, major league baseball was good to me. And I'd even get to see a pair of M's vs. Sox games at Fenway.

My expedition was officially scheduled. It'd begin June 16, 1985, at 1:35 P.M. in Seattle, Washington, and end sometime around sundown, August 6, in Atlanta. I was pumped!

With the schedule complete, I turned to other less important factors that needed attending to. My '77 Pinto was pushing 112,000 miles. It hadn't gone 65 miles per hour or over a steep hill in years, let alone taken on the Continental Divide. It'd never survive a worldwide crusade like the one I had in mind. Worse yet, my financial status was hard-pressed to get me to a Mariners game on a regular basis, never mind traipsing about the whole continent in search of baseball. However, with life's ambitions at stake, people make adjustments. Mountains are climbed, rivers forged, and, in this case, automobile loans taken out.

Ideally a Chevrolet seemed to touch the heart—baseball, apple pie, and all. But I did want something that didn't need to be dragged into the mechanics at each stop along the way. So it wasn't long before I'd migrated over to the oriental lots along with all the other true-blue Americans. It wasn't easy ...for 20 years my dad raised our family on paychecks signed by General Motors. Just thinking Japanese made me feel like a traitor. Yet with each glance at an American midget car, my guilt would evaporate. Why this country can't make a good small car that doesn't look like a gourd and run like a lemon is beyond me. But it can't! So I checked out the Toyota dealer.

And there I found it, a metallic-silver dream machine. Forty-eight miles per gallon, front-wheel drive for the rugged mountains, air-conditioning to combat Texas heat, four-speaker stereo system to rock away the boredom, and cruise control to preserve the muscles in my instep; I purchased options with a small Toyota Tercel attached. Although it struggled to get from 0 to 60, with Michigan State stickers slapped on all the windows and a little vinyl cover for the steering wheel, it was a beaut. If New York City traffic didn't eat us up, Texas sun didn't melt us, or we didn't end up being sold as parts out of the back end of some van in downtown Detroit, me and my car were gonna see 'em all. Whether either of us returned in the same condition that we left didn't really much matter.

Obstacle one was conquered: I had wheels. As for my second problem, it'd been compounded severely by the solution to the first. Being a teacher, I don't roll in the dough. At least not the green kind. So cutting financial corners became my new priority.

First off—where to sleep? Motels are probably the most overinflated ripoffs in the United States—$39.95 for a bed as soft as the front seat of a Ford pickup truck, a television set that gets three fuzzy channels, and a shower that inevitably runs out of hot water before you get to washing your hair just doesn't seem fair. Actually all I needed was a place to sack out and shower. While I'd never taken on such a venture before, my summer Bosox trips had taught me how to live on the road and still afford peanuts and hot dogs at the ballpark. Experience said that a tent and sleeping bags were as comfortable as most hotel beds. And that outdoor showers usually lasted as long as the ones inside.

So as in the past, KOAs (Kampgrounds of America), that fast-food chain of the camping world, came to the rescue. Only when my spine began to deteriorate from resting on tree roots for too long, or when setting up a tent at 2 A.M. in a pouring thunderstorm after a 600-mile drive, would I bend to the pressures of convenience. Then and only then would I lower myself to pay for a room. When I did it'd be the other modern-day lodging equivalent of McDonald's, a Motel 6. So I equipped myself with two essential Bibles—the asphalt campers' guide (*KOA Directory*) and the manual to those little clone closets about the United States (*Motel 6 Register*). They'd become my two blueprints to staying alive. Along with the *Rand McNally Road Atlas*, which can get anybody anywhere under any conditions, they'd be my trilogy of survival—the very works of literature upon which my existence would depend.

With the cost of sleeping frayed by KOA, and all my nourishment coming from ballpark dogs and peanuts, I had another major expense to contend with. I needed to get inside each ballpark without going bankrupt in the process. I figured all stadiums couldn't be like Seattle's. At the Kingdome I usually pay $5.00 for a ticket, then sit anywhere I please inside the empty place. In a normal baseball town ticket cost and availability would likely pose a problem.

So I decided to ask major league baseball to lend a hand. At the Mariner PR office I picked up a listing of all the leagues' public relations people. To each one I typed a short, yet sincere, request that explained my circumstances. I was a junior high schoolteacher and a baseball fan. That, I hoped, would win me instant sympathy. My wish was simple. I merely requested complimentary admittance to their stadium, a stadium that when I was there would probably have as many empty seats in it as filled ones. Tossing in at the end that I was writing a book on my experiences would be a meager attempt at intimidating them into helping me. I didn't bother to explain that I had the grammar skills of an eighth grader and hadn't written much more than bathroom hall passes since college. Still, I hoped my little ending might sway the undecided.

By the fifteenth of May, about a month before D Day, all were finished, typed, and mailed. I really had no idea just how the majors would react. Part of me expected, hoped, and prayed for a ticket from every park. Certainly a place like the Kingdome, with 36,000 empty seats a night, and Cleveland's stadium, with twice that, could afford me. The more realistic part of me said "no way." I was dreaming if I really thought they'd help. The two sides spent several nights fighting for recognition while I drifted off to sleep. Eventually the pessimistic side won out. I convinced myself my requests were idiotic. Baseball was a business not a charity. Even with the itinerary enclosed, there was no way they'd believe it. My pleas would probably be posted on the office wall, a joke for all to laugh at while they worked.

Those days after sending out the requests were the most nerve-racking. Two and three times daily I'd check the mailbox—looking, worrying, doubting, then checking again. Meanwhile I bombarded friends with paranoid questions.

"What do you think? Will they send me tickets?" Before there was time to answer I'd ask another. "Why in the world would they send me tickets?" As if anybody had the foggiest notion. I paid attention only to those who thought they would. Then the next day, just to feel a little more secure, I'd ask the same people the same question. It made those troubled times pass easier. Funny, most of those who really loved the game, those who braved the empty horrors of the Kingdome on a regular basis, expected aid for my journey. Those who merely saw baseball as another professional sport, no different from what the Seahawks or the Sonics played, thought not.

At last, six days after the letters went out, I got my first response. Up in the corner, the return address was a little orange and blue Tiger. It was Detroit, my first love, the team that had gotten me through puberty. I was petrified to open it. What would they say? How could they say no? Why would they say yes? Finally, convinced of total failure, I ripped open the Tiger-striped envelope and read, "We sincerely hope you enjoy your trip, Mr. Wood. However, it just isn't our policy to give out tickets in an instance such as this." My heart sank. I knew it. . . I was a peon. Nobody listened to peons. My request as a teacher, as a baseball fan, even my threat of a book had failed. The rest no doubt would be the same. I wanted so badly just to cry. So I did.

For the next week or two more letters poured in. Up in the left-hand corner of each was the ball club's insignia. They were neat to look at, but all said the same. Cubbies, Atlanta, and even my Red Sox, all cordial; all no, it wasn't team policy. Some wished me a good trip. They were sorry they just couldn't help out. Others bombed me with a flat-out denial. When Cleveland wrote back noting that their afternoon Oriole game was "Tribe Sun Visor Day" and that it wasn't policy to aid the needy, my hopes sank to a murky low. A place with 65,000 empty seats a game and all they could offer was full-price admission and some cheap sun visor. If the Indians were unwilling or unable, then how could those who didn't have the luxury of a huge park and nobody coming to it do any better? Even so, Christmas in May, running to the mailbox to find three more rejections on colorfully headed stationery was fun. At least they cared enough to write.

Still in shock from the Indian rejection, after eight no's in a row, somebody actually said yes. And not only that, but Ms. Van Aman wrote, "The Phillies will be happy to leave you two tickets.... Enjoy the game." With the ice broken, flood gates opened. L.A., Milwaukee, California—all in a day, all yes. A no here and there, but most were happy to help me out and would leave me two tickets. Some, like the Mets, said it simply: "Left two tickets for the July 31 game against Montreal." Others believed my excursion was fantastic. The White Sox referred to it as "That great, fun, and wonderful experience." Still others hoped for a copy of my writing. How little they knew about my authoring experiences!

With the personal invites, my trip took on a new meaning. To actually be asked to stop by a ballpark I'd never seen, in a town I'd never been in, by people I'd never spoken with carried with it the shot of excitement I needed. I was pumped, if not for Cleveland, then at least for Philly. In the end only four clubs ignored me; both the Canadians, San Diego, and my own hometown Mariners. Of those who wrote back, the Giants, Dodgers, Angels, Rangers, Astros, Royals, Brewers, White Sox, Phillies, Pirates, and New York's two teams sent a pair of tickets with their invitation. Suddenly I felt important. And I had another, even better reason for wanting school to end...as if I needed one.

Next on the agenda was writing a book. It had been part of the dream. Proof that I was a ballpark expert. Plus I figured it'd be a great way to tax-deduct the whole thing.

The layout of my masterpiece was simple. Something I'd pondered many a time in the past eight years. For most practical purposes, teaching has not really kept me in tune with the real world. At the ripe old age of 28 I had nearly become obsolete. Actually only one by-product was of any use at all— that "art" of grading things. Those people who condemn teachers for summers off, a week in April, two in December, four days at Thanksgiving, and an unlimited number of snow days and make-believe Monday holidays have no idea as to the horrors of grading papers. Reading 150 reports on Thomas Jefferson, nearly all of which are copied straight out of the encyclopedia, and having to put a comment on each is indefinable torture. However, with the help of lifesaving seminars on skimming, I've learned quite well to evaluate without "losing it" in the process.

Besides grading *World Book Encyclopedia* rewrites, report cards have also become a personal forte. I figured I could, God forbid, write an objective report card on anything. So, why not ballparks? All I needed was to decide on the criteria. What were the necessary categories that made up all ballparks? Okay, I thought, I'm a baseball fan. I am a normal hot-dog-munching, beer-drinking, peanut-shucking bleacherite.

What do I look for in a ballpark? What is it that first hits me? That's easy—the stadium itself. That first view of a ballpark always makes me shudder. The excitement of peering into something as huge and colorful is an unequaled thrill. Thus, the ballpark itself would have to be my first category—the so-called "layout." And while I was at it, why not upkeep as well! A baseball stadium should be clean. It didn't have to be as antiseptic as a hospital operating room. But it certainly should be clean enough so that the stench didn't mix with the grilling dogs and spoil the flavor. Either way, *Layout and Upkeep* was a good intro to each park.

Next: once inside, no matter the ballpark, the first thing I do even before getting in the hotdog line is to look at the grass. That explosion of green, the fresh scent of the grass rising up from below, it's always been my second ballpark chill. A virtual garden in the concrete confines of a stadium, the turf is so important to a ballpark's total feel. *Ball Field*, I figured, would be a good second category. And if it was going to pass, it just better not be plastic.

What then would be category number three? After making it through the packed-in walkways and taking that first look at the grass below, a seat search always follows. The find remains yours for the day. Regardless, if it's way out in the center-field nosebleed section or in the high-priced boxes down behind the third-base dugout, a hard, wooden-slatted chair or a comfy contoured orange plastic fold-up job, your seat is an essential part of a day at the ole ballyard. So *Seating* is an essential part of a ballpark's makeup.

After you find the right seat and settle in for batting practice, your eyes wander about the place. Inevitably, they come to rest on that ominous supplier of information, the stadium's front page—its scoreboard. More than any other item, the scoreboard is an extension of the stadium's consciousness. If the atmosphere is lifeless, usually the scoreboard will be as well. On the other hand, if a feeling of pure baseball oozes from the stadium, the scoreboard is usually real and traditional. A crazy place will have a crazy board, a quiet place a silent one. Most of the shows they put on, however strange or normal, will usually be a look into the very heart of the park. An underrated ballpark necessity, *Scoreboard*, I decided, would be category four.

With rears, eyes, and ears satisfied, next it'd be the tummy's turn. A ballpark dog and an ice-cold beer go with a ball game like sunshine and green grass. They give baseball that "I don't care if I ever get back" allure. For a stadium to shine in the eats department, it has to cover four basics: 1: Accessibility; 2: Selection; 3: Taste; 4: Cost. A hot dog, regardless of its quality, must be available without having to get up and go get it. Sometimes when the old stomach cries for another beer and a dog with mustard, the score is tied in the bottom of the seventh, Clemens is on the mound, a flock of Blue Jays cram the bases, and George Bell's at the plate. A loaded-down vendor better be somewhere close by. Less significant than accessibility, but a nice little luxury nonetheless, is the variety of food offered. Third, good food must taste good or it isn't quality stuff. Finally, I'd take a look at food costs. To do so I'd go back to basics. A good day's intake for a normal fan, I figured, might be two hot dogs, two 16-ounce beers, and some peanuts. So I decided to total their cost, then index it against the rest of the stadiums. *Food* would be my most scientific category.

While the game at hand and temperature of beer are more important, a good stay at the ballpark is also influenced by the folks who work the place. Ushers who usher and are easy to find are necessary—especially to a lost soul. Vendors should be fast and efficient. The aisles up in the stands flooded with them. Underneath, pleasant people peddling souvenirs and food provide another nice touch. Security that secures rather than bullies, and is approachable, make for a safer feel—particularly around many of the not-so-tidy neighborhoods. Taken together, the actions of those who wear the team colors in the stands are as important as those with the uniforms on the field. Good *Ballpark Employees* give the place a touch of class.

Finally, I wondered how to favorably compare the Kingdome with Tiger Stadium? Wasn't there anything Seattle's monstrosity was better at? There had to be. I thought, "What was it that I feared most as a kid back in the sixties and now in the eighties in those Eastern stadiums?" The answer was easy: "Going to the bathroom and parking the car." Each was a hazard with life-threatening implications. *Facilities*, I decided, would judge both. I wasn't excited at what would have to be the condemnation of Comiskey and Tiger Stadium for creepy bathrooms and lousy, if any, parking lots. But by combining them into a single category I could give some of the newer, "more respectable" places their antiseptic A. And provide moms and dads driving four kids to the ballyard in the family station wagon something special to check out.

With seven categories from bathrooms to ball fields covered, the single most important one—atmosphere—was still left. Those feelings that float about the place, while maybe not touchable, are just as real. They're why the game's so romantic. They keep people coming back, parking in the same dingy front yards, munching the same stale peanuts, and braving the same dangerous rest rooms year after year. They provide a special allure that almost tugs at your shirt sleeve and says a day inside me will wash all your troubles away. At some parks it may be a resilience to a seedy section of town that gives it such a special character. At others it might be the shape and smell of the field or the presence of a wall or a monument. Always, the atmosphere is the people inside, the fans and their intensity for the game... whether packed in by the tens of thousands as in Dodger Stadium or scattered about almost isolated by the masses of empty chairs as in Cleveland. For the sake of fair grading, *Atmosphere* would merely count as one-eighth of the report card. Deep down, though, it would be the stadium's most crucial test. And the one that mattered most to me.

With categories fixed, all that was left was how to grade 'em. Back to the classroom. I decided to letter grade each, divide the total, and produce an average. The final grade would be my opinion of how all the major league ballparks compare. By assigning point totals: D = 65, C = 75, B = 85, and A = 95—I could send a report card home to Milwaukee just like the one Billy's mom gets. As a teacher my philosophy's always been, nobody fails that tries. I figured all ballparks tried, so I didn't have the right to fail any. By the same token, it takes an extra special effort to pull an A. Here, as well as in the classroom, they wouldn't be tossed out like confetti. Also, to separate the most magnificent from the mere great, and the pure pathetic from the just plain lousy, I would assess an A+ and a D−. Worth 100 points, an A+ would reveal "par excellence" in a category, while a D−, at 60 points, would show the way to the bottom of the barrel.

All avenues were laid out. My single expertise as a teacher, that of grading papers and writing report cards, would finally come in handy in the real world of baseball, hot dogs, and peanuts in the bleachers. My sojourn, which had given direction to a career, was ready to take place. For those who wished that they could see the major league game from Boston clear across to L.A., I would be a test pilot. For fans who dreamed of sampling the differences between a peanut packaged in Kansas City and one raised in Georgia, of sucking down a Coors in Jack Murphy and emptying 16 ounces of Old Style Beer at Wrigley, my travels would be a guide. My thoughts, my feelings would hopefully inspire others to become teachers, and thus save the educational system within the United States. Then in those days of sunshine and baseball, of sitting out in the bleachers munching bratwurst and catching rays, when everybody else puts in an honest nine-to-five, they, too, might have the pleasure that I was about to experience... to fulfill a lifelong dream.

REPORT CARD

	BALL PARK	R	%	L/O	BF	SE	SC	FO	BE	F	ATM	PTS
A	Dodger Stadium	1	93	A+	A	A	B	C	A+	A+	A	745
A	Royals Stadium	1	93	A+	C	A	B	A+	A	A+	A	745
A−	Milwaukee County Stadium	3	91	B	B	B	B	A+	A+	B	A+	725
A−	Baltimore Memorial Stadium	3	91	B	A+	A	A+	B	A	D	A+	725
B+	Wrigley Field	5	86	C	A	A+	A+	C	C	D	A+	685
B+	Fenway Park	5	86	B	A	A+	A+	D	C	D	A+	685
B	Oakland Coliseum	7	85	B	C	D	A+	A+	B	B	B	680
B	Jack Murphy Stadium	7	85	B	A+	D	A+	B	C	B	B	680
B	Anaheim Stadium	9	84	A	A	B	D−	C	A+	A+	D	675
B	Busch Memorial Stadium	10	83	B	C	C	B	C	B	B	A	660
B	Comiskey Park	10	83	D	B	D	A+	A+	B	D−	A+	660
B	Tiger Stadium	10	83	B	A	D	C	B	A	D−	A+	660
B−	Yankee Stadium	13	82	B	B	A	A	D−	C	D	A	655
C+	Arlington Stadium	14	79	C	C	A	A	D−	A	D	C	635
C+	Olympic Stadium	15	78	B	D−	D	B	C	B	A	C	625
C+	Riverfront Stadium	16	78	A	D	C	D−	B	C	A+	D	620
C+	Veterans Stadium	17	77	D	D−	D	B	B	A	C	B	615
C+	Three Rivers Stadium	18	76	B	D	C	C	B	B	C	D	610
C	Shea Stadium	19	74	C	B	C	A	D	D−	C	D	595
C−	Metrodome	20	73	B	D−	D	D−	C	B	B	B	580
C−	Fulton County Stadium	21	72	D	C	C	C	B	D−	C	D	575
C−	Cleveland Municipal Stadium	22	70	C	D	C	D−	C	D	D	B	565
D+	Kingdome	23	69	D	D	D	C	C	C	C	D−	555
D+	Candlestick Park	23	69	D	C	C	D	C	D−	C	D	555
D+	Astrodome	26	67	C	D−	D	C	D	D−	C	D−	535
D+	Exhibition Stadium	26	67	C	D−	D−	D−	D−	C	B	D−	535

R = rank; % = final average; L/O = layout and upkeep; BF = ball field; SE = seating; SC = scoreboard; FO = food; BE = ballpark employees; F = facilities; ATM = atmosphere; PTS = points.

1

KINGDOME,
SEATTLE MARINERS

Let Me Out

REPORT CARD	Kingdome
	BASEBALL PARK
June 16, 85 vs Orioles	*Seattle Mariners*
GAME	BASEBALL CLUB

CATEGORY	GRADE	POINTS
Layout and Upkeep	D	65
Ball Field	D	65
Seating	D	65
Scoreboard	C	75
Food	C	75
Ballpark Employees	C	75
Facilities	C	75
Atmosphere	D-	60
Total Points		555
Average		69

D+	23rd
FINAL GRADE	RANK

"Only the greedy concrete contractors who rushed this thing
up could truly appreciate it.... No wonder nobody goes."

PREGAME THOUGHTS

What a place to start from... Here I was in Seattle, the city of April showers
throughout the year, of empty seats at baseball games, of Seahawk fans in a
Seahawk town, about to drop their second baseball franchise in 20 years, due
at least in part to that hideous concrete monstrosity—the Kingdome. At least
things would only get better.

In 1981, fresh out of Michigan State, and the Midwest's long, hot summers, I headed out to the Pacific Northwest. Why Washington, I'm not really
sure. I was just another first-year teacher in a state where Toyotas and Hondas
were beginning to hammer away at an already oozy economy. Chevys and
Fords weren't selling, consequently auto plants weren't hiring. Parents weren't
having children; schools weren't expanding. Teachers had decided to stop retiring, and I'd just graduated. A history teacher with a coaching minor, I was
still dazed that no longer would every Friday night be a giant kegger across the
hall and every Saturday afternoon an excuse to finish up Friday night's keg.
After five years of having fun, I finally had to make a real-life career decision.
Not only that, I had to make it in a state that hadn't hired a teacher in years,
let alone one with a major as worthless as mine.

Prospects seemed poor. So I decided to do what most college graduates
who based their major on a Friday-less schedule would do—I ran away from
home. The only problem was where to run to. The Midwest was swooning.
Michigan didn't have a janitor's job available, much less a teacher's. I had
already been East, but still had some of that explorer blood in me. Reliable
sources informed me that public education south of Ohio consisted of mem-
orizing the words to "Dixie." Anywhere in the Confederacy was out. With
only one other American choice, I turned westward. Because USC and UCLA
pounded on the Big Ten every Rose Bowl, I'd never live in California, so I
picked Washington. I packed up everything I owned, a whole Pinto-full-of-
things, and headed out for Seattle.

While my westward movement was providing new opportunities—a job,
some of that West Coast sunshine (I obviously never peeked at a Seattle weather
report), and a real hometown baseball team in the Mariners—I was leaving
behind a lot of memories. And a lot of them were baseball ones.

For the whole family, baseball had been much more than just a game. It
had been a summer way of life. Milwood Little League in Kalamazoo, as *Bad*

News Bears-ish as it was, still did its character-building job on me from ages nine to fifteen. For Drew, my five-years-younger brother, and for me, those summers were spent daily at the ball diamonds. Dad coached both of us to league championships. And on a couple of occasions took All-Star teams to district play. He was the best coach I ever played for.

Mom headed up bake sales, was a team mother three seasons, and put her time in at the concession stand. With all that to do, she still never missed a game that either of us played in. Whether it was one of those cold, wet, windy May openers where spring refused to wilt into summer, or a hot humid July night, she was always there. If we played at the same time, one of us would get Mom in the first three innings, the other for the last four.

As for my sister, Amy, she also got in on the act. A decent second-base person for the summer rec softball team, she came around too soon to play girl's Little League softball. It wasn't proper yet for girls to be athletes, so she sat up in the stands and watched ball games, ate snow cones, and worked at the ice-cream social. Once she was even voted "Little League Queen."

After Drew and I grew out of Little League, we moved on to the big time— high school ball. Nevertheless, it remained a family affair. Mom kept her string of consecutive appearances intact. Amy came when her boyfriend wasn't running track. And Dad traded the third-base coaching box for a bleacher seat. Seems like there always was a Wood or two watching.

While neither of us tore up the Big Six Conference, both Drew and I were pretty good center fielders. I had the better range, he the stronger arm. Unfortunately, neither of us really hammered the ball. Absolutely void of power, I just .265'd my way through each season. Still, I was tough to strike out and must've set a career conference record for sacrifice bunts and infield singles. And my claim to fame: I even stole home once in my senior year. For six seasons, with a two-year gap between us, fifth-place finishes in a six-team league and lifetime .265 averages kept us from being discovered by the big leagues. But we had a grand time just the same.

Playing wasn't my only love affair with baseball. As a kid I lived with a transistor radio. The voices of Ray Lane and Ernie Harwell were always play-by-playing Detroit Tiger games around the house. Night after summer night I'd join the pair. They put me in touch with the majors and offered some incentive for collecting so many bubble-gum cards. Up through junior high, I knew every Tiger statistic that ever was, every Tiger player that ever played, and in '68, "Year of the Tiger," when they took the Series, practically every pitch of every game.

After seeing Fenway in '74, the Tigers faded and I adopted the Sox. Road-tripping all about the Midwest, I found out that it wasn't Fenway that de-stroyed Red Sox pitching. They got hammered everywhere! Despite those eternal Sox frustrations, I was still in love with baseball. Whether it was to play or watch, listen to or read about in the boxes, the game was magic to me. Never did I plan on leaving it all behind. Little did I know, by moving to Seattle I was doing the next best thing.

Nestled softly between the Cascade Mountains' pine-covered slopes and the salt waters of lovely Puget Sound, Washington's "Emerald City" is an aesthetic jewel. In June of '81, when my packed-up Pinto putted into town, I was mesmerized by it all. I'd never witnessed anything so beautiful. Mountain ranges climb up all about the city. Water is everywhere—salt, fresh, and rain. Neat old ferry boats, something Michigan had never shown me, plod between the many green-covered islands. Slow-poking it all around Puget Sound, their deep horns cut the fog and provide the Northwest a special charm. To the south, Mount Rainier thrusts up into the heavens. It's huge! As dominating to Seattle as the "Green Monster" is to Fenway, the mountain snow-cones all of Puget Sound. Even sporting a climate where the gray morning drifts into gray afternoon, which drifts into gray evening—when the sun goes down, I think; it's so seldom seen—Seattle is purely beautiful.

In a baseball sense, though, Seattle provides as much tradition to the game as might be found in downtown Moscow. Having grown up where box scores in the newspaper's sports section were more significant than front-page world wars, I'd moved to a place where doing the wave was the foremost ballpark occupation. Seattle has absolutely no appreciation for baseball. As a town it neither understands nor supports the game, all the while insisting on its right to keep it. The city government refuses to allow baseball to pack up and leave again; still, folks go in apathetic groups of only 8,000 to watch. Newspapers and television stations, even during football's exhibition season, play it second fiddle to the football Seahawks. Regulated to second-page sports columns, the cellar-dwelling M's are forgotten in the glow of glorious Seahawk fourth-place finishes. Not exactly sure why Seattleites resist what so many others crave, I can only sit back and sort out the feeble excuses.

"Seattle's too small for the big leagues," some say. "We can't be expected to keep up with L.A. or New York." How 'bout just trying to match Milwaukee for a season? Seattle can't do it.

Others moan, "The Mariners are lousy. When they start winning we'll start showing up." Had that been in vogue in Chicago, both Comiskey and Wrigley would've closed down for nonsupport years ago. The M's have gone only a decade without making it to the Series; the Cubs seem to be closing in on a century.

A real biggie with the pro-wave masses: "We've got the Hawks, who needs the Mariners?" What a joke! Pro football captures all the charm of international kick boxing. Plus the two seasons overlap for only a couple of weeks.

It's just that doing the wave is more fun at Seahawk games. There you don't have to pay attention to figure out what's going on.

My personal favorite, and what seems most typical for such a cruddy attitude is "Seattle's just too beautiful for baseball. With mountains to the east and west, snowskiing, waterskiing, sailing, and the ocean within a couple of hours' drive, there are better things to do than to waste time watching the Mariners." Once in a while maybe...but not every day. Half the time the mountains are unseeable due to an ever-present gray that covers the city. And how many people own sailboats or ski every single day of baseball season? Priorities are just a bit confused. Boston surely provides as many cultural benefits as Seattle. Cape Cod is as naturish as Puget Sound. Yet at Fenway a fan can't enter on a $5.00 ticket and then climb down into one of a hundred open front-row box seats. They're already filled. Simply put, the Mariners, as bad as they may have been in the past, deserve better than the Pacific Northwest.

The only real support for the Seattle disease of nonsupport is the ugliest structure on the face of the earth. A concrete glob, the Kingdome is a festering pimple on one of America's loveliest urban faces; it exists to test true baseball loyalty.

Still, as repulsive as the Kingdome is, baseball inside it endures. Within its gray cavernous walls, locked away from the fresh saltwater breezes and patchy Seattle sunshine, I still enjoy the game; I guess even concrete closets can be adapted to with baseball at stake. Unfortunately I reside within a Northwest minority, the 7,000 or 8,000 a night who apparently feel as I do, that baseball in the Kingdome is better than no baseball at all. We few keep coming back because the game, which has triumphed over far worse circumstances in its past, still offers us its special magic. As for the rest of those poor misguided souls who would rather complain about the M's lack of talent, they can go on skiing and sailing, digging clams, and feebly searching the clouds to find the mountains. That, or they can just stay at home and wait for those unbelievably exciting Seahawk Sundays...all eight of 'em.

LAYOUT AND UPKEEP: GRADE D

Rivaling Olympic Stadium in Montreal as the largest free-standing concrete structure in the world, the Kingdome is not Seattle-ish.

Aside from San Francisco, West Coast cities look wholly modern. As a rule they lack the old-building charm that embraces the East. For some it's even tough to tell if construction began before 1960. In many respects Seattle breaks the mold. Stately Victorian houses hover above the city up on Capital Hill. Pike Street Market hustles and bustles through the day, much like the streets of Frisco's China Town. Close by the Dome, Ivar's old clock tower and Union Station stand. Each look almost colonial, something you might expect to see in downtown Philadelphia.

Seattle's not without the big boys though. Skyscrapers dot its skyline. The brand-new, big black Columbia Center, 76 stories tall, shadows the city. Ten blocks north, centering the 1963 World's Fair grounds, is Seattle's calling card— the Space Needle. Tall, thin, strange, and groovy; it looks like something a drug-induced celebration of the sixties might come up with. From the Needle to Market, Seattle is about as architecturally hodgepodgeish as the West Coast gets. Perched on a pleasant little waterfront, it actually looks like a miniature San Francisco without the cable cars.

The Dome, on the other hand, looks more like the work of Stone Age man. Bad enough when first built, its roof, now covered with a coat of white paint, makes for an even sillier sight. Chain-link gates at the stadium base allow folks to ease their way inside—kind of like slow torture. Heavy concrete walkways rise up the outside and encircle the stadium. Trudging up them provides a last-gasp view of nature before entering into the pits of despair. On a cool summer evening, as evenings usually are in the Northwest, gazing out at the town's twinkling lights, at the big old ferry boats plodding in and out of port, opening up the steel doors and entering into the Dome creates all the excitement of walking into a tomb.

Just a circular, covered, concrete glob, the Dome makes you seriously consider the idea of random drug-testing all modern-day architects, or at least letting only people who know what a baseball is design ballparks.

BALL FIELD: GRADE D

A standard necessity that results from blocking out the sun, the Kingdome floor is fake. Pretty much the norm as polygrass goes, surrounded by a phony red tartan track, any reminder of nature is quickly replaced by an indoor-tennis-club atmosphere. Only the three bases, home plate, and the pitcher's mound, all surrounded by real live dirt, remind one that outdoors there exists something organic that might benefit from Seattle's many showers.

I grew up on grass. I played on it; I watched others play on it. Until Seattle, other than on the tube, it was all I knew. And while the stadium has mega-problems, the one I've had the hardest time adjusting to is its plastic floor. Baseball under a roof as opposed to blue sky is criminal, but I've adapted. Since Seattle skies are seldom blue, I tell myself I am better off warm and dry than molding in a constant drizzle. Although the stadium itself is pure ugly, I've learned to handle that as well. Before the game I stop across the street at

Sneaker's Tavern and have a couple or I just close my eyes and feel my way inside. Either way I can live with its pathetic looks.

But the grass—I can't get used to. It neither looks right nor smells real. It kills any baseball feel that the Dome struggles to create. And it changes the way the game is played. It turns normal ground-ball outs into two-hop doubles to the outfield wall. Gutsy fielders on grass turn into one-hop play-it-safe guys on the plastic turf. Bunts become worthless force-outs; timely bad-hop singles, prayers of the past. While its proponents claim that fake grass speeds up the game, allows Harry Reynolds to bebop his way to 35 more stolen bases per season, and makes things more exciting, for me it only cheapens baseball.

SEATING: GRADE D

One of the Dome's few pluses is that it actually drives people away. Whether it's the perennial crummy record of the M's, Seattle's lousy baseball attitude, or the Dome's homely looks that keep numbers so low, there is a hidden lining in it all; one that the truest of baseball fans can readily accept. Buying a ticket to a specific seat means nothing with the M's in town. With so many empty ones around, nobody cares where you sit. For five years now the price of a seat in the nosebleed section has allowed me, without so much as a hassle, to watch baseball from the baseline boxes.

My first Mariner game back in '81, I sat in a prepaid, two-month-early-order box seat. Aside from its original inflated price, and a couple of $1.50 early-order surcharges, the seat was all right. At least until I found out that the guy next to me, who was supposed to be miles away in the third level, bought his ticket ten minutes before game time. Since then I've learned. Now when I stroll up to a lineless ticket booth during "The Star-Spangled Banner" I ask for a seat way up top, miles from the action. If the polite man inside the little house asks if I have a preference where, I always answer, "It doesn't really matter, I'll figure that out when I get inside."

Actually, Kingdome seating is typical of the newer, multipurpose places. Since a baseball diamond and football field don't have a lot in common, none of the views are great. Too much foul territory prevents that Wrigley Field look. But plastic and comfortable, with plenty of leg room and wide aisles, lower boxes at my special cheap seat prices are nevertheless a good steal.

Unfortunately, as you span back from the field, and into the second and third levels above, seat quality and view drastically decline. General admission seats, as well as a number of the back-half reserved seats, are cold, hard aluminum benches. Not only that, vertical obstruction abounds. Toward the rear of both lower levels, fly balls vanish, lost behind the low-hanging roof.

To counter the obstructions, the Dome features the world's largest accumulation of hanging television sets outside of Sears. Positioned nearly every 20 seats apart, they hang from the roof of the second level, which is the floor of the third level, and from the roof of the first, which is the floor of the second. Watching a ball game underneath them is a bit like doing so with all the comforts of home—minus the comforts and what little baseball atmosphere your living room might provide.

SCOREBOARD: GRADE C

Keeping in line with a lackluster consistency that runs through the gray walls and phony turf, the Kingdome's scoreboard show is boring.

Wedged between the gray concrete ceiling and gray concrete walls, the scoreboard hangs high above the center-field seats. Completely engulfing it is a barrage of advertisements: the Marlboro Man, Coca-Cola, McDonald's french fries—the billboard pileup looks like what you'd see along an interstate highway. Aided by a boomy sound system, it probably does a better job selling cigarettes than baseball.

The system does, however, have one saving grace. At its center is a huge Mitsubishi Diamond Vision screen. Diamond Vision—its crystal-clear and colored pictures can be a godsend to a boring ball game. Highlights from someplace more exciting jazz up the place. If nothing else, they prove that somewhere folks are cheering. Yet, as entertaining as it can be, at most of the other stadiums that use it the screen gets some electronic help. In Seattle it almost flies solo. Aided only by a small, line scorekeeper, every bit of visual information is attended to by Mitsubishi. As a result, the big screen is wasted on simple things that primitive technology could handle.

While it's overworked on the simple stuff, replays, a Diamond Vision specialty, don't get nearly enough time. It's not that the quality of the picture isn't good. With no sun to glare it, it comes out better than the millions of hanging TVs. But actual replay time is so little, it's embarrassing. If a play is even the slightest bit controversial, it's forever filed away in the computer's memory banks. Certainly don't want to rile the 7,000 dozing fans!

Not only are the M's games mishandled, so are everybody else's. In a good ballpark updates from around the league have their own permanent sight. In the Dome the already overworked giant movie screen handles the chore. Busy wasting time on simple game stats and noncontroversial replays, it seldom gets around to updates. As a result, other games in progress get your basic first-, third-, and ninth-inning Kingdome looks.

FOOD: GRADE C

Selection: Fair   Accessibility: Fair
Taste: Fair   Cost: 12th

Hoody's are the major league's tastiest peanuts. While today they're best bought before the game, there was a time a few years back when the greatest vendor in the business tossed 'em.

I'm normally the type who picks up a pound at the grocery store (always Hoody's) and finishes 'em up by the fifth inning. But my first couple of Mariner seasons I'd pay twice the price and buy 'em at the park, just to watch the guy in action. A small fellow, *he* was the pride of the Dome. From 20 rows up and two sections over, he could hit you in the lap. He had an arm more accurate than any catcher the M's have ever had. And probably as good as Mark Langston's. In fact, I can't figure why the Mariners never gave him a tryout. Always testing his range, I'd wait until he passed, then yell out, "Hey, Peanut." Without so much as a glance, he'd wing the two-ounce bag through the air. Sometimes he'd toss it behind his back, once in a while over the top in a windmill fashion, and on long throws to the plate he threw overhand like everybody else. Every pitch plopped flat into your lap. In the three years I watched him, I never saw a wild toss. His show alone was worth the price of admission. But now he's gone, peddling beer at a better commission. While the Hoody's are as good, vendors delegated to handle his peanut-tossing chores are bad enough to catch for the M's.

As for the rest of the Kingdome's lifeless menu...it fits the place. Basic baseball food, hot dogs and popcorn-type stuff, is available. Not particularly good, neither is it really bad. Actually it's Dome-ish. A stab at the out-of-the-ordinary eats, some sausages and imported beers, are so few and far between that the search isn't really worth the time it takes to find them. Only televisions are plentiful. In pairs at every concession stand, and at the center of each of the Dome's four plastic liquor lounges, they serve to remind that whoever dreamed up the place had absolutely no thoughts of baseball in mind.

BALLPARK EMPLOYEES: GRADE C

Kingdome employees are without a doubt the majors' worst dressed. Vendors strolling about the place, attired in gaudy orange jackets and brown polyester slacks, look like walking pumpkins. Ushers trade the orange smock top shirts for beige plaid ones, then plop dumb-looking brown berets on their heads.

And they, too, get the brown polyesters. Neither wears even a sock that might link them with Mariner blue and gold. A sad sight indeed; just looking at the poor folks is enough to make you feel sorry for them.

Most Dome employees act embarrassed. Ushers are considerate enough, but strangely quiet. Even when checking ticket stubs they look down and mumble. Dressed in such goofy clothes, I think they'd rather nobody recognize them. Even vendors whose paychecks depend on how loud they can be act ashamed. Like kindergartners forced to dress up on school's opening day, they, too, silently fade into the plaster.

Decent enough, but with no real personality, Kingdome employees just quietly go about their business. Not nearly as efficient as most on the Coast (nor as rude as some back East), they just finish out the game and go on home. As a result, they fit right in.

FACILITIES: GRADE C

Typically, West Coast ballparks offer the finest in facilities. Inside, the Kingdome is typical; outside, it isn't.

Large, clean rest rooms, easily accessible telephones, and plenty of drinking fountains line the inner stadium walkways. With glass mirrors and enough paper towels for the meager crowds, the bathrooms are actually an atmospheric improvement over the rest of the place.

Parking, however, is more East Coast-ish. Only the fact that nobody goes makes finding a close, safe spot to leave the car fairly easy. Unlike most West Coast suburban stadiums, the Kingdome sits adjacent to downtown, only a block from Pioneer Square. Supplying a large parking lot was not foremost in the minds of its makers—ugliness was. As a result, a majority of parking places are in small private lots and under the nearby highway viaduct. However, most are close to the stadium, and the stroll is pleasant. Since the place is usually more empty than full when the M's play, a lack of spots doesn't pose much of a problem.

But God forbid if people ever do start to show up for baseball—the place could get as zooish as it does for all eight of those slam-banging Seahawk Sundays. While odds are against it, considering the M's history and Seattle's baseball attitude, the mess could be enough to drive folks away.

ATMOSPHERE: GRADE D—

Actually, Seattle's dreary Dome doesn't have an atmosphere. Tearing away from the lovely view of Puget Sound is bad enough, but sitting down inside is even worse. Gray dismal walls climb up to form an equally blasé ceiling, which nothing can brighten up. Baseball being played inside better be good, for the stadium itself offers all the charisma of a night out in the closet.

From its ill-dressed attendants and millions of hanging color television sets to the overdone red, white, and blue banners that droop from nearly every upper-deck railing, tackiness seems to be a consistent Kingdome quality. Arranged in a circle, high above, at the ceiling's apex, long, gaudy, patriotic banners hang, a futile attempt to brighten up the depressing place. Also draped from the third-level railings, and posted on the out-of-play fences down each line as well, they make each game feel like some cheap "Yankee Doodle Dandy" celebration.

The absolute worst in the Kingdome tacky department "floats" out beyond the center-field wall. Booming off cannon shots upon each M's home run, propped up by wooden beams so that the blue wall in front of it is supposed to look like Puget Sound, is the SS *Mariner*. A tiny fake schooner, it's not only laughable but obnoxious too. It doesn't matter how many games I go to, with each homer I forget about the boat. After a blast has hit the bleachers, and I'm up clapping and dreaming that the M's really do have a chance in the AL West, it fires. Startled, I jump and curse the little tug, then watch it sink back behind the wall. I promise myself next time Presley dings one, I'll be ready. I never am. To lessen the chance of ball-game heart attacks, I cast one vote for scuttling the SS *Mariner*.

As tacky as the place is, the Dome's biggest liability are Seattle fans. Each night, regardless of the score, they exit early. Like there's really gonna be a traffic problem. While the M's have had some great finishes the past couple of seasons, a couple of fireballers every year, and Presley, Bradley, and Alvin Davis light up that fake schooner on a regular basis, not a lot of folks have been around as witnesses, particularly past the sixth. As dreary, empty, and quiet as the place is, it must be tough for any of the players to get pumped about a homestand.

Charismatically, the Kingdome is simply a concrete disaster. Baseball, Seattle, and the Dome just don't mix. The stadium only desensitizes the already lackluster feelings for baseball that the city has. Seattle doesn't deserve America's finest game. And the game doesn't deserve to be buried inside the covered dump that it is. A ridiculous combination, only the presence of so many empty chairs offering anybody a front-row view for cheap-seat prices is a plus. A beautiful game and a beautiful city, the two never mix. Like a retarded child, baseball is hidden away in the closet. Yet, that's the way Seattleites seem to like it.

2

CANDLESTICK PARK, SAN FRANCISCO GIANTS

Stick in the Mud

REPORT CARD — *Candlestick Park*

BASEBALL PARK

June 19, 85 vs Reds

GAME

S.F. Giants

BASEBALL CLUB

CATEGORY	GRADE	POINTS
Layout and Upkeep	D	65
Ball Field	C	75
Seating	C	75
Scoreboard	D	65
Food	C	75
Ballpark Employees	D-	60
Facilities	C	75
Atmosphere	D	65
Total Points		555
Average		69

D+

FINAL GRADE

23rd

RANK

"Windy, rainy, cloudy, sunny, hot, and cold, all within the span of nine innings...A disappointing ballpark and a weatherman's nightmare."

PREGAME THOUGHTS

Finally I was on the road—5:30 A.M., a six-pack of Coke on ice, three ham sandwiches cut and ready for a late lunch, sunroof popped, and Sinatra on the stereo. Heading out of the country of clouds and domes, I was on my way south to where baseball was played outdoors under sunny blue skies.

That new-car smell that lures the weak-willed into the palms of the car dealer's hands still flowed from the dashboard. As for me, I was being rejuvenated. It had been far too long since I'd been on a good voyage—actually about four years. My aging Pinto and I had cruised a few hundred miles north for a couple of weekend softball tourneys. But that was just round-the-block stuff. We hadn't gotten the chance to really take off. The old horse just wouldn't make it. Now here I was, new ride and all, rolling down I-5 with the sun peeking up into the sky and Mount Rainier bidding me farewell. Life couldn't be more grand!

As I drove farther south the sun rose and dipped alongside me, Washington highways gave way to Oregon country and finally to California. It was getting late. We (me and my Toyota) had been going for nearly 14 hours. Except for a short stay in some small Oregon town to play a little blacktop hoop, and an afternoon visit to a highway McDonald's for a couple of burgers, things had gone pretty smoothly. The ole car, I figured, probably needed a rest. So I decided to take on San Francisco John Wayne style. The Duke spent weeks in the saddle without food or sleep. Only for the sake of his horse would he ever take a break. I decided to follow his lead. For the sake of mine, I'd stop for the evening.

I'd just turn to my trusty *Motel 6 Register* and search out a decent resting place. Since they're all about the same, it didn't really matter which one I chose. So with two or three more of 'em in my path before the Bay Area, I judged my tiredness and hopped from one to the next, finally pulling off in the small, dingy town of Williams. My Rand McNally map barely recognized it.

It was about 10 P.M. when I pulled into the motel's parking lot. The city's lone police squad car rolled quietly by. I went inside, paid my $21.95, and got a room. Key in hand, I hopped back in the car and swung around to the rear end of the lot, scoping it out as I drove. Out back, on the lower level, I found my room. Its gaudy orange door was labeled with the same numbers that graced my plastic key chain. I backed the car up, nearly onto the sidewalk, within spitting distance from my bedroom window. With the outside porch light beaming away, I was quite satisfied that all would be well. I could retire in peace. So I did, and closed out my first day on the road dreaming of baseball, hot dogs, and peanuts in the shell.

The following morning I awoke to a lovely day. Up on my own by 7:30, I didn't even need the old garage-sale alarm clock that I'd picked up just for the trip. I was ready to roll without it. Walking to the door, I opened her up and stretched in the quickly rising sun. What a day! The parking lot was nearly empty. Semis rambled by on the expressway, which hadn't seemed as close the night before. All was well with the world. Back inside, a hot shower, a little background television sports reviewing the late games, and I was ready for the road.

Grabbing the few necessities that I had needed for my motel crash, I stuffed the odds and ends into my backpack and headed outside for that warm California sunshine. Resting against the doorway, soaking up just a few more rays prior to locking up, I scanned the lot one last time. Something wasn't right. My car, just a few feet in front of me, looked peculiar. Something that I hadn't noticed before was missing. Cautiously, I approached it. I looked closer. My heart sank. It wasn't true. It couldn't have happened. Nothing was smashed, no dents, no rips—the hatchback window was just plain gone. I was dazed, sure it wasn't real. I prayed I was still snoozing away inside and it was all just an idiotic nightmare.

Now, I don't handle catastrophes too well. Especially ones of such magnitude. I usually swear and scream. And I did. "Goddamn this," "Goddamn that." I didn't even have the nerve to look inside. Everything I could find I kicked. Garbage cans, my car, the nearby motel door. I kept kicking until it was the pain in my foot, not the car, I was screaming about. Meanwhile, everybody that hadn't already awakened did, to shrieks of "I can't believe this. I just can't believe this!"

After the tears ran out, and with no more cans left to kick, I gathered what was left of my rattled composure. Deep down, I knew I was history. That everything I owned was gone. But as long as I put off looking, there was still that chance it wasn't. Finally working up the nerve, I reached for the unlocked door. Ever so slowly I creaked it open. Maybe, I prayed, the vandals had become guilt-stricken in the middle of their heist and listened to their conscience. Or a cop had driven by and scared them off before they got to the good stuff. Fat chance—like Karl Malden says, that crime that always happens to some other guy had finally happened to me. I'd been cleaned out. "DAMN!"

For weeks before leaving Seattle I'd put together the best of road-tripping music—Frank Sinatra, Bruce Springsteen, Bob Seger. They all were there the night before, now all were gone. And my simulated alligator-skin tape case gone with them. At least the deck remained. Figured, it was a cheap one. What else? My suitcases, both of them ripped off. My clothes, socks, all those T-shirts I had collected for years had disappeared. The teaching résumé I had written up to get a job back in the Midwest was history too. My binoculars, new $22.50 antiglare road shades, even my Red Sox baseball-cap bank filled with quarters had been ripped off. All that remained was my lousy, rusting camping stuff stashed away in the trunk, an ice cooler with three warm Cokes floating inside, a couple of hanging shirts on the bar in the back seat, and my driver's-seat weapons. Flashlight, hunting knife, and billy club, stashed under the seat, there if I was ever to be attacked. Why couldn't they have worked on their own?

I returned to the hood. Not feeling a thing, I just sat there, opened one of my three remaining warm Cokes, and wondered what on earth I would do. My life's goal—so ready, so happening—was ruined. And I sat so helpless, on a windowless car, in some slime hole of a motel watering stop in Northern California. Just then a squad car, probably informed of the raving lunatic, crept up. A young officer, short-haired, well-groomed, stepped from the car and approached the broken shell of me that sat crumpled on the hood. He was pleasant. I wasn't; not rude, just sullen. I explained dejectedly what had happened and asked, as if he knew, why it had happened to me. Oddly enough, he was very concerned and felt almost guilty. He'd been on duty the previous night and had cruised the lot on several occasions. It was his job to catch those thieves that had taken from me and bash their brains in in this process. Williams being the town of nothing, and he being the lone night officer—while I'd been hit, it was his territory. He felt as taken as I.

As I sat there on the hood, the officer questioned me. After we finished filling out the papers and worked out what to do next, a little kid who'd been watching came over. "Hey, mister," he said. "I think I found your window. It's over by the Dumpster."

So the officer, myself, and the kid stumbled over to check it out. Sure enough, the window and the ripped-up rubber strapping were there. Not able to shatter it, like some tin can, they had just pried it open. After eating all the goodies inside they had thrown the lid away, leaving me the empty can. We checked for anything else that might have been tossed out and left to rot: not even a tape. So I stuffed the window and its ripped molding into the back seat behind what was left of my hanging clothing. The officer apologized again, shouldered a large part of the blame, and drove off to the station two blocks away, probably to check up on wanted posters. Still in a state of shock, I wandered off to call my insurance company, to see if they'd be as caring as they always were on television.

I dragged myself into the motel office. The same lady who had checked me in the night before was working. I explained what had happened and asked to use her phone to make a toll-free call to my insurance company. "Sorry," she popped back, as complacent as if it was a weather update I needed, "this telephone's for business use only." And she pointed to the pay phone outside. I looked at it, its one-foot cord hanging there amid all the noise of the semis rolling by.

"You serious? It's toll-free." I wasn't sure she'd heard the toll-free part the first time. She nodded. It figured. Too worn out to argue, and certain it wouldn't change things anyway, I made my way out to the phone, dialed the number, and against the whooshing of each passing truck strained for an answer.

"Hello," a bouncy-voiced secretary greeted me. My agent wasn't available, but she'd try to help. I explained my situation, stopping every few seconds for the semis to pass. Then, crossing my fingers, I asked, "What do you guys cover?"

"Oh, we don't cover any of that," she reassured me. She sounded like some bubbly cheerleader campaigning for homecoming queen.

"Then what do I pay $700 a year for?" I pleaded.

She reminded me, "If you read your policy, it clearly states on page 12-D, in the small print at the bottom of the page, that comprehension covers only the car. Your homeowner's insurance should cover the possessions." That figured; it had lapsed three weeks ago.

She said she was sorry she couldn't help me and then politely hung up. Her happy attitude made it even worse. Muttering obscenities into the empty mouthpiece, I finished and slammed the phone into its plastic jack. Once again drained, I slumped against the wall, slowly sliding down it and turning as I slid. Curled up on the floor, nearly wedged under the scuzzy telephone, I closed my eyes and prayed everything would disappear.

About then a baseball bounced up and landed on my stomach. I looked up. It was the same kid who had found my window in the Dumpster. This time he had a ball glove with him and was chasing down his ball.

"Sorry, mister. Hey, you all right?" He probably wasn't used to seeing grown men sitting under telephones and crying.

"Yeah, I'm okay," I mumbled, tossing him the ball.

"Hey, mister, you a Giants fan too?" The kid was. His black ball cap with that orange SF was staring almost straight across into my face.

"No, not really. I like the Red..." And right about then horror flashed its face one more time. My God. The orange SF. The Giants. Candlestick. I'd forgotten my sojourn. I had to get to San Francisco by noon.

"Oh no... What time is it?" Between the two of us I had the only watch. And I reached for my wrist to check it as I jumped up. Wummp. My head slapped the steel bottom of the phone. I slid back to my seat. A good-size knot rose on the top of my head.

"You all right, mister?" the kid asked again. I was too worn out to feel any pain as I crawled out from under the phone and pulled myself up.

I thanked the kid, rubbed my head, and started off at a jog to what was left of my car. "Where you going?" the little voice called from behind.

Backpedaling, I answered, "To watch the Giants. See ya later."

Around the corner, I jumped into my popped tin can and started her up. A couple of beeps on the horn to the tiny waving Giant fan who had followed, and I sped out of the parking lot. And toward the expressway. Open rear window, clothes flinging in the smelly diesel fumes of the semis, tape deck empty, and Barry Manilow playing on the AM radio. Off to the civilization of baseball parks, only because I didn't know what else to do and I couldn't cry anymore.

LAYOUT AND UPKEEP: GRADE D

Leaving that warm central California sunshine behind, the nearer I got to the Bay Area, the darker the skies became; 175 miles to the east, home of my nightmare, California was preparing for another scorcher. San Francisco, on the other hand, looked like it was readying itself for a hurricane. If that wasn't enough, the nearer I got to Candlestick, the more intense the blackness became and the less time between raindrops pelting my back seat. Things couldn't get much more pathetic. Driving through the middle of Frisco in a windowless car that had just been emptied of all its worldly possessions, I was on my way to a Candlestick rain-out. For a brief, fleeting moment even the Kingdome sounded good. Still I had tickets and figured I might as well go.

When I was a kid Candlestick was one of my favorite parks, the Giants my favorite NL team. I'd never seen either, I just had this fairy-tale image of the ballpark. Our family spent every Thursday night in front of the tube watching *Ironsides*. Plus, I'd seen all of the Dirty Harry movies at least three times apiece. Each is filled with shots of Frisco. Every other week episodes of *Ironsides* had Perry Mason wheeling around Coit Tower chasing bad guys. Detective Harry Callahan usually shot two or three scumballs at its base. For some reason I had come to associate Coit with Candlestick Park. It had forced me to fall in love with the Giants.

Perched upon one of the city's tallest hills, Coit is a beautiful ivory-colored observation tower. A memorial dedicated in 1933 to Lillie Hitchcock Coit, it really is a stunning sight. I guess because the structure, to a teenage mind, resembles a giant candle, I believed for the longest time that it was a press box at the Giants' ballpark. When I found out later that the ballpark was named after Candlestick Point, the land it rests on, and that Coit had absolutely nothing to do with the stadium, I was crushed. When I saw what Candlestick actually looked like, I felt much worse. Unlike majestic Coit, "the Stick," as it is called by its few regulars, is very ordinary. From the outside it looks like it deserves the fate thrust on it by the absence of sun. Just a plain arena, it stands on the fringes of a seedy neighborhood, wedged between a shabby, grassy ridge and the water.

Besides ugly, from first glance the park looks to be loaded with all sorts of problems. In fact, just getting into its rusting gates was a hassle. Prepaid tickets are handed out at the same window where game-day sales take place, at least on Wednesday afternoons. So even if they're already bought and paid for, it takes a frustrating wait in a snail's-paced line to reach them. As for its upkeep, winds rushing in off the bay do a number in and around the stadium. Hot-dog wrappers and empty peanut packages flutter about through the walkways underneath the stands, among the seats themselves, and down onto the playing field. At least, with all the wind constantly blowing, the mess is a continually changing one. Unorganized and unkempt, set in very plain surroundings, the result is a littered junky ballpark with just a neat name. It seemed only right that after the morning I'd had, the afternoon would be spent in a place as dumpy as "the Stick."

BALL FIELD: GRADE C

Baseball was made to be played on grass. Natural ball fields buried in a sea of plastic seats, surrounded by acres of concrete, carry about them an almost divine quality. One of the game's grandest feelings is lost when the fresh scent of grass is replaced by the stench of a synthetic copy. For five years I'd watched baseballs bounce upon the Dome's man-made field. God, I hate the stuff, yet it's all the M's have and I am a regular. Just entering into Candlestick and once again feeling the thrill of the grass was breathtaking. By the fourth inning, though, Candlestick's glow was wearing off.

The ultimate in a crisply trimmed, well-tended field is the checkerboard cut. Kansas City's old Municipal Stadium used to be the best. The light- and dark-green outfield squares were almost perfect. I used to watch the Tigers and A's just to look at the field. And that was on TV. Candlestick begins the same way, but then takes the traditional style a few steps too far. Not content to merely cross the cut, the ball field looks as though it can't really decide which way to grow. It seems to suffer from an identity crisis.

Instead of just a normal checkerboard cut, "the Stick's" grass grows in three different directions. Foul ground down both baselines is trimmed so that it runs parallel to the foul lines all the way out to the warning track. A nice touch, the idea in itself would be fine if the infield grass weren't cut in an entirely different pattern. It's as if an imaginary line runs from home plate straight through the center of the pitching rubber out to second base. And all infield cuts parallel it. The contrast is just too great. Worst of all is that following the semicircular shape of the outer edge of the infield dirt, radiating all the way out to the wall like ripples in a puddle and covering the entire outfield, the grass announces its third and most commanding cut. In addition to being a whole lot different, all three cuts are deep and wide. They don't blend quietly into the field; rather, they scream for attention.

The whole design is just too strange. It gives the park a Picasso-ish look. Baseball is more in tune with Norman Rockwell. Relieved to see and feel real grass again in a baseball park, I just hoped that down the road in the other stadiums things would be more normal.

SEATING: GRADE C

Typical of most of the West Coast stadiums, Candlestick's comfortable seats don't feature the best of sight lines. Double-tiered all the way around, each level is filled with plastic fold-up seats. Either up and out in the huge upper deck, or separated from fair territory by too much foul ground, for many the game is in a different world.

Like in Seattle, where Mariner fans leave more empty seats than those they fill, Candlestick offers the same blessing. With lousy turnouts and a laid-back group of ushers, you can sit most anywhere you please. Like at the Dome, your best bet is to pay cheap at the gate then sit in luxury in one of the many available higher-priced models. Yet even at general admission prices, a "Stick" box seat isn't a steal.

The setup does add one little specialty, that on TV at least is kind of amusing. Left-field bleachers, besides being miles from the plate, are a pretty good ways from the chain-link outfield fence. Thirty feet or more of empty space separates fan and fence. Every time Jeff Leonard blasts a towering fly toward it, kids pour out of their seats. Climbing and stumbling and crawling all over each other, they usually get to it just as the homer's bouncing up and over their heads, behind them into the second row. It's a riot watching, but must be frustrating as hell to the kids. This may sound stupid, but why not push the fence back a bit? Then the kids could see what was going on and get their souvenirs. Of course, ESPN highlights wouldn't be as entertaining.

SCOREBOARD: GRADE D

Candlestick's scoreboard is a bore. Not simple enough to be traditional, or electronically gifted enough to be considered exciting, it fits well in the unkempt facility.

Technologically, the system is not up to date. Nor is it imaginative. No special tidbits of baseball knowledge, no updates of games from around the league, no starting pitchers or starting times, no reflection of the standings, even a general lack of info about the batter—the electronic screen is just a waste of space. Buried in a sea of billboard advertisements, like the Kingdome, the only thing it does a good job of selling is cigarettes.

Musical choices are kind of neat though. San Francisco down to the bone, the recordings are a throwback to the sixties. "King of the Road," some old Beatles tunes, America, and the Stones fill the idle moments. Although not really baseballish, at least they're original and in tune with the colorful city. Even the seventh-inning stretch throws off the traditional "Take Me Out to the Ball Game" with Glen Miller's "In the Mood." It's a feat that only a city like Frisco could get away with. And actually a nice move. Too bad it's about the only thing going for the place that is in the mood.

FOOD: GRADE C

Selection: Poor   Accessibility: Very Good
Taste: Poor   Cost: 6th

Clad in yellow shirts, loaded with beer, hot dogs, and peanuts, Candlestick's "Golden Flashes" are the majors' fastest vendors. Sprinting up and down wide-aisled stands to the few that brave attending, they perform at a McDonald's drive-in-window pace. To each raised hand they race, kneel, serve, and leave—all before you're even able to thank them. Their intensity is remarkable. Their food is cheap. Too bad it tastes awful.

Although buying food at "the Stick" is relatively inexpensive, drinking beer is even cheaper, and although getting anything at the snap of a finger is a piece of cake, eating is not recommended. Foil-packaged hot dogs that are pushed through the stands are horrible. Outside, in concession booths, things aren't much better. In addition to the normal stuff, a few burgers, sunflower seeds—a treat for somebody, I suppose—and a couple of California wines, there really isn't much available. Not even pickle relish or onions—7-Eleven has a better selection.

BALLPARK EMPLOYEES: GRADE D−

Normally, California ballparks are served by top-notch facilities and catered by an extremely professional group of individuals. Candlestick breaks both molds. Aside from their speedy vendors, the Salvation Army probably employs a more intense work force.

In complete contradiction to the speed that food motors through the stands, everything else at the stadium moves in turtle time. Ticket sellers, whether it be that their job is just so confusing or due to mechanical error, are unbelievably slow. Concessionaires under the stands, although they outnumber customers nearly two to one, are equally inefficient. But it's the teenage ushers standing at the top of nearly every aisle who best exemplify the "I really don't know what I am doing here" attitude. They are dressed appropriately enough in Giants warm-up jackets, and I expected, since they looked like they had a clue, that they might prove it. I was wrong. I did find a consistency among them though. None were really sure where anything was. Rest rooms, security offices, even aisles—the do-it-yourself method works better than asking the kids.

Not only were employees ill-informed, but some, like my personal motor-scootered parking-lot attendant, were rude as well. Pulling into misty, windy Candlestick with an open hole for a back window, I was concerned for the safety of the few possessions I still owned. Until I could get something burglar-proof installed, like a plastic sheet, my meager personal items were pretty easy pickings. At each stadium, before my plastic was in place, I'd ask about parking in the secured lot. Usually guards working the gate helped me out. Whether it was by direction to a more restricted part of the lot or just a few kind words, most people were helpful... but, not at Candlestick.

Even though the lot had eight times as many empty spots as filled ones, the pompous fellow on the motor scooter had no time to listen to my problems.

"If we do it for you, we'll have to do it for everybody."

I looked about the place. Everybody, all 7,500 of them, had already made it inside. I asked the mirror-sunglassed worker one more time, "How 'bout just the back row of the press lot?" It was almost empty. I even explained the pathetic circumstances that had brought on such a request.

Candidly, he told me, "Look, buddy, I told you once it's not stadium policy. Now I am pretty busy, you had better find someplace else to park."

So, sheepishly, I did. Mr. Cool sped off to capture somebody else who had inadvertently steered into the empty restricted zone. While the guy surely didn't do much for Giants' public relations, he was one of the few at the stadium who seemed to know just exactly what his job was.

FACILITIES: GRADE C

Everywhere else in California, ballpark facilities are great. Only by crummy Eastern-city stadium standards, where rest rooms match the size of West Coast ticket booths, are Candlestick's decent. In the Bay Area alone they come in a distant second.

Tucked off the freeway, accessible by only a couple of roads in and out, Frisco's parking lot is at least better than the front yards used in Detroit. Although not much easier to get to. Bordering the stadium, and plenty big enough for puny Giants crowds, it's the lone accessory that puts the ballpark in its California class.

Rest rooms, on the other hand, are East Coast-ish. Since not a lot of people are around to use them, they don't need to be real big. That's good, because they're not. They do, however, feature one of the stadium's few luxuries. Instead of normal, useful, paper-towel dispensers, hand blowers are tacked to the walls. As if the place didn't already have enough problems with cold air blowing all about, these hot-air blowers only make matters tackier. Half of Candlestick's weather problems probably come when the two fronts come together. Arctic temperatures from the bay and tropical winds from the rest rooms mix and probably cause all those clouds to hover over the park.

ATMOSPHERE: GRADE D

All I really knew about beautiful San Francisco going in was that in the 1960s hippies had hung out there, that it was the self-proclaimed gay capital of the universe, and that everybody complained how cold it got in "the Stick." Since baseball fans can come in any sex or cross-sex without too much trouble, and since the beauty of a city has absolutely nothing to do with what goes on at the ballpark (Seattle certainly was proof of that), whether the town was pretty or pink didn't much matter. Its sixtyish atmosphere, and the weather, if it really was that bad, I figured would somehow make themselves noticed.

The weather complaint bothered me though. When it comes to the cold, Californians don't have a clue. It's always amazed me that people in a land so blessed with sunshine will cry about a little occasional wind and rain, of having to go to the ballyard wearing jeans instead of shorts, and shoes instead of thongs. A few years ago I spent a spring vacation in the Bay Area. Every day in the *Chronicle* sports section and each evening on the six o'clock news, some reference was made to the fact that only a real man could brave the bitter cold and swirling winds of Candlestick. Just the conversation turned my stomach.

That was before the game. By the end I was wondering if it was the Giants or the 49ers that I was watching, and if the calendar read January or June. When I had escaped from Williams, only a few hours to the east, the thermometer was reading 90+. Dressed in shorts and a cotton T-shirt too heavy for eastern California, by Bay Area standards I was encouraging pneumonia. By the seventh inning in Candlestick, I'd made more wardrobe changes than the chorus line of a Broadway musical. I'd worn shorts, jeans, a T-shirt, and a coat. I had gone bare-chested and bare-footed—all with an umbrella along my side that was opened but never rained upon.

The wind swirls, then shivers, then disappears. The sun shines, warms, then disappears. Clouds roll in and over, get black and forbidding, then thin and harmless-looking. Always threatening to wipe out the contest, they never follow through on their threats. The scenario, explained to me a number of times by those accustomed to it, and entertained by my constant wardrobe change, was standard for the park. While not the icy Siberian wasteland that some would like to make it out to be, an afternoon in Candlestick nevertheless would cause chaos in the mind of a weather reporter. It proves, if nothing else, that all of California's not sunshine and palm trees.

While the sun struggles with the clouds overhead, the game struggles as well. Nobody seems really intent on presenting baseball as it should be. Ushers, although noticeable, seem lost within the complexity of their job. Concessionaires and ticket sellers are frustratingly slow and not really enthusiastic. Fans, what few show up, are vocal if ever there is a reason to be. But since the pair of Willies (McCovey and Mays) left, there hasn't been much reason to be. Just the fact that the sky, whatever shade of gray it happens to be turning at the time, is not covered by a dome and the place has real grass, even if it is weird-looking, makes "the Stick" bearable. And then just barely.

Something about everything in Candlestick somehow doesn't seem right... maybe in another place, maybe in another time. *People* magazine has always insisted that if marijuana was ever legalized, it would be in California. After experiencing just what it is that makes up the atmosphere inside San Francisco's middle-aged ballpark, I guess that if a baseball stadium ever sold the non-baseball-type grass, it would be in "the Stick." That way the 36-year-old fans would have something to do. They could kick back, light up, toke out, watch the swirling patterns on the turf, and groove to the tunes of rock stars of years gone by. That or they could just sit there and soak up some clouds.

3

COLISEUM, OAKLAND A'S

Let the Good Times Roll

REPORT CARD		**Coliseum**
		BASEBALL PARK
June 21, 85 vs Indians		**Oakland A's**
GAME		BASEBALL CLUB

CATEGORY	GRADE	POINTS
Layout and Upkeep	*B*	*85*
Ball Field	*C*	*75*
Seating	*D*	*65*
Scoreboard	*A+*	*100*
Food	*A+*	*100*
Ballpark Employees	*B*	*85*
Facilities	*B*	*85*
Atmosphere	*B*	*85*
Total Points		*680*
Average		*85*

B
_____
FINAL GRADE

7th
_____
RANK

"From the Dixieland jazz band roaming the parking lot to the rock 'n' rolling scoreboard system inside... just a great place to have some fun."

PREGAME THOUGHTS

Candlestick was history. Back inside my popped tin can, the heater running full blast and minus a back window, I was at my crossroads. Although "the Stick" hadn't been the greatest, at least it'd temporarily relieved my nightmare. The whole thing seemed so unreal. Two hundred miles away somebody was rummaging through my things, probably throwing out half of the worthless stuff and cursing the fact that they'd spent their time on a teacher's car with Frank Sinatra music. The satisfaction that they couldn't be too pleased with their haul didn't help me any though. I had no place to go and no idea what to do. And none of my stuff to do it with. I wanted to give up and go home but I didn't have the guts. I wanted to stay the night and head over to the Coliseum but I was out of T-shirts, tapes, and underwear. I was dazed. After half an hour of just sitting there feeling sorry for myself and with really no alternative, I decided I had to return to the scene of the crime. Maybe, just maybe, something had turned up. It was either that or a one and a half gainer off the Golden Gate Bridge.

It was a bit past sundown when I revisited Williams. Just reading that "Welcome" banner over Main Street almost made me puke. I did have a job to do though. And only a few hours of daylight left to do it in. I promised myself I'd search out every filthy corner where the lowlifes might have abandoned my useless valuables. So I roamed. First the motel Dumpsters, then the gas station, looking to find any clue. Interviewing people who might've witnessed the act, my confidence grew; I felt like Sherlock Holmes. A lady working the cash register at the all-night gas station across the street, a couple of drunks getting soused at the local tavern, three school kids roaming by the city high school—nobody knew. I kept digging. By midnight, after exhausting all my leads and having thoroughly checked out the two city blocks that made up the wretched little place, I finally realized I wasn't going to find my things.

Yet, the search had given me new purpose. Revitalized me. Given me a reason to live. No longer would I drive back to San Francisco just to jump from the Bay Bridge. I decided I'd go to see an A's game. Even if I didn't change underwear the entire trip, I'd go to the rest as well. I'd buy Sinatra tapes, get some new shades, obliterate my Visa credit limit once again, and be off. I wasn't about to give up after just one ballpark.

So I headed back down Main Street under the "Welcome to Williams" banner and toward the expressway. But just before turning onto the ramp I thought maybe I'd give the police station one more try. Maybe the officer who had taken my loss so hard was back on duty. Maybe he'd have some good news. What'd I have to lose?

I checked out the station. Sure enough, he was on. I went inside. He apologized again and said that there had been a breakthrough in the case. Progress had been made and some items recovered. My heart, having been bounced about like a Ping-Pong ball all day long, leapt.

"What items?" I asked.

"Various things possibly of yours and the other three cars broken into," he replied. "We found them scattered about the inside of one of the motel rooms this morning." The criminals were gone, but at least some of the loot was left.

Crossing my fingers, I asked if I could see what was recovered. He was troubled. It wasn't policy. The chief was supposed to handle such matters in the morning. Still, the young officer felt partially responsible and reluctantly agreed that I could see what'd been found. I'd have to describe the item. He would then go to the safe and see if it was part of the stash. I recited, he retrieved.

"Binoculars?" I asked.

"No," he replied. I figured so, they were good ones. "How 'bout sunglasses?"

"Uh-uh." Strike two.

"Suitcases?" I guessed, holding my breath.

"What kind?"

I described them. Around the corner he came, with both of them. I jumped and clapped! Together we opened them. Full—my shorts, undies, my blank checks, all of my green-and-white Michigan State T-shirts. I was ecstatic. We continued, I describing and he sifting through the loot. My résumés all alive and well, forty copies and the original. Even my plastic Red Sox bank. They had emptied it, stolen all the quarters, but at least hadn't taken it with them. Not Sox fans, it told me; if nothing else, they were smart. Almost everything, except for the expensive stuff, was recovered. And being a teacher, those items for me are quite limited in number.

Purposely, though, I held off on the tapes. I couldn't face up to the answer if it was no. Finally, while silently saying my Hail Marys, I asked, "My music, I don't suppose you have my music? A simulated alligator-type tape case with the finest tapes ever recorded inside?"

He checked. He brought it in. I couldn't believe it. It was like Christmas in June. I was going crazy. I closed my eyes and unlatched the case. The tapes would be the most irreplaceable of all my items. Binoculars could be purchased at any Sears, sunglasses I could go on without. Even my custom-made backpack, as much as I liked it, could be picked up in some sporting goods store someplace in the country. But my music... I gulped and looked down at the simulated alligator-skin case and ever so slowly hinged the case open. "Please, God," I said, "at least let them have left the Sinatra." I looked. I screamed. They were there! All of 'em! Every single one! I counted, all twenty-four. I couldn't believe it! Pounding up and down on the counter, I was in heaven. My life was saved. America was wonderful. Even Williams was tolerable.

Feeling like the Grinch must've when he slid back into Who-ville with all the ripped-off Christmas presents, arms loaded, I stuffed everything back into my car. Once again it bulged with junk. Only now beautiful new junk. Never again would I leave even that plastic Bosox bank alone at night in my car. And my journey—it not only would be continued, it'd be better than ever. The greatest of all time. I grabbed my favorite Sinatra and Basie tape, the one in which they really swing. Thanking the officer for the umpteenth time, I hopped behind the wheel of my packed-up car, popped open the last warm Coke, turned up the tunes, and rolled back onto the highway... out to see some baseball, lots of it!

LAYOUT AND UPKEEP: GRADE B

Oakland is a workingman's town. Unlike that romantic place across the bay, Oakland's skyline doesn't twinkle in the twilight; instead it's dark and dreary. Cable cars don't clang up and down hillsides that plummet to the water's edge. There's no China Town, no Fisherman's Wharf, no Golden Gate Park. People don't flock from around the world just to soak in its cosmopolitan atmosphere. Tony Bennett has never left his heart in Oakland. In fact he probably did as much as he could to avoid even entering into its filthy city limits. Dirty and dangerous, the Bay Area black sheep, Oakland seems more a sister to a hole like Cleveland than the "City by the Golden Gate." Simply put, Oakland is a dive. Staring across the water at San Francisco, it must go through life as a comparison: of bad to good, dangerous to exciting, homely to charming. The last thing I expected from such an unholy place was baseball to feel at home. Instead my beliefs would be confirmed—pro football's baddest bad guys, the Raiders, still belonged.

For a long time the Coliseum housed Al Davis's silver and black, as well as providing the A's a place to play. From first glance the Raiders seem a more worthy renter. Trapped on the city's seedy South Side, the stadium sits amid bumpy train tracks and dingy warehouses. The tour to reach it is a nasty one. Confusing, chuckholed, one-way streets stumble through a shady neighborhood. Like a prison wall, a tall, cold, chain-link fence surrounds the complex. Peering through the metal links at the plain-looking stadium inside, I figured Oakland and its Coliseum would be a good match.

Once inside its gates, though, a strange transition takes place. A huge well-lit parking lot eases away the frightful area. Acres of open asphalt dotted by tall, slender light poles separate the stadium from all the outside filth. Grassy rolling hills, lined with teenage eucalyptus trees, are neatly landscaped. The Coliseum itself is plopped smack-dab in the middle, as far away as possible from the sleazy streets. A modern concrete bowl, it sits side by side with a matching covered arena. The other one hosts basketball. The two go well together. Between them is a clean open plaza. Ticket booths from each are so close that on a common game night their lines would probably intertwine. The setup actually looks like it might be the tidiest in town.

Through the ballpark turnstiles simplicity continues. Walkways that circle the circle lead up and into the various levels, then back down closer to the field. Beyond the bleachers more grassy green hills roll. They, too, are well kept. While it may not ooze with baseball, the Coliseum nevertheless escapes its foul elements. From inside nobody could guess that Oakland even existed. In fact, looking out at the ball field from a third-base box seat, it appears that those evil Raiders might be too tough for such a peaceable place.

BALL FIELD: GRADE C

It probably wasn't fair that I visited Oakland when I did. The USFL still had a few gasps of breath left in it. Football still had a home in the Coliseum—even if they played before empty seats in the slushy springtime. In '81, when the Raiders ran off to bigger crowds in L.A., they took that 100-yard rectangle with them. For a couple of seasons, at least, the A's ball diamond wasn't shared with anything that remotely resembled a fifty-yard line. However, in '85, for one last season the "Invaders," from the fake football league, attacked the Coliseum. They laid out their rectangle, chalked up the grass with hundreds of one-yard hash marks, and ripped up the turf every Sunday afternoon.

To the groundkeepers it must have been a never-ending horror picture—*Pro Football the 13th*. Frazzled turf can be patched. Goalposts can be torn down. Yard markers are even easy to hide away in some dingy closet. Yard-line lime, though, takes a bit longer to disappear. Like ghost footprints, it tends to leave its mark long after helmets have stopped crunching. The imprint on a baseball field draws from its charm. In the summer of '85 those pitiful hopes of the "Invaders" still lingered.

Most of the time the turf probably looks great. Graced by California sunshine, trimmed closely, and not showing the slightest patchiness, later in the year, when the footprints faded, it was probably sharp. Too, with miles of foul territory, it's got to lead the league in grass.

SEATING: GRADE D

Lousy sight lines are the Coliseum's greatest weakness. Pure multipurpose, it has a lot of problems in taking on baseball. The biggest is that a ball diamond just doesn't fit real well inside.

Foul territory down the baselines is enormous. More than at any other major league park, it just floods the place. Consequently, box seats are lousy. Now that's all right if the ball club's filled with Catfish Hunters and Reggie Jacksons like it was in the seventies. Folks will sit anywhere to watch a team like that. But for a ball club that struggles each season just to reach .500, ten bucks ought to put you in the dugout. In the Coliseum it barely lets you make out jersey numbers.

Other than megadistances, things are pretty standard for an all-purpose park. Three levels work their way around to both foul poles with a field section down in front. All four have easy access and are filled with comfortable fold-up plastic seats. A huge bleacher section fills in the land beyond the fences. Like the seats everywhere else inside, it, too, is a long way away. But bleachers are supposed to be that way. Their only promise is a tan in hot sunshiny weather. Or an occasional chance at a Canseco dinger. At the Coliseum they're also pretty crazy. Considering all the cheap fun and the new round of A's kid sluggers, it might be the ballpark's best hangout.

SCOREBOARD: GRADE A+

The Coliseum is a rock 'n' rolling place. Probably the biggest reason is its good-timing audiovisual show. For simply having fun, it's the majors' best.

Beyond the bleacher section stand three bigger-than-billboard size, totally separate scoreboards. While their sheer size alone dominates the place, what they have to say is even more eye-catching, besides being a little weird at times. In the middle a Diamond Vision screen sets the tempo—the stadium drummer, everything and everybody follow its fast-paced beat. Nowhere else does Diamond Vision work so hard. At some stadiums the giant TV is the only effective screen. Besides getting to show off once in a while, its flashiness is wasted on simple things like posting runs, hits, and errors. To use Diamond Vision genius for that is a bit like requisitioning Michelangelo to design postal stamps. Other places it's a useless ornament. There to dazzle on a few occasions, most of the time it sits blank. At the Coliseum I'm not so sure it's even got an off switch. From a pregame "This Week in Baseball" special to a constant replay of "even the close calls," it's almost obsessively in use. Crazy plays, good plays or lousy ones, baseball highlights, people highlights, even animal highlights—you name it, they show it.

Flanking the big screen in center field, each longer but not as tall, are two traditional scoreboards. As hardworking as their drummer, they allow the more talented machine between them to be imaginative. In right field a line score of the game at hand is in constant motion. Batting averages as well as other basic baseball stats light 'er up. Aside from hot dogs and peanuts, it's about as traditional as the Coliseum gets. In left field another board completes the symmetrical balance. There different items are handled. Upcoming events, special give-away nights, and future home stands are in constant rotation. The trio do a great job of complementing each other.

As good as the visual show is, without music it might go on routinely about its business. But its business is anything but routine. The Coliseum features, without a doubt, the majors' finest sound system. The place explodes in high-fidelity rock 'n' roll. All night long, stadium speakers belt out Top 40 tunes; Springsteen, Madonna, Huey Lewis—it's got whatever's hot. Together with the Diamond Vision's crazy antics, the pair buzzes Oakland with a continual current of energy.

Typical of the crazy place that it is, the Coliseum runs what has to be the world's strangest "Upcoming Home Stands" number. Folks sit around all night long just waiting for it to appear.

Things started quietly enough. Two little bobber-head dolls silently bobbed away up on the Diamond Vision screen. Another catchy tune kicked out on the stadium speakers. Boinging to the music's beat, the little fellows' oblong ceramic heads each sported the same doofy-looking smile. One wore a green-and-gold Oakland A's uniform painted on his tiny body, the other a Blue Jays outfit. The Jays were next in town. Folks must've been used to the show because the number had the perk-up effect of a two-out seventh-inning rally. Kids started pointing to the screen, telling their dads to watch. Dads tapped moms on the shoulder to take a look. With the heads still bobbing, A's vs. Jays dates flashed on the screen. Nobody cared though. They all watched a baseball glove slide in front of the little Blue Jay, then slide away. With it went the miniature Canadian. A zoom-in on that doofy A's smile, still somehow bobbing away, brought a mild round of applause.

Later in the game the dolls appeared again. Again folks took notice. Only this time dad was doing the pointing. While the little Oakland fella was back, he had a new buddy—a Boston Red Soxer. Like before, dates flashed announcing the upcoming Sox–A's series. Like before, a ball glove appeared. Only this time it came down from above. Grabbing the Bostonian, it pulled his oblong head up and out of sight. Only the spring neck rose with it; his ceramic body stayed aground. Folks cheered a little louder as the body finally followed. The doofy little Oakland A just kept on bouncing; his doofy little mouth kept on grinning.

By the seventh, when the last show flashed, everybody was pointing. This time as the two gents bobbed, a bat eased its way into view. Folks howled. They knew what was next. In super-slow motion the Louisville timber cranked up and slugged the puny Milwaukee Brewer. Its dumb-looking ceramic head shattered into a trillion pieces. The park erupted. Back and forth a couple of times, just to let anybody else who missed it see. Then one last zoom-in on the bouncing Oakland A.

If I didn't already know it, I knew it then—the Coliseum was a wild place.

FOOD: GRADE A+

Selection: Excellent   Accessibility: Excellent
Taste: Excellent   Cost: 10th

Baseball food galore! Featuring a Milwaukee Brewer-style sausage menu and a whole bunch of other stuff, the Coliseum makes Bay Area ballpark dining a pleasure—at least on one side of the bridge.

Organized into separate specialty stands, the most striking asset of the menu is how it can be so varied and organized at the same time. Each of the separate booths offers the basics—hot dogs, peanuts, beer, and pop. Each also features some special dish as well. Not only that, but they're spread evenly all about the park. And you can even see the field from their lines. Trotting up to the concessions doesn't cost you two innings of baseball.

The array of eats at the separate stands is amazing. Each has a single theme—nachos at one, juicy one-third-pound burgers at another, even baked potatoes at a third. For more extravagant taste buds, fancier foods are added. An Italian menu is spiced up with meatball sandwiches, Italian sausage, and Italian beef. Another presents barbecued beef and Mighty Rib sandwiches. Most impressive, though, is the Coliseum's line of sausages. In the same class with Milwaukee County Stadium, the variety outnumbers even the sausage masters six to four. Knockwurst, brats, kielbasas, Linguisa, Louisiana hots, and British Rangers all roll about the grill. Doused with a little kraut and washed away with another Old Mil, they're a great ballpark meal. Then it's back into the stands to enjoy whatever's next on the crazy Coliseum menu.

BALLPARK EMPLOYEES: GRADE B

Across the bay I found that Candlestick's employees weren't quite sure what they were doing. Aside from speedy hot-dog and beer vendors, most of the folks dozed through the day. No so in Oakland. The Coliseum is run by a good, hardworking group. From helpful parking-lot attendants to the friendly kids in the souvenir stands, the Coliseum aims to please.

The parking lot's a good one and a big improvement over the crummy streets flowing into it. An old gray-haired gentleman was working the gate when I pulled up. He took my couple of bucks and directed me where to go. The terror of leaving my new car anywhere without a back window, even in his fenced-in lot, must have shown. When I asked how secured things were he noticed that I wasn't just curious. He couldn't promise that my plastic window wouldn't be popped again, but he did offer a little special treatment. He pointed to the lot's tallest light pole.

"Leave 'er under that," he told me. Then he wrote down my license plate number and promised that he'd keep an eye on it. Whether or not he watched I'll never know, but just the peace of mind was enough. It made the show inside much more fun.

Inside things also click along without a hitch. Souvenir stands are stocked full with college kids. Talking baseball all night long with the fans seems to be standard practice and gives the place another happy feeling. While not as speedy as across the bay, vendors still beat the turtles up in Seattle and the beerless ones to the south. Security has a good grasp on things without squeezing too tight, and ushers are pleasant. All in all, the Coliseum is probably the best-run business in Oakland.

FACILITIES: GRADE B

If nothing else, California provides major league baseball with giant parking lots and clean rest rooms; Oakland, while it's not a sunshiny wet-and-wild West Coast paradise, at least gets high marks for both.

Bathrooms are big and clean, equipped with all the pleasures of home. Glass mirrors, paper towels, and clean floors serve as top-notch standard features, while the piped-in play-by-play ball-game broadcast is a nice added luxury option.

Outside things are also well kept. Despite being trapped on the iffy side of town, the stadium itself seems safe. Its large well-lit lot is secured throughout the game. Uniformed attendants, like my gray-haired friend, roam the grounds. They make sure no unsavory characters squeeze between the chain-link holes in the fence. The couple bucks it cost to keep my car off the street was probably the night's most sound investment.

ATMOSPHERE: GRADE B

Oakland's Coliseum provides major league baseball a different kind of excitement. Lord knows the place has problems, and the seedy neighborhood it lives in is its biggest. From first glance, although a little tidier than Candlestick, the ballpark looks like just another Bay Area bomb. Even up close, with the elements locked out, filled with concrete and plastic, it looks pretty plain. Inside, lousy sight lines and an average ball field don't instill any lost confidence. But once that switch is thrown, the scoreboard turns on, and the park kicks into high gear, the Coliseum becomes as unlike Oakland as any in the major leagues.

In order to have a good time at the stadium, you don't need to be an A's fan. In fact, you need not even care for baseball. The only qualification necessary to enjoy a date with the Coliseum is an ability to loosen up a little. Dancing in the aisles is also encouraged. Music belts out in high-tech stereo. Outdoor movies flash all night long. Strange between-inning numbers put the place on a happy edge. And the food is out of this world. After tasting a little Coliseum craziness, it's tough not to go away grinning.

Folks inside respond to their ballpark's lead. Oakland may not have the most, but they surely have some of the wildest fans in the majors. They sing and dance. They scream and shout. They even watch a little baseball in the process. Whether it's to cheer another Canseco blast or cheer another of one of all those K's, they get into the act. Just like when Reggie was around. In fact, if you look really close, almost every strange *This Week in Baseball* people excerpt features somebody in a green-and-gold ball cap. Usually for television their faces are painted and their shirts are off. The ones I saw swinging in the aisles were at least wearing clothes.

Celebrations at the Coliseum begin long before game time. Tailgate parties splash the huge parking lot. Second only in pregame get-togethers to Milwaukee, folks get properly prepared for fun. Beer flows, sausages grill, and people laugh and gab, all getting ready for more of the same on the inside.

Even an official welcoming committee roams the lot. "The A's Swingers," five old gents dressed in green-and-gold warm-up jackets, provide the parking lot that little extra pizzazz. Traipsing about back and forth, they fill the concrete up with "Oh! Susanna"-type requests. In between their lively numbers they visit and, with a twisted arm, will even drink a toast. They set a happy tone for all those who'd like to dance on inside for some more fun. With such a great intro, a night at the old ballyard can't help but be a good time. For even if the game is dull or your seat too far from the field to tell if it is, with happy folks all about you'd have to be a pro football zombie or a real hard-core Giants fan not to want to come back for more.

4

DODGER STADIUM, L.A. DODGERS

Camelot

REPORT CARD	*Dodger Stadium*
	BASEBALL PARK
June 23, 85 vs Astros	*L.A. Dodgers*
GAME	BASEBALL CLUB

CATEGORY	GRADE	POINTS
Layout and Upkeep	*A+*	*100*
Ball Field	*A*	*95*
Seating	*A*	*95*
Scoreboard	*B*	*85*
Food	*C*	*75*
Ballpark Employees	*A+*	*100*
Facilities	*A+*	*100*
Atmosphere	*A*	*95*
Total Points		*745*
Average		*93*

A
FINAL GRADE

1ˢᵗ
RANK

> "Luxurious automobiles and expensive women, bright sunshine, beautiful blue skies, and the game of baseball all come together at the majors' most stunning palace... splashed of course in Dodger blue."

PREGAME THOUGHTS

Road tripping—not much better for the soul than a five-hour drive to no-place-in-particular from anywhere else. Add a cold one, the stereo kicking out some tunes, and you've got an atmosphere that even a Caribbean cruise can't offer.

Actually, the need for a long overdue road trip was one of the main reasons I decided to go when I did. It was a shock for those who'd heard what I was up to. Back when I said I was making all the ballparks in a season, most people who gave a rip assumed I'd fly.

"You teach school, don't you?" they'd say. "That's certainly gonna cost a lot, to fly to all those places."

When I told 'em that I was driving they just looked at me kind of strange-like. "By yourself?" was the usual response. Outside of my circle of friends, who knew that I was weird and thought nothing of it, I was a certified loony.

What these people didn't realize was that half the excitement of the trip was driving 15,000 miles in 60 days. They obviously didn't know a car is more than a mere transportation machine. Probably 'cause they gave up on long drives after suffering through them in childhood. I haven't forgotten what it was like to be 12. Back then, piling into the family station wagon to go anywhere other than the ball diamond was torture. A half hour on the same road, without an ice-cream cone or a bathroom break, was a killer. I now know why Dad would go crazy. And why we went on only one real family vacation.

Fortunately, in this one endeavor, I've matured. I now know that a highway is not an obstacle but a haven, a cradle of creativity. Actually if I had to do it all over again, I'd probably bag college and become a truck driver.

Not all journeys are great though. It doesn't just happen. Certain factors are involved, which with the right mental preparation can make a cruise through nowhere land actually more inspiring than a trip down the ultrascenic California coast. For in order to appreciate long periods on the empty highway, a true road tripper can never be on the way just for the scenery. Scenery—whether it be mountains, sunsets, or even ultrascenic seacoasts—gets boring. The mental state of an efficient driver cannot tire. Instead it reaches for a zen state, totally void of physical feeling, pleasure or pain. This state can come only from hours of intensive preparation.

The last thing you want on any journey is to end up lost. Getting lost can destroy the peaceful feeling that 600 miles at a shot creates. Also considering the neighborhood can get pretty dangerous. For years I've become more and more experienced at highways and byways of the U.S.A., always guided by my *Rand McNally Road Atlas*. Every state is covered in poster-size paper, every highway highlighted. Nothing's unconquerable. Even big Eastern cities, buried in summer construction projects, have special inserts. And the whole thing folds neatly into a book that can slip in the pocket on the side of the door. With *Rand McNally* no land is out of reach. Without it, any trip is most likely to reach a confused and bitter end.

Just as essential as the "Highway Bible" is a dependable auto—one that's hopefully maintenance-free. Shady garage repairmen drool at the sight of out-of-state plates. Dollar signs register in their eyeballs. Nonworking parts finally find a place to go. The cost of a breakdown, in bucks as well as sanity, is often enough to haunt the entire voyage. That's why I bought a Tercel, Japan's most dependable jewel, a car for which a 25-year fully covered parts warranty would've been a waste of money. The only real problem was in breaking the news of a Japanese car to Dad.

Besides foreign and maintenance-free, the car must be loaded with options. AC, sunroof, cruise control, and a well-tuned radio-cassette deck—I chose options, then had the car built around 'em. Thus I own the world's only economy Tercel that costs more than Toyota's top-of-the-line Camry.

Of all the options, the radio-cassette is most important. Music is its most important function, tapes the most important music. For me three fellas in particular make a road trip right. Seger and Springsteen are the best for good-mood, beeping-the-horn to, rocking-out music. The dashboard makes a great drum set. And unlike the stuff my school kids tune to, they have lyrics that make sense, even when played forward.

Yet, even as good as the two rockers are, the master of a road trip is the "Chairman of the Board." Leo Durocher once said, "It's Frank Sinatra's world, we only live in it." How true. The guy is great! Nobody is as good at capturing the moment. Whether it be lighthearted times or the end of the world, Sinatra makes me feel it. Frank can light a fire that nothing can put out. When he rips into a chorus backed by Billy May's swinging brass band, I can't help but burst out singing. If I'm alone, I'll always join in. If somebody's with me, sometimes for their sake I'll resist. Usually, though, I don't care. Wherever or with whoever, if Frank's rolling, so am I. Besides brass-banding it, he knows how it is when no one cares. A savior for shattered romances, ole Frank has saved me a couple of times. Whenever I feel like wallowing in self-pity, I just pull out a few Sinatra saloon-song tapes. I feel so sad I get better.

I started listening to Frank in college. At first it was just a joke. A little cornball Sinatra music at a Friday-night kegger was always good for a few laughs. Girls thought it was cute if you knew the words. And I needed all the help I could get. But Sinatra was like drugs. Pretty soon I'd put him on on Tuesday or Wednesday nights. I'd get some crap from my roommates, but I didn't really care. Things got really serious when I started listening to him by myself, then borrowing albums. Finally shelling out some of my beer money for my own albums. My senior year I came all the way out of the closet. I listened to him outside. Our second-floor apartment balcony was great for Friday-night sunsets. Some Sinatra, a couple of beers, a few burgers on the grill, and the sun sinking below the telephone wires...what a way to start a weekend!

When I left Seattle I expected to cassette-deck-it all the way. I wouldn't need a radio 'cause I'd never get tired of my tapes. Inevitably, though, even five hours of Sinatra wears on the brain. So I turned to the radio. FM stations from town to town are all pretty much the same Top 40 promoters. Some show a little imagination, but their signals are so weak, they're out of range after a half hour. Consequently, you end up hearing the same songs over and over again. It allows a tune or two to become a lifelong memory. Years down the road, whenever it pops up, it brings back road-trip thoughts. In '74, when Bob and I took our first Fenway voyage, it was "Please Come to Boston." My sojourn of '85 it was Madonna—not a bad lifelong memory.

The longer I was on the road, though, the less I tuned to FM. In crucial times it was the AM dial where I found satisfaction. Local news became an obsession. Southern Oregon farm reports kept me up to date on the going price of hogs. In Northern California I learned about grapes and how they changed to wine. Later Missouri corn futures and Texas steers would join me.

Talk shows, too, were enlightening. Once in a while a local one would turn me on. But it wasn't long before I found a national favorite. Bruce Williams's "Talk Net" is the best. By my fourth night on the road I was searching the dial for his voice. Intelligent and friendly, Bruce's show, which runs for four hours straight, is all about business. Folks call in with a problem. Bruce helps solve it. If he can't, he asks other people who can to call in. Every conversation he ends with "I wish you well, my friend." He seems like such a good fella.

Besides the two Bruces, Frank, and Bob, baseball games are a great way to kill three hours at a time. Ball games on the radio are nearly as good as in person. Sometimes, considering the weather, better. Guess I've just been lucky to live where I've lived. And tuned into the announcers I have. As a kid Ernie Harwell and Ray Lane gave me the Tigers. Ernie's voice was like one of the family's. A weeknight regular on my transistor. And a Sunday-afternoon must, blaring from the old porch radio while that scent of barbecuing chicken drifted about the neighborhood. Now Dave Niehaus and Rick Rizzs do the M's, and are so convincing that I enter spring training each season honestly believing the M's have a chance.

On the road, ball games are especially good. Besides baseball you get world events in the background. Local weather reports, traffic tie-ups, and national catastrophes are talked about in their proper perspective—between innings. With a signal that must stretch from Anchorage to Mexico City, the Dodgers became my road team.

In addition to an atlas, an option-filled auto, and an efficient radio, a cooler with a reachable hinged lid is essential. It needs to be close enough to the driver's seat to be opened without you having to look away from the road. That way ending up in a ditch isn't as likely. Before MADD cleared my brain, a couple of six-packs of beer was the stuff that road trips were made of—that and a big bag of Doritos. Now caffeine, especially on long voyages, is required. Coke is a must. Still a few beers are kept on ice to wash away chips or just capture the moment. However, today they serve only as supplements, not the main staple.

With sufficient preparation even a meager road trip can settle the most distraught of minds. Not really a time for me to get in touch with myself, rather, I find the brain's chance to void a more pleasant experience. Just drifting off into oblivion, becoming conscious again, to see that L.A. is 100 miles closer, then returning to sing along with Frank is what it's all about. In the right frame of mind nirvana can be reached, even without crossing the legs or burning incense. Incense, however, is not out of the question, and with cruise control the lotus position at 65 miles per hour is quite possible.

LAYOUT AND UPKEEP: GRADE A+

If ever a baseball park welcomed a fan into its arms, Dodger Stadium is it. A virtual palace, it stretches five levels into the bright blue California sky. Colors explode from the inside. Oranges, reds, golds, but most of all Dodger blue splashes the open stadium seats. Glittering in the sunlight, they create the ultimate in a Sunday-afternoon masterpiece.

My first look at Dodger Stadium, a sunny Sunday afternoon, nearly took my breath away. From the parking lot, mouth agape, I just stared. Only a few ballparks offer such a wide-open view and none climb so high. Below the Washington Monument, or standing at the base of the Great Arch, I've been as awed. At each, my head tilted back as far as it'll go, I shield my eyes and search the clouds for the top. If I look away, just its presence lures me back. Dodger Stadium wields that kind of power. It didn't matter where I was or what I was fumbling with, my eyes kept peering up and in.

When the spell loosened I headed for the gates. Every few paces or so I still glanced up. In between looks I surveyed the grounds. They're as ordered as a feudal estate. Outdoor concrete steps and well-placed escalators lead up to multileveled entrances. Grassy landings with sturdy trees surround the walks. The invitation is grand. Had a drawbridge lowered, trumpets blared, and my arrival been announced, I wouldn't have been surprised.

Inside, too, the estate is elegant. Brightly painted hallways, conveniently placed escalators and elevators make traveling through its corridors like a walk on Olympus. Almost slippery, shiny, gray concrete floors stretch throughout the passageways. They reminded me of white castle marble, the kind where Errol Flynn dueled the evil Sheriff of Nottingham. No dirt, no garbage, no sign of mustard packets or hot-dog wrappers, nothing exists to hint that mere peasants traipse about it daily.

After roaming the castle grounds, and feeling the flavor of the park, I decided if King Arthur had owned a baseball team, this is where they'd have played. In Los Angeles, amid the sunshine and fair-weather breezes, in the "City of Angels," this is where Camelot would have been standing.

BALL FIELD: GRADE A

What else would you expect from a palace but the loveliest of gardens? A beautiful grass field nourished by the healthy glow of constant California sunshine, it's one of the majors' most handsome.

Perfect weather isn't the only reason the grass glows. Chalk is laid only for foul balls, not first downs. Baseball is the royal game, and everything inside the garden, especially the little things, gets constant attention. A Mercedes-Benz hood ornament has nothing to do with the guts of the car, but polished and clean, it symbolizes pure class. Dodger quality is obsessed with such items. Sixth-inning replacement of the pearly white bags is exactly on cue. And the ground crew that takes care of it is dressed to the nines. Rubber mats with matching team logos cover both on-deck circles. And the infield, which is dragged over and over again, gets one last sprinkle just before game time... seconds before the first pitch.

With the gorgeous grass and rich brown dirt, beautiful skies and a Sunday-afternoon old-timers' game, I was in heaven. Then when Koufax strolled to the pitcher's mound and hummed a couple across, for a moment I thought baseball had finally found its time machine.

SEATING: GRADE A

Huge but intimate, Dodger Stadium dispels the rumor that small is always better. Some of the other 50- or 60-thousand-seat monsters take on baseball as a mere renter. They also invite in anybody else who's got a buck—football, soccer, or track, and on occasion the inside ones even host basketball tourneys. Thus seats point every which way. Not in Camelot. All 56,000 face one direction—home plate. It's the biggest pure baseball park in the world.

Behind home plate five levels climb high into L.A.'s always sunny sky. From the very top, hovering over home plate, the view's unreal. It's how God must see the game. Level five is the pinnacle. Serving as a crown to the castle, it reaches only from first base around to third. The other four stretch all the way down each foul line. With seven front rows, no stray posts to hold it up, the place just bursts with good baseball seats.

Not only do the seats provide a good look at the Dodgers, at no additional cost, but they offer other extras. A bouquet of reds, golds, and blue (only the Dodger shade), just the seats' colors add a little pizzazz to the place. And sitting is a joy. Comfortable plastic, with wide aisles between them, seats within the foul poles are just about as good as they get. It's a great combination that the ballpark uses: only the most advanced technology, one sport allowed, and typical Dodger attention to the little things. Final result—a super place to watch baseball.

As good as reserved chairs are, beyond the outfield fences in the general admission seats the park is at its very best. Many of today's new stadiums, in order to pack in more folks and make more money, cover the outfield with three tiers of plastic. They enclose the place, ruin the gaze to the inside, and dispose of bleachers. No designated place is set aside to drink beer, talk dirty, and let loose a little. Sophisticated as the place is, Dodger games can be watched from bleachers. Fans can soak up the suds and bleach their bones, even watch the ball game if they care to. There, as well, a little Dodger extra is provided. For those who'd rather not bake but still like the cost and spirit of the bleachers, a small overhang shades the back rows.

At a place that prides itself on providing all the extras, isn't it grand that you can still enjoy baseball in the old simple style... kicked back in the sunshine on any seat you choose, out behind Guerrero in left?

SCOREBOARD: GRADE B

Most of the palace is perfect. Not the scoreboard. Other than not providing enough to eat, it's probably the ballpark's only flaw. And even then that's like saying Marilyn Monroe's teeth could've been just a wee bit whiter.

Before it's turned on, the setup is typical Dodger top quality. Unlike its crosstown neighbor in Anaheim, commercials don't obliterate it—only those orange Union (76) balls. In fact, those little logos are the only advertisements in the whole place. And they brighten it even more. Two huge screens, both behind the bleachers, looked simple enough to be good. Then, when the switch was thrown, and the left-field screen revealed Diamond Vision, I figured, well, just another Dodger A+. Not true—it has a couple of problems. The biggest is the screen itself. It just doesn't get enough playing time. Good systems exist without it, but if it's there, you might as well use it. The Dodger one never really gets into a groove. Replays and baseball shorts light it up once in a while, but most of the time it's blank and some wonderful possibilities are wasted. The other board around in right is more typical of the stadium. A simple electronic panel, it line-scores the ball game and posts the lineups. Together the two are all right. Their show's a traditional one, just a bit underdone.

Music also stays away from overdoing it. Nothing remotely Top 40-ish bombs the park. That's okay. Madonna, claiming eternal virginity, wouldn't fit in a palace. But like the Diamond Vision screen, tradition could be saved without silence. The organ could be turned up a couple of notches.

FOOD: GRADE C

Selection: Poor   Accessibility: Fair
Taste: Excellent   Cost: 18th

Castles are best remembered for their parties. Whenever I think of the Middle Ages I picture some fat king and all his buddies tanking up at the feast table. Beautiful damsels dancing about and singing songs, servants groveling in with the dishes, and all the guys getting loaded. Three-foot-long turkey drumsticks, roast pigs stuffed with apples, tankards and tankards of ale; while the peasants starve, royalty stuffs face. Since Dodger Stadium is the closest I've ever been to a castle, I expected to stuff-a-little-face. But after Dodger Dogs, one of baseball's best wieners, the rest is pretty much parsley and bread sticks.

Dodger Dogs are great. Both grilled and steamed, the almost-foot-longers overlap the bun two inches on both sides. Add a slap of mustard and crispy cold beer and you've got the turkey leg of the menu. After that carmel corn's about as fancy as it gets. A stab at the special stuff is available down on the lower level at the Club Cafeteria. To get there, though, depending where in the gigantic place you are, can be as far as a 15-minute walk and escalator ride away. And it doesn't even have a feast table.

With so little to choose from, at least the food service is conveniently set up. Concession stands are efficient. Placed in view of the field, waiting in line for something to munch on doesn't disturb the flow of the game. And although not as plush as having the peasantry pour it, beer is easy to find too. Express lines pop up everywhere. That's good, since only peanuts, popcorn, and ice cream work their way around the stands. To munch on a Dodger Dog or guzzle a cold Strohs, you gotta leave your seat. It's strange that a place so dedicated to baseball the traditional way comes up short in the peanut, popcorn, and Cracker Jack department. When the stadium finds a way to deliver that tasty Dodger Dog and some cold suds to the seats, and the stands are filled with "Get your cold beer here" and "Hey, hot dog, how 'bout a hot dog?" then the castle will be complete. I also wouldn't mind seeing some turkey leg or a little roast pork on the menu.

BALLPARK EMPLOYEES: GRADE A+

Without a doubt Dodger employees are the majors' best-dressed. In fact, someday *People* magazine will probably recognize it and put one of them in their "Best-Dressed Top Ten" issue. Not only do the folks that don the uniforms look good, they're also nice. Smiles must be a uniform requirement. And, thank God, none of 'em dine on a regular basis with Tommy Lasorda. You can actually get around their bellies.

The best of the bunch are the ushers. Decked out in blue and white, their dress is comfortably formal. For a hot Sunday afternoon, white short-sleeved shirts are pleasant. The white's spiced with a blue Dodger-inscribed necktie and navy-blue slacks. A flat straw hat with a Dodger-blue sash and a good clean spit shine to the shoes finish out the dress. Ladies look as good as the gents. A Dodger-blue logo in script splashes the front of their white shirts. A blue skirt matches the script. The two complement each other well. In pairs, at the top of every aisle, they know everything there is to know about the stadium. They do all they can to help with any problem. They are the classiest part of a pure class operation.

Others who work the premises are also on the ball. And, like the ushers, they wear happy faces. Vendors, although not allowed to carry much, push what they have hard. Sweepers armed with brooms and dust pans roam the palace halls in search of nasty spills. In a job that isn't as glamorous as ushering, even they seem to give it their all. It's amazing to watch the Dodger folk go about their business. Good wages, positive image seminars, even incentive bonuses couldn't inspire such efficiency. They must really love their jobs!

FACILITIES: GRADE A+

All the K Marts in the state of California can't have as much parking space as Dodger Stadium. Before a game the lot's covered by thousands of yellow-and-white parking strips. During it, jammed full with a normally packed house, glaring windshields take their place. Afterward the setup's so efficient, within a half hour it's nearly empty again.

At some stadiums lots are pretty much open. Drive-where-you-want-to and park-where-you-can make for a harrowing experience. The Dodger one, however, is the essence of proper planning. From the main gate, all the way in, road signs are set up. Highway-like directionals hang above the entrances. Stop signs, yield signs, this-way and that-way markers make inside travel a piece of cake. If, however, you can't read, cops are everywhere. L.A.'s finest interpret anything that isn't understandable...which ain't much.

Rest rooms sparkle. Checked every half hour by the roaming broom boys, any mess or potential mess is attacked before it spreads. Paper towels are in constant supply; everything works. I didn't see it, but I wouldn't doubt it if sinks were scoured and toilet-water temperature checked on the hour. It's amazing that a stadium can do so many things so perfectly. But it does!

ATMOSPHERE: GRADE A

Southern California is gorgeous weather, expensive women, and luxurious automobiles. All converge at Chavez Ravine inside the most traditional of places, at a palace that the Dodgers call home.

Approaching the ballpark, buried in another of the city's endless traffic jams, I worried. I couldn't help but think that L.A., with all of its hoopla, would bury baseball beneath mounds of glitter. Tradition would disappear, victim of another trendy takeover. Gone would be that hard-core Dodger tradition. Memories of Drysdale and Koufax mowing down Giants, of Jackie Robinson fighting to break an unbreakable barrier would be obliterated by Diamond Vision close-ups of Lasorda's overhang. Instead of gritting it out on the field, Dodger players would kick back in the sunshine and spend batting practice hobnobbing with movie stars. That's the California way. It changes things; gives 'em its own version. Even things that need no tampering get the California stamp.

I needn't have fretted. One glimpse across the gigantic parking lot put my fears at rest. Staring in awe at the five-leveled castle, I realized baseball could only love such a place. Not only would it flourish, but it'd do so in a style worthy of royalty.

Sunshine, 78 degrees, and blue skies—this is Los Angeles. And the scenario transfers so perfectly to baseball. Nowhere else is weather so suited to a game. With such elements come all the festivities that grace its presence. All the senses intensify in sunshine. With the sun warming cloudless blue skies, cold beer tastes colder, salted peanuts saltier. Sounds have a crisper ring to them, sights a more beautiful glow. The park explodes, like a rose in full bloom.

As for the California way, like the sunshine it only makes the place more sparkling. Dodger seats are graced not by just mere baseball fans but movie stars too. Television faces dot the baseline boxes. Stadium speakers announce "A Dodger Welcome" to a Frank Sinatra clientele. The Hollywood feel excites the place. Best of all, lovely ladies are everywhere. Box seats, bleachers, upper and lower levels, no place else are baseball fans so beautiful. California's finest offering, their presence dazzles the park, much like the damsels did in kings' courts long ago.

Even with such cosmetics a true feeling for the game could be lost. Just because beauty surrounds doesn't mean it enters into the heart. In L.A. traditions are well kept. A handsome grass field and tens of thousands of pure baseball seats adorn the grounds. Old-timers' day brought back a cast that only the Yanks could possibly match. And batting practice for both games was still, well... batting practice.

Dodger Stadium, like King Arthur's palace of long ago, stands graced by the very finest of luxuries. It rises up as the most stately structure in the game today. Yet in the custom that Arthur's Knights of the Round Table maintained, true to their principles even amid all the glory showered upon them, Dodger Stadium remains virtuous. In all its elegance it remains in touch with those simple qualities so necessary to the game. As a result Camelot exists in all of its splendor, sparkling in the California sun, dedicated to the justice of the game of baseball, now and forever.

5

ANAHEIM STADIUM, CALIFORNIA ANGELS

Country Club Baseball

REPORT CARD		*Anaheim Stadium*
		BASEBALL PARK
June 24, 85 vs Indians		*California Angels*
GAME		BASEBALL CLUB

CATEGORY	GRADE	POINTS
Layout and Upkeep	A	95
Ball Field	A	95
Seating	B	85
Scoreboard	D-	60
Food	C	75
Ballpark Employees	A+	100
Facilities	A+	100
Atmosphere	D	65
Total Points		675
Average		84

B

FINAL GRADE

9th

RANK

"A scotch-and-soda atmosphere in a hot-dog and beer world.... Even with all of its glitter, Anaheim and baseball just don't mix."

PREGAME THOUGHTS

Surrounded by freeways and flooded with BMWs, Anaheim, California, just doesn't have that old-time baseball feel. In fact, it captures every argument ever needed to condemn the big leagues for selling out to the suburbs. Street signs actually point left to the Angels' stadium while at the same time remind you that Disneyland's just a few miles in the other direction. For Peter Pan that's great—baseball and Tinker Bell in the same neighborhood. But for a kid raised on a couple of trips a summer to Tiger Stadium's bombed-out, riot-torn streets, baseball and Anaheim just don't fit.

It's not that California threatens baseball. The Dodgers revel in L.A., just because... well they're the Dodgers. Everything is first-class—from their ball club right on down to the dress of their ushers. Hollywood glitter does them justice. They play in a palace, claim royalty, draw 10 million a home stand, and it never rains on them. But the Angels are a different lot. While the Dodgers have a long rich history, the Angels' is short and sour, and filled with disappointments. If they somehow make the play-offs, it's only to find a new way to lose. Usually, though, they don't even get that chance.

Despite my doubts, I arrived at the park a couple of hours early. Like L.A.'s other gigantic stadium, nice men in uniforms took my money and directed me to a gigantic parking lot. They told me my early arrival had been made earlier due to an hour's delay... something to do with television. Figured: Wrigley had held out without lights for nearly a hundred years and Anaheim was giving into TV for a single night game. The delay did, however, give me an extra hour to kill. And a few ballpark bars were planted directly across the street from the stadium. There I could have a cold one, settle back down into my Midwest mentality, and try to forget that Mickey Mouse and Donald Duck were probably going to make a duet of "The Star-Spangled Banner."

Back where I come from a ballpark bar is someplace special. Not just a spot to stop for a cocktail, it's a home away from home, especially from April to October. Although football seeps inside on autumn weekends, even during the winter months baseball seems a main topic of conversation. Or at least a central thought. While props inside are minimal—a big bar, a well-seasoned bartender, plenty of bar stools, and a 19-inch color TV above in the corner—a simple friendly spirit hangs about the place, a feeling that only Christmastime or folks talking sports over a couple of brews can capture. To a baseball believer, someone who sees the Series as more than just another sports championship, the place offers an invitation. It calls to you "Come on in... at least for one." Then convinces you to stick around and provides a love affair with baseball.

Until Anaheim I'd been hard-pressed to find a sports bar, let alone one within striking distance from the ballyard. California has yet to discover the importance of the simple yet spiritually elegant "hole in the wall." Even if they did, there'd be no place to put 'em. Dodger Stadium, nestled in Chavez Ravine, and Candlestick, slipping into the Back Bay, don't have a 7-Eleven nearby, much less a place to drink beer and talk baseball. Crammed in between railroad tracks and dingy warehouses, Oakland's Coliseum, if it borders on a watering hole, would be best to advise folks to pass 'er up and go on home. Oddly enough, only the atmosphere-void Kingdome sits near a real live West Coast ballpark bar. And even though the city as a whole has no idea about the game, the few that do hang out at a pleasant little place called Sneakers. The problem with "Sneaks," is that by the time you cross the street to the M's concrete-covered closet that wonderful pregame excitement is drowned out by empathy in the dome.

Nothing to worry about... or so I thought. Anaheim was a different city—even if it wasn't a real city. And the Angels were in first—even if it was only June. With the game an hour and a half away, and finally a California ballpark with a couple of pubs close by, I decided to expose myself to a little pennant fever California Angel style. For the first time in five years I'd talk baseball with fans whose team wasn't in the cellar by June. So after waiting five minutes for traffic to clear, I darted across the highway-like four-laner that rolls past the stadium. Through thick wooden doors I entered into the lush, comfortable, air-conditioned confines of a ballpark bar—Hollywood style.

I guess I should have expected as much. But being so close to the stadium, it being June, and the Angels in first, I thought the place would offer more of a magnetism than Denny's. Brushing through the hanging green ferns that grew like mold from every corner, I walked into a nearly empty room. It was dark... and spiced with lavish decor. Quiet, respectable music played from tapes selected behind the counter. Quiet respectable men, most in conservative suits and ties, sat whispering about something that I was sure wasn't baseball. The carpeting was clean; Chicago it was not. Still that was okay. I'd just suck down a beer, get into the proper frame of mind, forget about the ferns, and be off across the street to see the Indians and Angels.

I strolled over to one of the plush booths and sat down. Above me, over the booth, hung a chandelier-type light fixture. It gave off a soft light. The kind that movie-star close-ups are always taken under. The wooden frame for the booth was solid. Its thick tabletop was layered over and over again with coats of clear shiny varnish. I could see the reflection of the fancy chandelier. The booths were lined with something soft and expensive that engulfed patrons. I sank down deep into it. The shiny varnished table came up nearly to my chest.

"Hello, sir," the bartender almost whispered.

I looked around, not sure who he had in mind. "You talking to me?"

He nodded, "Can I help you?"

"Sure. How 'bout a draft?"

"Nothing on tap." He said it so matter-of-factly that I guessed they hadn't just run out. "But we do have Löwenbräu in a bottle."

I wanted to ask the quiet fellow if he'd please let him out. In junior high when we were bored we'd pick numbers out of the phone book and call for Prince Albert's release from his can. After a few beers in college it was Mr. Löwenbräu. The guy looked too sophisticated for much humor though. So I asked for a burger instead. He pointed to the 53-course salad bar across the room.

"No draft? No burger?" I asked again, just to make sure.

The bartender looked down. I told him I'd go to the rest room, then make up my mind. Instead I sneaked out, leaving the bottle of Löwenbräu, the hanging ferns, and the quiet respectable businessmen in their three-piece suits behind. Granted, I wasn't in Detroit. I realized that life in a California suburb was based on ideals far removed from a huge Midwestern city. But nobody, especially across the street from a major league baseball stadium, should have to suffer through a Löwenbräu and salad before a ball game. So close to the ballpark, even Anaheim could do better.

Undaunted, I wandered farther down the street. A small 7-Eleven-type store sat on the corner. I went inside. The fellow behind the counter looked rough enough to direct me to a good tavern. I asked. He mentioned Charlie Brown's was just a few doors down. Great, at least it had a good name. I plodded the few doors down, still with a good 45 minutes left to relax and talk baseball. Up the steps and through the big, thick wooden doors, I entered into... another fern bar. Darker and more elegant than the last, it, too, was a place you'd take a date on prom night, not the type that offered a pregame pint. I wondered how long the two Anaheim bistros would last in Chicago. Across from Wrigley or Comiskey, maybe two weeks at the most and they'd be laughed out of town. They were as misplaced across the street from a baseball park as was I standing in the doorway.

I felt like Ole MacDonald goes to Hollywood. Decked out in my spiffy blue shorts, stinky sandals, Mariner shirt, and shoulder-slung backpack, I surveyed the room with disbelief. Everywhere I looked healthy green hanging plants, big-screen TVs, cutesy-pie waitresses in skimpy outfits—everything that the quiet, respectable, non-baseball type people enjoyed. Still not really sure what I was doing or why I was staying, I took a seat. When I looked to my left and saw it! At the very table that I'd stumbled to, only a few paces in front of me, in a bar only blocks from where the first-place Angels were going to play was a shrine to West Coast baseball mentality...an ornament that typified California fern bars. There it sat on the lush carpet, splashed in full and living color—its bright blue hue set against the orange curling horns. Built permanently around the lounge chair to which it was attached, so that you could sink inside, like on a carnival ride at Knott's Berry Farm, was a gigantic plastic Los Angeles Rams football helmet.

I felt sick. Just then a waitress in a short skirt bounced up and asked if I was all right. I looked ill, she said. I was okay, I told her. I just needed some air. Staggering to the door, back out into the sun and away from the Ram Club, I found the corner 7-Eleven. After buying a Bud from the same fellow who moments ago had sent me to Charlie Brown's, I returned to the curb. Across from Anaheim Stadium, between Löwenbräuville and Charlie Brown's, smelling in all of the premium unleaded fumes that a constant parade of European sports cars could exhaust, I finally settled back into my Midwestern mentality and enjoyed my Bud.

LAYOUT AND UPKEEP: GRADE A

Miles of highways, millions of cars without rust, and blocks upon blocks of two-car-garage split-level houses—Anaheim city limits are typical suburban California...and then some. With Disneyland down the street, and the ballpark usually more crowded than not, the neighborhood is never quiet. In fact, the only thing that ever slows are the unending lines of cruising automobiles.

As for the stadium, it dominates its plastic neighborhood. Pushed back off the crowded four-lane streets, backdropped by the San Gabriel Mountains, and set inside a palm-tree-peppered landscape, it's actually quite sharp. Add to the fact that it rises up out of acres of concrete parking spaces, that it's the only building around bigger than a corner drugstore, and it seems to triple in size. Although it doesn't throw a Dodger Stadium five-tiered knockout punch, the ballpark is nevertheless impressive.

Convenient and clean are Angel Stadium bywords. Once inside, an atmosphere of explicit, spotless, almost perfect detail serves a very efficient facility. Escalators usher fans swiftly up the three-tiered inside. Getting around the place couldn't be easier. If, however, for some reason it isn't, large plastic directories nearly 8 feet square are spaced all about the inner aisles. Outlining and color-coordinating separate walkways and seating sections, the directories handle all basic questions. They also highlight more important items, like special dining and drinking clubs. Telephones, first aid, and security stations are identified as well. Even rest rooms are marked. Everything that's bigger than a coat closet is featured on the plastic boards. The idea is a good one—particularly at a place that provides so much entertainment.

BALL FIELD: GRADE A

The grass is beautiful...the dirt ain't. Like Dodger Stadium across town, and south to Jack Murphy, Anaheim gets the most from its Southern California sunshine. No place else in the world does ballpark grass grow so well. Summers in the pleasant 70's...winter plummets into the nippy 60's. Just enough rain, hardly ever a frost. California's three southernmost stadiums probably don't even use fertilizer.

Although Anaheim's grass is soft as a putting green, and probably smoother...the dirt can't keep its color straight. Shade number one, a dark rich brown, covers the warning track. The color scheme blends nicely with a perfectly trimmed outfield. If all the dirt was warning-track brown, the field would be gorgeous. But infield dirt portions feature a second color. Kept as neatly as the other, shade number two is much lighter, almost grayish. Finally, pitcher's mound and home plate pick up a third reddish tone. While the three-pronged color wheel isn't dream-shattering, it does taint the flawless carpet in between.

There's probably not a ballpark in America with more handsome grass. Maybe Jack Murphy, maybe not. It's tough to tell the difference between perfect and perfect. But A+ material? Not until the dirt gets fixed.

SEATING: GRADE B

Used to be Anaheim was set up just right for baseball—before '79, when they kicked out the Big A scoreboard, invited in the Rams, 20,000 more chairs, and enclosed the place.

Back then most of the seats were great baseball ones—no obstructions, good sight lines, close to the action. Now three levels surround the field. To-day the place still has good sight lines and no obstructions, good views are still good. But close to the action? With a capacity of over 65,000, now most of the chairs are in tier number three. That's a long way from the ball game. If the place is packed, which it often is, and you don't get there early, chances are you'll end up in it. If that's the case, better bring along a radio so you'll have a clue who's up to bat.

As for comfort, there aren't many better. Typically suburbanish, roomy and plastic, almost everywhere inside a body is able to stretch out and relax. Aisles are up to California standards both in size and number. Rows are plenty wide enough. Plastic chairs fold up and down and provide all sorts of leg room. In fact, folks can even sneak to the rest room without forcing a chain-reaction rise by everybody in their way.

SCOREBOARD: GRADE D−

Not much more than a revolving television commercial, the scoreboard is Anaheim's crummiest feature. Hovering three tiers above ground level, flanked on each side by a pair of giant billboards, its primary concern seems less base-ball than—more important—that everybody watching knows once and for all...that Coke is it!

Each of the four billboards rotates its advertisement. That way twice as much money can be made renting them out. In addition, each by itself is as big as the single panel concerned with baseball. With so many ads crammed together, it's tough to find any baseball stats. Searching for even a batting av-erage is about like feeling out the corner pieces of a jigsaw puzzle. One glance away, even if it be for just a moment, and it's impossible to refocus on the original stat. If the permanent posted advertisements weren't enough, while baseball took its inner inning breaks, more commercials flashed across the screen. In fact, it wasn't until the sixth that any major league updates even made it up, and then just for a fleeting moment. And that for a Red Sox fan like me is pure torture. Since the Sox usually go through four or five pitchers a game, and more in Fenway, I usually spend as much time checking out scores someplace else as I do the ball game in front of me. At Angel Stadium I was lost...with absolutely no idea who or how many Bosox hurlers were in the process of getting hammered on.

Fortunately the sound system's not so bad. A deep, booming public ad-dress system echoes throughout the stadium, while between innings organ mu-sic grapples for control with tapes. None of the three, thank God, sells anything.

Even so, they can't offset the rest of the mess. It's too bad the scoreboard's patterned after prime-time TV. But then again I guess it does offer Angel fans a little hidden extra. Although they might not have a clue as to what the score is, at least by game's end they do know what cigarette to smoke, what kind of car to drive, and what gas to put in it.

FOOD: GRADE C

Selection: Excellent   Accessibility: Fair

Taste: Very Good   Cost: 17th

If the Hilton Hotel was ever hired out to cater a baseball park, they'd copy Anaheim. Gluttony and convenience side by side. Cocktails are never more than a short elevator ride away. Lounges cover every turn. Best of all, almost everybody takes Visa. Just like Charlie Brown's across the street, the menu's probably great for a pre-prom dinner or a polo match. But baseball...I doubt it.

From a pure quality standpoint, the menu is, as would be expected at any country club, par excellence. Sports Corners, featuring specialty sandwiches, pastrami, and beef dip au jus, are about as blue collar as the menu gets. From then on things get rich. Bud, while on tap at the peasant booths, isn't quite exotic enough for royalty. So upstairs at a separate site, and stocked with imported brew, is Beers of America. Also for the pickier palate, a fancy seafood station graces the upper deck. Stocked with fresh shrimp cocktail, oysters on the half shell, and crab salad, all exquisitely laid out on ice, the "We Take Visa" sign that hovers above tells the financial story.

The stadium's most lavish productions, however, flow from its endless number of cocktail lounges. And they come in all shapes and sizes. Four Grand Slam Clubs spaced throughout the place are perfect for someone who, totally bored with baseball, still wants to be social, enjoy the evening, and get sloshed on martinis. A ticket to one of the four clubs offers groups not only the game but all sorts of luxurious extras. A catered picnic dinner during batting practice, out behind the center-field fence, is course number one. Blocked-off ball-game seats right next door to one of the ritzy hangouts is a second added privilege. And of course number three's the big-screen TV. Traipsing back and forth between the TV and seats is encouraged. And even there you get a little help. If, after the picnic and cocktails, you feel faint from too much booze, an Angel doorman is especially assigned to the club doorway and available for you to slobber on.

You don't have reservations to the Grand Slam Clubs? No need to worry.

Like old-fashioned ice-cream wagons, portable rolling bars roam the stadium hallways. Each is loaded with liquor and manned by a real bartender. He even mixes drinks just the way they do it at the club. Thus nobody, regardless of financial status, ever has to go more than an inning without a favorite cocktail.

With Sports Corner taverns and Grand Slam Clubs available for those only mildly wealthy Southern Californians, folks with the big bucks, those who go just for the thrill of the game, visit the luxurious Stadium Club. After seeing the fringe benefits to being a "normal" Angel fan, I had to find out what luxury Anaheim style consisted of. So I talked my way inside. There, during batting practice, "beautiful people" were going through their pregame warm-ups. Elegant ladies with movie-star faces joined gentlemen clad in "non-rented" tuxes as they sampled a prime rib buffet. I was really happy for them, that after leaving their Mercedes in the lot, wolfing down a 12-course dinner, and retiring to their luxury box for the fourth, fifth, and sixth innings, they wouldn't have to even look at a hot dog.

As a wining and dining experience the place is unreal... at least when it comes to the credit-card stuff. But the basics? You'd think that getting a hot dog and a Bud would be a snap. Not so... nobody carries 'em. The only way to get either is to leave the game, go out to the concessions, and after passing a couple of rolling liquor carts and a club or two, waste an inning standing in line.

BALLPARK EMPLOYEES: GRADE A+

Spiffy and friendly, dressed in orange blazers and bright blue slacks to match the Angels, Anaheim's employees are some of the league's best. Concessionaires, security people, and ushers are not only well drilled on what to do, but treat you like one of the family. In fact, only in Milwaukee did I find a group as concerned with my well-being.

The best example of such genuine hospitality was shown me by a little old black gentleman. As he told me later, he had worked at the stadium for some fifteen years. Judging by his friendly manner, he must've loved most every one of those fifteen.

Having fled the clutches of that giant Rams helmet, I still had a half hour to kill when I got to the ballpark. And with Anaheim early on the trip, I was still camera crazy. Anything touristy I came across, I double-shot. I'm always like that, until I start paying for developing. The stadium's "Big A" reader board caught my eye. A huge 230-foot A-frame structure, it used to keep score on the inside. When they closed up the ballpark in '79 the huge haloed board was deported to the edge of the stadium parking lot, condemned to a life of listing upcoming events. For my obsession with anything that was remotely related to each stadium, and on my eighth roll of film in four days, the Big A was a monument that had to be three-by-five glossied.

I ran into a problem though. Although it stood outside of the park, coming from the direction that I had, I didn't notice it until I was already inside. For the better part of a half hour I roamed the near empty stadium searching for a good shot of the Big A. Each separate escalator ride would take me to the top of a different section. Each search would end with a locked chain-link fence. After being turned away at each of the lower outfield levels, I made my final attempt in the upper deck. It was there that I encountered the old fellow.

A rolling gate just like all the others guarded the entrance into the deep, deep sections of the third level. The old man guarded the gate. While everybody else was down watching Reggie smash batting-practice slow balls into the bleachers, it was his job to protect empty areas from roaming vandals like me. For all he knew my backpack could've been loaded with Crayolas drooling for some rest-room wall to draw on.

I stopped at his gate. We exchanged hellos. I told him my story. I even tried to explain the photographic significance that the Big A held for a scrapbook photographer like me. I didn't anticipate much sympathy, though. Expecting the obvious—"It's not park policy"—I began walking away before I was even through asking.

The old fellow caught me off guard. "Hold on there a second, young man," he commanded. I stopped.

Peering in both directions, and examining the aisles up into the stands, he scanned the immediate area for roaming bosses. Convinced that none were nearby, he rolled the gate aside and welcomed me to walk on in. His offer both surprised and delighted me. I thanked him and entered. Not wanting the fellow to get into trouble on my account, and noticing from his thorough search that he was concerned, I quickly went about my work. It was a poor angle, but better than any I could've gotten outside of the gate, and I focused and clicked twice. Content with my good fortune, I thanked him again and headed back out the gate.

He stopped me. "I thought you wanted a good one. That's not a good one." He was right, it wasn't.

"For my scrapbook, it's good enough. And what about your job? I don't want you to get in trouble."

"Don't worry about it," he assured me. "I've worked here for fifteen years, nobody's gonna hassle me. I've got a soft spot in my heart for that old A myself. Now follow me, let's get you a real picture."

Hesitantly at first, then happily, I followed the old Angel. Clear around to the back of the third level, he led me to a place that *National Geographic*, if they were to shoot a layout on the Big A, would have shot from. All the while we strolled we gabbed about really nothing in particular. Away from the gate and his roaming bosses, the old man carried on as if he hadn't a care in the world. Satisfied that he had ushered me to the city's finest view of the halo-covered A-frame, he halted. "Now give it a shot." Three more clicks and convinced I had the Big A in its most photographic pose, I put my camera away. We headed back for the gate.

On the way I told him that I was from Seattle. He was delighted. He wondered if I knew Don, an old buddy of his. They'd been good friends.

"For seven years Don and I worked together here at the stadium. Then he transferred up to your Kingdome. He was a good friend, Don was. I've often wondered what's become of him."

While he couldn't remember off-hand his buddy's last name, he gave me a complete description. He hoped that I might've come across him in my travels to the Dome. I hadn't. I felt bad; it would have pleased the old man. But Kingdome employees had never been so kind. Consequently, I knew them only as ticket takers and popcorn peddlers, orange-clad attendants with no names.

Back at the rolling iron gate, we paused and talked some more. We discussed baseball—outdoors and indoors—talked of Reggie and Carew... and other pleasant things that come to mind at a ballpark on a warm California night. He asked if the next time I went to the Dome I'd keep an eye out for Don. I promised that I would. We wished one another well and parted company, each heading our separate ways—me to roam the rest of Anaheim, he to guard his empty third level.

More than just a couple shots of the Big A, the old fellow left me with a great feeling. In a time when everybody is in a hurry to do nothing in particular, he wasn't. He had all the time in the world. In an age where employees are indoctrinated, and justifiably so, to believe that people out of assigned areas are there to destroy something, he believed me. That old Big A was even special for him. He and his good nature bless Anaheim with a *real* touch of class. One that all of its floating cocktail lounges and fresh seafood shops will never produce.

FACILITIES: GRADE A+

Hotels normally feature only the finest facilities. Valet parking and plush rest rooms are a couple of the flashier reasons they can squeeze $99.95 a night out of a client. About the only difference here is that fans have to park themselves.

Five highways surround the stadium. So getting to it's not much of a problem. Neither is finding an open parking spot. The lot is typical of California: humongous, well-lit, well-marked, and overlooked by plenty of well-mannered folks. What makes Anaheim's parking lot unique isn't the layout but what fills it. I've never seen so many Mercedes in my life. European sports cars, American luxury models, they all had one thing in common—sticker price. Most probably tripled the cost of my Toyota. Usually in any parking lot, regardless of how secured it is, I worry about my car. Not at Anaheim. I could've left the windows down and doors open. Prying into my Tercel amid all the ritzy mobiles would've been like breaking into a bank, then stealing plastic pens.

As would be expected, inside facilities are also well kept. Plenty of freshly painted rest rooms with full-length mirrors provide ample relief from roving stadium bars. Water fountains, telephones, and other items considered luxuries at some parks are easy to find. If they can't be, all you have to do is ask a friendly employee or search out a giant plastic directory. A well-organized stadium, it's the best-kept place in the neighborhood, which, don't forget, includes Disneyland.

ATMOSPHERE: GRADE D

Typical of baseball in the burbs, although blessed with the best cosmetics and friendly staff, the spirit of Anaheim is lifeless. It's a movie-star stadium with a Hollywood feel. Glittery around the edges, it's shallow in the center. Something inside the luxurious place just doesn't fit.

An evening out with the Angels is safer than catching the Tigers in downtown Detroit. A sunshiny plastic paradise, streets about the ballpark crawl with cops not hoodlums. And not only is a body safe, but so is the car. Odds are that it'll have four hubcaps by game's end. Cleanliness is also a top priority. Neighborhood roadways aren't like in South Chicago, cracked and narrow. Big-city garbage that Yankee and Met fans wade through doesn't engulf the Southern Californian. Instead, streets are cleaned and pressed, four-laned, neatly asphalted, and getting to a ball game is no frightening nightmare. Inside, as well, white-glove standards are strictly enforced. Even the folks who greet a body are warm and friendly. Norman Rockwell couldn't have chosen a more cheerful group. On paper Anaheim Stadium's got everything that should make a ballpark grand.

But something in the heart is missing. While the ballpark flourishes with elegance, it ignores the simple, and baseball at heart is simple. With clubs, "corners," taverns, and lounges all spaced within stumbling distance of one another, alcoholic possibilities are amazing. So much effort to provide just the right booze. But up in the stands where it really counts, no dogs or beer.

Besides a ritzy but hollow menu, folks in the stands are lifeless. A classic 3-to-1 pitchers' duel, the ball game was my journey's best. After roaming I spent the night watching Bert Blyleven drop curve balls over the plate like they were rolling off a kitchen table. And wondering if the Angel bats had holes in 'em. But I was in the stadium minority. Although folks flooded the place by the tens of thousands, most chairs were empty by the ninth. During the game lounge-covered walkways under the stands were packed. . . even when the Angels batted. Clubs were filled, televisions tuned in, a great game was being played, but unless two were on and two were out, I got the idea nobody paid much attention.

All the doubts I had rolling into Dodger Stadium—the glitter, that Hollywood hollowness, that baseball just wouldn't be baseball—hit home in Anaheim. For me it's the ball game that plays center stage. Not the clubs, not the booze, not even the comfortable plastic view. Baseball's what matters most. And in an edge-of-the-seater, half the Angel folks left early. Meanwhile, the rest carried on like it was just some sideshow to another perfectly pleasant California night. Anaheim's not real baseball, it's another Disneyland production—a scotch-and-soda ballpark serving a Budweiser game. While the Rams might go great with a fresh shrimp salad and a glass of white wine, for a baseball fan. . . I don't think so. One can only look up at the scoreboard, searching for the score amid all of the commercials, and wonder forever when the hot-dog guy will arrive.

6

JACK MURPHY STADIUM, SAN DIEGO PADRES

Let the Sun Shine In

REPORT CARD	*Jack Murphy Stadium*
	BASEBALL PARK
June 26/27, 85 vs Dodgers	*San Diego Padres*
GAME	BASEBALL CLUB

CATEGORY	GRADE	POINTS
Layout and Upkeep	*B*	*85*
Ball Field	*A+*	*100*
Seating	*D*	*65*
Scoreboard	*A+*	*100*
Food	*B*	*85*
Ballpark Employees	*C*	*75*
Facilities	*B*	*85*
Atmosphere	*B*	*85*
Total Points		*680*
Average		*85*

B
FINAL GRADE

7th
RANK

74

"Hot sunny days, cool clear nights... beautiful weather and a ballpark that knows how to have a good time."

PREGAME THOUGHTS

When I set this trip up back in May my San Diego stop posed a bit of a problem—I wasn't sure where to spend it. In Oakland I was gonna stay with a friend of a friend. His place was only a few miles from the Coliseum and just a bridge ride to Frisco... worked out great. I was able to get in both games and find an auto shop to reseal my car. For L.A. as well, everything was all planned out. A high school buddy turned DEA agent lived in Corona. I hadn't seen him for a few years, but he told me to come on down. So I did, crashed there a couple of nights, saw two ball games, and listened to real live *Miami Vice* stories.

San Diego was a little different. I didn't know anybody in town. Nobody I knew had any friends there either. Not only that, I had my first real break—four days off in a row. Originally I thought about sleeping on the beach, but my little excursion in Williams had cured the need for stimulation outside of the ballpark. Motels were a possibility, but in such a touristy, sunshiny paradise, they were bound to cost way too much. If I crashed in the car for four days, I could guard my things, but I'd probably never walk normally again. I wasn't really left with an alternative. For the first of what would be many times, I turned to my bible of survival—*Kampgrounds of American Directory*. I opened it, crossed my fingers, and searched under San Diego. There it was! San Diego Metro: "Open all year round, swimming pool and showers"—four stars. A quick phone call and a four-day tent reservation in downtown San Diego was mine.

This wasn't to be my first experience with KOAs. I used their grounds a few years earlier when I moved west from Michigan. A combination McDonald's, 7-Eleven, and Motel 6 all thrown into one, they're everything a fake camper like me could ask for. From Bugtussel, Kentucky, to San Diego Metro, they absorb almost every other highway exit in the U.S.A. Cheap, quick, and cloned, they're as American as hot dogs.

While each has little variances that only a KOA regular, like I was to become, can notice, they cover the basics in pretty much the same manner. All of 'em, even in Alabama, have hot showers. Another life-saver, besides checking folks in and out, the office doubles as a 7-Eleven. Milk, bread, pop, and postcards—it sells all of a traveler's necessities at only triple grocery-store prices.

Protection, too, is added cost-free. With Fidos and Rovers all over the place, cars continually pulling in and out, smart thieves stay away. My worthless stuff picked over up north was safe as long as I kept camping. Finally, for the social life, KOA's most luxurious models feature a swimming pool. Five feet in the deep end, it's always filled with hundreds of undisciplined screaming kids and fat people dozing in lounge chairs. Overnight crashers like me, or a mobile-home family socked in for a fun-filled, two-week vacation, it's a strange mix that hangs around the fake campgrounds.

Camping itself is probably the most overrated occupational disaster that befalls the human race. However, in the Pacific Northwest, with a populace that ignores baseball, it's an obsession. Back-to-nature freaks, and otherwise normal folks, love it. They find nothing more refreshing than hiking into a thick rain forest and smelling the pines for three days. Setting up tents in the rain, eating bark, and listening to birds chirp is the only true way to recoup from that weekday nine-to-five rut. They don't even care that the closest rest room is over the river and through the woods on the other side of Granny's house. And all for what?...fresh air and the chance to get in touch with themselves.

No thank you! I'll take a living-room couch for snoozing, a good 19-inch remote-control color TV to flip back and forth between ball games, a cold beer, and a couple of microwaved roast-beef sandwiches. I've always wondered how you could get more in touch with yourself than stretched out in front of the tube with all the goodies of the fridge only a commercial away. It's our payoff for winning so many wars. To spend each day like a typical South American, traipsing about in the woods and peeing behind trees, doesn't quite compare to all plug-in things that make America great.

Despite an anti-camping philosophy, I do own those items essential to the sport. Back in college everything, even camping, sounded "neat," and I actually gave it a whirl. Garage sales and swap meets had lured me into their clutches—my reward a KOA survivalist accumulation of junk. I owned everything that was too heavy to carry but a requirement if living out of the back end of a '77 Pinto.

My first purchase was a tent. It seemed like a logical place to start. A $39.95, three-man, yellow-on-green Montgomery Ward special, complete with necessary rain flap, was my portable house. When I bought it the rain flap was nice. In Washington it became more important than tent stakes. Next on my list—a fat foam pad. It resists the lumpy roots that the tent always seems to find. And prevents overnight recurvature of the spine. Even more important than a pad is the sleeping bag. To be useful it must feature a double zipper on Rip-Stop nylon, since otherwise the zipper always gets stuck and rips the nylon, and quickly turns the bag into shreds. Tent, bag, and pad are the basics. These three musts, along with a bag of nuts and berries, are what Pacific Northwest campers carry into the woods for their back-to-nature romps.

I have added a few Midwestern touches. A double-burner, ten-pound, green Coleman Camper Cooker, and a gallon of white heat to run it, is fundamental. These little stoves, while not as convenient as a portable microwave, beat the hell out of roasting rabbit over an open-pit fire. And they're wonderful for preparation of chili dogs, the only food I've ever eaten in the wild. Plus, the white heat is a great way to cheat on campfires.

A Coleman lantern, which gives off enough light to land a plane by, is another critical item. A cooler large enough to ice down a 12-pack yet still contain room for the hot dogs and OJ is as standard as the cooker. A combination radio-tape player is important for sanity's sake. AM must be able to capture local ball games, while the cassette deck is nice for cranking out a little Sinatra. Both are reminders that civilization still exists somewhere outside of the campground.

A few final luxuries round out the package. To find the KOA rest room after another chili-dog episode, it's nice to have a Durabeam flashlight handy. A can opener to get into the chili to mix with the dogs and a heavy no-stick frying pan to cook 'em is also crucial. Two place settings complete with silverware, one to eat off, the other to replace the one that will eventually be left at a campground, are the final necessities.

This is Chicago-style camping. This is how I camp. This is how normal Americans should camp. If the campsite is within two blocks of a tavern, 3.4 miles of a movie theater, and 11 miles from a shopping mall, the layout is complete and the situation ideal. I hoped, as well, that San Diego Metro would be a short hop to Jack Murphy and real civilization.

LAYOUT AND UPKEEP: GRADE B

Jack Murphy is a "neat" name for a baseball park. Just like "one of the guys," its name personalizes the place. "Going to Murphy's" or "I've got tickets at Jack Murphy tonight" is more fun than just seeing the Padres play. That, plus my flashy KOA tent site and all the nice weather, got me a little more pumped for my last California ballpark.

First impressions of the stadium, however, weren't so great. It is plopped in the middle of nowhere, with not so much as a four-story building nearby. No skyscrapers, no factories, no big-city excitement—suburbs don't even consume it. Convenient expressways drain into acres and acres of concrete parking spots. Typical West Coast multipurpose, its only real game-day scenery consists of thousands of glaring windshields.

The ballpark does, however, add a feature of its own—a touch of strange. Finished in '67, Murphy has that weird Space Needle flare about it. "Wow" or "Groovy" are the best ways to describe it. Huge, odd-looking concrete swirls surround the place. They look like giant upright Slinkies squashed down to normal size. My fifteen-minute walk from car to front gate was spent wondering what on earth they were. Missile silos, modern light standards, giant water or beer towers—I had no idea. Between each of the six swirls are gigantic outside escalators. Three-story ones piggyback up and over shorter two-story models. Each runs from ground level up into the stadium. An open concrete plaza dotted with small trees fills the rest of the space in between. Locking in the Slinkies, electric stairs, and real trees, a wall surrounds the plaza. The setup is odd-looking, even for California.

Although it looks weird, Murphy works. Its strange-looking structures have a common purpose—to provide the simplest of strolls inside. For traditional folks who enjoy walking, they can. Straight in from the concrete plaza to ground-level seats. For those in a hurry, alternatives are available. The concrete swirls are one. Not missile silos at all, the swirls are actually giant walkways. They spin their way up to the top, allowing drop-offs at each level along the way. Finally, for no-hassle direct deposit upstairs, the three-story and double-deck escalators work great.

Jack Murphy is different. It's California but it's not. It's weird-looking but it works. While it's set up like a typical West Coaster, typical white-glove standards aren't enforced. Not nearly as breathtaking as a gaze into giant Dodger Stadium, it brings on puzzlement instead. Never having been inside, I didn't have a clue as to what to expect. I knew only one thing. With such a neat name, it had to be a decent place for baseball.

BALL FIELD: GRADE A+

Baseball's most beautiful grass! Maybe the world's finest, Jack Murphy's turf is pure gorgeous. A deep rich green, cut to checkerboard perfection...I could have stared at the empty playing field all night long and gone home happy.

Grass just doesn't come any prettier. As lush as a putting green, its cuts are absolutely perfect. Nowhere does it splotch or fade or show even the slightest scar. And the checkerboard is wonderful. Crisscrossing light and dark squares take turns bathing the ball field in green. At most places, with two outs and the runners moving, a screaming line drive, the crowd roaring, pitcher turned and watching—an outfielder sprinting to the gap to kill a triple in mid-flight is thrilling. Even in high school for me, on our stone-spattered field, with mom- and dad-filled crowds it was. But for Tony Gwynn to do it while gliding across the San Diego green is a work of art.

I've always figured "If you've got it, flaunt it." You might not have it for long. Murphy must feel the same. Besides the grass being perfect, it's everywhere. In places where sod normally gives way to dirt, at the San Diego Stadium it doesn't. Instead of dirt running on either side of the right- and left-field foul lines, they're green. Foul-line lime is laid right onto the grass! The effect is marvelous. Coaching boxes aren't standard dirt boxes, instead just lines on the grass. And even those are so well kept that they look as if nobody stands in them.

One thing's for sure—whoever invented the concept of astro grass never watched a ball game at Jack Murphy. If he did, he'd have destroyed his plastic formula.

SEATING: GRADE D

While walking into the stadium is unbelievably simple, finding a seat makes up for it. For a first-timer it can take longer than the five-mile journey from parking lot to front door.

Tickets don't have a simple number dashed to a normal letter. Instead event # PD 31N-1 (my first Padre–Dodger ball game) was followed by section ID letters dashed to double-digit numbers. The seat was further specified by a row and chair. To reach my secretly coded seat I searched for a ramp. My first choice, a kind of shot in the dark, dead-ended into a wall. My second was no better. It brought me back out to the field at the wrong place. A few ushers were lounging around shooting the breeze, but by my third try I felt compelled to accept the challenge on my own. Finally, after a frustrating struggle, I managed to match ticket to chair. And like a typical Californian I sat just in time to stand for the national anthem.

It wasn't long, though, before my victory gloat was dashed. In the middle of the first my chair was claimed by its real owner. It's the first time that's ever happened to me. I illegally sit at the Kingdome every time I go. There at least I know I risk the embarrassment of "You're sitting in my seat." At Murphy I really thought I was right. I wasn't. The usher, who the ticket holder dragged along with him, showed me my error. Silly me, I had misread the double-digit section number by one. No problem, I figured, I'd just slide over one section. Not possible at Murphy! To get to the right place I had to exit my miscalculated section via a crowded ramp and go back under the stadium. Then I had to come back out through another walkway. All just to move some twenty feet.

When I finally stumbled down the right aisles, to the right seat, somebody else was sitting in it. Normally I'd just find another one close by, but I'd worked too hard to get there. The chair was an obsession. I showed my ticket to the mis-seated fellow. Embarrassed, he apologized. I told him I understood and suggested he try a section over. It worked for me. Sheepishly, he left. Had I kept a close eye on the situation, I probably would have noticed a domino effect on the entire stadium. People all over Murphy were probably sitting one section too far to their right. Like the dreaded wave, I'll bet it rippled back to me. Come to think of it, a couple of innings later the guy to my right was asked to move.

Once the proper chair is finally found, its view, at least along the baseline, is just okay. It wasn't really worth the trip. At what looks to be another comfortable, fold-up, plastic-filled stadium, sharing armrests is a problem. Baseline boxes, like the one I fought for, are packed too tightly together. Not only that, but they also have a shallow rise. A tall person's head can turn out to be a major pain in the rear. Normally I don't mind such mild inconveniences, but I'd gotten used to the California stadium code of ethics. Such horrors were not supposed to be allowed.

While close seats aren't so good for the price, ones up and away are better. Four plastic fold-up levels swing from the right-field foul pole back around down the line in left and end in left center field. Behind home plate the rise is so steep, I felt like I was hovering directly over the batter. But at least I didn't have to look through two rows of heads to see him. Only in right is the high rise halted. A gigantic scoreboard limits general admission seats to one huge section. And they might just be the best. With so much sunshine, and such a handsome field stretched out in front, you can't help but have a grand time.

SCOREBOARD: GRADE A+

Jack Murphy's scoreboard setup is simply awesome. Completely dwarfing the right-field skyline, perched up behind the plastic bleachers, it commands total attention. No matter where my eyes roamed, they were always lured back to the screen.

Besides being huge, it's the West Coast's best pure-baseball board. While Oakland's Coliseum may do more, Murphy's does more baseball. Actually the gigantic setup is four boards in one. At the center, in almost constant use, is a Diamond Vision screen. Unlike in L.A. and Seattle, where the jumbo TV is usually turned off, San Diego gets its money's worth. Replays, highlights, and upcoming events are in constant full-color motion. Above it, line-scoring Padre games, is a long rectangular board. Finishing out the setup, a pair of smaller screens flank the Diamond Vision. With AL updates on the right-field side, and NL on the left, other scores are as easy as the Padre one to find. San Diego fans couldn't ask for a better setup. Neither could a visiting Bosoxer. .

While the scoreboard is one of baseball's best to look at, the system might be even better to listen to. Traditional organ music mixes with crisp Top 40 tunes; it keeps the mood lively. Crazy little numbers created just for certain occasions hit the speakers regularly. The old standby "Charge" gets a frequent Murphy workout. Best of all, folks join in. If it asks for a "Charge," they give it one. If it kicks out a special number, they acknowledge the work with a little hand clapping. It's not typical that California fans spend so much time involved in the game, but then again Jack Murphy's not typical.

FOOD: GRADE B

Selection: Very Good   Accessibility: Poor
Taste: Very Good   Cost: 15th

Just like at Southern California's other two ballparks, beer isn't delivered into the stands. It really doesn't make much sense. I could see if Fenway wanted to cut off the taps with the Yankees in town. It'd probably save a few broken noses. But the problems that an extra draft might cause in the land of the mellow are too small to comprehend. Nevertheless, to get either is a bother.

At least the food Murphy does offer is good. Unlike L.A., with its puny menu, and the Anaheim country club reception, the San Diego stadium menu is baseballish. Hot dogs come with chili, cheese, or kraut. A "South of the Border" theme runs through the separate Specialty Corners. Some feature burritos and chili, others churros (Mexican doughnuts). Although the stuff is made in the U.S.A., fortunately it doesn't taste like it. The "un-American" burritos are actually better than the plastic wrap they come in. And the chili is tastier than its Styrofoam bowl.

If gringo food is craved, that's around as well. Just inside the concrete plaza walls are a couple of circular food bars. One has fish, chips, and chicken, the other, good ole American burgers. The setup is quick and the food is tasty, just like at the golden arches.

Actually about the only problem is how the stands are set up. Aside from the small fast-food houses inside the gates, everything else is arranged haphazardly. Upstairs concession booths are packed in at odd locations. Some are plopped on an already busy corner, others along skinny side aisles. As a result most are slow. Beer lines, too, flow like molasses. Third-level lines, from tap to back, stretch for sections or, worse yet, innings. Without drinks delivered into the sunny stands, and an eternity's wait in line, a no-win dilemma is posed—either go thirsty or sacrifice a couple of innings. Neither's a happy thought on a hot day.

Jack Murphy wouldn't quite be West Coast-ish without the overpriced pair...lounges and televisions. The stadium at least isn't saturated with them. A few tubes, to lessen frustration in the always-long concession lines, are a good thought. Also the plastic "Sports Club" is only mildly annoying. In typical Southern California style, it's open most of the night. Yet, unlike at Anaheim, people only visit, they don't move in. Murphy's even got one lounge that's actually kind of cute. In the uppermost level, facing out toward the parking lot, is a small German Hofbrau patio. A little imported beer, some German potato salad and sausages—the menu as well as the place is enjoyable. While you'd never find it in a place like Fenway, providing, God forbid, the chance to break from the game, at least it's tasteful and relaxing. Kind of hazy and lazy, like Southern California.

BALLPARK EMPLOYEES: GRADE C

Padre people dress typically Californian. Their brown blazers and matching tan pants look like they could've been designed up in fashion-conscious L.A. As for organization and efficiency, though, San Diego's crew just gets by.

Maybe like fans who must constantly get lost in the complicated maze of seats, ushers disappear with them. Or maybe they hide from all the potential questions. For whatever reasons, there just are not enough of them around. At Dodger Stadium and in Anaheim, ushers guard the top of each and every aisle. They know exactly what's going on. Most can answer a question even before it's asked. Padres, on the other hand, are splashed here and there and not always so sure.

Speed doesn't seem to be a San Diego forte either. L.A. helpers are Marine-like in their "Yes, sir, no, sir, three bags full, sir" attitude. And they smile a lot. Anaheim radiates that pat-on-the-back, ole-grandpappy feeling. But in San Diego a yawn and "Sure, we'll find you a seat, just hold your horses" attitude is more the norm. If it's a nice day and the question isn't life or death, chances are they'll take their time in answering.

FACILITIES: GRADE B

All day long Murphy bounced me back and forth. In some ways it looked and acted like a real West Coaster. In other ways it didn't. Surrounded by acres of concrete and cars, I thought it normal. That was until I saw the concrete swirls. Seats are plastic and fold-up just like in L.A. and Frisco. But they offer all the arm and leg room of an old Eastern park. Even folks working the aisles are confusing. They look like they've been dressed by the U.S. military but trained by the Mexican government. I was confused.

The facilities offered no relief. In model West Coast fashion, parking lot spaces reach into the millions. As far as the eye can see, it swallows up the stadium...typical for the West Coast. Not typical is how it's organized. About as well as a democratic Central American government. At the other stadium lots I was directed to a particular spot. A morning meeting had probably mathematically calculated an exact predicted automobile arrival estimate; my spot was waiting. At Dodger Stadium they even used street signs and real cops. Jack Murphy's parking is based more on come-and-get-it freedom of choice. Once inside the gates folks are pretty much free to fly at will. Confusion reigns, particularly after the game.

Inside as well, facilities are just okay. Rest rooms are clean but not spotless. Big enough, they could stand to be a little bigger. Located in a state known best for sparkling rest rooms and well-organized parking lots, in an honest-to-goodness California category Jack Murphy is just an average Joe.

ATMOSPHERE: GRADE B

Blue skies, 90 degrees, and sunshine...what more could I ask for? For the first time on my trip I'd be able to fry under clear blue skies. Seattle's sky had been blotted out by concrete, Candlestick's with clouds. My brief visit to Oakland found a chilly Coliseum, while in L.A. the weather was perfectly pleasant. In San Diego, finally, it was hot—not humid, not warm, not nice, just sunglass squinty-eyed sunny, sitting-in-the-bleachers, baking-in-the-Coppertone hot. Swimming through Seattle's June monsoons and gray summer days for the past five years, I'd forgotten that 90 degrees existed...let alone could feel so good.

With the heat comes an atmosphere to baseball all its own. Unlike normal people, who seem to melt in broiling temperatures, baseball fans revel in it. As the mercury rises fans just pour on the lotion, soak up the suds, and get more intense. Ballpark festivities find a higher high. Brighter colors fill the stands. Beach balls bounce, beer flows, and cheering for most anything becomes the vogue. The bleachers become the house's best seats as near-naked bodies attempt a month's worth of tanning in a single afternoon. At 90 degrees, on a sunshiny day, baseball's at its very best.

Southern California's summer high finds a good friend in San Diego. A mixture of hot sun, fans that finally get up off their butts and cheer, and a scoreboard of such magnitude that it dwarfs all else inside make a game in Jack Murphy California's most energetic. With such electricity, a situation exists for those special baseball moments, the kind that I enjoyed my second day in town—a hot weekday game in June between the Padres and L.A. On a weekday afternoon in most U.S. cities, even in June with the Dodgers in for a three-game series, people go about their daily routine. Not in San Diego, especially when the guy on the hill for L.A. is Fernando Valenzuela. His mere presence ten miles from his native homeland changes a normal sunny Southern California day into a festival.

In Mexico, Fernando is a saint. A Mexican superstar in an Anglo-American sports world. Idolized by an entire culture, so close yet so remotely different from our own, his visit to Murphy's is like a homecoming. For once it's actually legal traffic that floods the Mexican border. While most folks come 'cause they hate the Dodgers, the Spanish-speaking crowd is there for the love of Fernando. Primarily because of him, plus the soaring temperatures and blue skies, some 45,000 others and myself crammed into the concrete cooker of a stadium for an afternoon of sunshine and baseball.

The night before Jack Murphy had proved to me that baseball in California could have a little pizzazz. Fans really got into it. But no way was I ready for the hoopla that Fernando brought. The stadium was a zoo. By noon, traffic was jammed up all over the efficient freeway system. The acres of concrete parking lot were filled and even closed off. People streamed in from all directions into the stadium. Ticket lines bulged. Folks waited for a break in the crowd at the bottom of the three-story escalators. The concrete swirls were packed. An excitement engulfed the place, a feeling that even Dodger Stadium, with its multimillions, or the crazy Coliseum hadn't manufactured. I was pumped.

Obviously on such a lovely day the bleachers were my goal, but they were sucked up three hours prior to game time. Unsuspecting me had to settle for a left-field reserve, way up in the third level. No problem. Since general admission seats have no corner on the sunshine market, my left-field section was as colorful as the bleachers. Bright pink chests and lily-white legs were bared all about me. Others were protected by their own artificial shade. Small parasols popped up at random throughout the section. Nobody took on the sun in normal attire. They either hid from it or embraced it.

As all true Seattleites do, I sported a tan—a shade as deep as a pale peanut shell. It used to embarrass me. Now I accept it and hope I'm not molding. I always half expect to see something green growing on my arms. So moments after finding my seat my shirt was off and my body frying a bright pink. A Coke in one hand, a burrito in the other, I sat miles from the field in a nearly full third-level section. Only the three seats to my immediate left were vacant. As high up as I was, I could barely make out Fernando's number, let alone keep track of his screwgie. So I just relaxed in the sunshine. For confirmation of calls, I focused in on the giant scoreboard and roaring approval of the crowd. They'd tell me if the Dodger ace was off or on. On such a beautiful day baseball would have to share center stage. I'd spend half the time checking out people. The afternoon was prime for both.

Both sides went down in order in the first. Fernando cruised. As the Dodgers came up to hit in the second, the three seats to my left were filled. Three Mexican gentlemen took them. I'd guess they were between 30 and 40 years old. I don't know, I'm lousy with ages. All three looked ready to take on a September frost instead of the June sunshine. Each wore old worn-out boots that stuck out from under faded blue jeans. Long-sleeved flannel shirts partially covered dingy T-shirts. While two wore hats, the fellow closest to me had on a red bandana. It circled his shiny black hair. They must have been field hands of some sort. Worn bodies, weathered faces, and tired clothes showed the toll of a life working in the hot sun. That same sun fish-belly white me was so desperately soaking up.

Historically, at the ballpark I am a bit friendlier than in most other social situations. I feel more at ease talking baseball with a stranger than asking one to dance. I guess that's why I spend most of my bar time at ballpark taverns instead of discos. Also, in the right setting, I even get curious...enough to ask questions. This was the right setting. Plus, I had a year of high school Spanish under my belt. So I tried to strike up a conversation. My neighbors, of whom Pedro sat closest to me and was the most talkative, happily responded. He was a bit better versed in English than I in Spanish...not much though. Our how-do-you-do's were in English.

From Mexicali, Mexico, Pedro and his two friends had bussed up to watch Fernando. The Dodger pitcher was their hero.

"In Mexico he's everybody's hero," Pedro boasted. "Television stations, newspapers, radio shows, whenever Fernando pitches it's a front-page story. And if it is here and we have the money, we take the bus to see him."

Pedro couldn't have been more proud of the Dodger if he had been his own brother. He even talked like they were brothers. Never once the whole afternoon did Pedro mention Fernando's last name. To him it didn't exist. Everything that Fernando'd ever done, Pedro could recall. And I benefited. A couple of innings at least were dominated off and on with stories. Fernando's life, his family, his best pitch, and at least half a dozen of his finest ball games. Along the way Pedro'd lapse back and forth between Spanish and English. When he was most excited the story was in Spanish. I'd get confused. He'd slow down, apologize, and repeat it in English. For two people whose only real common words were "Dodger" and "home run," it was amazing how well we got by.

Pedro knew much more than just Fernando. He knew baseball. Particularly proud of Mexico's contributions to the game, he rattled off name after name of Mexican major leaguers of the past twenty years. Many I recognized but wasn't sure from when or where. Still, when one rang a bell I'd guess what I thought was his team. Sometimes he'd go so fast I'd have to shout out the team. He'd slow down and apologize. Then he'd nod, confirming my guess if I was right, correcting me if I was wrong.

After Pedro provided his list I named some ball players I thought were Mexican; a few played for the Mariners. Most of my guesses, while I found out they were from "south of the border," were from some other country— Cuba, Puerto Rico, or Venezuela. With each one I'd cite, Pedro would name their natural country. He must've known every Latin American player that ever played in the major leagues. He certainly knew everyone I'd ever heard of. After names were exhausted, he revealed his favorite team. Although his hero was a Dodger, Cincinnati was his ball club. I figured it was because the "Big Red Machine" had rolled on the wheels of such great Latin stars. Perez, Concepcion, and Geronimo all were from somewhere south of the Rio Grande. I in turn revealed that I was Red Sox fan. He mentioned Luis Tiant. I nodded, noting that in '78 I saw the Cuban pitch.

Tiant revived our memories. The thought must have hit us at the same moment. We both forgot 1985. San Diego, Los Angeles, and even Fernando vanished. Without a word to one another, almost instantaneously, we each recalled an event that Red Sox and Red fans all remember, one of the game's most eloquent moments. Before I was able to, Pedro leapt to his feet. Waving his arms to left field, he signaled fair ball, home run, and game six of the '75 Series. Thinking the same thought, I jumped up and joined him. Like two little kids on a school playground, we jumped up and down together, laughing and yelling "Carlton Fisk, Carlton Fisk!" Anyplace but a baseball park, people probably would have thought we were nuts.

The very sight of the Boston catcher coaxing his eleventh-inning fly ball fair over Fenway's "Monster" was emblazoned in Pedro's Spanish mind as it was in mine in English. What our languages had struggled with, Fisk erased in a single swing. And since laughter and friendship, like baseball, know no national bounds, we raised a Coke to each other. We toasted Carlton's home run, Fernando's arm, and the game of baseball. Sitting back down, we finished out the afternoon as friends taking part in a wonderful day. Fernando didn't get the win. Yanked in the seventh, he didn't even finish the game. That didn't matter though. Pedro told me, "We just came to see him. It's the excitement of seeing him throw that we come here for. He'll win his next. He is the greatest of all time!... *Si?*"

7

ARLINGTON STADIUM, *TEXAS RANGERS*

Texan Hospitality in a Frying Pan

REPORT CARD	*Arlington Stadium*
	BASEBALL PARK
July 2/3, 85 vs Angels	*Texas Rangers*
GAME	BASEBALL CLUB

CATEGORY	GRADE	POINTS
Layout and Upkeep	*C*	*75*
Ball Field	*C*	*75*
Seating	*A*	*95*
Scoreboard	*A*	*95*
Food	*D-*	*60*
Ballpark Employees	*A*	*95*
Facilities	*D*	*65*
Atmosphere	*C*	*75*
Total Points		*635*
Average		*79*

C+

FINAL GRADE

14ᵗʰ

RANK

"Round-the-clock dripping humidity, and 103 degrees at game time. This ex-minor leaguer struggles in her outside oven... but always she's a-smiling."

PREGAME THOUGHTS

Leaving San Diego wasn't easy. Sun, surf, and staring at bikinis have a way of making you quite content. When paradise is found, tearing away from it, especially to head for Texas, takes an awful lot of mental toughness. The kind that separates mere *NBC Game of the Week*ers from real baseball fans. From my KOA campground I got to see Southern California at its sunshiny best. The weather was wonderful. A hot, dry 90 degrees throughout the day, every day, was followed by a cool 75 at night. Jack Murphy, with its handsome field, and some good Dodger–Padre ball games even showed me a little East Coast-style intensity. And I got it all for that KOA special, only nine bucks a night.

Besides business, non-baseball vacation time was also well spent. San Diego is California at its very best. While the whole state has ocean sunsets, San Diego's are my favorite. They seem just a bit more golden than the others. The beaches, too, are gorgeous. Sunny and sandy, loaded with babes, they're probably America's most colorful ocean welcome mat. Hell, they're even safe at night, and those are the public ones. As for private beaches, I found a couple of those too. One is mind-altering.

My last day in town I spent in search of La Jolla's totally stark-naked Black's Beach. It took most of a hot morning to find it, but what a find! Nakedness is not only allowed, it's encouraged... and legal. Swimming trunks and bikini tops are nonrequired material. You can actually watch the application of a perfect tan. Black's was the last straw. A sandy beach on the Pacific, with naked women all over the place. If I needed any help in making the decision before its discovery, I needed none afterward: someday, should I get too old and worn out to challenge the seasons, San Diego's where I'd go. I'd live at the KOA campground, just ten miles from Murphy's. I'd pick up box season tickets for all Padre night games. Afternoons would be spent catching rays with the kids out in the bleachers. When San Diego was out of town I'd take my radio down to Black's, listen to the Padres, and stare at the scenery until my eyeballs popped out. After that I'd spend the rest of my life basking in the sunshine and listening to ball games.

As grand a plan as it was, my retirement would have to wait. I still had a baseball journey to finish up. Duty called. Next stop... aughh... was cowboy country—home of Lone Star Beer, a lot of cows, and not much else. I couldn't put it off any longer. It was time for Texas. I dreaded the thought. Leaving San Diego for Texas has all the appeal of being kicked out of a honeymoon suite at the Hilton only to spend the night on some filthy park bench. If it's legal to have an arch-enemy state, Texas is mine. Ewing Oil, the A & M Aggies, University of Texas and that idiotic hook-'em-horns sign, the list goes on and on. Every time any Texas team plays any sport, I root for the other guys. If both are Texans, I just turn off the tube and hope for a tie.

More than any other organized Texas entity, I despise the Dallas Cowboys. "America's team" was never mine. From fifth grade until ninth, when pro football was important in my life, every Sunday was "Cowboy Sunday." It didn't matter where they played, they were always on the tube. And it didn't matter who they played, I always bet against 'em. Consequently, from the ages of nine to fifteen, I lost somewhere around 872 25-cent bets. Only when they froze their butts off, up in Green Bay, did I make a little of it back.

The Dallas Cowboys and San Diego crawling with beautiful naked women were not, however, the only reasons for me dragging my feet. I wanted to live to see another World Series. Texas weather, I was sure, would kill me. People who say the desert is a lovely nighttime paradise should pick up a newspaper once in a while. I did and was terrified. My first baseball stop, Dallas–Ft. Worth, had been peaking at 106 for four days straight. Houston, scheduled for the Fourth of July, was rolling in a few degrees warmer. But that wasn't all. To get there I was going to have to pass through cactus country. Phoenix topped 110, Yuma was pushing 114. San Diego sun was already cooking me at a cool 94. And even with its pleasant ocean breezes, I still felt like an ant frying under some fat kid's magnifying glass.

Between me and the Rangers stood 1,400 miles. I had three days to cover it. To survive, I needed a plan of attack. Ordinarily I wouldn't have worried. Driving all day long, stopping for a swim now and then, and a Mcburger or two, a normal 500 miler is a piece of cake. The Great Southwest, however, was not normal country! I was heading into a land where 95 degrees was a cold front. Where backyard swimming pools were the closest things to a real live lake. And heat waves even pulsated off of ice cubes. The only way, I figured, not to bake alive would be to sleep through the sunny times. At least until I reached Texas, I'd drive when the sun was down and the temperature dropped into the high 80's. Arizona and New Mexico deserts I'd conquer at night. During the day, while everybody else cooked, I'd Motel 6 it. AC, swimming pools, cold showers, and buckets of ice would get me through.

So on Sunday night, as the sun dipped into San Diego's Pacific, I bid good-bye to paradise and headed out for Arlington. For two nights I cruised the empty desert highways. A roasting Monday afternoon I slept away in some air-conditioned motel. I survived. My car survived. By Tuesday morning neither of us had suffered anything remotely close to a meltdown.

But as I tooled along in my rolling oriental oven, entranced by the tumbleweed-covered sand and continuous string of mirages, weird thoughts raced through my mind. I wondered if there was such a thing as a baseball sun-out. For years I had to live with all that moaning about Merideth and his frostbitten fingers, how he shouldn't have had to play on Green Bay's frozen tundra. Well, was it any fairer that the Brewers would have to bake in a Texas home stand? The Midwest had it all. Slushy snow in April, icy-cold winds in October. Rain, too. Monsoons bombarded Midwest ballparks all year long. But baseball continued. And nobody died.

The heat, I wasn't so sure about. To pitch a complete game without collapsing would take a miracle. And probably take 20 pounds away in the process. To catch it, twice as much. To watch one...I could only hope wasn't quite as dangerous. I prayed for a little help from the Rangers. That they delayed games on account of the temp. Or at least had the forethought to schedule me a late-night one. Like midnight. That way I'd fry only the last couple of innings, when the sun came back up at dawn.

LAYOUT AND UPKEEP: GRADE C

Whenever I see a baseball park, be it for the first or twenty-first time, a shiver of excitement passes through me. I may be pulling into the parking lot on a crisp April afternoon. Or it might be a night game in September. I shudder even in the winter if I am driving down the highway and pass a stadium. No matter when or where, they always get a double-take.

Besides intimidating, ballparks have a special talent to pack all those cares away. Like a happy dream, they make sad things disappear. All other thoughts save baseball are forgotten. That's how the game survives its element. And God knows it's got some nasty elements to survive. Old broken-down Comiskey is able to escape the filth of South Side Chicago. A psychological barrier is built, and you forget the crummy neighborhood outside. For three to five hours a night Oakland's Coliseum turns a nasty little town into a tourist trap. Tiger Stadium, for years, has taken on the horrors of Detroit. Everything from race riots to triple-digit unemployment has been eased by the stadium on Michigan and Trumbull. I hoped that Arlington's little ballpark could destroy its element. Somehow it would have to cool off the heat.

I had confidence it could. When I walked through the gates I expected a blast of cold air to greet me. Float me in through the aisles like I was inside a refrigerator. Heck, J.C. Penney could do it, and it was just a department store. But the blast never hit. Instead of AC, hot-air blowers met me at the front door. More heat. It almost oozed from inside. Like a sauna set in the middle of the tropics. I wilted. It was then that I realized the sad truth. Although they take on magical qualities at times, baseball parks are only human.

From my Freon-filled front seat I got my first look at the ballpark. It was actually kind of cute. Across the street from Wild Waves Amusement Park, set in a decent part of town, a peek at the inside reveals an upper level filled with seats and a scoreboard overhead. Sort of open and sort of enclosed, the place looks friendly. But that's from the car. Once I got out and started to roast, it looked a little different.

Inside its gates the place is worn. Anything would be, pounded day in and day out by the Texas sun. Things in other ballparks that might escape being noticed are ugly. Junk that probably wouldn't look so bad in a normal climate finds ways to spoil the stadium flavor. Smells that only team with constant warmth linger nastily in the air. Not obsessing the place, just kind of hanging around. Narrow hallways painted a dumb-looking gold run briefly under the stands, then back out into the weather. They serve as hot-air ducts. The odors mingle with the heat and flow to the stands. It's not the most storybook of ballpark strolls.

It's too bad the stadium sits in the middle of the desert. In normal weather it'd be delightful. In Arlington it's only hot.

BALL FIELD: GRADE C

Surprisingly enough, the ball field seems to resist the heat better than the building around it. It's impossible to water down and cool off the housing, but round-the-clock sprinklers have the ability to save living things from sunstroke. Green things get greener when they're watered. With almost constant care, Arlington's turf survives. But like the stadium, it also tires in the process.

The infield is bright green and well trimmed. A checkerboard cut, the outfield's sharp too. Where the two come together, however, the mesh isn't so fine. Fading yellow spots wrinkle the inner portions of the outfield grass. A course patchiness creeps about its edges. In a less harsh climate the imperfections would be pure ugly. In Texas, though, they're forgivable. Just the fact that most of the grass is a living color is a wonder.

Dirt, however, is a different story. You'd think in a stadium where rain is almost nonexistent, items that don't depend on water would look sharp. Just the opportunity to work on something and win should spur on the ground crew to create the major's finest soil. But it doesn't... mostly because of a tacky three-wheeled scooter. The scooter zips around the infield pulling a flimsy wire screen. Pregame swirls and sixth-inning touch-ups, instead of taking pressure off of the grass, add more. On a field that has to struggle just to be average, something that can be improved should be. Dirt should get a normal human drag. The scooter should be shot.

SEATING: GRADE A

Arlington's roots go back to minor league ball. In the late sixties it could hold only 10,000 people a night. Now it's up over 40,000. To get the extra seats, sections have been crammed in wherever there was room at the time. Each addition, a separate square, like lines on a tree trunk, almost tell the stadium's age. First it moved out, then back, and finally up. Rather than planned out, the ballpark looks like a spur-of-the-moment hot-fudge sundae, something thrown together for the hell of it. Impossible to copy, it just happens to work... in fact very well. Seats are great!

While it was put together in pieces, the basics are the same as at most places. Two levels of seats slide around from foul pole to foul pole. A third plaza level, one of those piled-on additions, tops the middle tier. But it just hugs the space up and over home plate. Almost all reserves are good. No surprise problems pop up once the game starts. The upper deck isn't so far up that walking around in it brings on vertigo. And the lower level doesn't stretch way underneath, causing seats that look good in the program to sour as soon as a fly ball is hit. With no iron supports and little vertical obstruction, sweet seats stay that way.

Beyond the outfield wall is the stadium's only part that actually looks planned out. A single gigantic section of aluminum benches (enough for 18,000 fans) forms probably the world's biggest baseball bleacher section. And without a doubt the largest-ever open-air human cooker.

Hugging both the left- and right-field lines, another little hodgepodge addition, are the ballpark's best seats. The Rangers are like the Mariners—they lose more than they win. As a result Arlington's like the Kingdome—not a lot of folks show up. General admission roam-around prices will get you almost any seat. So I moseyed about and sampled them all. Batting practice I checked out from behind home plate, then an inning or two in the upper deck. By the fifth I had made my way on down into the left-field corner. There, wedged between bleacher benches and reserved chairs, I found my favorite seats.

Actually the tiny section, not much larger than a few rows up and twelve seats across, is an extension of the bleachers. But crammed into each of the two outfield corners, it's some forty feet closer to the field. Also, instead of aluminum bleacher benches, it's filled with plastic chairs. Only a few feet from the foul line, and not much farther from the foul pole itself, from the front row I could almost reach down and touch the chalk. The whole section is great, the front row of it, exciting. It provides baseball a refreshing look, even if it's just to watch the Rangers... lose.

SCOREBOARD: GRADE A

Talk about a tall order: with crummy food, a soaring thermometer, and a consistent loser on the field, the duty to rescue Ranger fans falls squarely on the shoulders of the scoreboard and public address. Both come through nicely. All night long major league baseball in Arlington is treated with a friendly minor league flair.

Faceless and nameless, a "stadium's voice" is a special part of a ballpark's character. Hidden away inside speakers, we seldom think of it as a person, rather just a sound. But it's so much more! An inspiring voice can carry a ballpark. It can pump up the fans or bring 'em down. In the majors "the voice" is just a part of the ballpark feel, but in the minors it runs the show. A drawing card in itself, it adds a separate dimension to baseball—"Bingo at the Ballpark." Being a minor leaguer at heart, Arlington's voice dominates. All night long it keeps folks checking their ticket stubs with "Well, it's time for another lucky number giveaway" and "We've got another winner." Baseball things are also handled well. Bellowing out the Ranger's batting lineup, it starts the night out with a bang, then keeps up the pace till it's over. Its cheerful attitude is fun, its optimism catchy. As wired as an early-morning DJ on his fourth cup of coffee, it never lets the temp bring it down.

Joining the minor league P.A. is a minor league-looking scoreboard. From foul pole to foul pole, a continuous stream of billboard advertisements stretches around the upper rim of the stadium. Only an occasional scoreboard breaks their run. At most parks so many commercials would dampen the atmosphere. At Arlington it's just the opposite. Triple A ball clubs survive on stadium advertising. TV doesn't care about 'em and ticket costs are too cheap to add up to anything. Each one I've ever been in, just like Arlington, is obliterated with billboards. By turning the scoreboard into a rotating commercial, Arlington just adds to that minor league feel. Consequently, the Texan can have its cake and eat it too. It gets all those big bucks for covering its walls, but doesn't sacrifice atmosphere to do it.

While the setup is delightful, baseball coverage is pure business. All the basics are reported. Sandwiched between Dr Pepper and Delta, a single panel in left updates scores from around the league. Immersed within the right-field sea of commercials, Ranger games are taken care of. And in center, paid for by all the surrounding propaganda, is a Diamond Vision screen.

The Rangers get their money's worth from the big screen. Pregame highlights of the previous day's loss are set to music. In between innings, shots of "This Week in Baseball" and short baseball videos liven up the place. As lively as the inside of a charcoal cooker can get. Little fan motivators, however, are the big screen's forte. If anything can drag Texans from their heat-induced catatonic state, it's the Lone Ranger number. William Tell's Overture blares from stadium speakers. Meanwhile, the masked man rides across the giant movie screen. Pounding on bad guys and hi-ho-Silvering it away, it's as though he was there to save everybody—the Rangers from their drive to the cellar and their fans from being baked alive...two almost impossible tasks, even for a pair of six-shooters filled with silver bullets.

FOOD: GRADE D−

Selection: Poor Accessibility: Poor
Taste: Poor   Cost: 26th

Eating at this Texas stadium is a nasty experience. And expensive. In fact, according to my highly scientific rating system, it's the majors' most costly.

Crummy food at inflated prices could only be served in the sloppiest style. It is. At 6:30 I found my seat. For forty-five minutes I sat there and cooked, hoping that I wouldn't evaporate before "The Star-Spangled Banner." A beer, I knew, would be the only thing that'd get me through. But no beer salesmen were around. As the game wore on, and the temperature plummeted into the middle 90's, still nobody showed. The Rangers don't employ a whole lot of folks to carry around eats and drinks. In fact, I saw only a couple the whole night. And they weren't old enough to drive, let alone drink.

Thirsty and hungry, by the fifth I felt like I was in the middle of the desert, marooned by a broken-down stagecoach. Just another episode of *The Big Valley*. With nothing to eat and slowly dehydrating, I gave up on the vendors. The next stage wasn't due for three days. So, with everybody else who was starving or dying of thirst, I was forced into the concessions.

I should have gone hungry. The only thing worse than Ranger food service is the food itself. Most everything stinks. Hot dogs, however, are particularly lousy. Right down there with Fenway Franks, and whatever it is that the Blue Jays sell, they're tied as the world's worst. Pizza looks like it's been scraped up out of some grocery-store frozen-food department. In fact, the food service produces only one worthwhile product. In the grips of constant heat stroke, crispy cold beer tastes oh-so-good.

BALLPARK EMPLOYEES: GRADE A

Talk about down-home hospitality. Only visiting the folks at Christmastime am I treated as well as I was in Arlington, At the ball game I received a special Ranger welcome. Flashed on the Diamond Vision screen long enough for me to snap off a half-dozen shots was a "Welcome to Texas, Bob Wood" paragraph. They even revealed who I was, and why I was there, and that I was a junior high schoolteacher.

That was just the beginning. The next morning I drove to the public relations office. I had to thank somebody. I'd never been in pictures before. There I was showered with gifts. Everything the Rangers had freebied out for the past three years was mine—hats, thongs, beach balls, and bags. I had to make two trips to the car just to get all the stuff in. Not only were folks generous, but very nice as well. Big brass was interested, secretaries impressed. PR bosses told me all about the Rangers and asked all about me. Where had I been? What had I done? How'd I like their place? And they were sincere. Any warped ideas I had about Texans before my visit vanished. I found out they were just as normal as... well, Iowans.

One person in particular was especially kind. Terry Southern, director of the Lady Rangers, Arlington's "teenage girl work force," was really taken by my trip. "It's a great idea.... Where do you go to next?"

"The Astrodome," I replied.

Everybody kind of looked at one another and rolled their eyes. The old inner-state rivalry I figured. I do the same when University of Michigan is brought up in a conversation. I found out later there was a lot more to it. Looking back on it now, I'm surprised they didn't hold their noses too.

"Why don't you stay another night?" she suggested. "We can show you around a little better." I had two days scheduled in Houston. An Astrogame couldn't be rained out. Two in Arlington was just as good. Besides, I didn't want to hurt anybody's feelings, they were all so nice. Without even a twisted arm, I was convinced to catch another Ranger game.

What a great idea. An afternoon thunderstorm cooled the place off. At least enough for pregame to linger in the middle 80's. Meanwhile I got to see all there was to see. I visited the field during batting practice. And with the Angels in town watched Reggie orbit a few shots from ground level. After that I was toured through the upstairs luxury boxes. Baseball and big bucks—lavish furniture, good crystal, only the best liquor, even waiters. All surrounded by AC. The Barkleys and Cartwrights would've loved it. Me, I'd do better drinking beers and roasting out in the bleachers with Kittie, Doc, and Matt.

The Rangers even set me up for the night. I'd already checked out of my Motel 6. Its clone awaited me in Houston. Being the third before the Fourth, it was too late to get my old room back. I didn't really want to spend the night in the car, especially in 80-degree heat. No problem! Terry gave me a couple of Sheridan Hotel coupons. Twelfth floor, overlooking the ballpark, it was my only night of luxury on the entire trip. The next morning, just for the hell of it, I even ordered up a little room service. My first Egg McMuffin-less breakfast in a week, and a perfect way to cap a pleasant Texas hospitality-filled two-night stay with the Rangers.

Even kids working the game treated me great. The second night I got to the game early. I had to if I was gonna enjoy my royal tour. Since I'd canceled motels, and my luxury accommodations weren't yet official, all my junk was in the car. It bulged. After picking up the armloads of Ranger souvenirs, it bulged even more. I needed a safe place to leave it, so I pulled in and asked for a special spot. Sometimes, like at Frisco, when I requested help the attendant would look at me like I was from Mars. Other times, if my story was good enough, I'd get a little sympathy. They'd direct me to a tall light pole and promise to watch the car. At Arlington they rolled out the red carpet. I explained the problem. That I needed help. The kid I asked looked at me kind of strange.

"You're the guy, aren't you?"

"What guy?" I thought. Geez, what'd I do now?"

"You know, the teacher from Washington. The guy that's going to all the ballparks. I saw your name on the scoreboard last night."

Relieved, I admitted he was right. In fact, I even bragged a bit. The kid got into it. He had a few of his buddies come over. They all thought my trip was "cool." They even thought it was "neat" that I was a teacher. That was something I wasn't used to. Nor was my car... press parking, front row!

Inside the ballpark things were a little different. Parking-lot work, even on a hot night, is cake. What little breezes exist in the state flow through it. Public relations air-conditioned offices, too, are a better environment for smiling than the plaster halls of a ballpark cooking in the high 90's. Nobody should be made to take a ticket or roll up hot dogs in the midst of such heat. And basically nobody did. Ushers were invisible. As were vendors. And concession stands, flooded with 13- to 15-year-olds, looked like junior high detention wards. In fact, the ballpark employee average age is lucky if it's legal.

Kids were everywhere. All of 'em decked out in Ranger duds. Some passed out programs, others souvenirs. Most hung out at food booths underneath the stands. Crammed together like 95-cent goldfish stuffed into some department-store fish tank, they lollygagged the night away. And also passed out food if time permitted. Darting back and forth, munching and fooling around, they had a grand time. Which in itself would be a challenge. Considering that just waiting around for a dog and soda was like sitting in a sauna, never mind pulling one off the grill.

The kids weren't the only ones who had fun. So did the legal-aged security guards. And like the kids, their number one priority was enjoyment. Anytime, anywhere, the cops were willing to kick back and discuss the trauma of the Rangers' latest losing streak.

The place isn't quite as businesslike as Dodger Stadium. In fact, it's run more like a high school football concession stand than a major league ballpark. But big deal! Texas Rangers are friendly people. The cops and the kids have an upbeat attitude that makes the heat bearable. Sure, there are problems, but if the folks weren't so neighborly, there'd be a lot more.

FACILITIES: GRADE D

Arlington's rest rooms rank right up there with the hot dogs. While the heat can hammer many a stadium luxury option, things like toilets and urinals should be indestructible. There's absolutely no reason why a ballpark bathroom, frying in the Texas sun, can't faintly resemble one cooking in San Diego. When only 10,000 people a night are around to use 'em, they shouldn't be too difficult to clean up, sinks too hard to repair. Paper-towel racks shouldn't take a lot of work to restock. Apparently in Arlington they do. Joe's Service Station down the street has a more luxurious setup. Drinking fountains aren't any better. At a place where water should be at a premium, where each spilled droplet should cost somebody's job, Arlington features water fountains nearly as old as the Roman aqueducts. Too bad they don't work as well. Water dribbles out of cracked faucets. Handles have a 50-50 chance of coming off with a spin.

While inside facilities are tired, the parking lot is everything a sleek Texas Eldorado could ask for. Big, well lit, and in a good part of town, although it doesn't bring Dodger efficiency to its knees, it gets the job done. Still something's gotta be done with the bathrooms. Stadium fixer priority number two should be to provide inside facilities the same care that the outside ones get. Number one—a giant-size nuclear-powered air conditioner.

ATMOSPHERE: GRADE C

Sunny blue skies, 75 degrees with 10 percent humidity, a slight breeze blowing out to left, and all is right with the world. Baseball weather can get that good. Unfortunately not every ballpark in the majors sits under L.A. skies. If it did, we'd have no more domes, no more rain-outs, no 35-degree April openers, or no 103-degree night games in Texas. But that just ain't the case. As the old Western saloon saying goes, "We all gotta play the hand we're dealt." In Arlington a five-card discard would be in order. Days of 100+, nights at least in the 80's, take a toll that almost nothing can rescue. Even so, somehow baseball survives. It shouldn't. In fact, at such odds in most places it probably wouldn't. Yet something in the heart, a special sincerity, fights the heat and makes the Rangers' home a happy one.

Arlington Stadium is a people place. Only a positive attitude could keep it from the evil clutches of "Mr. Sun." And the Ranger workers have it. Public relations offices set a happy tone that filters into the ballpark's steamy concession booths. Kids in the booths survive, and in doing so give the place a lift. Of course things are taken care of in their proper perspective. Instead of getting out early to peddle popcorn, teenaged "Lady Rangers" use the time to curl their hair. You can never be too sure. Selling popcorn at a ballpark, a girl can meet a lot of guys. A rush to fill another order at the food counter isn't always top priority either. First, the 16-year-old waiter has to throw one more cup of ice at his buddy. Couldn't wait on someone if you didn't give paybacks first. Not professional you say. Hell, who cares? They smile, they giggle, they laugh and have a good time. They make the place more bearable.

Like the kids, the park itself fights the heat. Instead of moaning, Arlington's attitude is pumped. The peppy stadium voice helps. It volunteers a happy-go-lucky feeling. The giveaways, contests, and inspiring introductions provide a type of mental air conditioner. With friendly folks, and a happy ballpark frame of mind, the fact that you're slowly roasting is nearly forgotten.

The smiles, though, are just not enough. All summer long the ballpark bakes. And all it can do is sit and take it. It gets no shade, no relief. It's not able to take a break in an air-conditioned office or sip on a cool glass of lemonade. Wrinkled and ragged, like a middle-aged sun worshiper, Arlington Stadium looks older than it is. And feels old too. The weather, the unpleasant odors and cluttered junk wrap around the park and choke it. And as a result the frolicking spirit sooner or later wears down. Eventually even the folks in the stands feel it. As hammered as the park itself, they sit quietly through the ball game, only once in a while really getting into it. And that's usually for a pitching change, about the only thing the Rangers do consistently well.

It's really kind of sad. Arlington deserves a better fate. It's entitled to a little more rain than it gets each year. It's too nice a place to be the home for an eternal cellar dweller. Or to just slowly evaporate in the Texas sun. Yet just when all hope seems lost, and the sun will finally eat it up, just when nine straight days in the 100's and another double-digit Ranger losing streak threaten to melt away the spirit, out from behind the bleachers, high up above on the Diamond Vision screen, rides the Lone Ranger. He gallops across the sky. A symphony announces his arrival. His duty—to drive away the bad guys. Folks stop, they watch, they listen, and wearily cheer. Arlington looks up into the sun—smiles and survives.

8

ASTRODOME,
HOUSTON ASTROS

Just Another Dome—Only Worse

REPORT CARD	**Astrodome**
	BASEBALL PARK
July 4, 85 vs Expos	**Houston Astros**
GAME	BASEBALL CLUB

CATEGORY	GRADE	POINTS
Layout and Upkeep	C	75
Ball Field	D-	60
Seating	D	65
Scoreboard	C	75
Food	D	65
Ballpark Employees	D-	60
Facilities	C	75
Atmosphere	D-	60
Total Points		535
Average		67

D+

FINAL GRADE

26th

RANK

"A parking lot filled with chuckholes and an inside year-round 72.8 degree temperature are its finest features.... A place actually tackier than the uniforms its ball team wears."

PREGAME THOUGHTS

Always came down to the same two—a fat-handled 34-inch Jackie Robinson or a 33-inch flame-treated Clemente model. My last two years in Little League and the first in high school, Dad would take me downtown to Miller Boremans Sporting Goods. He'd buy me a bat. Just the first one of the year. If I cracked it, or God forbid somebody else did, I'd be on my own. That first one, though, was on Dad.

I was 14 the first time we went. Before then my hands were too puny for much more than a 30. And 30-inchers were pretty much all the same, Adirondacks and cheap. Dad was a Little League coach, anyhow. We had a bag full of bats in the garage. If I needed one, they were there for the picking. Our last trip I was 16. After that, being "cool" was more important than a good Jackie Robinson. I still can't believe it—my last two years in high school I used aluminum.

To a teenager, a baseball glove is a personal friend. I loved my chocolate-brown, MacGregor Willie Mays. From April to August we were inseparable. Bats, on the other hand, were status. Only a privileged few owned their own. At least a real one...a Louisville Slugger. The flame-treated Roberto Clemente was probably the best of all time. It was sleek. Not thin-handled like the Yastrzemski, it was made for a normal grip. The barrel eased gradually away; it had just the right proportions. And the flame treating made it look great. The wood grain burned to deep rich brown on the sweet spot, softened to a more golden color down the barrel. The handle was untouched white ash.

I'm not sure if flame treating did anything for the wood. Mike Walsh, my best friend and first baseman on our Lees Sports Senior League team, swore that it did. He was a baseball-bat wizard. He knew all about 'em, or at least as much as a ninth grader can know about bats. Mike could read flame treating. He could tell if the wood was good or bad. If the grain was too close together or just right. Even if the trademark was misplaced. Mike would go down with Dad and me. He'd read the wood and okay my purchase.

Bats are different then ball gloves—they break. Gloves can only get lost or be left out in the rain. If circumstances were right, I'd lend out my Willie Mays. Circumstances were right only if the user was a good friend and I was playing in the same game. That way I could keep a close eye on it. Bats, on the other hand, were not exchanged. Besides me, only Mike got to use my Clemente. And only because I figured he was my baseball-bat agent. Friendship had nothing to do with it. Even then I'd cringe each time he'd swing. Most of those two seasons we played together, I hit second, Mike fifth. When I was on he was up. Half the time I was more concerned with my bat than picking up the signals down at third.

Until high school the Clemente was my only choice. Then, because of a basketball-season jammed thumb, I decided on the 34-inch Jackie Robinson. The Robinson wasn't nearly as glamorous as the Clemente. Nor was it flame treated. A plain, nine-to-five, working-joe bat. It had a hard, ugly yellow finish. But one very special option—the handle was almost as big as the barrel. Even with my bent thumb I could grab it tight, and it was great for choking up. After my thumb got well I still used the Robinson off and on. With a handle bigger than most bat barrels, even a wrist shot got more wood than some of those other no-name bats. And God only knows, the way I bailed out on a good curve, I needed all the help I could get.

For the three seasons when I was 14, 15, and 16, I bounced back and forth between the Clemente and the Robinson. Occasionally, for a change of pace or to break a slump, I'd go with the Yaz. But always wood. The aluminum just lay around. It was okay for batting practice, but on game days, when it counted, even in the cold springtime, I used wood. My junior and senior years, just to be cool, I sold out to metal.

Aluminum bats are a curse to baseball. They belong on the end of a lightning rod or in a golf bag, not in an on-deck circle. Their rubber handles are too comfortable. Names on 'em are of a company not a ball player. They can't be flame treated, they never break. Worst of all, they sound sissyish. A "ping" instead of a "crack" has taken over Little League and high school practice fields. They've tainted baseball at its most important levels.

Bats aren't the only thing changing—all of baseball is. It's being invaded by technological efficiency. Aluminum bats, plastic grass, and domes are symbols of a new major league age. The one that the Tigers conquered in '68 isn't the same today. Players are different, their values aren't the same. A good contract, lots of bucks, and free agency seem to be today's priority issues. Not "how on earth" to touch a Nolan Ryan fastball. Getting to the Series and beating the Yanks isn't enough incentive anymore. Now contracts are locked into how many folks are in the ballpark when you pitch or if you can get to the All-Star break without crashing on the 21-day DL. And the big payoff isn't that Series ring, it's more green. Baseball's just not as pure as it used to be.

I guess it's only natural, if ball players aren't the same that the ballparks aren't either. They're not ballparks anymore; the new ones are multipurpose stadiums. Roomy and comfortable, their biggest concern's no longer baseball, it's let's see how many sports we can fit inside. And let's do it as technologically efficiently as possible. Plastic chairs, plastic food, but most of all plastic grass has laid its roots. Durable and cheap, artificial turf has found a home. If a stadium is built today, odds are it'll have a plastic floor. That's just not right. Baseballs belong on grass, not skipping along some synthetic tablecloth. Half the spell of a ballpark is that first glimpse of the turf. Its fresh fragrance after a soft summer rain, the cut, the texture are locked into the very spirit of the place. To replace it with a sheet of plastic is criminal. It's like dining at Denny's on Thanksgiving or putting up a silver aluminum tree for Christmas. Tradition is ruined. Baseball becomes just another modern sport.

Seattle was my introduction to artificial baseball. My Midwest ballparks—Chicago's, Milwaukee's, and Detroit's—are as traditional as turkey on turkey day. But Seattle introduced me to the horrors of the ultramodern game. Not only did it provide an intro to synthetic grass, but it also showed me baseball's ultimate villain—THE DOME! For five summers now I've suffered through domed baseball. And unfortunately become somewhat of an indoor baseball expert. Domes destroy the notion that baseballs are meant to float high up into a blue sky and that sunshine is beautiful. In regions where Mother Nature won't allow the game to be played normally, domes have attempted to make it work. They've failed...miserably.

Baseball needs Mother Nature. It doesn't matter where—every climate offers something positive to the game. If a ball game is slow, sunshine and blue skies make the afternoon an enjoyable one. Sometimes in April or October cold biting rain pelts the stands. Not enough to call a game, it makes sitting there miserable. If I brave one of those, I feel significant. I tell myself only a real fan would've stayed all nine innings. Pride and hot coffee get me through. In a dome the excitement, the challenges vanish. No hot sunny days, no starry, starry nights. Like lukewarm bathwater, a dome is safe but boring. Instead of nature's surprises, year-round 72.8 degrees sterilizes baseball.

Only in extreme emergencies should a dome be considered necessary. Houston, I thought, might just be the emergency. There, in the thralldom of a dripping steam kettle, maybe a little AC would be nice. In a place where there's more water in the air than in the lakes, a little cool might let the fans enjoy themselves. Up north I watched sweet little Arlington Stadium nearly die in the heat. Her heart was just sucked out of her. From what I'd heard, Houston was worse. If Arlington was baseball in a frying pan, then Houston was baseball in the fire. If the Rangers staggered outside, the Astros certainly would die there.

It's not like me to think anything good about domes, plastic, or aluminum bats. I still feel guilty for selling out those last two years in high school. But in this one instance, in Houston, a dome just didn't seem like selling out. These thoughts ran through my brain as I left the AC of my Japanese import. I slipped from my cool car. My shirt clung to my chest. Sweat splashed down my body. The heavy air squashed my shoulders. For the first time in my life, since I was a "cool" senior in high school, I was on the side of metal bats, plastic grass, and indoor baseball. Maybe in Houston, "The Humid Capital of the World," a dome was the answer.

LAYOUT AND UPKEEP: GRADE C

From the highway Houston's not much of a treat. Scattered all about, it looks like eight different cities in one. Buildings cluster in with skyscrapers at different places along both sides of the expressway. Each cluster looks like it's the main hub, then after a few miles it stops. More of nothing follows... until the next grouping. None look too awfully exciting, unless you enjoy watching concrete bake.

The Astrodome, on the other hand, is rather stately looking. Located on the south side of official Houston, it sits inside a so-so neighborhood. Decent houses surround the stadium. Suburban streets feed into it. Expressways make it accessible. Neither homes nor roads are too terribly quaint but they're okay—somewhere in between those on Tiger Stadium's battered streets and the safe, suburban clones in Anaheim. It's a place you'd make sure to lock the car but could watch the game in peace without having to check it on the hour.

At its highest point the neighborhood skyline reaches a second-story-bedroom peak. The dome, though, is much taller. Pushed back off the road and raised up in the middle of its huge parking lot, it dominates its Astro neighborhood. A sparkling silver finish covers its perfectly round base. Actually it's kind of sharp. In fact, if major league baseball were to have a dome beauty contest, the Astro one would win. Of the three, Minnesota's funny-looking bubble top, Seattle's concrete tombstone, and Houston's, the Astrodome is easily the most handsome. Even so, that's like pitting Quasimodo, Frankenstein, and the Phantom of the Opera against each other in a beauty contest. Domes compare only with domes.

Inside, it's not as pretty. A few convenient up and down escalators make traveling about the place easy. Walkways are wide enough to get comfortably around, but halls are cluttered with junk. Minnesota's and Seattle's monsters might be uglier, but both are a lot tidier.

One fact makes Houston's dome livable. Only because all that humidity is locked outside is baseball even thinkable. At 72.8 degrees, depending on the day, it's 20, sometimes 30 degrees cooler than on the outside. Its air is filled with oxygen instead of water. That blast of cool that I prayed for in Arlington hit me on the way through the double dome doors. My pores reclosed. I stopped sweating. I almost floated through the inside hallways. I thought again, maybe a dome was all right.

BALL FIELD: GRADE D—

It took one look at the ball field to rekindle my hatred for artificial baseball. Houston's dome field is, without a doubt, the ugliest a baseball has ever rolled upon. And that includes the grade school blacktop I used to play wall ball on when I was a kid.

The grass is plastic—"strike one."

Houston's turf, however, isn't just normal fake green plastic. Carved directly into the heart of it, right down the middle, is a hundred-yard rectangle. One end zone is set up in dead center field, the other across the pitcher's mound. Yard lines are almost as clear as baselines. And that's in the middle of July. I'd hate to see it in September—a base runner would need a compass to find second base. He'd probably end up sliding into the goalpost. It's nothing more than a lousy football field—"strike two."

There's more! Around the stamped-on football field runs a normal dirt warning track. Not only out of place in plastic land, it's also tacky, unkempt, and splotchy, as if it's been hammered by a good rainstorm—"strike three."

As ugly as all this is, it's sad to think things could get even worse. But they do! The coup de grace is its huge, grotesque seam. Stretching from foul line to foul line, just above the infield–outfield circle, the seam is the ball field's Frankenstein forehead scar. And proves that besides striking out, the entire field ought to be tossed out of the league.

I was embarrassed to have to look at it. To play on it could only be worse. Astro players could justify a strike on "ugly grounds" alone. The saddest part of the whole matter, though, is that somebody, somewhere, on some occasion must admit, "Yes, I am a member of the Astro ground crew."

SEATING: GRADE D

As gaudy as the Astros' uniforms are, one day long ago they must have really turned on the right folks. That same hideous combination—orange-orange, lemon-yellow, raspberry-red—besides striping the unis, splatters the seats. The mix might taste good in a bowl of Trix, but in a ballpark it's a nasty one.

Despite their coloring, chairs are comfortable. Aisles are wide, leg and arm room abundant. Even the butt gets a break. Seats are made from a soft cushiony material. Almost movie-theater quality. Views are also pretty good. Vertical obstruction is limited, and construction poles aren't used. Problem is that most chairs in the five levels wedged under the ceiling are a long, long way from the field. Only field-section seats are close. The rest just get farther away as they rise.

Behind home plate, Astro seating has real problems. While all ballparks hang a net, most of which you can see through, the dome net literally hugs the seats. Trying to pick up a baseball out of the mesh is almost impossible. Which is too bad with Mike Scott and Nolan Ryan smoking the plate a few times a week. You'd think management might want folks to see the best of the Astros do what they do best—strike people out. On the other hand, maybe the net's left alone for a reason—a little fan relief. It takes so much energy to find the pitch that somebody sitting behind the net can't muster up any more to look at all the other ugly stuff.

SCOREBOARD: GRADE C

It's billed as "The World's Biggest Scoreboard," but looks more like a pinball machine at full tilt. Once again the product isn't worth its Astro hype. Much like the beauty in Oakland's Coliseum, two large electronic information panels flank a Diamond Vision screen. The dome, however, adds something that fortunately the A's left out—tackiness.

Unable to decide which colors to use on the board, stadium planners decided to use 'em all. As a result the wall-mounted signs have all the charisma of an aluminum Christmas tree. The scoreboard abandons traditional soft white lights, just as the ball field abandons traditional grass and the roof blocks out traditional sky, to instead flash stats, scores, and pitching changes in reds, greens, and bright white. You need sunglasses just to sneak a peek. Only Diamond Vision features a watchable screen. Instead of creating imaginary colors, it reproduces real ones.

As overdone as normal baseball coverage is, it's nothing compared to what happens on an Astro homer. All hell breaks loose. Lights flash, neon flags blink on and off, little cartoon cowboys shoot their little guns, and cannons boom. The whole background between the boards, and the boards themselves, goes crazy. The show's almost blinding. And it is probably the real reason why Houston always comes in last in home runs.

The sound system, on the other hand, at least tries to be normal. For the most part, though, it falls on deaf ears. Fans still reeling from the flashing scoreboard show, and mesmerized by the hideous-looking field, focus any left-over energy on the game. It's a wonder they can see at all!

FOOD: GRADE D

Selection: Fair   Accessibility: Poor

Taste: Fair   Cost: 23rd

Slow lines, messy setups, and boring food highlight just another cruddy dome offering. Astro food, like the Astro floor, Astro seating, Astro scoreboard, and everything else in Astro world, is pretty lousy. It's also Astro-nomically expensive.

Sleepwalking vendors never make it to some corners of the tomb. So hungry fans are forced down under. There ungodly slow lines provide a Christmas Eve post-office wait. After standing around for too long, many folks just give up and go back to their seats. If they're lucky, they don't buy anything, and may only starve to death. The alternative is worse.

Texas ballpark food up in Arlington was the pits. I didn't think there was a possibility it could get worse. I was partially right—none tastes as bad. But there it didn't take a four-inning wait to be disappointed. At the dome, torture's slower. Lines are enormous. Not, God forbid, because the stuff they serve is tasty, but because for some reason more booths are closed than open. So everyone crowds the same ones. It's a total mess. If the wait is braved, and the front of the line finally reached, Astro food is the prize. No biggie! Offerings, while a bit imaginative, are nothing to get excited about...and, as expected, quality's not an issue.

About the only really intelligent food-service provisions are concession-stand televisions. They allow you to actually eat and watch baseball at the same time—only a dream up in the near vendorless stands.

BALLPARK EMPLOYEES: GRADE D−

As uninspired as I was watching Astro baseball, it was nothing compared to the excitement that dome employees showed working it. It might have been that they were too drained from the afternoon off. Just breathing in Houston's steam kettle is enough to bring on near exhaustion. Or it could've been that the scoreboard's electrical light show dazed them so that they were unable to perform. Whatever the reason "domers" carried on like extras practicing for another sequel to *Night of the Living Dead.*

Everybody who wasn't somewhere snoozing was sleepwalking. Whether selling hot dogs or programs, vendors crawled through the stands. Ushers, if the stadium had any, must've taken private-eye courses in the art of disguise. They listened well in class; I couldn't find 'em. Concessionaires, though, were the most inspiring of the group. Absolutely lifeless, they can turn a quick hop down to get a chili dog and beer into a three-inning marathon. Bumbling about, bumping into one another, I kept expecting one to fall asleep and collapse face-first into the popcorn popper.

Following in the truest of Texas traditions, only security people seemed to really know what was going on. Astro deputies were all over the place—helping out, keeping order, and basically doing their job. They did their best to make sure fans didn't receive any permanent damage from the place. Plus, when the game ended they were probably the only group not asleep. Which is fortunate. Somebody had to wake the rest of the work force.

FACILITIES: GRADE C

Parking lots are probably the twentieth century's greatest gift to baseball. A necessity desperately needed in the downtown streets of some big Eastern cities, they flourish in the West. If nothing else, at least the dome has a big one.

Heavily guarded, the Astro lot provides safety from everything but itself. It is littered with potholes and broken bottles, and driving around inside it was like cruising through an obstacle course: two smashed beer bottles and a swerve to the left, slam on the brakes before vanishing into a crack in the asphalt. If you handle a car well, or have a couple of spare tires in the trunk, it's not a bad deal. A good cleaning and some hole filling wouldn't hurt though.

Good-size, tidy bathrooms are probably the stadium's finest feature. And while they're not quite California clean, at least they're better than the pits up in Arlington. And considering the rest of the place, they're probably highlight film material.

ATMOSPHERE: GRADE D−

Going to Houston, I had sought to keep an open mind. I tried to forget that it was the Astrodome where that first polyseed for the first polyfloor was planted. That it was the first ballpark ever to kick out Mother Nature. I even tried to forget that the Texas dome was related to my retarded dome in Seattle. I promised myself I'd be objective. That I'd look at the bright side of Astro world. After baking in Arlington's oven, I figured I was ready for a dome. Not aluminum bats, not plastic grass, certainly not prima-donna clause-covered contracts, but maybe a dome.

Instead what I found was awful. Astro world convinced me of what I'd suspected all along. Baseball will never adapt to the computer age. Sophisticated equipment, faster playing surfaces, even fake cooler temperatures don't have a role. Baseball's almost oriental in its philosophy. Its beauty is found in a reflection of the past, not in a high-tech world of efficiency. And it must have Mother Nature. To feel right, it needs all the good and bad she has to offer. Sun, sky, even heat have to be around.

With outdoors removed from the dome, the game's left to the mercy of man and his man-made Astro things. For it to be anything better than dull, everything must perform perfectly. And even if it does, that's no assurance that indoor baseball will survive. It only means the place won't feel a total disaster. Disaster is a good dome description. In every traditional offering, the place is either too little or too much. It never lets baseball be itself.

At the top of the "too much" category is that obsession with its Astro color scheme. Everywhere inside those same colors flash their ugly faces. Uniforms, plastic seats, and, most revolting, on the scoreboard. Instead of baseball I was ready for Barnum and Bailey to bring in some circus acts.

Too little is almost as bad. Sleepwalking employees contrast with the loud colors. All night long in zombieville, they acted as though they didn't even know the temperature had fallen below 90 degrees. Fans followed their lead and spent most of the game in a trance. Rounds of applause were as wild and crazy as those at a funeral home. Lunacy and death! Together they create a strange, strange mood. An atmosphere for baseball it is not.

And still there is that plastic playing surface. Uglier even than the streets that lead into the stadium's potholed parking lot, it's the single biggest reason why the place has such a dull, dark, and dreary tone.

Not long ago Houston's Astrodome was considered a world wonder. People marveled at the brilliance of man. It was amazing how indoors could be made as good or better than the real thing. The Astrodome was the greatest discovery since the aluminum bat. Now that its personality has crystallized, its true character has emerged. And the result—a stadium designed and maintained with all the tactfulness of a *National Enquirer* headline story. To the baseball world Houston's tomb provides a new low in charisma, a bottom-of-the-ballpark barrel.   ·

The Astrodome does, however, offer one single saving grace. Rejoice Seattle fans! There actually exists a place on earth that can make a night at the Kingdome seem natural.

9

ROYALS STADIUM, KANSAS CITY ROYALS

A Masterpiece...in Plastic

REPORT CARD

Royals Stadium
BASEBALL PARK

July 6, 85 vs *Orioles*
GAME

Kansas City Royals
BASEBALL CLUB

CATEGORY	GRADE	POINTS
Layout and Upkeep	A+	100
Ball Field	C	75
Seating	A	95
Scoreboard	B	85
Food	A+	100
Ballpark Employees	A	95
Facilities	A+	100
Atmosphere	A	95
Total Points		745
Average		93

A
FINAL GRADE

1st
RANK

"A truly magnificent work of art! An awesome sight, a flawless structure equipped with graceful fountains and hot
weather.... Only problem, plastic grass."

PREGAME THOUGHTS

I should've guessed the Fourth was gonna be lousy. Normally at a ballpark
it'd be great. Baseball, hot dogs, and beer, fireworks after the game...how
could I go wrong?

But I was in Houston, one of only three ballparks in the country that can't
celebrate with rockets' red glare—the roof's in the way. Instead I got Independence Day Astro style. From square one it was a dud. The old guy singing
"The Star-Spangled Banner" blew it! Left out half the song. And that was
probably the best part of the night. The stadium was a nightmare. The game
was boring. The hot dogs were raunchy, and I was beat. I could barely stay
awake for the festivities. Not even the announcement of "Postgame fireworks
in the parking lot" revived me. My happiest Astro moment was the final out.
Within twenty minutes I was back at the motel and sound asleep, dreaming of
Kansas City and fighting off Astro nightmares.

As rotten as the Fourth was, I was pumped for the fifth. I love challenges,
especially on the road. Having to get somewhere within a certain amount of
time makes driving so much more exciting. I feel like I'm on a mission in my
very own sixteen-wheeler. "I'll get this baby in on time if it kills me!"

Well, me and my baby certainly faced a challenge. In KC on July 6 at
1:30 the Royals were scheduled to play the O's. I was scheduled to join them.
And I'd promised Terry, my Rangerette friend, lunch back in Arlington. According to *Rand McNally*'s back-page mileage guide, that made for a pretty
tough haul. Houston to Dallas was 245 miles. Dallas to Kansas City, 505.
Arlington was a few miles out of the way. By tacking on at least another 60
getting-lost miles, I'd be up over 800. I'd never reached the 800's before. Three
or four times the middle 700's, twice already on this trip, but 800 was big
time.

Still, I felt up to the challenge. A couple of McMuffins, some Sinatra and
Tommy Dorsey sing-a-longing, and by 1:00 I was back in Arlington. Lunch
with Terry was my little thank-you to the Rangers for their down-home hospitality. *Rand McNally* joined us. And while we sampled a real chuck-wagon
special, barbecued ribs and Texas toast, Terry helped me with directions.

Terry's a homespun Royal. She lives and dies Kansas City blue, especially when it comes to George Brett. She'd driven the same route I was gonna take plenty of times; family and George were still in KC. According to her, I had two choices: one, I could stay on Interstate 35 and take it on up into Oklahoma. It had already run me boringly down and back from Houston. And continued boringly north to Oklahoma City. There I'd turn right, crisscross the state through Tulsa, and reach Missouri. A four-lane expresser all the way; time would be good. My alternative, U.S. 69/75, looked great on paper; headed straight for KC. Plus map-length-wise, it was at least four inches shorter than 35. Terry said it was slow and suggested 35. I didn't listen.

I have no idea why, but every so often I get this idiotic urge to take something other than a four-lane expressway. I guess I think I need the scenery. I figure a leisurely drive through the countryside will be calming. It never is. I lose four hours time, my blood pressure soars. The very notion that it was supposed to be a relaxer when it starts in reality turns into a nightmare. Stuck behind some haywagon doing 35, stopping every five miles for a local traffic light, I go nuts. Just one of those diversionary drives cures me for about two years. Then I forget the horrors and have to try again. Well, I was ready to try again. Sick of Texas expressways, and determined to see the real heart of Oklahoma, I chose 69/75. I'd failed, however, to notice the *Rand McNally* color of 69/75. It was red.

Now *Rand McNally* is good to people with brains. It lets you know when a four-lane highway turns into a two-lane, chuckholed street. Blue and green represent limited-access highways. That means people travel normally at 70 miles per hour—170 at night. Yellow is a four-lane divided highway. That's okay too. It isn't lined with McDonald's and Burger Kings, but still moves along fairly well. Red is a different story. Mapmakers color their principal highways red for a reason. It's a warning to stay away from them. They usually pass through every village in the state, where they evolve into a highway of main streets and railroad crossings.

My choice, 69/75, was both red and yellow, a color proportion close to fifty-fifty. It also ran through a host of little black dots... Armstrong, Caddo, Atoka. A normal human would've guessed that highway 69/75 in a place like Caddo, Oklahoma, featured at least three traffic lights. I was, however, not in a normal state of mind. I was on my way to Royals Stadium.

After lunch I hit the road. About 4:00 P.M. I cleared Dallas. Close to 6:00 I entered Okie country. I was fat 'n' happy rolling down my yellow-colored highway, singing to the afternoon farm report and munching on some Cheezo's. I even enjoyed the scenery. Somewhere along the way I'd picked up the tune "Kansas City, Here I Come." Probably 'cause I couldn't wait to get there. I didn't know any more of the song, so I passed the time making up endings. "Leaving Houston on the run" was my best. Over and again I saturated my brain with the theme song. Finally I got sick of it and put Frank back on. When I reached the Okie border I laid on the ole horn...a welcome to Sooner country.

Wasn't long, though, before my elation was dashed. Not only was Sooner country an early disappointment, miles and miles of nothing, but not far into it my expressway vanished...and turned into a normal country road. I took a serious look at Rand McNally. My God, red lines! Principal highways in a state the clone of Texas. About then I passed my first hay-loaded Chevy pickup truck.

The sun wasn't the only thing on its way down. So was I. Traveling in the opposite direction of the expressway, too far to turn back, I could only plod onward. Not only that, I was driving on "DWI" Friday night. Loaded up with caffeine, I wasn't much better. My impatience turned into stupid passing. If the situation was too frustrating, which it usually was, double yellow lines were ignored. I'd dart out past a dragging clunker, put my life on the line, only to be trapped behind another. When two lanes temporarily swelled to four, I'd push it to 70. But just for a while. Pretty soon I'd be back putting through some traffic light-lined main street or stopped waiting for a train to pass. Yellow-flagged at Indy, plodding through a clone of Texas, with another 400 miles between me and the Royals, Kansas City by Saturday was gonna be tough. McDonald's by dinner was out of the question.

Sometime after dark I decided to take a break. I'm not sure exactly what time it was, I just remember brights kept shining in my eyes. I'm not sure just where I was, but somewhere a long, long way from Houston. And a long, long way from Kansas City. I was wiped out. And I needed somebody to confirm my hopes that an expressway existed somewhere down the road.

The day's log had pushed up over 500 miles when I rolled into another of those puny Oklahoma highway dots. On the back side of town stood a tiny roadside restaurant. I pulled into the crowded parking lot, stopped next to yet another pickup, and got out of the car. The night was humid but not unpleasant. Insects swarmed around the lights outside. Exhaust from so many parked cars, some still running, consumed the place. Voices and lights came from inside the diner. It must've been the local hangout. I strolled up the steps and pushed open the screen door. I might just as well have walked into a time machine. Outside might've been 1985. Inside I found a different world; I looked for the Fonz. He'd have fit.

The diner stretched before me. Directly in my path was the soda bar. Stools that could spin all the way around and off, if you really wanted 'em to, lined it. Nearly all were filled. Two cops sat drinking coffee at the bar. One turned and nodded to me as I walked in. Off to the left, in the main room, were booths. Most were occupied by families. Howard, Marion, Joanie, and Richie worked their way through a meat-and-potatoes dinner. Mixed in among the Cunninghams, at some of the other booths, probably just killing time, were teenagers. Small towns and summer nights have always presented a high schooler's greatest challenge—what to do! Usually it involves trouble. Not here though. The kids behaved. No yelling or swearing. No vandalism. Just quiet laughing over fries and a burger.

On the wall that divided the booths from the counter was a sign. It announced the day's special. Pork chops and mashed potatoes, along with lima beans. I hadn't seen a real cooked lima bean in years. They probably even had homemade lemon meringue pie stashed away in the fridge.

The place glowed with a simple homey warmth. The coziest spot, an old-fashioned soda bar, lured me toward it. Ice cream in eight or nine flavors hid in cartons underneath the counter's stainless-steel lids. Malt blenders sat on the shelf behind 'em. One was running. Syrup squirters ran in a row between the two. Cherry, raspberry, strawberry, the others labeled with a smudge. Fancy soda glasses and big stainless-steel malt cups stacked behind them. The menu special repeated itself above the counter.

A lady approached me. She looked like she'd just walked out of a forties black-and-white, late-night movie. "Hello." She smiled with an Oklahoma drawl.

"Hi." I didn't say much more. I was still mesmerized. My eyes were just rolling back and forth soaking it all in. The cops, if they were real, probably unlatched their holsters. I must've looked like I was casing the joint.

"Can I help you, young man?" She got my attention the second time. With an eye on the fifties, I asked directions back to the eighties.

"Where exactly am I? How do I get back to an expressway?" I kind of put the two together.

"Tulsa's where you wanna go, just keep on up the road. You'll run into the turnpike." That'd run into the highway I'd forsaken back at lunch. I was relieved to know I'd be able to find it again.

"Would you like some dinner?" The question seemed genuine. Not just one that cared about another ring on the till.

I wasn't real hungry, but the soda fountain had caught my eye. It also brought back memories. As kids, every Sunday after church we'd visit Langs Drug Store. It was between home and Sunday school. Dad couldn't drive by without us begging to go inside. He did it on purpose, I think. He liked the place as much as we did. It probably was the only reason he went to church. Amy, Drew, and I didn't have a choice. Mom insisted.

Langs had a soda fountain that could mix any drink ever made. Soda water any flavor, Cokes—vanilla, cherry, lemon, even straight. A nickel for a normal glass, 10 cents for a big one. Ice cream too, sodas, sundaes, and on those days that Dad was in a really good mood, Langs specialty—chocolate malts.

Ruthie worked Sunday mornings. She was a nice lady... and Langs most famous malt-maker. Sitting on the main counter's red stools, Amy, Drew, and I would watch Ruthie create. I saw only half the project since I spent most of the time spinning. She'd scoop the ice cream out from under the stainless-steel lids and plop it into a big metal cup. After adding a little milk and lots of syrup, it'd be stuck on the blender. I'd drool just watching. Then she'd pour that baby out in front of me. Best of all, the rest was left in the big cup. When I finished round one, a second glassful waited. God, those malts were good! I'd probably still go to church if Langs was around.

I was lost in a Sunday-school dream. My Oklahoma waitress asked again. I hadn't yet answered her request about dinner. "Do you have chocolate malts?" I asked instead of answered. I didn't mean to be rude, but I am sure that's how I was coming off.

"Sure do. Vanilla or chocolate ice cream?"

A choice... I'd forgotten they came with a choice. "Vanilla." It was the one soda-fountain decision I could make with authority. Much better than chocolate. I added that I wanted scoops of malt in it. That was important. Turned a plain shake into a malt. Gave it that little extra pizzazz.

I sat at the stool and waited. I twirled a couple of times. She poured it out for me. Just like Ruthie used to. I took a paper-covered straw from the glass full of them. I was tempted to shoot it across the room. That's how we always prepared ourselves at Langs. Of course we always ran and picked it up off the floor. I resisted and pulled the paper off. Then buried the straw into the cold rich chocolate. I played with it for a moment. Blew a couple of bubbles. Then tested it. Each swallow I held on my tongue until it melted. I slurped the corners of the glass until it was drained. A loud *ssssppppp* sound finished 'er off. Mom always told me that was rude. But she wasn't around. The rest I'd take with me. I'd enjoy it halfway across Oklahoma. In the car I could make as much noise as I wanted.

Chocolate malt refill in hand, I took one last look around the place, soaked it in, and skipped outside to my car. I felt a lot lighter than a half hour earlier; time machines can do that to a person. Revived, my Kansas City tune came back to me. And as I started in on it I headed off for Tulsa. In between verses I worked down the malt. The rest of the night my mind cruised through Langs. Till Tulsa the roads stayed pretty much the same, but the drive was wonderful. Probably my favorite night on the road the whole trip. About five o'clock in the morning, the odometer sliding past 800 for my all-time road record, I pulled over just outside of KC. I leaned the seat back and pulled the quilt up over me. My dreams continued. Chocolate malts and strawberry sodas, even Sunday school.

I still stick to four-lane expressways when cruising cross-country. They're still more convenient. The time is better. But every once in a while, if I'm ahead of schedule, I'll pull off on one of *Rand McNally*'s red highways. I do it more often now than before. I guess I'll always be searching for another Oklahoma Langs.

LAYOUT AND UPKEEP: GRADE A+

Whoever designed the Harry S. Truman complex in Kansas City should receive a special induction into Baseball's Hall of Fame. Despite all the technological wonders of the Western World—long suspension bridges, cities full of skyscrapers, the ability of a man to walk on the moon, and the perfection of the Ronco Veg-o-matic—it wasn't until the birth of the Truman complex that man solved his greatest problem. Before Kansas City's brilliant setup, nobody had come up with a really good stadium that housed both professional football and baseball.

Time and again architectural genius has proved by default that, like water and oil, the two just don't mix. Houston's Astrodome is a stunning example of a blunder that offers two as one. California nearly ruined a beautiful baseball field by enclosing the stadium and taking out the Big A. All that just to let the Rams in. And the Blue Jays have proved beyond the shadow of a doubt that a baseball diamond cannot just be tossed together inside some football stadium. Exhibition Stadium is so funny-looking, it's almost sad. Kansas City and its revolutionary thinkers solved the problem by creating them side by side. In Arrowhead the Chiefs play football, while right next door major league baseball carries on. Then they went and made the setup even better by putting a Dodger-style parking lot around the whole thing. The idea truly shows the upper limits of the human brain.

Interstate 70 passes directly alongside and a bit above the complex. That's where I got my first feeling for the place. Actually I was lucky I didn't end up in the ditch. Of the pair of parks, the Royals' lies closest to the road. Facing out, its diamond-shaped field opens to passing cars. It is an explosion of color, and nothing blocks a look inside. Three levels of red seats hover above the synthetic green turf. The brightest reds and greens I think I've ever seen. Instead of barriers out over the center-field wall, the scoreboard stands, 12 stories high, shaped like a royal crest. A huge blue crown decorated with the KC logo, the display's a giant name tag. On each side of the scoreboard, swirling, spouting fountains shoot water into the air. With the brilliant reds and greens, the cool water offers a soft touch. The view is awesome. It's gotta lead the majors in back-seat "oohs" and "ahhs."

Inside is just as grand. At a place that purposely separates the cowhide from the pigskin, you'd expect an exacting attention to baseball detail. And like Dodger blue in L.A., Royal blue in Kansas City doesn't disappoint. A clean, organized, very professional ballpark, finely tuned to the needs of baseball, everything's in its proper place. Even the paint on the inside hallway matches perfectly with the royal shade outlining numbers on the Kansas City uniforms. The whole complex is efficient. The idea is pure genius. And Royals Stadium... it's a masterpiece.

BALL FIELD: GRADE C

During the five years I went to college I spent summers working for my hometown city parks department. There I learned well from full-timers just how to lean on a shovel or a rake. Consequently, every tool that we used was around and happy when its lifetime warranty was up.

Royals Stadium's ground crew is not a hometown city parks department. In fact, brooms and rakes, as heavy a workout as they get, probably last only a single home stand. Most of the participants performing the operation are probably like I was, just college kids picking up summer work. But when they've finished they've practically pulled off the impossible. They almost make artificial turf breathe.

The game-day assault begins some 60 to 90 minutes prior to the first pitch. And that was only what I saw. The turf itself is probably read to each evening and sung a lullaby before the lights go out. To ready it for a game, sixteen gardeners dressed in Royal blue get down to business. Each triangle of dirt, the three bases and home plate, are worked over by three separate workers. One hammers down the dirt with a manual jackhammer device. Shaped like a replica of home plate, the jackhammer invention repeatedly pounds the ground. Following its packing, the small patch is raked, rolled, beaten, and watered. All the while a broom pusher circles the base, twenty times and more. Any microscopic creatures that bounce out onto the green are shoved back into the dirt. The rest of the space in between is massaged by a roaming sweeper made out of a golf cart. The sweeper and a cruising vacuum cleaner, complete with driver, spend the entire hour or so that the beauty treatment takes place going around the field like nervous goldfish in a rocking aquarium. Nothing, absolutely nothing that doesn't belong, remains behind.

To cap off the production, a final dusting and watering occurs. At home plate, the last to be done, it's as ceremonial as the Ohio State halftime dotting of the "I." All hoses are rolled in. One worker stays out on the field; he stands alone with only an old tin watering can. One last time he sprinkles the dirt about the plate. Then he steps back, making sure nothing has ruined his artwork. Finally, before he heads to the bull pen and his other 15 comrades, he towels off his shoes. Quietly and carefully, he tiptoes away.

While the pregame ceremony was exhausting enough to watch, the sixth inning touch-up was even more intense. On cue the workers broke from their gate faster than the ponies at Churchill Downs on Derby Day. Each sprinted to his assigned duty, four to a base. One pounded, one sifted, one raked, and the other swept. Dumbfounded, George Brett just stood and stared. After the dirt was reperfected, and curious George picked up and moved, the kids popped on a new white base. Then the four groups of four galloped back to the pen. Unmatched in speed and intensity in the majors, I could only wonder how well they'd tend to a grass field. Pebble Beach's eighteenth green couldn't be more polished. The turf could probably be used for Kansas City lawn-bowling championships if Kansas City had them. If only it were planted with real fresh-smelling, soft green grass, the workaholics could create a masterpiece unmatched anywhere except at America' finest golf courses.

Yet even with all the effort, efficiency, and technology, the dedicated workers and their intense invasion, the grass remains synthetic. It doesn't live or die. It doesn't smell fresh after a soft summer rain or reach back to the sun after a drenching thunder shower. It just doesn't do anything but lie there, as clean and antiseptic as a hospital floor. The turf, as traditional to baseball as a living-room carpet, is perfect—but only perfect plastic.

SEATING: GRADE A

Royals Stadium was made just for baseball. Its three bright red levels have sight lines with one goal in common: how to best watch the only game in the house.

Three tiers of seats rise almost straight up and tower over the ball field. Each of the chairs is bright red plastic. From outside looking in, the scene is festive. From the seats themselves, views onto the field are great. A small second level is sandwiched between the larger lower level and a huge upper deck. All three run down both foul lines and curl cozily around the foul pole in the corner. Consequently, only a small portion of the outfield has seats. Instead of bleachers that space is reserved for fountains. The effect allows for the greatest number of people as close to the action as possible.

In addition to its great sight lines, comfort is a Royal Stadium byword. The many extra-wide aisles stream down from under the stands toward the field. Since there are as few as six seats per aisle alongside home plate, getting in and out is not a problem anywhere. Even the seats themselves are extraordinarily comfortable. They add a feature that few in the majors provide. With each standing ovation, when the plastic seat is folded down, it doesn't pop back up, it stays down. Consequently, if you miss center, you don't end up with your rear on the concrete. Another simple extra at a place just loaded with them.

SCOREBOARD: GRADE B

Kansas City's royal-emblemed scoreboard is one of the park's most impressive, yet at the same time most limited, features. Twelve stories tall in dead center field, shadowed by tall, thin light standards, and balanced on each side by graceful fountains, from the outside or in, it's an eyecatcher. Its work output, though, is restricted.

At first glance the arrangement looks perfect. Not until it clicks on are its few flaws apparent. First, the quality of instant replay is poor. A black-and-white video screen, wonderful 12 years ago, is no longer state-of-the-art. At night the pictures and replays are probably a bit fuzzy. In the glare of the sun, on a bright Saturday afternoon, they were worthless. Diamond Vision's clear crisp movies would seem much more in tune with such a high-tech place. Besides, it'd take a little pressure off the screen to do it all. By itself the setup's overworked; info's up and then just as quickly it disappears. Sometimes before you even have a chance to check it out.

Despite its problems, the screen handles pure baseball information efficiently. Its computerized face is split into four equal-size squares. At the base of the face, below the squares, is a line score. It runs the Royals game. The upper two boxes spend most of their time with the ball game, the lower two with the players in the game. Other baseball information, including league updates, is alternated onto any one of the four squares at the right time... usually between innings.

At most other parks the arrangement would be considered wonderful. The emblem's unique shape is enough to keep it around Kansas City forever. Yet it just doesn't match up to the stadium's high standards. For a place that ripples with excitement, the scoreboard, once turned on, is a yawner.

FOOD: GRADE A+

Selection: Excellent Accessibility: Very Good
Taste: Excellent   Cost: 2nd

After leaving Texas and suffering through horrible American and National League ballpark food, Kansas City was a welcome taste! Not only does the place have some of the majors' most delicious food, but it comes in wide variety at very low prices. And specialty-wise it might just be the best.

In Texas my taste buds nearly croaked. Since neither park provided any edible specialties, I was forced to live on peanuts, popcorn, and hot dogs. And even those were lousy. I made up for it in KC. Baseball's very best barbecue sandwiches served with a healthy scoop of baked beans top the menu. Tangy and oozing with sauce, they're the best I've ever tasted...in or out of a baseball park. Gourmet hamburgers, big, juicy thick ones, smolder on the grill. Onions grilling right alongside create an aroma that forces the mouth to water. At a separate stand, thick, cheesy, oven-baked "Fielder's Choice" pizza slides in and out of the oven. It almost bubbles as it's plopped onto its wax-paper slabs. Finally, for those Rocky Mountain diehards in from Denver, Coors and Coors Light move around the stands at a pleasant pace.

As if all these extras weren't enough, Kansas City vendors provide a wonderful special service. They scrap those crummy little mustard packets and let you enjoy a real hot dog with real mustard right there at your seat. Caring for my stomach, I've made it a policy to stay away from what's inside of those plastic envelopes. And since a hot dog without mustard isn't worth the trouble it takes to chew, and since on all my other stops mustard in the stands was only by the packet, I'd been forced down into the concessions. There I could get real mustard. But to buy the dog I had to wait in line. To squirt a little mustard on it I'd wait in another one. Then while the dog was handy and freshly mustardized, I'd take a bite or two. By the time I got back to my seat it usually had disappeared and was digesting somewhere in my tummy. In addition to being uncomfortable (walking and eating at the same time), the whole process would cost me three to six outs of baseball...critical time if the ball game was a tight one.

In KC I just kicked back and waited for the vendor. Armed with squirt bottles of real mustard (and ketchup for visiting football fans), vendors handle the chore. They do the squirting right there at the seat—no missed outs, no missed innings, no plastic packets. They complete a circuit of class. From parking lot to mustard, Royals Stadium does it all with style.

BALLPARK EMPLOYEES: GRADE A

Maybe it's the color blue that brings out professionalism in a stadium's work force. Be it of the Dodger or Royal shade, each shows why theirs is such a class organization.

Ushers and security people are not only well dressed but also pleasant. Basically very businesslike, should a specific situation come up that calls for adjustment, they can also bend a bit. A no-nonsense rule of one-time exit was altered so that I could return to my car to retrieve my camera. Considering the artwork inside, it would have been criminal to have left it behind. While I did get out and back in again, I got the idea that it didn't happen often. Even so, in order to leave I wasn't forced to sign over my firstborn or go through some bright-light interrogation.

Food vendors roam the stands with an intensity I hadn't seen since Candlestick. Most West Coasters just drift from section to section. And a lot of 'em don't carry dogs or beer. The Kansas City crew busts tail. With that high-quality Western menu kicked out at East Coast speed, I must've gained ten pounds on beer and peanuts alone. But it's those people who rake the dirt, sweep the turf, and change the bases who are the real class of the place. Managed by George Toma, Kansas City's head groundkeeper, they do for artificial grass what fertilizer, sunshine, and rain do for the real thing.

FACILITIES: GRADE A+

The Truman complex is the essence of proper planning. Facilities inside and out are the very best. From the big things like its monstrous-size parking lot to those little special touches inside, this category might find the stadium at its very best.

Each and every detail is attended to with the utmost care. Play-by-play radio broadcasting is piped through all the walkways under the stands and into the rest rooms as well. That way you never have to miss a Saberhagen strikeout. Rest rooms are spotless. Phones and water fountains are all over the park, all in working order. Everything is placed in just the right spot and works just as it's supposed to.

Set between the two stadiums, the gigantic parking lot is the last one before you move into big-city front yards in the East. Not only does it do a good job of taking care of cars, it backs up against the freeway. Just a short and safe walk from the ball field, just a short and safe drive from the highway, it's just typical KC quality.

ATMOSPHERE: GRADE A

A totally professional atmosphere makes Royals Stadium one of the majors' best. While the feeling inside is pure baseball, oddly enough, not everything that makes it so is traditional. A lot in fact is unique, only to KC. But nearly everything works. A first-class sight brings on that first-class air. Together they create a first-class feeling. Kind of like those old Imperial Margarine commercials, taking a bite of the flavor of Royals Stadium makes you feel like a king.

Oddly shaped, the scoreboard stands alone beyond the center-field fence. Its one-of-a-kind look is refreshing. Rather than strange, it's striking. Too unconventional anywhere else in the majors, inside the Kansas City ballpark it fits...like a crown.

Missouri summers are blue-skied and hot, perfect weather for lounging in the sunshine and soaking up suds. But the ballpark left out bleachers. Anyplace else the omission would be criminal. Yet Royals Stadium gets away with it. One reason is, with all the other seats so comfortable and close, even in such nice weather bleachers aren't missed a bit. The other is those folks that fill the place. Crazies in the bleachers wouldn't fit in KC, the park is much too stately. Instead it's crammed with normal folks. Almost every hot summer weekend Royals Stadium is packed to the gills. With three levels awash in a constant ballpark buzz, you hardly even notice that the only noise beyond the fences is that of splashing water.

Probably the strangest thing about the place is that its fountains actually find a home. After suffering through the Astrodome and seeing just what kind of horrors technology can bring to a ballpark, I wasn't too pumped to meet Kansas City's outfield waterfalls. But in Royals Stadium the fountains belong. They prove that weird and baseball can work together—as long as weird is also beautiful. And in the middle of Missouri, where 90 degrees in the summer is expected, it is. By adding a refreshing feel to what can be some beastly hot afternoons, the fountains actually soften the elements. Watching them quietly rise and fall between innings allowed me to forget that I was cooking.

I left KC with a little better feeling for baseball in the future. Before, I figured the only way to make the game better would be to invest in a time machine...drop backward 40 years and try to recapture some of the old magic. Tell the dome architects, the plastic manufacturers, the Japanese giant-movie-screen makers, "Go away! Bother someone else." Then bring back the old broken-down ballparks, the hand-operated scoreboards, the $2.00 ticket prices, and let tradition run the show. But Royals Stadium got me thinking. It gave me ideas...ideas I'd never thought of or hoped to think. That maybe some things can be improved. Maybe someday modern technology and baseball will be able to stroll together down the aisle.

If that marriage ever takes place, it's certain that plastic grass will never be the flower girl. Only the turf ruins a perfect 10. Only because of it does an afternoon at Royals Stadium lack a little something. Of all those new and exciting touches in the ballpark, it's the one that doesn't belong. You can only wonder what that ground crew could do with real grass. The stadium would be unflawed. An evening of baseball in Kansas City would be stunning—the equal of an afternoon at Wrigley. But as things stand now, it still lacks that one quality. Royals Stadium remains the limited beauty that it is. Merely a masterpiece...a masterpiece in plastic.

10

BUSCH MEMORIAL STADIUM, ST. LOUIS CARDINALS

Gateway to the East

REPORT CARD	*Busch Memorial Stadium* BASEBALL PARK
July 7, 85 vs Dodgers GAME	*St. Louis Cardinals* BASEBALL CLUB

CATEGORY	GRADE	POINTS
Layout and Upkeep	B	85
Ball Field	C	75
Seating	C	75
Scoreboard	B	85
Food	C	75
Ballpark Employees	B	85
Facilities	B	85
Atmosphere	A	95
Total Points		660
Average		83

B

FINAL GRADE

10th

RANK

"Finally baseball with a little of that hard-core Eastern tradition.... Historians had the right idea, just the wrong direction."

PREGAME THOUGHTS

St. Louis is pure Eastern, at least when it comes to baseball. Texas, California, the rest of the West, and all their clean rest rooms were finally in the rearview mirror. I was on my way home! I was going back to where baseball was played in the city, not the suburbs. Where broken-down ballparks rose out of broken-down neighborhoods. Where street crime was a game-night factor, and taking a taxi, considering the clientele, a better investment than Metro buses.

And I couldn't wait! I wanted to spend ten bucks to cram in behind some fat iron support post. If it meant my knees would scrunch up into my stomach, or I wouldn't be able to see home plate, I didn't much care. I needed the excitement! I longed to finally be surrounded by baseball fanatics, folks who lived and died baseball. Who spent the game sloshing down cold beer instead of sipping California wines. I was even willing to stuff my new car into some overpriced front yard in the welfare section of town. If that meant picking up a dent or two, tough. It would be the chance I'd have to take. While these wishes to some might seem strange, for me they were refreshing. I was ready for a little old-time baseball tradition somewhere east of the Rockies and north of Oklahoma. Above all I had to find a ballyard whose fans, when they rose for the seventh-inning stretch, didn't continue on out the door.

It's not that my first leg wasn't a treat. It was. I'd done the Western circuit— the only way it can be done—in first-class style. You see, baseball out West is luxurious. In Southern California, as well as at Royals Stadium, the game comes wrapped inside a perfect package. Played under blue, sunshiny skies, in temperatures that bake but don't burn, baseball's clean, convenient, and safe. Ballparks sit in neighborhoods where you don't need to carry a gun to the grocery store. Next-door neighbors own cocker spaniels instead of Dobermans. Station wagons pass by the stadium when the team is out of town. Tickets to most California suburban stadiums mean that families can actually do something together—even at night.

Still, even with all the conveniences, something's missing. It's true, the boundless, bright blue sky makes Dodger Stadium an awesome experience. Standing at its feet, you can only shudder. And Oakland's Coliseum rock 'n' rolls the night away. It's impossible not to have a good time. Driving by Royals Stadium and staring down at the sea of red is hypnotizing. It probably causes two dozen traffic accidents each year. Yet all three lack the intensity that the East relishes.

Why? Maybe it's because the West Coast attitude is too laid back. When folks spend their whole lives mellowing out, it's probably too much bother to be fanatical in three hours of leisure time. Or it could be the weather. Not having to shiver through an April ice storm or swim in your own sweat on an August afternoon with 95 percent humidity, just to watch a ballgame, might weaken your resolve. Who knows? It might even be genetic.

But whatever the reason, there's a difference. In the East emotions run much deeper. For eight months out of the year, baseball's not just some other professional sport. It's a way of life. Something to become totally infatuated with. This isn't to say that all Westerners are ho-hummers. Many likely show suicidal tendencies when their ball club blows it down the stretch. It's probably true, though, that more fans west of St. Louis than east of it fall asleep at night not worrying about divisional standings.

Well, right now I live far away from the problems of Detroit or Chicago. As big cities go, Seattle is almost crime-free. I can go to a Mariner night game and leave by myself with twenties hanging out of my pockets. And I'll make it to the car alive. It's restored my faith in America, in the morality of the human race. But when it comes to baseball, I relate to the "Midwest state of mind." For me the game's always been more typical of Chicago's dangerous South Side than the suburbs of Disneyland. I can live with the escalators and multipurpose stadiums and appreciate the parking lots where cars have a better than 50 percent survival rate. But I'll take that Eastern intensity any day— even if it means using the bathrooms at Tiger Stadium.

While a sunny summer afternoon in Dodger Stadium might provide the game its most gorgeous setting, give me the intensity of an autumn pennant race in Chicago. The air may be cooler, but the people won't be. They'll be going crazy, even if their car is down the road being cleaned out for the eighth time in a month.

LAYOUT AND UPKEEP: GRADE B

I'd never been to St. Louis before, but couldn't wait to go. I'd heard it was a real city. That it actually had a downtown ballpark surrounded by real street crime and parking problems. That it added a little character and excitement to go with baseball. Taking off from Kansas City's palace, on a clear blue-skied Sunday morning, I was pumped!

Through corn-covered country, I-70 links Kansas City's suburbs and downtown St. Louis. Three hundred miles, from ballpark to ballpark, it nearly connects their front porches. The transition along the way is as great as Dorothy's was from Kansas to Oz. KC is country; Royals Stadium is suburban. St. Louis is city; Busch is urban. The change takes time, but explodes when it hits. About twenty miles outside St. Louis, Ole MacDonald disappears. Soft rolling cornfields are replaced by smoke-belching factories. I passed cars instead of pickup trucks. Train tracks were everywhere. So were trains, and crossings, and traffic jams. Tempered steel, concrete, and industry—it was almost like cruising into Chicago. I was so taken with all the clutter, I got lost three times trying to find the right exit.

The ballpark itself doesn't look cityish. Born in 1966, it was the first in the concrete-bowl line. And like the two river ones in Pit and Cinci, it's simple concrete, round, and enclosed—not really much to look at. Instead, at Busch, it's all the downtown props that provide the excitement. The ballpark sits smack-dab in the middle of it and hovers over the freeway only a couple of blocks from where the Great Arch guards the Mississippi. City streets and sidewalks crisscross all about. Asphalt and concrete are its landscaping materials. No grassy hills roll about the outside gates. No palm trees provide a pleasant welcome. Nothing but fire hydrants and street signs grow in the curb lawn. Only a solitary statue of Stan "the Man" Musial out in front breaks the hard, flat, concrete entrance. Leaning out over the plate, bat cocked high, Stan's a good doorman to the ballpark.

Strangely enough, inside the stadium gates it's clean. Usually with the city comes garbage. But at Busch most of the crap either gets cleared away or never makes it in. The layout's efficient too. Nothing as California-ish as escalators, but wide concrete ramps run comfortably about the place. Seats are easy to get to and simple to find. The majors' westernmost big-city ballpark that's actually in the city, it isn't flooded with big-city problems. In fact, if you don't mind gray, the scenery's quite refreshing.

BALL FIELD: GRADE C

Unfortunately, like so many of today's modern stadiums, Busch's floor is made of plastic. But, like its Missouri neighbor, the ground crew does a good job with what it's got to work with.

No other state in the union tries as hard to make plastic perfect. Kansas City's workers are unreal. They literally attack the dirt. The St. Louis group, although not quite as fanatical, is still intense. Sweeping, raking, watering, both the dirt and plastic get a good pregame prep. The turf itself is also quality... top-of-the-line as plastic goes. Not nearly as sweet as the real thing, at least it's not like Houston's... hammered with extras: no 100-yard rectangle, no fat ugly seam. Nothing but acres and acres of plain fake grass.

Busch also adds a little gizmo to their field that not even KC includes: outside the first-base coaching box and running parallel to the foul line, the turf's cut. Under the cut is a rollaway tarp. On cue it pops up and is automatically rolled out to cover the infield. As soon as the game is finished, even if the forecast calls for 90 degrees and sunshine, which St. Louis summer forecasts usually do, groundkeepers get the tarp moving. And they do it as quickly and efficiently as they do everything else. I was impressed. As in Kansas City, while the plasti-feel isn't a traditional one, I couldn't help but admire the work ethic of the plasti-gardeners.

SEATING: GRADE C

At most of the modern concrete bowls finding a comfortable seat is no problem. Busch is the same. Sitting close enough to feel the game, however, is a different matter.

Two tiers circle the park. Field seats fill in the foul ground below them. Of the three sections, only the top one doesn't have a break. The other two pause at the foul poles, making way for a scoreboard and some center-field bleachers. Consequently, most of the stadium seats are in the huge, unbroken upper level. From way up high, baseball loses a lot of its intimacy. Numbers replace faces as ID markers, and sometimes they don't even help. You're left watching the little Redbird base stealers bounce around the diamond like marbles in a pinball machine. A program's needed to check who's doing the swiping. Ozzie or Vince Coleman or Willie McGee... or all three at the same time.

Although the eyes may get a little strained, none of the other body parts suffer. Typical multidimensional comfort spreads about the place. Wide aisles between the seats allow you to kick back and relax. The many aisles into the stands make for easy in-and-outing-it among the rows. Vertical obstruction isn't bad either. So many of the seats are in the upper level, the sky's their only overhang.

As nontraditional as the setup is, it does provide one feature from the old school. Most of the major league circle stadiums are plastic and fold up all the way around. They don't have bleachers. That's not only boring, it's un-American. In St. Louis the sun shines too bright, and the summer days are much too hot not to provide bench seats for at least a few thousand folks. So out under the scoreboards sit two big sections of flat benches. Under blue skies and sunshine, folks can carry on whatever way they please. They can drink beer, splash on the lotion, and let it hang out a bit. An Eastern ballpark necessity, in an Eastern park tradition, it's the rowdiest bleacher section west of the Mississippi.

SCOREBOARD: GRADE B

A feel for the traditional, a little imagination, and an upbeat way of doing things provide Busch with a pretty fair scoreboard show. In fact, it's one of the liveliest pure baseball ones around. Too bad half the folks inside can't see it.

Although the ballpark may not look conventional, it attends to everything that is. Keeping score's no different—all the basics get a good look. Small auxiliary boards provide constant updates from around the league. Meanwhile, a larger pair of outfield panels handle the more complicated stuff. Up over the left center-field bleachers hangs the traditional screen. It features a running line score of the Cards game, flashes simple statistics, and keeps track of all the stolen bases. Over in right center field is a giant color video board. Not many ballparks get more from the big screen. No call is too close to replay, no decision too controversial; everything gets a second look. In fact, whatever it takes to get the crowd in gear—chants, highlights, replays—the big screen shows it.

As good as the video board is during the game, it's even better before and after. Two times a night it runs a Cardinal highlight show. Set to music, yesterday's ball game gets a five-minute review. Fans love it. They sit and watch, and when the timing's right roar their approval. Ten minutes after the game, another show is featured. Diehards stick around. Again set to music, highlights that made or broke the Cards that afternoon are rolled. Together with the rock-'n'-roll music, it begins and ends each ball game with a bang... especially when the Cards win.

Only a shaky placement of the two screens taints the arrangement. Each hangs above the outfield bleacher sections and below the huge upper level. Hardly anybody beyond the fences can enjoy the fun. They're either too close, too far under, or too far over to join in. Music, on the other hand, is for everyone. Speakers are crisp and clear, even from the upper deck. And unlike the plastic grass, things stay pretty much traditional. Organ tunes float about and create a happy background for the game.

FOOD: GRADE C

Selection: Fair   Accessibility: Fair
Taste: Fair   Cost: 8th

If nothing else, Eastern baseball means fans are able to stay planted all afternoon, eating, drinking, and watching the game. A wiener is only a "Hey, hot dog" away. A beer is no farther than a wave of the hand. Like in Kansas City, the Redbird vendors make sure you never go an inning without either.

Too bad the food isn't as good as those who carry it. A hot dog I bought came packaged in a mangled soggy bun. Rather than tossing it after I ate it, I decided I'd toss it before. So I let it rest in peace in the nearby trash can and tried again. The second one I tried was dry but not much better. Other stuff hitting the stands was all right but certainly not in the same royal class as Kansas City.

Quality rises under the stands. The setup, though, is a bit awkward. Food booths stand at spots already crowded by the walkway traffic. Instead of pushed off the main drag, they're in the middle of it. Folks searching for food get crowded in with those passing by searching for seats. Everything is clogged up. Still, it's worth the wait. Grilled red hots and a couple of extra sausage things team up with Cardinal burgers and are a lot better than the soggy stuff upstairs.

Beer, however, is the ballpark specialty. At a stadium with a name like Busch it better be. And since Augie Jr. owns the club, it only figures that 95 percent of the draft would be named after him. Cold Busch beer is everywhere.

BALLPARK EMPLOYEES: GRADE B

Out West a low-keyed style floats about the ballparks. Stadium employees, especially in Southern California, are just plain good folk. They dress well and act proper. But most important, they really look like they're having fun. With all the happy people around, you can't help but be happy. Smiles are a catchy commodity. In the East smiles are fewer, fuses shorter. Of all the Eastern ballparks, only Milwaukee's workers fit the friendly California mold.

Although Eastern at heart, the St. Louis staff isn't cold-hearted. Busch is a good, hardworking people place. Workers are businesslike, but also pretty nice. Their pace is quicker than in the West, especially up in the stands pushing the food and drink. Well-dressed ushers are easy to find and quick to help out. Stadium security is approachable. Even concessionaires are pleasant. That positive work ethic that the ground crew shows radiates up from the ball field throughout the rest of the place and bounces off the beer salesmen in the upper deck.

FACILITIES: GRADE B

Downtown provides baseball with excitement. Yet it also poses problems. Criss-crossing streets and buildings crammed together don't allow room for parking lots. City rest rooms are usually filthy. The same is true of most downtown ballparks. Not Busch. Even with the bigness of St. Louis hovering over her, she finds time to clean the bathrooms—and, oddly enough, provide space for all the cars.

Parking for a Cards game is unique. Unlike arenas in the West, which are surrounded by acres of parking lots, St. Louis offers only a few. That doesn't mean you're forced into front yards and back alleys like in Detroit. With no room to spread out, the city provides the only room it's got—up. Such a simple solution, it's a wonder it's not in use all over the nation. Just a short stroll from the stadium, a couple of three-story garages solve the problem. Big enough, and fairly easy to get to, the garages work great. Attendants even roam about them during the game. And if the nearby ones are filled, a few more farther into town are available. Also, tiny corner lots are scattered about downtown. As a result you don't have to go to a Cardinal game wondering what you'll return to.

Inside facilities aren't typical downtownish either. Rest rooms aren't fancy, but they're usable. They don't have real mirrors or tiled floors. They're not nearly as sparkling as on the West Coast. Still, they beat the aging closets in Comiskey. Hit with the broom at least a couple of times a game, for a city ballpark they aren't half bad. Plus they even add a Dodger-style option: throughout the game play-by-play broadcast is piped in.

Clean, safe, and convenient, at least for a city stadium, Busch offers that downtown feel without having to feel the downtown.

ATMOSPHERE: GRADE A

It had been a while, but it felt good to be back in the East. I'd almost forgotten that baseball was more than a game, that it wasn't just some sideshow to an urban sprawl with better things to do. Baseball in St. Louis is refreshing.

In the big Missouri city on the banks of the ole Mississippi the game is real. It's important. It's emotional. Summers in St. Louis are first the Cards and second everything else.

I am sure there are those in St. Louis who probably consider themselves Westerners. History even sees it as the West's Great Gateway. But the Missourian's roots stretch to the East. Emotions and problems that dominate St. Louis are more caught up in the whirl of a Chicago or Detroit, not San Francisco or San Diego. Even Kansas City, only six hours down the road, is in a different world. Spiritually it's a lot farther west than 300 miles.

Like other big Midwestern cities, St. Louis has big-city problems. Problems that only seem to get worse in summer heat. Gorgeous orange sunsets don't sink into the ocean to soften the weather. It has no Mount Rainier rising above to temper the highs and lows. Or even fresh-water breezes to just plain cool off in. Without nature's help, the town must find something to mellow it out. Baseball serves that purpose. To hot city summers, where even at night the asphalt doesn't cool, where street crime rises with the temperature, the game is a godsend. It allows the boiling pot to steam.

Looking at the empty stadium with the Cards out of town, you'd never know it. Busch itself isn't all that special. Rather it's the game-day electricity that is. Inside a very plain-looking place an excitement glows. When the Cards are playing Busch bursts with a passionate Eastern big-city spirit, a spirit that nobody else to the west can claim.

Cardinal red is the only game-day color allowed in St. Louis. Bright, almost fluorescent, it swarms on the city streets that lead into the stadium. Hats, shirts, shorts—almost everybody has on something that glows in Cardinal red. Streams of the brilliant color weave closer to the park gates, then glob together at the corners. Streetlights change, cars stop, and the colors ooze on. Meanwhile, up ahead, ticket windows, entrances, stadium walkways all swim in a people pool of red. The color electrifies Busch and bathes it with a big-time college football excitement. Nowhere else in the majors do hometown folks feature such a loyal wardrobe. No other baseball color is so passionate.

Festivities that sizzle outside on the concrete sidewalk ignite and explode inside. Fans are good and loud. They love to cheer. And every chance it gets, the ballpark lets them. Charges by the bugleful, and all sorts of little scoreboard tidbits, help the ballpark get down. Plus it adds a little personal touch. In the seventh inning, instead of baseball's *only* tune to stretch by, Busch picks a personal favorite. The Clydesdales prance across the giant movie screen. Budweiser's "King of Beers" theme song hits the speakers. It may not be normal baseball music, but a hometown tradition. Folks love it. Clapping along in unison to the catchy tune, they light up the place.

The East also has baseball tradition, a legacy that transplants on the Pacific don't. And the Cardinals' legacy is as intense as the folks who follow it. There's Musial, the Gashouse gang, Dizzy Dean, a long rich line of champions, and a World Series aura that only the Yankees can match. Even for me, a diehard American Leaguer, Busch brought back a '68 version of Cardinal red. Childhood memories of Bob Gibson smoking heat in on the fists of "Willie the Wonder" Horton. . . . Of 17 K'd Tigers opening the '68 Series. Of Lou Brock singling to right over and over again, then standing on third two pitches later. . . without the benefit of a hit. And in the end Brock coming in standing up, his shoe a quarter inch off home plate, Freehan with the ball, and the Tigers winning the World Championship. A great Cardinal legacy indeed, and one that intertwined that one season with a great one in Detroit.

Finally, there's the city skyline. As exciting as the vocal crowd and bright red colors, as stirring as the Redbird tradition. Skyscrapers hover over the park. The powerful *Clarion* Building shoots up alongside it. Peaks of smaller structures grow about too. Up and down, bordering the smooth stadium roof, they energize the place.

A fiery excitement flows through Busch. It can be found in many places. Loud and red, enthusiastic fans have fun under the push of the big city. St. Louis is a big-city baseball tradition in a vibrant Eastern mold. Its awesome ID marker even says so. Huge yet graceful, the Great Arch climbs up over the stadium. From the inside its sight is commanding. From the outside the Arch serves as a symbol. Serene and strong, it stands as a marker, a dividing point between East and West, a passageway to a different baseball way of life, a "Gateway to the East."

11

WRIGLEY FIELD,
CHICAGO CUBS

Baseball Pure and Simple

REPORT CARD		**Wrigley Field**
		BASEBALL PARK
July 9/10, 85 vs Padres		**Chicago Cubs**
GAME		BASEBALL CLUB

CATEGORY	GRADE	POINTS
Layout and Upkeep	*C*	*75*
Ball Field	*A*	*95*
Seating	*A+*	*100*
Scoreboard	*A+*	*100*
Food	*C*	*75*
Ballpark Employees	*C*	*75*
Facilities	*D*	*65*
Atmosphere	*A+*	*100*
Total Points		*685*
Average		*86*

B+

FINAL GRADE

5th

RANK

135

"Enclosed in ivy, attended by the sincerest of fans, tucked
away in a tidy little neighborhood known as Wrigleyville.
...Baseball forever in the sunshine has no truer home."

PREGAME THOUGHTS

Charley sells peanuts on the sidewalks outside of Wrigley Field. A college
graduate, and a former Peace Corps warrior, he now makes a living calling
out "Peanuts, three bags for a buck"...what a wonderful life! A friend of my
sister Amy, who lives in Chicago, Charley heard about my trip. Amy told
him. She hadn't really said why I was doing it, probably because it was too
strange for her to explain. However, as you might expect from a guy who
depends on the spare change of Cubbie bleacherites for a livelihood, Charley
thought the idea grand. Not only did he like it, but he invited me over to see
the ropes of his in-house peanut-packing operation. I was ecstatic. On the
ultimate journey, I'd get to see the inner workings of the ultimate career.

Plenty of times I've daydreamed as to what I'd like to be when I grow up.
Everybody does I am sure...teachers probably more than most people. When
you spend most of your kid life choosing whether to be a pro football quar-
terback or center fielder for the Detroit Tigers, your college career concentrating on Spartan football games instead of classes, and your adult life with
hundreds of kids, daydreaming becomes second nature. I've often wondered if
there's a job out there less mind-boggling than teaching ninth-grade history.
Of course, like teaching, it'd have to come with more days off than on. While
I'd never thought of it, being a peanut vendor at one of the majors' most historic places had definite possibilities.

My sister met Charley via the Cubs. They both lived in Wrigleyville, the
friendly neighborhood about the park. Wrigley, only two blocks from her apartment, had seduced her. Before the Cubs, like most normal Midwest girls,
Amy was an occasional sports fan. She knew teams, understood games, but
was basically uninterested—even in college! A State grad like me, she went to
Spartan football games only on "sunny" Saturdays and watched Magic Johnson
on television instead of in person at the field house. Her four-year schedule,
unlike my five-and-one-half-year version, was centered around a real major,
not how to best prepare for weekend ball games. A year out of school, she
moved to Chicago, got a graphic design job, and rented a little place two blocks
down the street from Wrigley. At the time it didn't seem like a big deal. Soon,
though, she was converted.

It was primarily due to the hex of the ivy that Sis became a baseball fan. And after just a few visits she fell in love with both the Cubs and their ancient park. She kept on top of Wrigley's "no lights" issue (day games only), so much so that when I asked about it she had all the legal details in their proper order for me. She wore her Cubbie's T-shirt and sat out in the bleachers. She even bought a cheap transistor radio to tune in to Cub's broadcaster Harry Caray during the game. And like everybody else in the "Windy City," Amy died a little when Garvey hammered a Lee Smith fastball into the bleachers spoiling the dream season of '84.

Charley's involvement with the Cubs was more financial. Unlike Amy and me, he went to a tiny Midwest college, Miami of Ohio. Like me, he also turned a four-year degree into a much longer, more leisurely stay. Inspired by a patriotic graduation speech about duty, Charley signed up for a two-year hitch in the Peace Corps. With nothing better to do, he ended up adding on another year. However, when living in Malaysian jungle huts became too much of a drag even if it was for a good cause, he opted out and moved to Chicago.

Amy met Charley through her boyfriend, Bruce. They kept in touch outside the stadium. Each time she went to Wrigley she'd see Charley selling peanuts. Each game she'd buy "three bags for a buck" from him. She set up a business appointment between the two of us—Charley the traveling salesman and me the traveling teacher. She thought I'd get a kick out of it. She was right. I was to meet him at the Peanut Plant, which doubled as his apartment, about 10:00 A.M. Tuesday, my second day at Wrigley. He was anxious, she told me, to explain the ins and outs of the peanut business. I was anxious to find a career more financially secure than teaching.

A bit late—typical for me—I got to Charley's place just as he was finishing assembly-line packaging procedures. He welcomed me in. Charley looked like what you might expect an ex-Peace Corps soldier to look like: thirty-two years old, six-footish, thin, almost pure white complected; he was also balding. It's funny, most every ex-Peace Corps person I've ever known is thin, bright white, and losing his hair. It must come from living in grass huts and eating bananas all day long.

I could tell Charley was glad to have me stop by. He was friendly. We talked a bit about my trip. He thought it was grand. We tried to figure out how a team like the Cubs could win it one year, then totally dissolve the next. After deciding that the championship of '84 must have been an act of God, and that this was just a normal season, he took me on a plant tour.

A small dining room was where major operations took place. It smelled like a peanut factory would smell, like the kitchen does if the Peter Pan's been left open on the cupboard all day long. Neatly stacked in the corner, nearly ceiling high, were a dozen or so 20-pound boxes of fresh salted peanuts. Peanuts were loose inside. A crate of plastic bags leaned against the boxes. They were crinkly plastic, the type that doesn't melt when it gets hot. On the thick oak table in the middle of the room sat 30 or so already home-packaged two-and-one-half-ounce bags of nuts. On one side of them stood a simple weighing scale. On the other was a folded red-and-white-checked tablecloth. An old worn iron, the kind that every garage sale features, sat on the tablecloth. The room was tidy.

"Well, this is it," he revealed. "Let me show you how it works."

Reaching into the open 20-pound box he scooped out a handful of shells and dropped them into one of the crinkly plastic bags. "That's about two and a half ounces. I used to measure. Now I just eyeball 'em." Kind of like me and grading papers—I used to read 'em.

"Then I iron over the fold. It seals the plastic—and we stack 'em over here." An empty peanut box was filling back up with freshly filled bags. "A couple of straps on the box and I've got a carrying case. *Voilà!*" Simple but effective, labor costs certainly were minimal. I asked if I could give it a whirl. No problem. It wasn't a union shop. "How'd you ever get into something like this?" I asked as I practiced packaging. It was a question I was familiar with. Most of my ex-college friends wondered the same about me.

"Well, after the Corps I had to fit into the real world. I thought about a lot of things. You know...sales, computers, even substitute teaching. Nothing seemed to do much for me though." I assured him that subbing, particularly in Chicago, would've done a lot...for the lining of his stomach.

He continued, "In college I worked at a drive-in hot-dog stand. It was fun. I love baseball and ballparks. There are two of 'em here. So I decided, why not sell hot dogs outside the stadium? Seemed like the thing to do."

After scoping out opening day, hot dogs turned to peanuts and the business venture began. As I packed Charley went through all of the financial aspects of his operation: material costs, overruns, advertising (a fat black felt pen on a cardboard box top), etc., etc.; actual investments were limited. He did have to use the El, Chicago's elevated train, to get over to Comiskey. It was $1.80 round trip. Wrigley was within walking distance. Besides being farther away, the Sox park wasn't as profitable either. Only about 25 pounds a night, compared to Wrigley's 40, the South Side stadium merely served to supplement his gold mine in the North. Between the two he figured to be pulling in enough to cover rent, food, and a ball game or two each week. Not bad. It was a good transition from the Corps to reality.

Things had not always been so rosy in the peanut business though. Like any other job, it took adjusting to. Hazards face every kind of traveling salesmen... I'd find that out later. "The first day I sold," he told me, "I was really ready to go. I went down to Wrigley with 50 pounds and wasn't even sure that'd be enough. I was gonna set the all-time world peanut-selling record. Ended up a little short, though... only sold $12 worth. Lugging those 47 pounds back to the house, after four hours of work, I almost quit. Things got easier though. I didn't give up.... Actually," he continued, "I began to watch the older salesmen and picked up a few new techniques. It saved my business from going bankrupt."

About three hours before the first pitch, and finished with the packing, we headed for the ballpark. It was a few blocks from the factory. We split the 40-pound peanut load and continued our business discussion. Along the way Charley filled me in on all the inner workings of the peanut world. I was going to give it an afternoon whirl, and didn't want to end up in the clink, so I listened closely. He'd been arrested once for selling without a license outside of Comiskey. "They're a lot tougher over there," he noted. But at Wrigley don't worry, nobody will bother you. Just don't stand outside the stadium turnstile. That's like selling food in a restaurant parking lot." I assured him that I wouldn't do anything so stupid.

When we got to Wrigley it was still over two hours before game time. Didn't matter, though, folks were already lining up. I couldn't blame them. What a way to spend a sunny Tuesday afternoon—sitting on the sidewalk, pounding beers, cracking peanut shells, and waiting for batting practice. The happy crowd, some 30 to 40 strong, shuffled between two lines—one at the tap in Murphy's Tavern across the narrow street, the other snaking its way up to Wrigley's bleacher ticket window. Leftover folks just sat in the sun or leaned against the stadium wall and shot the breeze with each other.

Besides the fans, other salesmen were starting to arrive. Even on the heels of a double-digit losing streak, Wrigley was getting ready for another sell-out. Portable wooden souvenir stands, full of T-shirts, hats, and assorted $5.95 junk, were on their way up. A couple of other peanut packers were there, mingling through the beer-soaked crowd. An old fellow carrying a big box walked past us. The box was filled with strange little items—whirly-gigs, inflatable things, and other assorted Cub stuff. "He's the birdman," Charley told me. Before I was able to ask why, the birdman whistled. It was a high-pitched whistle, sounded something like the mating call of a whippoorwill. "That's his sales pitch," Charley noted. "He doesn't even call out. I guess he's been doing this for twenty-some years."

All about, the place buzzed with excitement. Wrigleyville was alive. Charley added to it. For a while, I walked with him, making special note of his style. "Get your peanuts here! Three bags for a buck... 85 cents apiece on the inside." He had that old nasal-pitched tone down to an art. Like most of the other peanut packers, he found "his regular corner," stayed put, and let the hungry folks come to him. I was impressed; he came on like a 20-year veteran. After standing in the same place for 25 minutes, he began to circle the stadium, always returning to his corner. None of the vendors stole corners ... each of the four or five there by game time had his own. Everybody, though, was free to roam. The unwritten peanut vendor code of ethics allowed for that.

Finally, with the crowd thickening, I decided that I was ready. I was more prepared than I'd been for student teaching... I probably couldn't do any worse. Still, I was nervous. Calling out anything in front of strangers makes me uptight. Charley assured me I wouldn't have any problems. "I was nervous, too, when I first started. Just do your best."

He gave me my own homemade carrying case. Like his, an emptied loose-shell peanut box filled back up with bags. The box stayed draped along my side by a simple strap. Loaded down with 51 two-and-a-half-ounce bags of home-packed peanuts, I had to tilt the other way so I didn't tip over. I felt like I was 13 again, my first day on the route carrying the *Kalamazoo Gazette*. The big difference was, with newspapers I only had to toss 'em on the porch. Here I was really gonna have to sell. First I figured I'd case the joint. I didn't yet have the guts to yell anything. I'd just walk around with the box strapped to my shoulder. So I circled Wrigley twice. By the end of my first time around, I still wasn't ready. Had anybody come up and asked me if they knew where to get some peanuts, I'd probably have lost my voice and pointed to the tiny grocery store across the street.

Finally I figured it was time to give it a go... besides, the peanuts were getting heavy. I'd had 'em for almost a half hour without selling a single package. I swallowed hard. It brought a little saliva to my tongue and made speaking easier. "Peanuts, get your peanuts," I almost whispered. A librarian would've been louder. I tried again—first quietly to myself, then aloud. I improved. Pretty soon I copied Charley's "Peanuts, three bags for a buck...85 cents apiece on the inside." For 20 minutes I roamed. My voice got stronger, my confidence grew. Still no sales. Something was wrong. It worked for Charley, why not me? Hell, people weren't even looking at me.

Some kid came up and asked what I was selling. Excited, I answered, "Peanuts, three bags for a buck." He looked at me. "Try holding 'em up, maybe somebody will know what you're doing."

I looked down at my stash. God, I'd been walking around with my hand in an unmarked box, yelling inaudible sounds. Nobody had the foggiest notion what I was doing. Obviously, neither did I. Flushed at being so stupid, I thanked the kid for his observation and gave him a half-price deal.

A bad start but a start nonetheless. The ice was broken. I grabbed three bags, raised them over my head, and spoke up. With a sell and a little confidence under my belt, I experimented with sales songs: "PEA...nuts. Get your fresh peanuts. Three bags for *ONLY* a buck." I concentrated on the "only" and settled into my sales pitch. It was a good one. I was even getting a little cocky. Still, the main object, I figured, was to sell something, and nobody seemed interested. I looked closer at the folks walking by. Everybody that passed was already cracking shells. I turned. About twenty yards to my left some old codger was selling his peanuts in record numbers. For twenty minutes I'd been standing downwind from some guy doing the same thing as me. Stupid move number two, it was like setting up a barbecue at the end of the McDonald's drive-in window.

I decided to roam. With song down pat and game time approaching, I began circling the park. If it took twenty trips around the stadium, I'd sell until all 51 bags were gone. I was determined. Around and around I strolled, calling out, "PEA...nuts. Get your fresh peanuts. Three bags for *ONLY* a buck." Once in a while I'd mention that inside they were 85 cents.

As I walked I started recognizing familiar faces from the previous circle. They noticed me. Some of the folks, like me, were selling things, others were just standing around. A scalper wearing a bright red Wisconsin Badger T-shirt noticed my MSU 1984 Cherry Bowl T-shirt. He asked if I went to Michigan State. I always get excited when somebody asks me about State. He'd been there before, for a Spartan–Badger football game, back when both teams were good. After talking Big Ten "good ole days," I explained my goal—all 51 bags. He promised to take care of the last $2.00 worth. "Just come on back when you get there, I'll still be here!"

Meantime, I was on a roll. Once in a while I'd pass Charley, still standing at his corner. Each time he'd see me he'd ask how I was doing and remind me that I didn't have to sell 'em all. Each time I promised I would.

I had under a dozen left when "The Star-Spangled Banner" echoed over the stadium speakers. At a lot of places that only means it's time to be thinking about going inside. At Wrigley it's like last call at the bar. All the noise, the buzzing of people, and vendors...all that excitement on the outside vanishes and migrates into the stadium. The once-filled streets were empty. Only stragglers and scalpers remained. Down to six bags, for pride's sake not willing to buy them myself, I ran back to the scalper corner. Still there holding up a pair of unsold tickets was my Wisconsin buddy.

"Got your peanuts, here...saved the best for last. Still want 'em?" I asked, confident that a Big Tenner would never go back on his word.

"Sure," he answered. "How 'bout a half-price box seat?" A perfect deal; we made the trade. I sold out—all $17 worth after two hours of work—and got a cheap box seat in the process. He'd have to eat one less ticket and could finish the day with a fifty-buck profit. Plus he had some high-quality peanuts to munch on at the ball game.

I dug up Charley... still at his corner. He usually stayed selling for an inning or two after the game started, picked up stragglers that way. I thanked him for the business seminar and confirmed what he already knew: "You've got the best job in Chicago." He thanked me for the compliment and paid me for my day's work—six bags of peanuts. I slid across the street to Murphy's. Figured I deserved a little pregame beer. After all, I was a successful businessman... even if I only worked for peanuts.

LAYOUT AND UPKEEP: GRADE C

A ballpark takes on a whole different feeling when it's walked to. All those fears that normally haunt city baseball vanish when the pregame stroll is only two blocks long. From Amy's quaint Waveland Avenue apartment my Monday afternoon walk was a pleasant one. On time, not worrying about my car or the price of parking, I was able to concentrate on more important matters, namely baseball in the warm summer sunshine.

However, upon reaching Wrigley for the first time, I was disappointed. Coming up on its western face, the ballpark doesn't really look too baseballish. In fact, without light standards streaming into the sky and situated quite conservatively on a normal street corner of a normal neighborhood, it hardly takes on the appearance of a legend. More or less a shell painted white and trimmed in blue, it looks like a giant warehouse. With a couple of stop-and-go food markets next door, a fire station down the street, a few corner taverns across the way, and even a McDonald's nearby, the large building blends almost unobtrusively into its surroundings. Only the constant bustle of barking vendors and the sound of gay organ music inside hint that something very special awaits beyond the gate.

Continuing my walk east down Waveland to its intersection with Sheffield Street, where bleacherites line up, the stadium brightened up. At the corner the building itself looks no different. It still resembles just some plain city warehouse taking up space. Sidewalks bordering it are ragged; the street is narrow. But stepping back and looking up, its normalness vanishes. Rising high above the simple shell is the stadium's second level. Visible from the outside sidewalk, the upper deck opens to Sheffield Street. It hovers over the ball field, revealing thousands of chairs. Not nearly as powerful as a gaze into Royals

Stadium, Wrigley's look is more of a tease, there to let everybody know it's not just another building.

Inside, the ballpark is as plain as it is outside. Steel girders break up the open cavern inside the gates. Empty boxes lie stacked about. Narrow criss-crossing concrete ramps lead slowly from the entrance up to the left, then to the right, then back to the left again. Whatever's not directly related to base-ball gets second-class treatment. The layout is simple; the house is a plain one. Aside from its Sheffield Street view, it simply acts as a barrier, there to separate street from field.

BALL FIELD: GRADE A

Tiny walkways funnel folks into the stands. When gates open crowds just glob together. From street to seat, Wrigley felt like any other stadium not made in California—too cramped and crowded. That was until I stared back down at the field below. With a single glimpse I realized I wasn't in just another ballpark. Within its very normal walls and drab, thin concrete ramps, resting in a city of millions, Wrigley's field is an oasis. It's why the game belongs in the city, not the suburbs! To place a garden so lush in the middle of big-city filth makes that garden much more commanding of the senses. For a mo-ment I just stood and stared. The field seemed to glow.

It's the ivy that dominates the ballpark. I'd seen it before, but never in person. Chicago cable stations play Cub games all around the Midwest. Oc-casionally I'd watched baseballs bounce up-and get lost in the leafy green vines. A couple of times a summer, black-and-white *Kalamazoo Gazette* photos fea-tured umpires and outfielders searching in vain for a ball that rolled in but never out. Neither did the ivy justice. Even *Sports Illustrated*'s full-color spreads couldn't capture its spell. The thought was always charming, but the picture's just not real.

In person, Wrigley is the ivy! So much thicker than I ever imagined it to be, like a rich fur coat, it hugs the outfield wall. And the color, not just green, is a deep dark green. The plant hypnotizes. It overrides everything inside. Wherever my eyes roamed, it wasn't long before they came back to rest on the outfield vines. Just like when a very lovely lady strolls past me. No mat-ter how I try, I can't control my eyes. Usually I'll glance once, then follow it up with another quick look. Finally, as she passes on from sight, I'll just stare, wonder, and wish. The ivy has that power. It, too, without even ask-ing, gets a second and third look. It makes every other object inside back-ground material.

The outfield ivy-covered wall is made of simple red brick. Only occasionally do the bricks peek out. Just where a little pruning reveals yellow numbers to mark distances from home plate. Otherwise the bricks lie buried beneath the thick green coat. While the ivy ends in the outfield corners, the quaint brick wall continues around to circle the entire diamond. Only waist level at the backstop, the wall itself is delightful. Without its cushion of green, it provides a pleasant contrast to its vine-covered counterpart across the field.

In between the red brick and green ivy stretches real live grass. It'd been three parks and about 2,000 miles since I'd last seen the real stuff. I was relieved. Even so, Wrigley's turf is worn. Where dirt and sod meet, the cut is sometimes ragged. Wheelbarrows and other field fixers must be stashed away in the outfield wall doorways beyond the warning track. Their faded tracks stretch from the wall across the outfield. Age spots pockmark the infield's edge. Not nearly as smooth as the crisscrossing California fields, Wrigley's grass is merely average.

Still, it's forgivable. The ivy is a drug. Ragged edges that would cry for attention anyplace else almost vanish under the glow of the vine-covered wall. Like that stunning lady strolling by, all I ever notice is her. I never think to look that the sidewalk she's walking on might be cracked.

SEATING: GRADE A+

Wrigley's simple close confines offer up some of baseball's finest views. Featuring excellent reserves and exciting bleachers, only a few steel supports taint an otherwise perfect view. From almost anywhere inside you're right on top of the action.

The lower level stretches from foul pole to foul pole. An upper deck hangs over it. While upper boxes provide a great look down at the game, it's the lower reserves that are the best. I snuck down in 'em for the last three innings of game one. Sunken all the way to field level, with the meagerest of foul ground, seats behind the dugout feel like they're in the middle of the infield. So close that you actually look up the crest of the pitcher's mound. I now know the horrors of staring out at a six-foot-six-inch fireballer made another foot taller by the elevated rubber.

Only in Fenway is the game so intimate. Facial expressions, grimaces of satisfaction and frustration personalize it. Not only is it more intense to watch, but sounds and smells join in. The scent of the grass rises up from the field. The catcher's mitt pops with the smoke of a fastball. The bat cracks if it somehow manages to meet the ball. Even a helmet slammed against the dugout in frustration makes noise. Baseball is so much more real.

Beyond, the outfield breeds a different kind of excitement. Hovering almost directly over the ivy are baseball's closest bleachers. All are flat wooden benches. Meager, only a few rows deep in the outfield corners, they rise nearly straight up, some 40 rows high, and explode to a peak under the big center-field scoreboard. Sitting in them, a heckling cheering crowd, Cub's bleacher bums are baseball's most colorful. Their intensity and closeness to the action not only make for a good time, but also add to the total excitement for everybody inside.

Even with such great house seats, "the best seat in the house" neither costs a cent nor is even in the ballpark. On Sheffield Avenue, in back of the bleachers, looming over the right-field wall, rises a row of tightly packed apartment buildings. Facing toward the field, the three-flat brownstones are typical for the neighborhood. Box-shaped, and peppered with Victorian-style windows, they're almost molded to one another. Pleasantly simple, they're neither fancy nor run down.

Besides being charming little homes, they cling to Wrigley. Bleachers in the right-field corner are so meager, and the street outside so narrow, that the six or seven houses down the block are no more than a short pop up from the field. Baseballs regularly rocket out of the stadium and bounce into their front lawns. From behind the tiny stone guardrails around each rooftop people sit and peer down into the ballpark. With Chicago's skyscraper-covered skyline behind them, and the ballpark below, they are the finest seats in all of baseball. They were the ones I had become obsessed with.

In Kalamazoo, as a kid, I was able to pick up the Cubs on WGN TV—home games, away games, all of them. Never an NL fan, I used to choke down Jack Brickhouse's "Hey, heys," watch a few innings, then find some other afternoon rerun on the tube. But before I flipped channels my attention would turn to those lucky souls who perched upon rooftops, sat soaking in the sun and gazing into the park. I dreamed that someday I would share their view. Well, I'd just successfully finished my peanut-packing venture. To watch the Cubs from the rooftop in the same day would be a dream come true. And if I failed, I always had my University of Wisconsin half-priced box seat to sit in.

I figured that before me many had come and asked and been turned away, so what did I have to lose? I was good at begging. Equipped with a six-pack of Old Style beer and my paycheck (six bags of peanuts) to offer in exchange for a seat, and willing to give up my Visa card as well, I cautiously approached my first apartment building. Almost embarrassed at what I was doing, I sneaked through the iron gate and rang the doorbell. A thin pleasant lady, accompanied by a large dog, approached the door. She was smiling. So was the dog. I was safe. Her name was Nancy. I don't recall the dog's name. I explained my story to her, how I was on my lifelong dream trip, that her home was my lifelong dream seat, and the game of baseball my life. My destiny, I revealed, was to sit on her roof.

"No problem," she said. "I don't really like baseball. In fact, I've never been up there. All the other tenants use it, though. If you'd like to, go on ahead." I couldn't believe my ears. Accomplishing dreams wasn't supposed to be so easy. As primed as I was for rejection, I nearly stumbled getting up off my knees. I thanked her several times, patted the large dog, and was directed to the back stairway. Opening the old wooden door, I set out on my journey up to heaven.

Backed up nearly on top of the El, Sheffield's whole block of apartments lie squeezed almost directly between Wrigley in front and the noisy city trains behind. From the street, the buildings are quaint. But looking out their back doors at the four-lane train tracks, and the battered houses behind them, the scene's not so pleasant. In fact, from the puny back porch, the homes look kind of ratty. But I was concerned only with the stairway. From the porch, wooden steps rose almost vertically. More like a ladder than an actual set of stairs, the steps jockeyed back and forth. As they rose they connected each of the three tiny back porches, then ended at a trapdoor above.

Quietly, almost reverently, I started up them. As close as I was to making it up, the last thing I wanted was to be evicted. It would've been worse than being shooed away at the front door. So I tried with every step I made to be absolutely silent. Even with the El rumbling noisily behind, I held my breath. Before each step I felt and pushed on the creaking board, searching for a solid space to stand on. It was like I was in some slow-motion dream scene out of an Alfred Hitchcock movie. Oblivious to everything but the trapdoor above, one foot at a time, I stalked it. Finally at the top, with my head pressed against the door, I dared to breathe. I composed myself, pushed the creaking old wooden door open, and pulled myself up and onto the roof. Standing there in the warming rays of a sunny Tuesday afternoon, I gazed in disbelief at what lay before me. It was the essence of a luxury box. More beautiful than any of those high-priced West Coast models, it came equipped, best of all, with bright Midwestern sunshine.

Each of the six or seven rooftops were molded to one another. None was more than a foot or two higher or lower than its next-door neighbor. They reminded me of the rooftop dance floor that Dick Van Dyke and the other chimney sweeps "chim, chim, cheree'd" across in *Mary Poppins*. As grand as

I felt, I could've done the same. A few of the roofs bustled with activity. Most were empty, as was mine, except for one young lady in the corner. She sat in a lounge chair with her feet propped up against the roof's concrete guardrail. I was behind her.

The scene was inviting. The roof, which served as the floor for my luxury box, was covered with green indoor-outdoor carpeting. A huge American flag flapped quietly in the breeze. Available lounge chairs were neatly stacked in the corner. A stone grill stood to my left. Quiet at the moment, it probably was home for some of the finest pregame meals ever cooked. A simple single shower, there to combat the hot sun, stood idly by too. Adjacent to my empty roof, on the next one down, only a hop over the short concrete rail, a barbecue was in full swing. Harry Caray's pregame show blared from a stereo. Old Style flowing and sausages grilling filled the air with a blend of pleasant aroma and laughing voices. It provided a stark contrast to my quiet setting.

While all about me the feeling was warm and homey, across the way the scene was breathtaking. Opened up, arms stretching toward me, in all of her splendor, was Wrigley Field. Closer to the ball field than in a plastic park's third tier, I felt like I could reach right into the place. Like I was sitting in heaven looking down on a beautiful garden. I was a part of it, but at the same time above it all. All the senses that embraced baseball inside blessed the rooftop as well. Ballpark sights and sounds filled the air. Organ music drifted across the way. The buzzing, babbling of people, the call of cold beer by the vendors, even the game itself lay clearly in front of me. Only the deep right-field corner, overhung by bleachers, was absent from view. On my roof, too, out of a small transistor radio, Harry continued his pregame assessment of the Cub's recent 13-game losing streak.

As hypnotizing as the scene was, I hated to move. I figured, though, I should offer an Old Style and some peanuts to the soul who was already enjoying the magic. So I walked up and extended my peace offering. Introducing myself to Michele, whose boyfriend, Jon, lived downstairs, I received a cold, blunt "Hello." Later I found out that my presence on such hallowed ground was taboo. Non-tenants were not allowed up and usually didn't slip through the front gate. That pleasant "non-baseball fan" downstairs didn't realize what she'd done. However, after realizing that I was harmless and loved baseball, Michele welcomed me and became my self-proclaimed Wrigleyville tour guide.

She explained all the traditions that I might otherwise have missed. She told me about Ronnie, the black street person who blessed the bleachers daily with his high-pitched "Go Cubs" cheer. As we sat and visited we could hear him "Go Cubbing" it on the inside. She told me of the blue flag with the white L and the white one with a blue W. One of the two was run up the scoreboard after each game to inform the neighborhood and those El train passengers who won. If the Cubbies did, the white flag would fly from the scoreboard; if they lost, the blue one. She revealed that even after all the games she'd watched, she'd never seen it running up the pole, only noticed when it was finally in place. She'd turn her head and there it'd be.

It was her boyfriend, she said, who was the lawyer who during the '84 play-offs had brought suit against the owner of the building. Capitalism flourishes even in Wrigleyville. The owner had barred his tenants from the roof for the Padres games. Instead he planned to rent it out for high-priced parties. Jon, she told me, went to court and got an injunction to stop the bum. She also, gratefully, explained how through the entire trial the bleacherites across the street would turn in unison and chant "Landlord sucks," followed by a round of applause. Jon would probably get out the newspaper articles and explain all the intricacies of the case to me when he got home. He loved the Cubs.

Meanwhile, I just enjoyed my good fortune. Leaning back in a lawn chair, feet propped upon the short concrete rail fence, I soaked in the warm sunshine and the tradition of Wrigley. Peering into the kingdom below from my temporary throne, I'd found the grandest seat in all of baseball. On the roof-top of an ordinary apartment building, looking into one of the game's love-liest ballparks, so close that my cheers actually became one with the roar of the crowd, I guessed life just couldn't get any better. With an afternoon stash of Old Style on ice, six bags of peanuts at my disposal, Harry on the radio, a city of millions looming behind—in front of me unfolded the drama of major league baseball. All of it rising out of a simple neighborhood they called Wrigleyville. I'd found Eden on a rooftop in North Side Chicago.

SCOREBOARD: GRADE A+

Rising behind the center-field bleachers, a huge, faded green rectangle stands, backdropped by the blue skyscraper-covered Chicago sky. Characteristic of the pure simplicity of the entire park, it is baseball's oldest scoreboard.

Nearly everything about the relic is the same as when it was propped up in 1935. Even its sun-bleached color hints that it rarely, if ever, is painted. In a day and age of exact digital atomic time, a small round-faced clock with real clock hands perches innocently at the top. It serves as a reminder in Chicago that it's the tradition of history, not the exactness of science, that's important. Two cables sprout from the board, flank and attach to a tall center pole that anchors the Stars and Stripes. From them the pennants of each of the twelve National League teams fly in a column. Arranged by division, six on one side, six on the other, the pennants rise and fall daily according to the current standings.

Easily seen from anywhere in Wrigley's cozy confines, the face of the scoreboard is consumed with a listing of the current day's games, both in the American and National Leagues. Although only a few are in progress during the Cubs' weekday games, those that are get constantly updated by real people. Little human bodies roaming about the insides of the giant board replace white numbers on green rectangles. As for Chicago ball games, the line score is kept rolling, inning by inning, by the same human hands. The resulting drift back into baseball's past—the white numbers on green rectangles, the daily flying of a won or lost flag, the roaming humans in the big board—can best be explained like the ivy and the fans and so many of the park's precious features—"only in Wrigley."

By no stretch of the imagination is the setup the majors' most informative. Unlike the wizardry of computer-age screens, this one rarely even shows batting averages. About its only plug-in part is the short electronic message that runs along the base. And usually its main concern is trivia. As for batting averages, I finally found them posted on auxiliary boards camouflaged in the sun on the facing of the upper deck. So used to being dominated by computer screens flashing an electronic portrait, complete with every bit of little known fact about the human at bat, I found it somewhat of a relief to have to strain just to make out their season average.

Lively organ music trades off with recorded tunes throughout the game. Just enough of a mix, together they keep the pace pleasant. Pure and simple, the P.A. and scoreboard exist only to quietly serve the Cubbie faithful. For at Wrigley Field it isn't the organ or the classical scoreboard, or even the lush ivy that are most important. Center stage belongs to baseball!

FOOD: GRADE C

Selection: Poor   Accessibility: Excellent
Taste: Fair   Cost: 22nd

Wrigley Field is ivy and atmosphere. It's big-city baseball in a cozy park. Great food's not what it's known for... that's Chicago's other stadium. Wrigley doesn't need it. To enjoy baseball in Chicago's "North Side Museum," all that's required is sunshine, an Old Style, and a bag of peanuts in the shell. That's good, 'cause there's just not much more to choose from. Actually the good stuff is peddled out on the streets, or from the four or five taverns on each of the corners surrounding the stadium.

To make up for a puny menu, service is intense. Effort to get something to eat is minimal. Barren when the Cubbies bat, concession stands are speedy in the bottom half of each inning. Unlike the West, where aisles are crowded and food booths packed even when the home team's up, Cub fans stay put. Here, walkways resemble a deserted ghost town. Picking up the slack, hard-working vendors pound the stands and are seldom more than a shout away. Their speed and stock of necessities allows you to stay planted, watching base-ball the entire afternoon. And at Wrigley on a pleasant afternoon...what more could you want?

BALLPARK EMPLOYEES: GRADE C

While much of the place takes on an almost divine air, Wrigley's employees are merely human.

Vendors, while hardworking, add to their intensity a touch of rudeness. Busily tracking down the big buck in a packed house, they have very little time or patience for any comment other than "Two, please." Concessionaires under the stands are also content to go about their business without a smile. An occasional question is answerable, but never with more than a simple "Yes" or "No." They merely cash in and out. Ushers are easily accessible through-out the park. Usually stationed two to an aisle leading up into the stands, and regularly on nearly every turn of the winding ramps, they seem to be the most likable of the group. Yet they too lack that warm down-home attitude.

Just inside the front gates Wrigley offers its own special "people touch." Classic scorecard salesmen and the sound of their sales pitch add another East-ern feel to the park. Clad in dark blue shirts and Cubs ballcaps, the old gen-tlemen are pure Chicago. Calling out "Scorecards here!" and "Get your program" in their own distinct style, they look as though they could have stood in the very same place, and gone about their business in the very same fash-ion, 40 years ago. As precious as Wrigley itself, the old gents are timeless. As for the rest of its working class, they're just normal people putting in their normal nine-to-five.

FACILITIES: GRADE D

Parking's nearly impossible on the crisscrossing streets surrounding the stadium. With prime curb spots gobbled up in the morning long before game time, a car's only alternative is the limited $10 lots around the park. And even at premium prices, they, too, turn into temporary sardine cans. Needless to say, Wrigley by car is not a pleasant proposition.

Alternatives, however, do exist. The El runs 24 hours throughout Chicago and regularly deposits crowds across the street from the ballpark. Although haggard-looking, it's actually quite efficient, plus it's a great way to get that pregame pump. A noontime train ride to Wrigley, with all sorts of baseball folks, grabs that exciting big-city flavor.

From a suburbanite's perspective, the neighborhood may seem a bit seedy. But in the afternoon, it too is pleasant. And like the trains that pass through, it's safe. Suburban parking lots twenty minutes north and west of the park are convenient for those who don't care to search out an overpriced parking place. All they need do is to drive to one of the huge lots. And from there, for about a buck or two, take the El back down to Wrigley.

Inside, stadium facilities show their age. Rest rooms, furnished with out-of-date equipment, are large and decently maintained. While other niceties, typical of newer, more convenient stadiums, are old and not so accessible. Although not luxurious, facilities serve its crowds as well as any other city park—certainly well enough to keep baseball in Chicago without ever moving it to the suburbs.

ATMOSPHERE: GRADE A+

As thick as the ivy that hugs its red brick walls, the very essence of baseball hangs in the atmosphere of Wrigley. Not only the ballpark itself, with its vine-covered walls and hand-operated scoreboard, but the folks that grace the place are why Chicago's North Side park is the purest in baseball. Tucked into the northern corner of one of this nation's largest cities, complete with all the problems that accompany being a big city, Wrigleyville exists as a step back in time. Reminiscent of a day when life was simpler, it's the tiny neighborhood's love affair with baseball that makes the park so special.

Long before the gates open, Wrigley awakens. Fans stroll to the ballpark down narrow, crowded streets made more narrow by all the parked cars lining each side. Neighborhood taverns, like Murphy's, Berny's, and the Cubbie Bear, and souvenir shops bustle with anticipation of the ultimate—though merely the norm in Wrigleyville—day baseball during the week. Capitalism flourishes as ticket scalpers, hot dog pushers, and peanut peddlers find their corner and practice their sales pitch. And the bleacherites line up on the cracked sidewalks surrounding the stadium. Even on the heels of a thirteen-game losing streak diehards show up three hours early, laughing, talking, and enjoying themselves almost as much as they will hours later inside. Dressed appropriately for the hot July afternoon, they spill out from Murphy's Tavern, across the street to more entertainment in the bleacher line.

A four-foot-tall Padre voodoo doll, complete with San Diego hat and Steve Garvey's number, is carried along the waiting lines by a Cub fan, obviously experienced with black magic. Cradling the floppy four-foot-long doll in his arms, its head and legs drooping over toward the ground, he strolls up and down the bleacher line. Lured by taunts of "Stick it to Garvey" and "Goose the Goose," any soul is welcome to walk up, take one of the available needles, and pin-cushion the Padre free of charge. It's a cheap way to relieve some of that ever-present Cub frustration.

Ronnie—the "Go Cubs" guy, dressed in shorts and a Cub shirt, blue Cub baseball cap, and knee-high black boots—offers his specialty to the stew. Rumors whirl as to where Ronnie comes from and if he has a roof overhead. People even wonder how he gets into the ballpark. But nobody questions his voice. His piercing "Go Cubs, Go Cubs, Go Cubs" scream can be heard, inside and outside the stadium, all game long. Even from my rooftop seat across the street. As his voice carries throughout all of Wrigleyville, Ronnie rules inside.

While teams take their pregame batting practice, Waveland Avenue, beyond the left-field wall, serves as a congregation place for souvenir seekers. Usually about a dozen or so hopefuls, ranging in age from six to 36, all with ball gloves, hang around and wait. Some lean against parked cars. Others just sit on the curb and grab a few stray rays through branches of the overhanging maple trees. Most of the time is spent playing cards or talking baseball. Religiously they linger, with an eye on that outfield wall, waiting for a Sandberg batting-practice shot to clear it. For nearly two hours each day they lounge there on Waveland, friends until a batting-practice home run makes them all contenders for the single prize and causes a mad scramble for the ball. It's these kinds of happenings that occur daily under the Midwest summer sun. They offer a very special touch that can be found only within the city.

When the gates finally do open, bystanders are swallowed up in a flood of human bodies. Walkways into the stands are thin and insufficient. Slowly oozing up them, you can only follow, carried along by the multitude. All along the way baseball conversations buzz: batting averages with no names, ERAs with no pitcher audible, people preparing themselves for the ensuing game. Finally in the stands and away from the moving mass of humanity, gazing out over the pride of Chicago, "Wrigley's field" wills the onlooker into a dream. With red brick peeking from the ivy-covered walls, only the hustle and bustle from outside that's found its way in reminds a fan of reality.

Hovering over the ivy, covering every inch of wooden plank, sit the taunting bleacherites. Merciless to opposing outfielders, they put to work efforts of their earlier voodoo magic. Above them is baseball's most priceless antique. Wrigley's hand-managed scoreboard adds another touch of tradition to the already rich climate. Across from the ballpark on Sheffield, perched upon the crowded three-story brick apartment buildings, tenants settle in for the game. Far beyond them skyscrapers loom, adding another face to the neighborhood's many-sided character.

Besides adding to the color, Cubbie fans are true blue. Especially the bleacherites. In a ritual practiced by no other group of fans in the majors, it's an unwritten rule that bleacherites will not keep a homer smacked by a member of the visiting team. Instead, within minutes of the blow, play must be stopped. The baseball's almost always tossed back out onto the field. Shots out of the park have even found their way back inside on occasion. The most precious example of loyalty was told to me by a proud contributor. "One day," the fellow explained, "a guy in the stands sitting next to us wanted to keep a Gary Carter home run. No matter what, we couldn't get him to give the ball up." Unable to be convinced by those around him to throw it back, finally the pressure of the almighty dollar solved the problem. "We took up a collection, about $20, and bought the ball from the guy—then threw it back ourselves."

It's this crazy loyalty, not only for the Cubs and Wrigley Field, but for baseball as well, that gives rise to such a rich atmosphere on Chicago's North Side. The character of the neighborhood in which Wrigley lives, those blessed souls that love, live, and die daily with the Cubs, the treat of baseball bordered by ivy played forever in the sunshine, all under the shadow of the big city, makes Harry Caray's song so special. Every seventh-inning stretch, Harry, Chicago's beloved "Bud Man," leans from his play-by-play booth and leads Wrigley in baseball's most rousing rendition of "Take Me Out to the Ballgame."

Harry sings, everybody else joins in. They stand, in the box seats, upper and lower, in the crowded bleachers, on the rooftops across the street, and on Waveland below. All sing from the heart, for they truly don't care "if they ever get back."

12
METRODOME,
MINNESOTA TWINS

No Frills—No Thrills

REPORT CARD   <u>*Metrodome*</u>

BASEBALL PARK

<u>*July 16, 85 All-Star Game*</u>   <u>*Minnesota Twins*</u>

GAME   BASEBALL CLUB

CATEGORY	GRADE	POINTS
Layout and Upkeep	*B*	*85*
Ball Field	*D-*	*60*
Seating	*D*	*65*
Scoreboard	*D-*	*60*
Food	*C*	*75*
Ballpark Employees	*B*	*85*
Facilities	*B*	*85*
Atmosphere	*D*	*65*
Total Points		*580*
Average		*73*

<u>*C*</u>   <u>*20th*</u>

FINAL GRADE   RANK

"An inexpensive way to keep out the autumn cold...with a white ceiling, tacky plastic carpet, and absolutely no extra options...a real dud. At least folks who fill the place are nice."

PREGAME THOUGHTS

When I took off back in June I didn't even consider a player's strike. Sure, they'd threatened, but I never figured they'd actually go through with it. It wouldn't make sense. Grown men who made millions, living a life that the rest of us could only dream about, would just stay fat and happy in their perfect world. Besides, I was on the ultimate journey. I'd planned it for years, unknowingly chosen a career just so I could carry it out, a strike couldn't be its end...death or disease maybe, a New York City mugging, or a paralyzing foul ball bounced off my noggin, but certainly not some worthless walkout. Besides, there wasn't a damned thing I could do about it. If it happened, it happened. I'd deal with it when it came up. For my first 11 ballparks, 14 games, 20-some ballpark hot dogs, and gobs of salted peanuts, I never gave the strike a second thought—I just enjoyed.

Wrigley ended round one. From Sis's I headed home to Mom and Dad's—for a little golf, a little rest, and some real home cooking. There, too, I ignored the strike. Filed away in the back of my mind somewhere with all those lost Bosox Series hopes, I wasn't worried. Besides, I didn't have the time. I was a Kazoo celebrity.

Kalamazoo, Michigan, is a solid sports town. It's Midwestern, so baseball, college football and basketball, high school sports, all the meaningful things in life, are important. And close...each within a two-hour drive. Michigan State in East Lansing, the Wolverines in Ann Arbor, and Notre Dame's Fighting Irish all have a good Kazoo following. Especially come fall. Every sunny Saturday morning in September and October you can watch the streams of cars stuffed with folks leave town. Destination—the world's greatest tailgate parties. As for baseball, lying directly between Detroit and Chicago, options also come in triplicate. The Tigers have a flood of Kazoo fans. The Cubs a splash. The White Sox barely a trickle. Good golf courses weave throughout the county; June, July, and August early tee-off times are tough to get. And high school gyms and football fields get a better Friday-night turnout than the movie houses. It's a hardworking city filled with good folks who love their teams, and I couldn't have asked for a better place to grow up.

Kazoo's also got its own daily newspaper—the *Kalamazoo Gazette*. The *Gazette* has two major obsessions. The Tigers and local excitement. Needless to say, my trip was prime-time stuff. And Mom made sure they knew about it. A week before I left Seattle, she was at the *Gazette* Building looking up major league cities. A giant map covered my folks' living-room wall. A Magic Marker line followed me city by city around the baseball world. While she was researching, Mom ran into sports editor Jack Moss. He asked about the family. She mentioned my trip. He wondered if he could do a story on me at the All-Star break. With no agent to schedule interviews, she took the job and set one up. So when I pulled in for my week off I was pointed to the *Gazette* to go get some "ink."

Now "ink" is something worth living for in Kalamazoo—even dying for on the high school football field or baseball diamond. A line or two thrown your way by the *Gazette* is scrapbook material for life. And enough to turn you into an eternal sports hero. Way back when I was a teenager, and still resembled an athlete, I'd picked up a couple of lines. A little yellowed, I still have the articles pasted away somewhere in the attic.

This, however, was big-time: a full-page layout and a real live interview all about my voyage. Not only that, I was hailed as a "former prep standout." Me, who was once willing to die for "current prep standout" status. I was an official Kalamazoo folk hero...still am, sorta, thanks to Jack. Even now, home on Christmas vacation, at least a few times I get introduced as "the guy who went to all the ballparks." Offered congratulations and pats on the back, I just shrug my shoulders and remind them about the "former prep standout" part.

The whole week home was wonderful. Besides gloating in my newfound press coverage, I lived in luxury. Golfed every day. A trip or two to Lake Michigan, some of Mom's home cooking for my peanut- and hot-dog-riddled stomach. And some *Munsters* and *Big Valley* updates. I even got to stretch out on something other than a root-covered tent floor. All rotten thoughts, possible strike included, were placed on the back burner to simmer. My head was too swelled to think anything bad could happen. My belly too happy. My back too comfortable. A local celebrity, I was sitting fat and happy on top of the world.

A couple of days before the All-Star game, my dream world shattered. That strike I knew would never happen was given a date—August 6. The players said that if their "reasonable" demands for multimillions weren't met, baseball in 1985 was through. Like a high, hard brush-back pitch, it floored me. The whole thing just didn't make any sense. Not only that, but talk about *mistimed*. August 6 was not just any date. It was my grand finale. The day I was supposed to waltz into the Atlanta Braves' stadium and fulfill my dream.

But if the players weren't going to play, people wouldn't be eating peanuts and watching batting practice. Hot-dog salesmen wouldn't be pounding the stands. Fulton County Stadium would be locked up. Plus I had a feeling we weren't looking at some short-termed walkout. This one was for all the marbles. Both sides were already hammering on each other...and me and my trip, we were gonna get squashed in the middle.

I couldn't just sit there on my butt though. Something had to be done. I thought about contacting the Player's Association. Maybe if they knew what it'd cost me, they'd vote to push the strike back a day. Surely something as stupid could happen on the seventh as easily as it could on the sixth. No good. I knew ball players only by the backs of bubble-gum cards. That doesn't give you a whole lot of leverage. Maybe, I thought, I'd get ahold of the owners? Explain the significance of August 6 to them. No, I decided, no pressure on the owners. For the first time in their greedy history they were right. Baseball needed to be brought back to financial reality. Just not at my sake. I really didn't have a choice. At the mercy of history's most ridiculous strike, my only alternative was to take off, pray that the union came to its senses, and resume my schedule...even if it was only for 25 stadiums. So for the second time in a month I left the easy life for one filled with dogs, peanuts, baseball, and tent-covered tree roots. I hit the road for Minnesota.

For 585 miles, twelve hours, through portions of four states, three homemade ham sandwiches, four Cokes, and a big fat dill pickle, the strike was all I could think about. What was I gonna do? Missing one ballpark was like missing twelve. A year-long strike on the sixth would ruin me. I'd be labeled a fake, a baseball-park fraud. My accomplishments would be zilch. My return feature *Gazette* article might just as well be a back-page obituary. People would read it and shake their heads. They wouldn't say "Gee, that's really swell you saw so many ballparks." No, they'd just wanna know which ones I'd missed. If they weren't sick of all my earlier "ink," they might offer condolences. But I'd soon be forgotten. No longer a Kalamazoo folk hero, I'd just be another "almost statistic." Worst of all, how could I live with me? For the rest of my life I'd introduce myself as the baseball-park failure. In normal conversation I'd probably bury my head in my hands and just blurt it out. It'd be an obsession. Hell, it already was—and the strike was three weeks off. The horror consumed me.

Then it hit! Somewhere between 6 A.M. and noon, on the road just outside Chicago, I decided it was *my* schedule that had to change. Baseball's plans to destroy me would be sabotaged before they had the chance to work. I'd take destiny into my own hands. So for the next eight hours, driving north on 94, I attacked the situation. My *Rand McNally* United States map stretched out across the passenger seat, both league schedules crowded in my lap, my itinerary taped to the steering wheel, I took apart what was left of the three weeks of the season. Some way I had to make sure that I'd never have to tell anybody "Yeah, I missed Fulton County Stadium."

Where to start? Success hinged on finishing the fifth. That August 6 game in Atlanta, in a ballpark that happened to be 600 miles south of anyplace else in the baseball world, was just going to have to move up a day. The problem was that New York (August 2), Pittsburgh (August 3), Cleveland (August 4), and Cincinnati (August 5) were all booked the four days before it. In fact, on my final swing, from All-Star game until the strike, I had 21 days, 15 ballparks, and 5,500 miles to cover. Not a lot of leeway to play with. Still, I didn't give up. If I couldn't drive, what about flying? If the Cincinnati game August 5 was a day game, I could watch it, then fly to Atlanta for the 7:40 P.M. Braves start. No such luck, the Reds' ball game was at 7:30. Even if I watched only the first pitch in Riverfront, hopped on Flash Gordon's back to get to the airport, and took the *Star Ship Enterprise* down to Atlanta, I wouldn't make it in time to interview the clean-up crew.

For the next four hours I glanced back and forth between rolling office and the road. I checked schedules with dates, cross-checked teams with schedules, and tried to come up with anything. Nothing, but nothing, seemed to work.

And with each squashed alternative one particular problem made itself clear. The Indians had joined with the players' union. Both, it seemed, were bound and determined to destroy me. Every change I tried, that hulking empty Municipal Stadium, "The Mistake by the Lake," killed it. Three or four scenarios, all possible, all beating the strike date, all scalped by the Indians. Paging through schedules, checking and rechecking ball games, I began to wonder if Cleveland ever played at home. They sure as hell didn't in July of '85. It figured, though, they'd do me in. Year after year in September, when it counts most, they hammer on the Bosox....Why not a Bosox fan as well?

Still I searched. Back and forth, over and over. Then all of a sudden, in the middle of my last sandwich, on the road between Madison and Minneapolis, just when I was about to call it quits and pray for a settlement, like the "Ford's Got a Better Idea" light bulb, the answer just clicked on. After Minnesota (July 16), I had Milwaukee (July 18), and Comiskey (July 19) back-to-back. A day off, to cruise leisurely back through Kazoo to Detroit (July 21) was my opening. Instead of taking it easy I'd bust south and squeeze in Cincinnati. I could drive from Comiskey down to Riverfront, then back up to Detroit. Atlanta would be moved to August 5, the new last day of baseball for 1985, in place of the Reds. Aside from six parks in seven days after the All-Star game, and four in a row to finish up, I'd make it. If it didn't rain in

Atlanta, or the Indians, just to ruin me, didn't decide to strike on their own, my journey would be complete. Once again I'd be able to claim celebrity status in Kalamazoo. And never have to explain to anyone, ever, why I didn't make it to Fulton County Stadium.

Relieved that my world was righted, I put away my office equipment, popped my last Coke, turned up Frank, and bebopped off down the road to the All-Star game. My last visit to the world of domes.

LAYOUT AND UPKEEP: GRADE B

All-Star games, I've finally figured out, are played at places where nobody ever goes to baseball games. Execs must figure it a shot in the arm, and that the fever might catch on. As a result Wrigley, Fenway, Comiskey, the grand-daddies seldom get the "Midsummer Classic."

No big loss for Boston... "The Game" is usually anything but classic. I've seen plenty of 'em on the tube. Each year I sit down, usually with a beer and a burger, and watch the AL get hammered. Most have been boring—not as bad as the Super Bowl, but on the same track. The multihour pregame ruins what little flavor's left over. Which usually ain't much. A tensionless blowout, with absolutely no bearing on the standings, worse than anything else, it seems like they're always filled with Yankees. And that's on TV; in person it was even lousier. The Metrodrome All-Star pregame was as sappy as the closing of the '84 Olympics. All sorts of sports cars weaved back and forth across the plastic ball field. Sideline autograph sessions looked like a gigantic car sale. Drill teams and bands and people standing around dressed in gaudy costumes covered the turf, as thick as a World Series field rip-up celebration in New York. From batting practice until the last out, it was easily my trip's sorriest game. And as usual the AL was filled with pinstripes. And as usual they got dumped.

As for the Metrodome... it fit the game. Domes built to keep out rain and humidity are bad enough. Minnesota's, though, is the ultimate of pointless. Tossed up because of Siberian winters, in the middle of July it doesn't seem to make a whole lot of sense. The sky's too blue and the summer weather too pretty in Minneapolis to bury baseball under a season-long roof. Plus the thing's ugly. Easily the majors' funniest-looking ballpark, the Metrodome doesn't carry even a dash of baseball excitement. Instead, with its short gray walls, giving way at the top to billowing mounds of a white fabric roof, it's caught somewhere between being strange, sad, and laughable. White and roly-poly, propped up soft and fluffy by all the inside air, the roof looks like what's left of the Michelin Man at his open-casket funeral.

Despite its looks, the bubble dome at least is efficient. Grounds around the outside are well kept. Entrances are well marked. Inside everything is scrubbed and neat and ordered. In fact, if you just looked forward through the doors and ignored all the folks wearing ball caps, you might think you were heading into Sears. Even the walk inside is like a department store. So that all the air doesn't escape and collapse the roof, doors are the rotating circular kind. The ones that when you were a kid you let your sister go through first, then, when she was all the way in, you stopped the spin—a temporary glass cage. They're great fun at department stores, especially if Sis is along. At a ballpark, though, they fit about as well as a roof on a sunny day.

BALL FIELD: GRADE D−

Like most non-native Minnesotans, my only link to the Metrodome was the fine PR job Billy Martin had done on it earlier in the season. In his usual tactful manner, Billy had labeled the place a joke. He had ranted and raved about how a baseball was impossible to see coming out of the roof's white background. A Little League team, he said, didn't deserve the Metrodome. Certainly not the Yankees. Well, the Yankees and I are not close. And I pull for Billy only when he's squaring off with Yankee fans in some tavern. So I really hadn't paid much attention. Figured it was probably George's idea anyway.

When I saw the place I marveled at just how observant a part-time Yankee manager, part-time New York City boxer could be. About the roof, Billy was right. How the engineering whizzes who dreamed the bubble top up could have overlooked the similarities between a white baseball and a white fiberglass roof is tough to figure out. The two play off of each other about as well as a hard-boiled egg dropped into a bowl of vanilla frosting. My only question is why Billy didn't add the turf to his list of complaints. A light, almost grayish-green, the plastic grass contrasts a grounder about as well as the white bubble handles fly balls.

Being a fan is frustrating. All night long, in order to pick up the ball, I had to watch players' movements. If the first baseman lunged, I figured he was going after the ball. A left fielder on one knee meant somebody singled his way. While a strange way to go about things, at least I was safe. Too bad the ball players can't say the same; it's gotta be the majors most dangerous field to play on. Handling the hot corner would be like drawing a death sentence. Until the ball crashed between your lips you wouldn't know it'd even been hit. Come to think of it, isn't Gary Gaetti missing a couple of those front pearlies?

SEATING: GRADE D

Once sucked inside by the vacuumed air and spinning revolving doors, getting to almost any Metroseat is a cinch. That, however, is about their only good quality.

Although the stadium is the majors' youngest, Metroworld doesn't provide many of the new plastic-world options. Instead only those it could afford were added. Two levels of seats rise almost straight up around the inside. The upper tier runs completely around in a solid ring. The lower-level seats, except for a break in right where a purple Glad Bag of an outfield wall fills up the space, do too. Chairs are all fold-up and plastic, yet strangely enough, unlike those in many of the other modern stadiums, aren't real comfortable. Leg room is average. Sight lines are lousy. With air instead of iron supports holding up the roof, nothing's in the way—except distance. And there's certainly plenty of that.

Not only is watching a pain, but moving around in the lousy seats isn't much better. Usually at the new plastic places, aisles, particularly close to home plate, pop up everywhere. At the Metrodome you better know how to squirm through standing people. Or have great bladder control. Scarce enough along the baselines, aisles nearly vanish as you push out to the cheap seats. If that isn't frustrating enough, because both levels are so steep, climbing the steps to a walkway above is like scaling a mountain. Coming back down is as simple as stepping down a ladder, butt to the rungs. Either direction, the trip is discouraging enough to keep anyone, once seated, from leaving...and once left from ever coming back.

If the regular box and general admission frustrations aren't bad enough, left-field "bleachers," down in the corner, are the bottom of the barrel. Tacky Plexiglas shields, the kind that hockey arenas install so that people's faces aren't rearranged by flying wooden sticks, extend a few feet up over the wall. I guess they're there to keep Twins fans from reaching in and catching pop-fly home runs. That or visiting Sox fans from chucking things at Dave Winfield during visiting All-Star games. I didn't get a chance to look through the Plexiglas or chuck anything over it; "The Game" was just too crowded. I could only guess how bad it was. A poor fan already straining to pick up the ball off the white roof and hazy turf must be totally blinded by the fake glass.

SCOREBOARD: GRADE D—

"Inexpensive and built to stay that way." The Subaru jingle applies in Minnesota. While the Japanese car comes loaded with luxury options that work forever, the only reason the Metrodome is inexpensive is because it's got no options to break. Few aisleways, crammed-in seats, a flimsy white roof held up by air, but the worst example of cheap has got to be its overworked, undertalented scoreboard—a flashing reminder that quality costs money, much more money than it took to bring the Metrodome in under budget.

Tacked high above the left-field seats, packed into the middle of four full-size advertisements, baseball info is lost in a barrage of sales pitches. Even if it weren't, the thing would be tough to follow. History of ball players, averages, at bats, home runs, and any other informational tidbits are constantly rotated. Brief flashes, if caught at the right time, are watchable. Full-length paragraphs are out of the question; it's baseball by the glimpseful. Instant replays are almost as bad. Shown in fuzzy black-and-white, the only likeness to the original play is that it's just about as difficult to follow. Between the turf, white roof, and cheapo screen taking in a replay, it's nearly impossible to tell if the Twins or the Vikings are playing.

As horrible as it is, the scoreboard's better than the P.A. At least you can look the other way. The stadium voice, on the other hand, is impossible to ignore. All night long he barks out orders, as intimidating as a Marine drill sergeant in orientation week at Parris Island. "NO SMOKING!"—his favorite greeting—booms through the place. Actually, 'bout the only good sound that comes from stadium speakers is organ music. Simple and rolling, the tunes try to offset the rest of the over- and underdone dynamic duo. But they can't be saved. A wimp of a scoreboard and a monster P.A. hammer any good feeling that the organist creates.

FOOD: GRADE C

Selection: Fair   Accessibility: Excellent
Taste: Fair   Cost: 21st

The last thing I expected from a place as antiseptic as the Metrodome was good, greasy, home-cooked food. Almost everything, I was sure, would come in a plastic package or taste like one. For the most part I was right—Metro food tastes pretty much artificial. Fortunately, though, it's decent enough to go with a Bud.

Simplicity, the dome's finest asset, transfers perfectly over to the concessions. Evenly spaced throughout both levels, food booths aren't much more than rolled-up windows in the walls. Up goes a sliding aluminum door and—presto!—we've got a plastic diner. Consequently, huge crowds, even All-Star-size ones, are easy to handle. As for the food, aside from a few extra sausage things, it's not good enough to crowd 'em up anyway.

Probably the best of the eat features are hot-dog toppings. Only five major league stadiums don't toss a packet of mustard in with the sale of their in-stand wieners. The Metrodome is one of them. When picked up from a Metro vendor, while the dog itself may be no wonder, at least the mustard's added free of charge... by squirt bottles that he carries with him. Underneath, in the clean hallways, things get even fancier. Mustard, ketchup, relish, onions, and kraut, all as much as you please, are self-serviceable. They make the Metro dogs edible. Still, it's pretty sad when a ballpark's most lavish claim is a wide array of pickle relish.

BALLPARK EMPLOYEES: GRADE B

It's amazing what a good attitude can do for a lousy situation. A pleasant personality, dashed with an optimistic air, has turned many an average-looking gal into a heart throb. Look what it did for Mary Tyler Moore. She's not exactly what you'd call gorgeous. But that cheery personality and cute smile of hers have pumped many a TV-watching heart. I know... it did mine. Funny, isn't it? Mary was a Minnesota product too (at least on the tube she was), just like the Metrodome.

Dome workers are Mary Tyler Moorish. They dress neatly, like Mary. They smile a lot, like Mary. They're happy most of the time too. Just like Mary. It wouldn't surprise me if Lou Grant was head of the Twins' personnel department.

Whoever it is did a good job hiring. Ushers are the best of the lot. Their bright red blazers and blue slacks match the ball club's colors. And paired at the top of every aisle, along with Metro security, they're quite helpful. Vendors, pushing food and drink into the stands, do good work too. And at the in-wall concession booths, plastic-food chefs are also nice. They don't seem a bit fazed that most of what they're serving isn't better than the relish that goes on top of it. In fact, most employees at the park are good people, just like Mary and her clan.

The Metrodome has a good heart. Too bad it does up baseball about as well as Ted Baxter did the six o'clock news.

FACILITIES: GRADE B

Minneapolis is not a normal city. It's much nicer!

As for Metrodome facilities, they're better than at most city ballparks. While the stadium doesn't provide a lot of parking spots, alternatives are safe and simple. The best are nearby lots and garages. And as tidy as downtown is, the walk back from the stadium, even if after a late-start extra-inning marathon, is pleasant. In fact, you'd probably be safer soloing it through the streets of Minneapolis at 2:00 A.M. than surrounded by a squad of Boy Scouts at noon in some of the other major league downtowns.

Inside facilities are almost suburbanish. Big rest rooms, with glass mirrors and clean floors, handle the crowds easily. Drinking fountains are all over the place. So are telephones. Along with pickle relish, squirt bottles of mustard, and smiling employees, they're the bright spot of a dull dome.

ATMOSPHERE: GRADE D

The Metrodome is a classic example of what happens when a multimillion-dollar facility shoots for the budget...and makes it. It's goofy-looking on the outside, uncomfortable and boring on the inside. It should stand as a warning to all future ballpark builders trying to blend economy, technology, and baseball...DON'T! Spend the extra bucks, blow the budget, and put up something decent.

By all rights the state of Minnesota should be furious. Twin City residents should be up in arms. Baseball fans should picket ball games. They should take city planners hostage until the dome is destroyed...or just pack up and move south to Milwaukee. They should, but they won't. In fact, I got the feeling folks were "damned proud" of their bubble. In a world of overblown budgets, wasted tax dollars, and never-ending deficits, they stuck out their chests and claimed fiscal responsibility.

Since the All-Star game was *soooo* boring, and since getting in and out of the Metro chairs was such a hassle, I just sat and listened to the financial reports. Stadium cost underruns buzzed all around me. One young couple took turns. "You know it came in under budget," the happy husband explained.

Meanwhile, his wife chirped in, "On time, don't forget on time." Then together they told the exciting story.

Another fellow, during the pregame parades, reminded me, "It's the only major league stadium that has ever cost less than was planned." Then he told me why. I had no idea of whether he was right, I'd never thought of such things when it came to baseball. Then again, balancing the checkbook doesn't thrill me either. But if they're happy, I guess it's all right. It'll make things a lot easier in the long run. As cheap as it was to build, at least when the "new stadium shock" wears off, and Twin City folks realize they've been had, it won't cost so much to tear it down and start again.

From the air-blown fabric roof to the cheap overworked scoreboard, it's obvious that the only real motive in building the thing was cost. And that just doesn't mix well with atmosphere. Neither pleasant nor homey, about all the thing does well is keep out the autumn cold. Still, the Metrodome's a good people place. Fans are friendly and extremely loyal to their bubble. Workers are pleasant. And with the exception of the public address announcer, everybody seems to enjoy themselves. It keeps the place from being a total rip-off, which for a twenty-five-buck ticket and another NL blowout was a good description of my All-Star visit.

Too bad, the town deserves better. Maybe the next time Minneapolis decides to put something up in their lovely city they won't mind adding in a few options, paying a few more dollars, and buying something other than the stripped-down economy model. It's a shame ballparks aren't like cars. At least then they could trade the dome in or junk it and sell it for parts... what few there are.

13

COUNTY STADIUM, MILWAUKEE BREWERS

Roll Out the Barrels and the Brats

REPORT CARD

County Stadium
BASEBALL PARK

July 18, 85 vs Mariners
GAME

Milwaukee Brewers
BASEBALL CLUB

CATEGORY	GRADE	POINTS
Layout and Upkeep	B	85
Ball Field	B	85
Seating	B	85
Scoreboard	B	85
Food	A+	100
Ballpark Employees	A+	100
Facilities	B	85
Atmosphere	A+	100
Total Points		725
Average		91

A-
FINAL GRADE

3rd
RANK

"Beer, bratwurst, and baseball...what a combination! In the parking lot before the game and in the stands during the game, this is major league baseball served up the way it should be in Big Ten country."

PREGAME THOUGHTS

The season after the '78 Sox collapse, and Bucky Dent's chip shot over the "Monster," was my first visit to County Stadium. Since then I've probably seen the Sox play at least ten games there. Each has been fun, as well as tasty. The only thing better than watching baseball in Milwaukee is eating bratwurst, drinking beer, and watching baseball in Milwaukee. It was that first trip, though, that was best. Stuff like that is what cold drizzly February daydreams are made of.

Bob, my Bosox buddy, and I were in for a four-game weekend series—Friday night, Saturday afternoon, capped off with a doubleheader on Sunday. The Sox, still reeling from Bucky, were somewhere back in the pack. The Brewers...I'm not sure just how they were doing. It didn't matter, though, we were on another Red Sox road trip. And those were always great. Milwaukee's not far from Kazoo; the drive over is only about five hours, minus one for the time change. It's so close we probably could've taken off at a normal hour and gotten to the ballpark in time for batting practice. Road trips, though, are always better at night, so we left Thursday, a little after midnight... from the Pantry.

Paul's Pantry is a tiny neighborhood grocery store. Like a 7-Eleven, prices are triple what they should be. But at the Pantry employees smile at customers and even know their names. Regulars make their rounds, pick up a loaf of bread, a quart of milk, and give their opinions on the current sports season. It's a good place. For 15 years Bob's family's owned it; Bob's the manager. Back during our Red Sox road-trip years, summer nights when I didn't have anything to do, I'd just hang out down at the Pantry, welsh free pop and Doritos and talk baseball. It was one of those Thursday nights, about 15 minutes to midnight, when we decided to go. Simple as that, we grabbed a twelve-pack and a bag of ice out of the cooler, some chips, a couple of Slim Jims, and hit the road for Milwaukee.

Our five-hour drive piddled into more than seven. This side of the Indiana border, we stopped for breakfast at a truck stop. Every road trip has to include at least one greasy spoon, at its greasiest time, or it doesn't qualify. Eggs over easy and some hash browns is a great way to take care of any need for sleep—

the stomach's in too much pain. We also brought along our ball gloves and threw pop-ups over the parked semis. Indiana toll roads, empty highways, and another beer got us past Chicago. Farther north, Ohare Oasises (enclosed rest areas) span the expressway. There we killed another hour watching cars roll underneath. A few more cups of coffee, a cruise through the *Tribune* sports section and talking Sox, by the time we finally hit Milwaukee we were buzzing. Between the beer, caffeine, and baseball we didn't even notice the sun come up.

It must've been about 8:00 A.M. by the time we came to "Welcome to Milwaukee" signs. Even then, though, it was hot. I remember one of the bank-building clocks already showing 80+. Before going out to County Stadium, we cruised downtown. It was empty, but so very clean. I've never really seen Milwaukee crowded. It doesn't seem anywhere near the half-million population that *Rand McNally* claims. Nor is it dirty like you might think a factory town would be. Bright blue Lake Michigan washes against the shore. Beautiful little parks are everywhere. Flower gardens fill in many of the street medians.

County Stadium's right off the expressway a few miles from town. The drive between the two is lined with big and little factories. The Miller plant, name-tagged with a big red Miller High Life sign, is easy to see from the road. Side streets branching off and below are covered with machine shops and warehouses. They, too, like downtown, are ordered, not globbed together and hovered over by smoke and soot. Since it was my first trip, I just gazed out the window and carried on like we were cruising through a National Park.

In no time at all we reached the stadium, pulled off the highway down into the parking lot, got out, and headed to the ticket window. The August morning was muggy. Lake Michigan thunderstorms blackened the horizon and threatened to wash out the series before it'd even begun. We weren't worried, though, we'd been around long enough to know what Midwest summers could do. In 15 minutes they can turn the most beautiful of cloudless blue skies pitch black, lost in a downpour, only to be even bluer a half hour later. During June, July, and August in the Midwest one tends to roll with the weather and go about his business. So we did. We ignored it and stepped into line.

A few folks were already waiting for tickets. Most were Brewers fans. We could tell who the Red Soxers were—they wore caps, either the new red ones with the blue B or the old classic blue hats. Baseball souvenirs are like military uniforms. On the road they symbolize loyalty. Bob was wearing a painter's cap he had picked up the past summer in Boston. Red and white, with the Sox logo on top, all the '78 nicknames—Dewey, Louie, Rooster, Pudge— circled it. It was a good hat. Sold only in '78 at Fenway, "fair-weather" fans couldn't buy it. Me, I'm not a hat person. But being on the road I knew my duty: I had on a plain gray "Property of the Boston Red Sox" T-shirt, the kind you can pick up in any Sears.

Sox fans, especially on the road, are talkative. Misery likes company. We found a couple at the end of the line and joined 'em. Together, all the way to the window, we moaned about Bucky's bloop. Concentrating on the Bosox and Yanks, instead of Brewer tickets, when we reached the window the line globbed. We were too busy with our "See ya later's" and tossing parting cheap shots at New York to notice that it was our turn. Nobody seemed to mind. Milwaukeeians are basically good people; they hate the Yankees too. Besides, everybody was too busy second-guessing the weather.

"What do you need?" the old fella inside asked us.

"Well, we're here for the series. What do you have?" Bob did the talking. I was still thinking about that goddamned home run.

I'll never forget that day back in '78. I was going to State. Skipped my Physiology 240 class to see it. In fact, I think I took the whole day off. I was too nervous even to think. The two weeks until then had been a gut wrencher. Late-night sports reports, a Monday night *Game of the Week*, and a couple of Saturday afternoons with Kubek and Garagiola, I watched, listened, and prayed while Boston scrambled back into it. State's library carried the *Boston Globe* on a two-day delay. Each day I started with New England's version of the race. The Sox picked up four games in two weeks, and on number 162 caught the Yankees. The clincher Tiant spun a beaut. He was on the front page smoking a cigar. The headline read, "Play-off Tomorrow."

Me, a couple of roommates, and two freshman girls headed into Lansing to see the game. One of them was a cutie...I kind of liked her. Play-off day, I didn't even know she was alive. Actually I should've left everyone back at the dorm and just gone by myself. We were in different worlds. They all wanted to watch the game on a big-screen TV. I'd have settled for an eight-inch black-and-white. They wanted to get loaded; me, I just wanted a win. The game was too big to be clouded by alcohol, plus I was too nervous to keep anything down. It took us until game time to find a place that they'd agree on. And as "The Star-Spangled Banner" filled the bar we ordered a couple pitchers and packed in, five feet from the screen.

Everybody was having a grand time—afternoon beer, pretzels, skipping class—just like "senior skip day." Not me, I knew better. Torrez on 12 days' rest was no match for Guidry. I'd prayed they'd go with Eck. But Zip Zimmer played the odds. It makes no sense, your ace with an hour off is tougher than number two on three days. And Torrez wasn't even number two. To this day I know if Eckersley had thrown, the Sox would've won.

At game time my confidence level was zero. When Yaz curled one around the foul pole in right, and Torrez made it into the middle innings with a shutout, I started to loosen. Then it happened. I still cringe thinking about it. Bucky hobbling around in the box, a squirt of freezo on the instep, and Torrez sets up the fattest pitch I've ever seen. Wham, Bucky pops it out, and just like that the season's over. Crushed, I gave up and started pounding beers. The Sox trickled back in the eighth, but in the ninth, with two on and two out, were finished off by the Goose.

Something as traumatic usually brings out my best, and at least one good tantrum. Not this time. I didn't speak. I just wanted to be left alone. I drove everybody back to the dorm, then disappeared for ten hours. I'm not even really sure where I went. I just drove around East Lansing, sat at bars, and mourned. I've never felt as miserable.

But this was '79, a new opportunity for the Sox to blow. Bob was still figuring out our seats. The fella selling the tickets suggested we pick 'em all up. "Crowds are gonna be big," he warned us.

"What do you think?" Bob turned to me. I looked up at the sky. Damned clouds! They were just hanging there, waiting for us to make up our minds. When we did they'd open up and it'd be too late.

"Whatever you think." I couldn't stop thinking 'bout Bucky.

We finally decided to split the series. Shelled out for the Friday and Saturday single games, but held off on the Sunday doubleheader. We made the trip only once a summer. Rain checks weren't something we liked to collect.

Satisfied we'd gotten decent enough seats, we headed back for the car. We still had the day to kill, plus we had to find someplace to wait out the monsoons if they broke. Each of us had picked up a stadium guide. Paging through 'em, trying to find out where our seats really were, and glancing up at the clouds overhead, we bumbled along the sidewalk. About halfway to the car we came upon a large, rolling, chain-link gate. The gate that led into the stadium wasn't guarded. Its padlock was opened, the gate unlatched.

We both saw it about the same time. I walked up and gave it a little kick. The gate opened a crack. The chain slid with it; the lock fell to the ground. We looked inside . . . and out at the parking lot. We turned and looked at each other. Nobody but us was around to stop us.

I'd never had such a choice before. I'm sure Bob hadn't either. In Kalamazoo we both lived reasonably sheltered lives. Drawing the high school stamp on the back of my hand and sneaking into basketball games was about as illegal as I'd gotten. Bob had been a night watchman at the flower shop for a while. Everybody in town who visited would get a dozen free roses for Mom or a girlfriend; whoever they were in the most trouble with at the time. Stamps and roses were excusable.

Trespassing was not. Sometimes with trespassing you can play dumb, say you didn't really know where you were, apologize, and get out of it. Not this time. The 12-foot fence and the padlocked gate would give us away. If found inside, it'd be impossible to talk our way out. Not only would we get thrown out, but if it was by some hard-ass who wanted to prove a point, maybe tossed in jail as well. The Sox and the Brewers'd be history. When I got back home and Dad found out, so would I.

On the other hand, this was a once-in-a-lifetime opportunity. Morally we really had no choice but to go. It was as if a voice inside whispered, even if I spent the weekend in the Milwaukee County Jail, picked up a criminal record, and was kept from ever teaching in a respectable school, it was just a weekend, only a profession. If I didn't go, I'd regret it my whole life and wonder why. Something similar must've been going through Bob's head. We didn't discuss it, but came to the obvious decision. We'd go.

Neither of us is really the James Bond type. But if we were to make it, some high-class sneaking around was called for. Adrenaline pumping, I made the first move—looked left, right, up, down, repeated the search two more times, then eased open the squeaky gate. After looking in the same directions for twice as long as me, Bob followed. At first we didn't go anywhere. We just stood there—halfway in, halfway out. Not really having the nerve to follow through. But knowing we could never live with ourselves if we blew the chance. Deep down inside I hoped that some crusty old guard would yell at us and shoo us away. The fateful decision would be out of our hands, an easy way to weenie out. No such luck.

After finally slithering inside, we slipped quickly under the stands and into the shadows. We lost each other on the way. We were moving together, but since we didn't dare breathe, explorations were solo. Nobody was around. Chills raced up and down me. The concrete hallways, which seemed so normal during a game, were silent, like hallowed ground. I forgot that normal people walked about them every day, that workers got paid minimum wage to sweep 'em. Quieter than funeral-home quiet, I was hesitant to even whisper, fearing capture, and, horror of horrors, being kicked out on the verge of ecstasy. I turned back to see how Bob was doing.

"You okay?" I mouthed it. No sounds came out.

He nodded. And stuffed his hat into his back pocket. First time it was off his head since we left Kazoo. Must've done it in case we were caught. Sox fans in Milwaukee would be the last straw. They'd imprison us for sure.

We continued. I had to find a ramp to the field before somebody found me. I had to see the grass. It's like peering into the very soul of the park. Bumbling around searching for sign numbers that match ticket numbers, stepping on people's heels in the same shoes as me, I never remember the stadium until I feel the grass. Then I never forget it. Sunlight colors it a brilliant green. At night lights illuminate it. That fresh grassy scent hovers above like a cloud of mist at dawn. When I finally reach it, touch, taste, and smell it, my insides explode. On that sultry August morning in Milwaukee, they were about to.

Hide-and-seeking it behind the iron beams, I darted from shadow to shadow. Finally a break in the darkness. I ran to its source—an aisleway up into the stands. An iron handrail joined the rise. I grabbed it and eased my way up and in. Peering out of the dark, the sun hurt my eyes. I staggered out into the light, blindly reached for a nearby seat, and sat. Bob followed and sat in the chair next to me.

In boxes behind the third-base dugout we looked out over the field. The place was empty. No human being save us breathed, and we barely did. Red and green seats, 50,000 of them, climbed above. Overhead the summer sun was being cooled by the storm's strengthening breezes. Before us lay the ball field, quiet except for the rhythmic clicking of an old worn-out sprinkler. Tools of its absent keeper, a couple rakes, a shovel, a small cart, lay scattered about. Freshly cut grass raked to the third-base foul line sent up a scent and allowed my nose to join in on the blessing. Empty only of people, not spirit, in all of its splendor it was as silent as I.

I dreamed a rush of stored-up dreams. My greatest catches since I was 12 all came rushing back, all on the County Stadium turf. Diving grabs by me, the new Red Sox center fielder. The empty stands filled with cheering. The catches were a splash; as quickly as they'd come, they left. My heroics vanished. I looked again at the field. God it was gorgeous, and so very quiet. What a wonderful life it had. The memories, the moments that must've been filed away in its heart. If only it could tell me. The clicking of the sprinkler awoke me from my dream, a gust of wind swept stray grass and sprinkles of the drink into my face. It could talk. I was being thanked for such thoughts.

LAYOUT AND UPKEEP: GRADE B

County Stadium lies off I-94, less than five miles outside of town. Tidy neighborhood streets border the hillside across the expressway from it. Breweries and other plant smokestacks rise up all the way back into town. While it sits down and off the road like Kansas City's stadium, it's not nearly as dazzling. Instead, plain and enclosed, it has a giant warehousish look about it—much like Wrigley.

Game night is when the Brewer house really lights up. Every time I go I feel like I am on my way to a giant family reunion. Two hours before the ball game the parking lot bustles with activity. People milling about, hatch backs open, small single grills fired up, big trash-can cookers cooking. Closer in, friendly sounds and pleasant aromas join the party. Kegs of Miller and Pabst are tapped and freely flowing, the mouth-watering scent of brats charring over an open flame, the sounds of people laughing—this is the scene that draws a body so warmly into County Stadium. It's the majors' friendliest greeting.

Inside, the stadium takes on a West Coastish flavor. It's clean and well organized. Aisles stretch efficiently all around. Rest rooms are easy to find. Set up in an orderly way and evenly spaced throughout the walkways, concession stands are almost Californian. The park even hides a few convenient elevators to the upper deck. Not shown off like out West, the Brewer ones are strictly functional. In fact, all those luxuries that grace the West Coast parks can also be found in Milwaukee, only in Brew town they're just a little more shy about it.

BALL FIELD: GRADE B

Whenever I think of why grass is better than plastic, I dream of County Stadium. The ball field's not baseball's prettiest. The Southern Californians and two or three in the East are sharper. But I saw the Milwaukee field in its finest hour. Smelled it at a silent moment. It was quiet and empty. The vision is one of my baseball favorites—the ball field a personal friend.

Midwest weather can be tough on grass. Hot, humid summers provide little consistent rainfall. Those giant thunder boomers pour buckets of rain for ten minutes, then disappear for two weeks. In winter the grass hides under mounds of snow. In fall and spring it floods and freezes back and forth, not ideal growing conditions. A lot of TLC's needed to keep it from getting patchy. County Stadium's turf gets its TLC. It's as nice-looking today as when I sneaked in years ago to watch it grow.

Without California's natural greenhouse, in places it's a little worn. Still it's lush, green, fresh, and, most of all, like everything else at the park—natural. It's Milwaukee.

SEATING: GRADE B

County Stadium gets the best from both worlds. A big parking lot and efficient stadium layout say Western, but up and in it's got that old traditional Eastern feeling. It makes for a delightful combo.

Two levels of dark green and reddish-orange chairs run from foul pole to foul pole. A tiny mezzanine section is sandwiched between them. Beyond the fences sit bleachers. With some of the majors' sunshiniest days, the U.S.A.'s freshest beer, and the world's tastiest sausages, bleachers might be the best seats in the house. But they sure aren't the only good ones.

Reserved chairs don't have to mess with much foul ground—everybody's close. Especially those in the front-row boxes; they're stuffed right into the infield. Good seats are great. Decent ones are good. Unfortunately, like some of the older places, bad ones can get awful. Just like in Chicago and Detroit, iron posts hold up the roof. And they're just as tough to see around. At least, though, the Brewer park doesn't use many. Odds are, if the view's not obstructed, it'll be good. Odds are, unless the place is really packed it won't be obstructed.

Completed in 1953, as far as ballparks go, County Stadium's a middle-ager. It's got all the flashy technology of the fifties—plastic chairs, wide aisles, and room. But it keeps its old-time character. Someday the oldsters will be torn down. Fenway, Wrigley, Comiskey are too inconvenient to live forever. When they go, and we're left with the lifeless multipurpose models, County, along with Baltimore's Memorial Stadium, will be the vets. It's comforting to know, at least until I die, there'll always be a place to watch baseball...from behind an iron post.

SCOREBOARD: GRADE B

Milwaukee's scoreboard is friendly. Fans are treated like one of the family; players, like they were born and raised in downtown Milwaukee. A good visual production and a snappy organ blend well together. They ensure that a night out with the Brewers will be more than just a pleasant dining experience. Although that's not such a bad fate.

Small auxiliary screens located on the facing of the upper deck rotate scores from around the majors. Everything else is handled on the giant screen above the right-field bleachers. Its size alone dominates the place, and it has plenty of good things to say, but it also has a problem. Replays are bad. Black-and-white-dot matrix isn't quite the same as crystal clear and colored Diamond Vision. Even on the huge screen, in slow motion and at night, pictures are tough to follow.

While it may lack flash, the setup has plenty of heart. Ball players are treated great. To begin the game all nine Brewer starters are separately announced. As the crowd cheers, each runs from the dugout to his position. The feel is almost high schoolish and puts a little innocence back in the game.

A few years back, when the Brewers featured that World Series "All-Tough-Guy Team," the ones that looked like it secretly agreed never to wash, shave, or comb their hair. It was a riot. To see guys like Vuckovich and "Stormin Gorman" trot out to their positions as the P.A. rolled through their names and fans cheered told you that baseball in Milwaukee, at least in '82, was more than just another professional sport.

Player introductions aren't the end of special treatment. For each batter a player profile dominates the screen. Not only season and game stats are shown, but a mug shot (with Gorman it was a quick flash) and personal facts as well. The baseball-card information makes the players human.

Meanwhile, fans are encouraged to have a great time. "Roll Out the Barrels" and "On Wisconsin" ring through the place and spur on the bratwurst- and beer-soaked crowd. Sing-alongs get a response from the happy people and consequently the atmosphere becomes even more fun. Even as good a time as everyone has, things seldom get out of control. A big reason is the attitude of the scoreboard. All night long the big screen and P.A. suggest that everyone please be considerate of others. Some numbers are short and funny. Little comical characters are cute, their message quiet. Other times it's more serious. Everything from how to find lost keys to lost children and what to do about obnoxious drunkards is explained. Each ends with a reminder of where the Fan Assistance Center is located and encourages the use of it.

The arrangement seems typical of the people and the place. Drink beer, eat sausage, watch baseball, and have some fun, but please be kind to others. Everybody does, and is. Ballparks don't get much nicer.

FOOD: GRADE A+

Selection: Excellent	Accessibility: Excellent
Taste: Excellent	Cost: 10th

Baseball food just doesn't come any better—even in the University of Wisconsin parking lot on Saturday afternoons in October. Everything is barbecued, and in all sorts of quantities, from bushel-barrel numbers to pairs. Chicken, steak, wieners... after roaming around the lot before the game, I always wonder if ballpark food inside could smell so good. That's before I get there. Inside, County Stadium presents its own version of baseball, brew-'n'-bratwurst style.

In Milwaukee, a city with a strong German heritage, sausages are king.

And the ballpark is flooded with 'em. Four kinds, brats, Polish, Italian, and Bavarian, join an equally scrumptious ballpark dog sizzling atop almost all the stadium grills. Their good smells linger in the hallways and drift up into the stands. To resist 'em is impossible; sooner or later you're lured to the mouth-watering lines. Up close their spell takes over; you can never buy just one. Buried in a soft fresh bun, smothered in kraut and doused with a splash of that secret stadium sauce, baseball doesn't feature a tastier wiener.

Fortunately the menu doesn't end there. Real deli corners serve roast beef, corned beef, and Philly sandwiches. Piled high with meat, each a meal in itself, you can get 'em on a plate with hot German potato salad. Tangy and tasty, only Mom's is as good. At other booths steak sandwiches and thick juicy burgers are cooked up on smoking grills—lettuce, tomatoes, cheese, and horse-radish are available to dress them up.

And beer...it's everywhere. Cold and crisp, in the stands and down un-derneath—just knowing that the keg was probably rolled in from downtown that morning makes it that much more refreshing.

BALLPARK EMPLOYEES: GRADE A+

A host of Norman Rockwell gray-haired grandpa models, and a few middle-aged kids, Brewer workers are some of baseball's best. Like out in Anaheim, that pat-on-the-back, down-home feeling radiates about the place.

I made sure I got to the ballpark early. I'd cruised the parking lot before. And even though I wasn't cooking, I didn't want to miss out on all the good smells. Plus after living on hot dogs for a month, I was down a few pounds. I hoped somebody would notice, feel sorry for me, and feed me.

At the entrance I ran into my trip's first Brewer employee. I rolled down the window to pay. "How's the neighborhood?" I asked. "You think my car will be all right?" I knew it was a dumb question. The neighborhood was fine, I'd been in it before...before my California break-in that is.

The fella accepting payment was taken by such a question. Probably wasn't something a lot of folks worried about. He laughed. "You must be from Chicago." I thought about it and laughed along with him. "Don't worry, son, we'll take care of it for you. You just go on in and have a good time." He pointed me to the best spot to leave it. And promised to keep an eye on it. I felt like my car was left sitting between those palms of "You're in good hands with All-State."

Inside the attitude's just as homey. Ushers are stationed regularly around the park. More than willing to track down a lost seat, they also help out with more important matters, like the one I'd come across. Five times on my trip

I was gonna get to see the Mariners. Milwaukee was one of the places. I thought it'd be neat to send word back to Murph and Hendy, my two Mariner buddies, that all was well and that I hadn't died of indigestion. All I had to do was get a message up to the broadcast booth. I've tried that before at other places; usually it's impossible. In most the booth is miles away, off limits to everybody but the team owner. In addition, all avenues to reach it are surrounded by armed Buckingham Palace-type guards who don't breathe, let alone smile. That, or somebody takes the slip of paper and, as soon as you leave, eats it. I figured I had about as good a chance of getting my message on the air as the M's had at winning the pennant....Not so in Milwaukee.

I explained to the old gentleman in charge of the broadcast-level elevator what I wanted to do.

"Well," he said, "I can't promise you anything, but let's get you as close as we can."

I was traded twice, first at the elevator, then out at the walkway underneath the broadcast booth. Front-door service with all three. I even saw my little slip of paper hand-delivered. My "Hello" was read on the air, promises were kept, and I was happy—all because the three old gentlemen working for the Brewers were kind enough to lend a hand.

In fact, all of the Brew crew I came across were good people. A friendly bunch of folks, just their presence around the park reassures a body that one can still drink a little beer, eat a little brat, watch a little baseball, and stroll out to a waiting, nonvandalized car at eleven o'clock at night without being mugged...all just two hours north of South Side Chicago.

FACILITIES: GRADE B

From the open-armed parking lot to a tidy inside layout, County Stadium pulls the best from the West and the East and blends a satisfying baseball flavor. It comes through strongest in a solid facility presentation.

Besides serving as the world's largest open-air barbecue pit, the parking lot is huge. Although not as perfectly laid out as the monsters in California, for an Eastern model it certainly is well cared for. Along with the decent neighborhood that it's in, it provides Brewer fans a pretty good place to leave a life's investment.

Inside facilities also break with Eastern tradition. Bathrooms are clean and spread evenly throughout the place. They feature uncracked glass mirrors and paper towels, and walking into one doesn't make you long for a nearby Standard station. All in all, County Stadium shirks its Eastern park allies at just the right time...and bathrooms and parking lots are just the right time.

ATMOSPHERE: GRADE A+

Beer, bratwurst, and baseball—what a combination! When the beer flows as freely in the parking lot as in the ballpark, brats are grilled to smoking perfection both outside and in the stadium, and baseball is played on lush, green grass under blue Midwestern skies, the result is major league baseball served up on one of its finest platters. An evening at County Stadium is truly a joy.

Roaming through the pregame parking lot of open tailgates and smoking grills is like getting ready for a Big Ten football game. As early as four hours before game time, preparations begin. One area, across the street from the stadium, is reserved ahead of time. Long tables are set up and tableclothed. A portable stage goes up for the five-piece polka band that'll kick out some tunes a little later. Kegs fresh from the downtown breweries are rolled out and readied for tapping. All are signs of a Brewer game in the making. Closer to the stadium, in fact engulfing it, groups of 100, 20, or even 2 on a single grill barbecue everything from burgers and steaks to kielbasa and kraut. With the different aromas meandering together amid the parked autos and the sounds of people having fun, pregame at County Stadium, even if it's just a stroll through the open-pit barbecue, is an experience in itself.

Once inside, the atmosphere only intensifies. More good food and baseball add to the brewing stew more good times. Everybody and everything seem to really enjoy what's going on. And the ball game only makes things more exciting. Typifying the good-feeling place, the P.A. has fun with the fans. And the fans have fun with the game. From the players' rousing introductions to the organist's rolling clap-alongs, a ball game at County Stadium is a treat for all the senses.

Taste buds, however, get the royal treatment. They must think they've died and gone to heaven. All that good hearty German food served in Sunday-dinner portions and a cold Old Style make a good game of baseball a "cure for whatever ails ya."

Finally, workers dedicated not only to the safety of the stadium's fans but to a professional presentation of the game round out a wonderful evening. Always pleasant, the County Stadium staff carries on as if they were the ones who were supposed to be having the good time. This is baseball as it should be in Big Ten country—full of beer, full of food, and full of good times—whether it be on a Saturday afternoon in September or a warm summer evening in July.

14

COMISKEY PARK, CHICAGO WHITE SOX

Welcome Snakes and Snakettes

REPORT CARD — *Comiskey Park*
BASEBALL PARK

July 19, 85 vs Indians — *Chicago White Sox*
GAME — BASEBALL CLUB

CATEGORY	GRADE	POINTS
Layout and Upkeep	D	65
Ball Field	B	85
Seating	D	65
Scoreboard	A+	100
Food	A+	100
Ballpark Employees	B	85
Facilities	D-	60
Atmosphere	A+	100
Total Points		660
Average		83

B
FINAL GRADE

10th
RANK

"Old and decaying, squeezed in between the ghetto and the expressway, this South Side Chicago park is still the majors' craziest.... Where else would reptiles get a special invite?"

PREGAME THOUGHTS

Since 1910 baseballs have bounced around Comiskey Park. No other major league stadium still standing can say the same. Even so, it's far from common knowledge. Most folks think the game's oldest home lies north of town enclosed in ivy, not to the south surrounded by low-income housing projects. Wrigley gets such good PR around the baseball world, some people don't even know Chicago has two stadiums. Comiskey, to a casual nonbeliever, unlike Wrigley, is nothing special. It's just another over-the-hill baseball park. A place that probably once upon a time had its day, but is no longer useful. A stadium that could best serve baseball by quietly going away. I know different though. I've soaked in Comiskey's tradition a number of times. One thing about the old South Side park that I know for sure... it's not just another ballpark.

In the press the two are incomparable—Wrigley is everything that is beautiful about baseball. It's living history, a museum piece, that even with all their conveniences the West Coast stadiums can't claim to top. In the midst of a quaint city neighborhood, it is ivy-covered walls, a hand-manipulated scoreboard, and day baseball. To many Wrigley Field is a reminder of what baseball once was. The ultimate martyr to tradition, it will die before allowing technology to change it. Comiskey, on the other hand, sits on the fringes of poverty and crime in the South Side ghetto. Cheap tenements and broken-down low-income housing projects submerge it. Getting there is supposedly as bad as a subway visit to see the Yankees. Rumor has it that the ballpark is decaying, that with each gust of wind off the lake something else falls off it. Even its fans have a bad rep. Unlike Wrigley's good Chicagoans, Comiskey is home for the less fortunate, an unruly group who just can't get tickets to see the Cubs. Along with Detroit's Tiger Stadium, the South Side Chicago park is the very reason baseball has made a mass exodus to the suburbs.

These, however, are the doubts of those who've never been, never sat inside it. It'd been six years since I had, but I remembered. Those were the days when I'd go anywhere to see the Bosox. As long as Eckersley was on the mound, and Rice out in left, I was happy. Where they played was really no big deal. At least the first few visits it wasn't. But Comiskey has a way of growing on you, and it grew on me. I just had too much fun not to want to come back for more. Bosox in town or not, I became a twice-a-summer regular.

Fun is only part of the Comiskey character. When a body lives to be 75 it becomes a part of many weird events... and grand events as well. Ruth, Gehrig, all the famous ancients filled its stands at one time. In '33 the first major league All-Star game was played inside it. "The Babe" even smacked a home run in it over the same wall and into the same stands that people sit in today. The 1919 Sox left their mark too. Instead of white, though, theirs was "black." "Shoeless Joe" and seven others confessed to playing to lose a World Series at the South Side park, one of baseball's darkest events. Good and bad memories, the place just oozes with history.

It's the park's less historic, more crazy recent past that I best recall. Of all the weird things that have happened to baseball in my lifetime, most occurred in South Side Chicago. I've always loved controversy—guess it's the *National Enquirer* in me. As a kid I kept a close watch on the master of it, White Sox slugger Richie Allen. His dark shades were cool. So was he. He said things that Reggie only dreamed of saying. His face, his shades, his stats were always grabbing sports-page headlines. Usually he was just shooting off his mouth. Once in a while, though, like in '72, when he was traded to the Sox, he made sense. Richie hated plastic grass. I'll never forget his comments on it. "If a horse don't eat it, I don't wantta play on it." Guess what Comiskey, his new home, was made of? Half real grass, half plastic. For four years the place actually had an artificial turfed infield with a natural outfield. Poor Richie! He had to play a plastic first. And the ball field looked so strange. Yet somehow in Comiskey both Richie and the combo grass seemed to fit.

Nowhere else in the majors was a home run more fun to watch. The mammoth exploding center-field scoreboard made Chisox blasts a real cause for celebration. Whenever one reached the stands multicolored whirligigs perched on top would whistle and spin while they flashed different colors. Simultaneously fireworks would shoot off into the dark Chicago sky. For three minutes a few times a week all summer long, South Side Chicago celebrated the Fourth of July. Each time I'd go, even when it was Sox vs. Sox, I pulled for a couple of Chicago blasts to ignite the powder keg. I hoped it still put on a show in 1985.

Then there was Bill Veeck, the bizarre little man famous for the introduction to—and banishment of—midgets from baseball. With him at the controls in Chicago's fun house, baseball was never really the same. I heard before games he'd had cow-milking contests and chicken-catching races on the field. I never saw 'em, but believed it. It was Veeck material. On the bicentennial Fourth he dressed up as Yankee Doodle Dandy. Covered with red, white, and blue, he led a patriotic march around Comiskey. Of course all the while the scoreboard was exploding. Nothing was too offbeat for Veeck. He even dressed the Sox strangely. Rainbow-colored Astro uniforms dominated the seventies. I think every City League softball and high school baseball team for the next ten years must've copied 'em. Not the Sox. Veeck had them decked out in unis that looked like pajamas. Jerseys, modeled after maternity dresses, weren't supposed to be tucked in. Instead they hung out over bottoms that looked like cheap sweat pants. He even had 'em wear matching shorts a few times. The players looked silly. It didn't matter, though; anything went at Comiskey.

And almost everything did go in the summer of '79. A *Saturday Night Fever* disco rage swept the country. Well, most of the country, not South Side Chicago. Veeck'd support anything that bucked the current, so he allowed a "Disco Sucks Night." Officially it was called "Disco Demolition." But, since disco really did suck, the more colorful title caught on. Anybody could get in for 98 cents if they showed a disco album at the gate. Between games of a Tiger–Sox doubleheader, all the albums were to be burned in a great bonfire, a symbol of protest to crummy music. Problem is they never got through game one. Albums make great Frisbees. They started flying all around the place. Rock fans came unglued, spilled out onto the field and trashed it. The ball field was ripped to ribbons. The Sox had to forfeit.

Other folks left their mark on the place as well. Before I left for Seattle I followed the Sox on Chicago TV cable stations. Harry Caray and Jimmy Piersall announced the games; once in a while from the bleachers even. They were as crazy as the park. Harry would hang out of the booth, Bud in hand, singing "Take Me Out to the Ballgame." Piersall picked on everybody in the organization, from the players' wives to the owner's dog, and tore them to ribbons. They lasted until Harry jumped ship, switched allegiance to the crosstown Cubbies, while Piersall, who finally accused too many people of too many things for far too long, just disappeared. A strange mix, they seemed right at home with the sideshows taking place all about them.

Comiskey certainly had been the home for many a strange happening. Maybe they weren't all healthy, but most were harmless. They only made the game more fun, a quality hard to argue with. It'd been some time since I visited, though. I wondered if the old place, after leaving the reins of Mr. Veeck, and after obtaining some decent respect that comes with age, had changed. I hoped not! I hoped that it still retained the old flavor, that it carried on in its own strange and surprising way. In this predictable world of suburban parks, with their boring food, plastic grass, and lifeless atmosphere, I longed for some of that old Comiskey craziness.

LAYOUT AND UPKEEP: GRADE D

There's only one way to take on Comiskey—by El. The city train makes its White Sox stop at Thirty-fifth Street before swirling deep into the South Side ghetto. Train tracks and platform sit just above the expressways that sandwich it. Stairs rise to the filthy street that crosses above. Cars whoosh by. Across and above the expressway southbound traffic, only a few hundred yards from the road, sits the stadium. Dripping in white, accented by a gaudy fluorescent green, the old place almost glows.

Not much has changed with it since 1910. It's still enclosed by the same brick shell that it was born with. Open archways still dot its face. People walking up the inside ramps can look out through arches at the seedy neighborhood below. Although the openings are dangerous, simple to jump through down two stories to the street, nobody seems to worry much about 'em. In fact, Comiskey doesn't look like it's been worried about for years. Face-lifts that have softened Tiger and Yankee stadiums, and even Fenway, have skipped by the Chicago ballpark. Not much has been done to keep it young-looking, just gobs and gobs of paint, so thick now, you can barely make out the lines of the bricks underneath.

While outside, layers of whitewash try to hide its age, inside they don't even bother. Wires hang from nearly every beam, bunched, taped, and painted over again and again. Concrete floors are broken by chuckholes. Asphalt that runs under the stands, around and behind the outfield walls, rises and falls as often as a midway roller coaster. Uncomfortably thin aisleways leading from seats to concessions are blocked by all sorts of iron beams. Nothing's up to date, not even of 20 years ago. It's not what you'd call tidy, either. Papers litter many of the inner aisleways and are kicked around constantly by frequent breezes off the lake. Junk and assorted important objects sit stacked or lie piled together, cluttering the back walls of the walkways. As worn as it is, though, the place drips with character. An old broken-down lovable sincerity floats about. For me, anyhow, it more than makes up for its many faults.

For others more concerned with convenience, the ballpark must be a nightmare, the ultimate test of baseball allegiance...for the plastic yuppie generation. Folks born and raised in the safety of the suburbs, those who think that big cities only crawl with slime, could have a field day picking it apart. Although the concrete floors are classic, they're dangerous. Unless you watch yourself, one of the holes might just swallow you up. While walkways that lead gradually into the upper deck are quaint, they can be slow and sometimes frustrating. Crowds constantly bottleneck. And with the wiring having been taped over and over again, it amazed me that the stadium's lights didn't just flicker with the wind.

Taken together, the inconveniences, the junk lying around, even the gobs of paint make for a bad rep. They add fuel to the fire that classic places like Comiskey are more bother than worth. That they'd be better off dead, so baseball could find a new, clean, safe home in a more normal neighborhood out in the burbs. Eventually they'll get their wish... but in doing so will leave a lot of character behind.

BALL FIELD: GRADE B

The grass is thick. Like a fat down-filled quilt, it pillows the field. For a fan it's pretty, soft, and full. For a player, it's probably too clumpy.

It had been a while since I'd last seen the South Side grass. Memories, though, have a way of rushing back when involved with Chicago and baseball. I'll always remember Comiskey's fragrance. The ball field seemed to smell much more natural than any other. Something about the scent of recently trimmed and watered grass is captivating; it allows my mind to lapse back into grander times. In most ballparks, even in the most finely tuned and best-manicured ones, the scent of the turf blends in with all of the other friendly smells hanging in the air. It's a portion of the whole, not able to be singled out from the rest. In White Sox stadium, with home plate so close to the stands, and the grass as thick as it is, entering up the ramp and into the open air, I was still greeted by that wonderful aroma. Fresher, cleaner, and probably more polished than any other patch of grass within miles of the stadium... just its fragrance is enough to bring on the feel of baseball.

It looks pretty good too... better than I remembered. A huge outfield dominates the whole inside. Everywhere you look seems to be outfield. Cross-cut and smooth, it's the turf's most elegant portion. As it creeps toward the dirt, though, the luster fades. Rough spots weave in and out along the mesh. The infield grass is only average. The dirt's nothing special. Still, with its friendly scent, and such a lush outfield, the ball field is the "Pride of the South Side."

SEATING: GRADE D

Views for a Sox game are about as standard as the flight path of a Hoyt Wilhelm knuckleball—you never know what to expect. Some chairs sit almost on top of home plate; others hide behind fat iron beams. Still others face away from the field, not even hinting that baseball exists below. Regardless of their location or direction, each seat offers something different—the chance, if you want, to see baseball from an entirely different perspective.

The old traditional setup for a big ballpark, like in Tiger Stadium, two levels work their way around the inside. Both are filled with bright green chairs. The same shade that fringes the white bricks outside. Since baseball was the only game planned for the place, each level hugs the field. And after turning the corner down the foul line, each level heads back toward one another. In dead center they stop; upper decks make way for the giant scoreboard, while the lower level breaks for baseball's most worn bleachers. Each is connected to the bleachers and consequently to one another by a walkway. Suspended over the bleacher seats, the aisles look like gangplanks. During the game people wandering 'em stop, lean against the rail, and watch.

Each level provides plenty of good seats... and bad ones as well. Between first and third, particularly in the front rows, sight lines are great. Hovering almost directly overhead, or down alongside the action, they make the game much more exciting. Behind home plate, in the front row of the upper deck, the seats almost overhang the batter, close enough to make out the smoke of a rising fastball. As rows push back, though, iron supports pop up. Views aren't so good, sometimes only frustrating. Down in both corners of the upper deck, straight back from the foul pole, wedged against the wall, chairs actually face toward center field. To see the batter you've almost got to sit crossways and flop your legs over the armrest... and that's just to point in the right direction. To see anything you might be hindered by as many as five or six iron posts, the overhanging roof, and whoever's lap you might be standing on at the time.

While sight lines vary, lack of comfort's pretty standard. For the most part, aisles are thin and leg room cramped. In 1910, when the place went up, ballpark plastic was still in the planning stage, comfort not a top priority. Oddly enough, just getting in and finding a seat, any seat, was enough. Today people need more. They need extra room for arms and legs and plastic for the rear. South Side Chicago's not the place to find it. The extra room is absent, and probably always will be. It does, however, promote fan unity. As for comfort, a few plastic chairs put in a couple of years back cover the front portions of each level. Most normal humans, who pay normal prices, get a normal wooden chair. It must be why Comiskey leads the league in standing ovations. It's just too painful to stay seated the whole game.

Between the two levels, backed up against the huge scoreboard, under the gangplanks, is baseball's oldest bleacher section. They're also the park's most special seats. Every time I go I make sure to make a trip out and watch at least an inning in 'em. Miles from the field, with the overhang from each of the upper levels in the way, the view's pretty bad, and the seats are certainly not comfortable. Some of the old wooden benches are splintered to half their original width. The ones that aren't need paint. All of 'em should be checked for slivers. Nevertheless they offer an insight into something as special as the game itself. They're real baseball in a real baseball town. Sitting in them is an experience that only the city of Chicago and a place as rich as Comiskey can offer.

SCOREBOARD: GRADE A+

No other park in the majors gets fans as involved or keeps them so entertained. The place is wild! A big reason is the giant exploding scoreboard in center field. Equipped with Diamond Vision, pinwheels, and rockets' red glare, it's one of baseball's craziest. And musically there are just none better than Nancy Faust.

The scoreboard is miles from home plate. Filling the gap between the left- and right-field upper decks, it perches atop the bleachers. It's gigantic—so big that even from outside on the El it dominates the place. A Sox logo sits smack-dab in the center. On each side of the logo is a billboard-size screen. The right-field screen is traditional. Digital lights handle the basics and cover most of the Sox game. In left is Diamond Vision. And the sucker's cranked up all night long. Highlights, good plays, bad plays, whacky plays—no other screen in baseball gets more replay time. It's free to mess around; scores from around the majors are taken care of on the facing of the upper deck.

If that was all it did—updates, messages, and baseball coverage—it'd be good enough. But there's so much more. Above the combo arise Comiskey's most famous ornaments. Nine colorful pinwheels climb the board to form an apex. Somewhere inside there's a rocket launcher. Each White Sox blast still gets a 21-gun salute. As the ball clears the fence the scoreboard goes bonkers. The whirligigs spin and flash. Fireworks explode above the stadium. Fans go wild. The cheering, the booming, the bright sky and whirling pinwheels still make it baseball's best home-run celebration.

As good as the scoreboard is, the musical show is even better. Known to Sox fans simply as "Nancy," she's baseball's best organist. Busy and imaginative, Nancy plays it all, from church music to circus music and everything in between. Some of the tunes are traditional. "Battle Hymn of the Republic" is great for clapping to. Others, like "My Boyfriend's Back," are corny. Arrangements unique to nearly every strange situation that can occur on a ball field get some kind of organ response. It might just be a few quick notes. Sometimes it's a whole verse. Almost always it fits. When Jim Rice, the Bosox slugger, walks to the plate in South Side Chicago it's usually to a few sharp notes of the "Rice-A-Roni" song. "I've Been Working on the Railroad" joins Spike Owen as he digs in to hit. If a ball player's got a workable nickname, regardless of the team, odds are Nancy's dreamed up a tune to introduce him.

Besides introductions, she's great at breaking the tension. My trip brought me to Chicago the same night Tom Seaver was going after win number 298. With two on and two out, ahead 1-0 in the eighth, Tony LaRussa headed out to the mound. White Sox fans greeted him with a crisp chorus of boos. How could he even think of pulling Tom? Fans got their wish. Seaver stayed in. Meanwhile, LaRussa was joined on his walk back to the dugout by "If You're Happy and You Know It, Clap Your Hands." Fans clapped their hands for Seaver and LaRussa.

Then there are the old standbys. The one that turns 'em all on is the "Good-bye" tune. It's a Chisox tradition, an escort to the showers for the other team's pitcher. Singing along to "Sha Na Na Na Hey Hey Hey Good-bye," the place rocks as the poor guy who just got hooked stumbles to the locker room. Sometimes, if things are going real good, she'll crank out "Good-bye" after the game, too, but only if the Sox blow 'em out.

Although always playing, Nancy never takes away from the game. Often the cleverness of the choice or the intensity of the situation will cause the quick verse to go unnoticed in the background. But when they want her, she's there. And as a result they love her.

FOOD: GRADE A+

Selection: Excellent   Accessibility: Excellent

Taste: Excellent   Cost: 15th

Visiting concessions along the cracked walkways underneath the stands is like wandering through a world ethnic food festival. I'm never sure if the trip or the food is more unusual. Both, though, are an experience that anybody who has ever bitten into a ballpark dog has got to take on.

If a Sox game wasn't being played inside… underneath, with all the people, the noise, and the food, I'd swear a carnival was going on. It's set up like one. Instead of cloned stainless-steel concession stands with roll-down doors, booths vary. Some are official ballpark ones that extend back into the walls. Just as many, though, are makeshift carts or tables. Instead of being spread evenly along the aisleways, they pop up everywhere. Behind iron posts, in a corner against the wall, alongside the already skinny walkways, if there's six free square feet, odds are, before the night's over somebody will be selling food from it.

Every carnival midway has game booths. Somewhere stuffed between all the food, Comiskey's got one. I've never seen it, but it's there, I'm sure of it. Each time I wander around the place I expect to be stopped by some shady-looking dude with a straw hat and cane. With that used-car salesman twitch in his eye, he'll walk up and put his arm around me. "Son," he'll say, "looks like you got yourself a pretty good arm. What's say you step up here and win your honey a White Sox doll? All you gotta do is knock over the six milk bottles." He's out there somewhere. One of these days I'll find him.

Until then I'll just eat, and eat, and eat. Nearly anything that can be thought of to create and eat at a ballpark is both created and eaten here. Mild items like pizza and submarine sandwiches, absent in other stadiums for being "too wild," are like bags of chips on a supermarket shelf compared to all the other stuff. Chicken dinners, regular and deluxe, are at one place. Hot roast beef and corn beef deli sandwiches, complete with big dill pickles, are at another. Burgers and even steaks are available someplace else.

Specialty stands are special! Particularly the one filled with tacos. Not plastic taco meat crammed into assembly-line shells, this stuff is real! Hard- and soft-shelled tacos, tostadas, and bean burritos get spiced up with real "hot" sauce. A single simple booth, it sits almost hidden behind iron posts down under and along the left-field line. But you better be good at pointing or know a little Spanish. The cooks might not have their translation book with them. Churros, a Mexican dessert, is available around the corner at an entirely different location. Pennsylvania Dutch funnel cakes, oil-fried and dipped in chocolate, are handled, fried, and dipped on location, probably by actual descendants of the Pennsylvania Dutch. The resulting mix of people and food up and down the walkways is as festive as the game inside.

With Old Style beer flowing from the taps, and vendors who pound the stands at a ferocious pace, with almost every other beer known to man in cold cans to prove it, drinking is a pleasure as well. Whether it be up in the stands watching the game or down underneath waiting in line, both eating and choosing what to eat are definitely a treat—and another act of "The Wonderful World of Comiskey."

BALLPARK EMPLOYEES: GRADE B

Like their workplace, most White Sox employees, although not the best dressed, have heart. They're a good match for the old park.

Security guards look almost as tacky as some of the other weird things inside. Slacks are whatever they happen to choose. Some wear blue jeans, some polyesters; at least most don't have holes in the knees. A corny black label on the back of their standard yellow shirt says "Security." I kept waiting for it to start flashing in neon. At the Western, dress-conscious, well-oiled stadiums, Sox security guards would look appalling. Dodger Stadium would never allow such a thing. It'd be a direct reflection on the quality of the organization, a black mark that not even a trip to the World Series could erase. In Chicago it's no big deal.

Concessionaires in the giant food fair seem to have a good time. They handle the Midwest summer heat efficiently and with a smile. Ushers are available and pleasant. In a strict Eastern tradition, vendors are busy. Unlike to the west, where even hot-dog peddlers and soda pushers will set their product down and have a short visit, moving eastward they're more intense. They have to be. Fans stay put, drink beer, eat dogs, and watch baseball instead of leaving every half inning to pick up a scotch and soda.

FACILITIES: GRADE D−

In 1910, when Comiskey opened its doors, where to park a car wasn't a major consideration. Neither was the quality of the town about the place. Today both are problems.

Getting to the ballpark, fringing Chicago's seedy South Side, can be a little harrowing, at least for the imagination. The train is worn and the scenery out the window is worse. The El ride is safe though—much safer than it looks. It's not nearly as iffy as a trip anywhere through New York City. Neither is it the frolicking ride north to Wrigley. It just gets the job done, and if you don't mind being stuffed inside a sardine can, it is kind of exciting. At prime time, within an hour of the game, baseball people saturate it. Baseball talk swarms it. Even so, it's not a recommended family transportation vehicle, particularly at night. The ballpark crowd isn't the problem. On the contrary, White Sox fans, while some of baseball's rowdiest, are good people. But Chicago subways don't require character references, and as a result, as in any other city of millions, it's not always a classy clientele that frequents them. Staying for a couple too many at McCuddy's Tavern after the game can make the trip home a little unnerving.

Parking can also be a pain. Puny overpriced lots next door to the ballpark are crammed full every game. But at least both fan and car are safe. Street parking can be had if you're not too picky about where you leave the car or what you plan on coming back to. Even so, it's better than in Detroit.

Inside, some of the facilities look like they haven't been touched since their original installation. Most work. And being so old, they add to the stadium's character. They are, however, way out of date. Drinking fountains look as though they need to be pumped, and some of the rest rooms are the size of a good high-priced West Coast closet. Throughout the game, lines extend back into the carnival's midway. Fans wait out the overused, nonaccessible rest rooms. This might make for an unpleasant situation if anybody cared. But hanging around in line is almost as much fun as sitting up in the stands.

ATMOSPHERE: GRADE A+

It's still there. That crazy spirit that thrived during the Veeck years, and played along with the "Harry and Jimmy" show, is alive and well. Like an enchanted castle, Comiskey infects those who pass through. It makes them a little crazier, a little looser, a little more fun-loving. It touches its visitors with a light heart and offers the kind of magic that only 75 years of good hard living can create.

The very heart of the ballpark, where it's at its weirdest, is down under the stands. Taking a stroll through is the only way to really taste its flavor. The mixture of people, strange places and things, resembles a drive-in flea market taking place at the same time with a world ethnic food festival. Nothing can be expected; except the unexpected. Aisleways of all different sizes, some no wider than four fat people walking abreast, force folks to cram together. The ceiling is low. It makes the crowds seem more squashed. And directions are all screwed up. Shoulder to shoulder, like little toy soldiers marching off to battle, people plod about. Pickpockets must have a field day. Passing by foods-of-the-world, and looking for the dude in the straw hat with the milk-bottle game, for three and a half innings I just wandered about, mentally sifting through it all. Some of the stuff I came across was neat, some too tacky to sell at a Saturday-afternoon garage sale. With each discovery, though, I found out why I love the old park so.

Out under the left-field stands, where the cracked concrete floor gives way to rolling asphalt, is the stadium's strangest corner—an inside picnic area. Only Comiskey could have such a place. Junk clutters it, just like everywhere else. Paper cups, All-Star ballots from God knows what year lie ground into the floor. Two ceramic, waist-high Greek-boy fountains welcome in passersby. Each carries an urn that fountain water trickles down. Each stands quietly in his own separate pool of dirty water. Quarters, nickels, but mostly pennies dot the floor of the pools...White Sox wishes for a winning season. Plastic green things, shrubs, and crushed rocks landscape it. The boys look over long wooden picnic tables, more than a dozen of them in rows, each with their ends pressed up against the lower left-field wall. Instead of brick the wall is open, filled with flimsy wire fencing. Anybody who wants to can wander out to the tables, sit there, gulp beer, eat dogs, and razz the left fielder. Yaz must've loved it! At any other park the setup would be hilarious. The Greek boys alone would probably give Dodger Stadium officials the hives. In Comiskey, though, they fit.

After finishing my midway stroll, I headed up and into the stands for the sideshow—White Sox baseball. Craziness isn't only underneath. I found it alive and loud above as well. To say Chisox fans are loud is an understatement. It doesn't take into account all the ways they get that way. And there are many! Nancy lights 'em up. Her sense of humor for choosing just the right music at just the right time controls a lot of the clapping. Yet fans also have minds of their own. They must; all the times I've gone, I've never seen the wave. If they tire of clapping, folks pound their old wooden seats up and down. When they get going real good the place feels like it's gonna collapse; someday it probably will. The scoreboard also gets in on the act. On homers the whirligigs still whirl, the fireworks still explode. The rest of the time, following Nancy's melodies, Diamond Vision works the place into a frenzy. The result is a crazy place, where cheering for almost anything is allowed.

Not only is the ballpark still wonderfully strange, but as our world by staying the same becomes more predictable, Comiskey actually grows stranger. Some may call it senility; I'd like to think of it as sincerity. It wasn't until the ninth that I was totally sure. Not until the Diamond Vision's rolling welcome wagon announced all the visitors was I convinced that none of the craziness had been lost. Like all normal ballparks, Comiskey recognized the various groups on hand. Everybody from the Moose Lodge to the Girl Scouts got a big White Sox welcome. I sat and watched. Name after alphabetized name rolled through. After the X's, Y's, and Z's it paused and, as quietly as with the rest, with no special explanation, gave a White Sox welcome to all "Snakes and Snakettes."

At first the message startled me; it didn't make sense. But after I thought about the place, I figured it out...and chuckled.

The message was pure Comiskey—the fact that they said it, and the fact that it's true. The "Snakes and Snakettes" are what make Comiskey so much more than just another baseball park. They're the different cultures roaming the flea market under the stands, the picnickers behind the fenced-in left field munching down under the watchful eye of the Greek-boy fountains, the crazies that stay to the very end to sing their songs with Nancy, the old decaying ballpark itself—these are the different faces of Comiskey. They were there years ago when the flamboyant Veeck held the reins, and they are still there today. It's these "Snakes and Snakettes" that make the ballpark so unique from all others—past, present, or future—in this world or any other.

15

RIVERFRONT STADIUM, CINCINNATI REDS

Shhh...Library Baseball

REPORT CARD	*Riverfront Stadium*
	BASEBALL PARK
July 20, 85 vs *Phillies*	*Cincinnati Reds*
GAME	BASEBALL CLUB

CATEGORY	GRADE	POINTS
Layout and Upkeep	*A*	*95*
Ball Field	*D*	*65*
Seating	*C*	*75*
Scoreboard	*D-*	*60*
Food	*B*	*85*
Ballpark Employees	*C*	*75*
Facilities	*A+*	*100*
Atmosphere	*D*	*65*
Total Points		*620*
Average		*78*

C+

FINAL GRADE

16th

RANK

"Even with the tradition of the 'Big Red Machine,' 35,000 people on Farmers Night, and Rose chasing Cobb... a peanut cracking in the center-field bleachers echoes through a strangely silent stadium."

PREGAME THOUGHTS

The "Big Red Machine"... what a powerhouse! To any normal red-blooded American League-loving kid—a nightmare. A dreaded technological horror!

Teen years are an impressionable time for a growing kid. It's important that they go well if you want to end up normal. A disastrous junior high or high school experience can change a kid for life. Junior high can do the same to an adult... if he's a teacher. A sound outlet is needed to make it through. For girls the release is boys. For boys it's sports. For me it was more specific. It was baseball.

For most, baseball's reliable enough to make even puberty a livable event. But my most crucial years were kinda screwed up. The reason: that "Big Red Machine." Through Little League I lived for the Tigers; after that it was the Sox. But since birth I've never swayed from the AL. In fact, it still takes till October each year before I realize there's another league. The seventies obviously was not my best decade. Detroit or Boston, or anybody else, it didn't matter who I pulled for, whichever AL team stumbled into the Series it seemed like the Reds were waiting there to bash their brains in. Crew-cut All-American heroes, dressed in stubby red stockings, they spent the seventies feasting on my American League.

Unfortunately, it wasn't just Series time that I saw them. Television, radio, newspapers, magazines, Cincy was everywhere. Every Saturday it seemed, *Game of the Week* was beamed live from Riverfront. The few times it wasn't they had inning-by-inning updates and postgame follow-ups. I couldn't turn the dial without finding another interview with some Red. TV wasn't their only invasion. For three years I skimped on high school lunches just to scrape together enough cash for *Sports Illustrated*. Brown-bagging it, no milk, and pocketing the dollar-a-day allowed a subscription. But what the hell for? Each issue I had to stare at Johnny Bench smiling on the cover or read about Sparky babbling on about nothing.

It's tough to say who of the Big Red Crew bothered me the most. All of 'em were fair game. Joe Morgan, he wasn't a second baseman, he was an NFL fullback. About as dainty as Dick Butkus, every time he flapped that elbow against his stumpy body I'd cringe. Then there was Bench. Catchers weren't supposed to be cute, just ugly, dumb, and dirty. That's why they wore masks. Girls who knew nothing about baseball were supposed to fall in love with shortstops, pitchers, or center fielders like me, not catchers. But they loved Johnny. He was everybody's honey. Even Mom's. Pete Rose, though, was my ultimate villain. "Charley Hustle" was pure ruthless. I never could forgive him for destroying Ray Fosse's career. An All-Star game, a game nobody cared about, nobody but Rose. And he buried Fosse... just to score a run. The Reds were the Dallas Cowboys of major league baseball. Their big red C as nauseating to look at as that blue Dallas star. For anybody who knew zero about the game, the "Big Red Machine" was T-shirt material.

I think it was the seventh game of the '75 series when my frustrations reached their boiling-most point. For that was finally time for the Reds to meet their maker. Fisk had coaxed his fly ball fair into Fenway's net for a reason. God was sick of Cincinnati too. No way would He have let Game Six go to Boston if He wasn't gonna help dethrone the "Machine" in Seven. I tuned in to watch. At least 112 $1.00 bets rode on a Sox victory. But it wasn't to be. Once again Boston stumbled. The boys in red battered 'em about the ring, then floored 'em with a couple of Tony Perez punches. Just another Bosox almost, just another Reds World Championship.

Well, I was on my way to Riverfront—the lair of the "Machine." The graveyard of my AL hopes. I felt like General Custer's great-grandkid heading out to the Little Big Horn. I wondered if I'd find a Red Sox tombstone.

But I approached Cincinnati with a different attitude. Times have changed since October of '75. A decade has slipped by. No longer your typical teenager— an unlicensed critic of anything conventional—I look at life a little more conservatively nowadays. Those traditional things that I once despised because it was "cool" to be anti-traditional, now appeal to me. Or at least don't give me stomach aches. Things like short hair, "Big Red Machines," and even school-teachers seem "cooler" than they used to be.

Baseball-wise, things are getting drastic; social security's right around the corner. Those old traditional unis, the ones I used to despise, the ones that fit like gunny sacks and featured three-inch stubby stockings—you know the kind the Reds used to wear—are now my favorites.

The ball players who used to wear 'em I've re-evaluated too. If the old "Machine" peaked today, I'd probably tune in to watch. Joe Morgan was not only a great player, but a great man. That flapping elbow, just pure intensity. Johnny Bench was probably the best catcher I've ever seen. Even if he wasn't ugly. And Charley Hustle, my most hated enemy, is now one of my all-time favorites. As hard-nosed as when he smashed into Fosse at the plate, he played the game the only way it was ever meant to be played...full speed. If Fosse were blocking that same plate today, in the same game, with nothing on the line again, he'd still smash into him. Even if it meant breaking them both in two.

In a day when prima donnas write more clauses than periods into their contracts, in a time when money and looks have replaced character as the prime personal reference, Rose is a shining example of what's still right with baseball. Rose played because he loved the game; he has a real passion for it. An intensity that with or without the big bucks would still be there. So do I. So do a lot of us. And some of us who do used to despise the Reds, just because, I guess, it was the "cool" thing to do.

LAYOUT AND UPKEEP: GRADE A

Cincinnati is a charming Midwestern city. Quiet and clean, packed in alongside the Ohio River, it's a model of American efficiency. For all towns not already obsessed with too much crime, too much pollution, and too many people, it should be a goal to shoot for. A kind of All-American city. A place where the Beaver must have gone when he grew up and moved away from home—if he ever did.

If ever a ballpark was matched to a place, Riverfront is to Cincinnati. Just a covered walkway bridge from downtown, it sits cozily between the river to the south and the rolling city skyline across the expressway. A perfect facility for such a pleasant place...the stadium belongs.

Organization is Riverfront's specialty. Every stadium thing seems to have its own tidy little purpose. A well-planned parking structure stands next to and underneath the stadium; cars always have a close, safe parking spot. Elevators usher fans from there up onto giant concrete plazas that surround the stadium quickly and efficiently. The plazas are dotted with tall, thin light poles and tiny ticket houses. Both are perfectly spaced out, and ticket lines probably never even clutter. Every slab of concrete gets just the right amount of light. And talk about tidy—not so much as a stray paper cup blows about the place. Inside or out. Riverfront is pretty close to perfect. It looks like something that might house a "Big Red Machine."

Still, the park's most delightful feature is its setting. Before going in you can linger on the concrete ramps outside and just relax. Down below, old-fashioned riverboats slowly plod back and forth on the big river. Their horns softly cut the still air. Lights twinkle off the nearby Kentucky-bound suspension bridge. The scene is peaceful. Across the expressway in the other direction, Cincy explodes. Skyscrapers dominate the scene. Not as intimidating as those in New York or Chicago, the buildings are so close to the park, they seem almost as big. Their bright lights hover over the stadium and ignite the place.

Quiet river below, big-city excitement across the way, and the "Big Red Machine" at Riverfront in between—it's strange to figure how baseball in Cincinnati could be anything but wonderful.

BALL FIELD: GRADE D

It isn't long before Riverfront's perfect little pleasantness is ruptured. Once inside, a place that cries for natural turf reveals instead one made of plastic. Not only is the ball field fake, it hints that footballs bounce about the place as well. Faded etchings of the Bengals sneak through to the surface. Although not as gruesome as in Houston, the effect is still depressing. And as always when the two sports meet on the same field, football gets the better of the deal.

You'd think a legacy like the Reds would've rolled on grass. That the machine would've munched on all those AL and NL pretenders on dirt. That's what champions are made of—dirt and sweat and blood. Old battered Crosley Field seems more in tune with the "Big Red Machine," not a plastic palace. But I guess if Crosley had been Johnny's home field, he'd have grass-stained his pants. And grass stains just are not that cute.

SEATING: GRADE C

What else to overlook a pure plastic field but pure plastic seats. Like most of the other modern concrete bowls, Riverfront's chairs are fold-up and plastic all the way around. The layout is predictable. You could stumble about the place blindfolded without so much as bumping into a roving peanut vendor.

In the late sixties and early seventies the same stadium floor plan must've been moving around the States. Pittsburgh, Atlanta, Philly, St. Louis, and Cincy all got ahold of it—they're all pretty much the same. In the Riverfront version three levels stretch around the enclosed space. A fourth, the field seats, fills in some of the foul territory down in front. The idea must've been to cram in as many folks for as much money, for as many sports as was humanly possible. Also, they probably figured to pull in a lot of extra bucks on concessions. The top tier is huge. On nights when the place is packed, most people sit in it. Somewhere in the upper stratosphere, much too far away to see a baseball game, fans turn instead to things like eating hot dogs and drinking beer.

While distance from the action is a problem, seat quality is not. Durable plastic chairs are kind to the rear. Legs have a chance to straighten out. Aisles are wide and plentiful, both between rows of chairs and sections of seats. Like most of the newer models, almost everything's added to make a day at the ole ballyard a pleasant one. All that's missing are some of those coin-operated telescopes. That way you might be able to tell which team was up to bat.

SCOREBOARD: GRADE D−

The scoreboard just doesn't fit. A Goodyear Blimp view from the action, its only saving grace is that it's actually too far away to read.

Drowned in a sea of advertisements, two tiny screens hang side by side from the center-field roof. Each, a simple electronic panel, is about half as big as it should be. And neither offers even a crummy instant replay. If they did, it wouldn't matter much. From that distance struggling to watch even a Diamond Vision screen would be like trying to make out a nine-inch portable TV from across the room of a crowded, smoke-filled bar. Not worth the eye-strain.

Besides out of sight, the show is pretty much out of mind. There's really no rhyme or reason to what goes up. And even less to what stays. Sometimes it'll leave worthless messages up for an entire inning. Sometimes almost an entire night. Cap night two months down the road seemed to be a ballpark obsession. At least three times for fifteen minutes straight it saturated one of the panels. Meanwhile, the important stuff—scores, stats, ERA's, and batting averages—was given the brush-off.

Not to be outdone, the musical portion of the program is just about as bad. Organ music reminiscent of a wake creeps boringly through the inner-inning breaks. Then during the game it is virtually turned off. Sometimes the two work together; the result nearly brings on sleep. Bad clichés, weak charges, and everything's mistimed. Such a cheap presentation for a well-planned stadium is almost criminal. It's like Earl Scheib spraying his famous $39.95 wash-away paint job on a vintage '57 Cadillac.

FOOD: GRADE B

Selection: Good   Accessibility: Very Good
Taste: Fair   Cost: 3rd

The beer is cold! So cold it almost hurts to drink it.

After sampling tap-water-temperature brew at so many ballparks, it's nice to know that at least in Cincinnati you don't have to go to the tavern after the game to get "colder than ice-cold" beer. Besides the majors' coldest, Riverfront offers the most on tap. Seven different kinds flow all night long. And at 32 ounces, barrel-size cups are per ounce the least expensive in baseball. All of it makes drinking one of Riverfront's finest pastimes.

Not only beer, but most every other edible or drinkable item is also affordable. Hot dogs are the cheapest in the States. Although not the world's tastiest, if nothing else they give you an inexpensive reason to pick up another draft. Hamburgers, cheeseburgers, and bratwurst, and a few other extras, while meager in comparison to the 12-course meals up at Comiskey or "sausage world" in Milwaukee, are good enough. Which is just fine. You see, they don't have to be great. The suds assortment pizzazzs everything else on the menu. That ice-cold brew makes the peanuts taste that much more peanuty and the hot dogs more hot doggety... even if they're really not.

BALLPARK EMPLOYEES: GRADE C

Reds fans are quiet and unassuming. So are ballpark attendants. Silent vendors roam the stands. Pleasant, almost shy concessionaires work the booths. Ushers stand in the shadows ready to help out, but only if called upon.

Vendors running beer, soda, and dogs throughout the aisles to hungry fans are most efficient when they move their mouths as well as their legs. In order to buy a hot dog you've gotta first hear "Hey, hot dog." To think of gulping a beer it helps to be reminded with "How 'bout a Bud?" Just silently strolling about with a loaded case isn't enough, even if it's in a packed house. Nobody's told that to the Cincinnatians. Beer and hot-dog vendors acted like junior was in the next room sleeping. Some, I swear, were even tiptoeing.

As for security... fans are so polite, the ballpark would be better off hiring officials to provoke the crowd rather than calm them. Consequently, the place isn't stocked with ushers or cops. At a less friendly place the situation could be disastrous. Unchecked by ushers, fights might break out. People would yell obscenities. Seats might even be stolen. Not in Cincinnati. The honor system would probably work. Everybody sits in his or her assigned seat and minds his or her own business. Why would anyone do differently? Not sitting in the seat you paid for would be wrong; besides it wouldn't be a very nice thing to do. At Cincinnati fans are nice, and so are the employees.

FACILITIES: GRADE A+

Cleanliness, efficiency, and organization were three of the "Machine's" finest qualities. Each season they just neatly took apart the majors. All without getting dirty. Cleanliness, efficiency, and organization are also three of their lair's finest qualities. With these kinds of pluses it only stands to reason that stadium facilities would be top-of-the-line.

Inside, Riverfront is not your typical city stadium. For one thing it's clean—even the bathrooms. Big in comparison to normal, tiny, city standards, bathrooms feature real glass mirrors and regularly restocked paper towels. Tidied up throughout the game, they provide a few more comfortable plastic seats in a ballpark filled with them.

Outside, however, the stadium's at its best. Easy to get to either on foot or by car, the place is about as accessible as they come. A covered walkway stretches from the city out over the highway to the stadium front doors. Walking from downtown is quick and easy. And also kind of neat. By car the trip isn't much more difficult. An ingeniously planned concrete parking garage piles in the cars. And the stadium sits on top. Ground-level lots also add to the almost perfect parking situation. All are well lit, well organized, and clean. Secured well enough in a city that doesn't seem to have too many security-related problems, the setup is great.

ATMOSPHERE: GRADE D

Talk about a transition. Comiskey bubbled with excitement. A full-housed Riverfront was almost soundless. Kind of like being sent from a ninth-grade gym-class-floor hockey tournament to the principal's office...to get a hack. And just about as exciting.

For my Cincinnati visit I coaxed my brother, Drew, along—at such a hard-core NL place, I needed a fellow Bosox backer to relate to. On the five-hour drive from Chicago we could only guess at how wild Riverfront was gonna be. Just the fact that Rose was closing in on Cobb and the legacy of that "Big Red Machine" we figured would set the place on fire. It'd be a ballpark in the tradition of those teams of the seventies. Everything Pete Rose style. Fans would come in family units. Mothers and fathers, each on their first marriage, and their 2.3 kids would all drive up in red station wagons. They'd all wear Cincy ball caps, red shirts, and wave pennants. Together they'd scream loud enough to wake those dead Red Sox Series hopes. Baseball "Big Red Machine style" could be nothing else. I shuddered to think of it.

Yet instead of a let-it-all-hang-out kind of spirit, we found a place that only a librarian could appreciate. Packed in 35,000 strong for "Farmers Night," Reds fans and their lovely little river park bothered nobody, not even the visiting team. Instead of screaming, folks whispered. Instead of cursing, they were polite. Sitting where they were supposed to and acting like human beings, their attitude, while commendable at the public library, was weird for a baseball game.

Now I've never been one to question silence. Each year, come class-change time, word around school is "You don't want Mr. Wood. Shit, you can't even breathe in his class." But at a ballpark it just doesn't feel right. Baseball's at its best immersed in cheering. Drew and I found out how strange it can get without it.

On the way to our seats we sampled some of that crispy-cold Riverfront beer. In those barrel-size cups, at cheaper-than-store-bought prices, by the third inning we were ready for another. But the shy Riverfront vendors were in hiding. So we flipped to see who'd buy. I lost and left. Out the walkway down a section or two, I picked up a couple of quarts and headed back. Problem was, in all the silence I'd forgotten where we were. Our tickets, I knew, had nothing to do with our seats. They were five miles from the field, and we were sitting only half that far away. The Reds were up, the place eerily quiet. It sounded like my classroom does on test day. I yelled for Drew. People turned and stared. I actually felt embarrassed. I half expected someone to put his finger to his lips and "Shhh..." me.

A couple of sections down, some 20 yards closer to home plate, Drew heard me. He stood up and waved his arms. People turned and stared. I looked for a hand to reach up and tug at his sleeve, asking him to sit. I wandered over with the beer. Quietly I sat and sipped. So did Drew. I looked at him, puzzled at what had happened. To find one among thousands wasn't supposed to be so simple. Particularly in the lair of a "Big Red Machine." Drew just shrugged his shoulders, put his finger to his lips, and told me, "Shhh..."

The rest of the night, so as not to get tossed out, we were more polite. We cheered only if everybody else did. We talked only if the subject was real important. We behaved as natives.

Yet, as quiet as the evening was, for a brief fleeting moment, in the bottom of the seventh, it wasn't. From out of eerie silence IT appeared. The wave, that disease that pro football has purposely infected baseball with so as to bring the sport down to its own level engulfed Riverfront. Only in the Chicago parks, both North and South, had I not seen it. Everywhere else to the west somebody had tried to start one. In each stadium somebody had stood up, yelled, and thrust his arms into the air. He hoped, I guess, that the fella next to him would do the same. Together they'd begin a perpetual circle that would run all the way around the stadium and back to its origin—just so it could be done again. The whole process makes you seriously question the intellectual development of the human race. Well, Cincinnati was no different, normal humans with normal brain capacity. Even in a park where people stood only to excuse themselves for belching, the wave rolled.

The Reds had pieced together a skimpy seventh-inning rally. A couple on and a couple out caught the attention of the quiet masses. People who'd whispered throughout the game almost instantaneously transformed themselves into wavers. Producing a scene that brought to mind *Invasion of the Body Snatchers*, clones burst forth from their silent pea pods to rise, thrust their arms skyward, and yell. Nine or ten times around and around Riverfront, in tidal proportions, the wave rolled. Dumbfounded, Drew and I just sat there, probably the only two in the stadium too confused to stand.

For almost seven solid minutes the place was drowned by rising bodies and voices. When a poor Reds rookie, as mesmerized as we were by the turbulent background, K'd for the last out, it stopped. Nobody groaned. No boos were to be heard. The wavers just silently sat down. I looked at Drew and started to speak. He just raised his finger to his lips and answered, "Shhh...."

Riverfront lulled back to sleep, quieter than the plodding riverboats paddling their way slowly down the Ohio.

16

TIGER STADIUM, *DETROIT TIGERS*

Some Things Never Change

REPORT CARD		
	Tiger Stadium	
	BASEBALL PARK	
July 21, 85 vs Rangers	**Detroit Tigers**	
GAME	BASEBALL CLUB	

CATEGORY	GRADE	POINTS
Layout and Upkeep	B	85
Ball Field	A	95
Seating	D	65
Scoreboard	C	75
Food	B	85
Ballpark Employees	A	95
Facilities	D-	60
Atmosphere	A+	100
Total Points		660
Average		83

B

FINAL GRADE

10th

RANK

"In 1984, 16 years later and another Series win; riots, drunken fans, and burning cars capture headlines. . . . But in its heart the old park is as sincere today as it was in '68 when Kaline roamed in right."

PREGAME THOUGHTS

What's happened in Detroit? Burning cars and rioting fans! Where has baseball's innocence of the sixties gone?

Back in the sixties, race riots turned the Motor City into the Mortar City. A summertime messiah—baseball—offered sanity to a people who seemed to have none. No matter what front-page horror story rocked Tiger town, the Tigers packed 'em in. Even in the throes of civil war, Michiganders, particularly those in Detroit, found a common friend in the boys in the Olde English D's. They were one thing true and tender in an otherwise hard, cold, and often dangerous place.

But now things were different. Race wars were over, or at least simmering on the back burner. Cops didn't live in a continual war zone, just an intermittent one. Fire engines weren't flying round-the-clock to every low-income housing project. World news reports didn't show burning city buildings with shot-out windows anymore. Now TV captured another grim side of Detroit news—one just as painful to watch.

The year 1984 found Detroit once again out of control. Only this time the cause was a happy event—a baseball World Championship. A celebration turned sour, the Tiger Series victory revived evil memories. Dinnertime news reports began with it. Late-night sports shows featured it. TV brought the sixties back to life. Drunken fans roamed city streets lusting for trouble. In their wake they left burning cars, beat-up bodies, and smashed windows. Once again Tiger town was going up in flames. And as Dan Rather tried to explain, the whole world looked on.

Not quite the same as when I was a kid. Back then, Detroit was wonderful. Each summer, for one Saturday afternoon, almost the whole of Milwood Little League would journey from Kazoo over to the Tiger den. It was a festive event. Squads of station wagons stuffed with eight kids apiece would meet up at the ball diamonds. Lunches packed, loaded with enough baseball cards for all-day trades, and money from Mom for at least five ballpark dogs, we had enough crud with us to stay a week. Decked out too . . . each of us wore our team jersey and ball cap; the parking lot splashed with color. We were about as wired as 11-year-olds could get. And why not? It was the biggest day of our lives.

After the grown-ups talked for what seemed hours, and everyone was accounted for, the station-wagon caravan would take off. Some coaches were cool—they buried the speed limit. Others, like mine, always seemed to plod. Regardless, about an hour or so from departure, just outside of Jackson, we'd all stop at the same rest area. There the tuna fish that had been stinking up the back seat, the chips we'd been nibbling on all the way, and the soggy pickle, along with the leaking pickle juice, were devoured. Ball gloves came out. And an I-94 rest area, halfway between Detroit and Kalamazoo, was flooded with hundreds of games of three- and four-way over-the-tree catch. After enough of the coaches' cars had been hit, we were gone—back on the road to Tiger town.

The rest of the way all we talked about was how hacked up the city was gonna be. And we knew it would be. All our moms had issued pretty much the same warnings: "Unless you're with the coach, don't leave the car for any reason." We got the message: Detroit was filled with weirdos.

When we finally hit town all the back-seat playing around stopped. Our noses pressed to the windows, and with dry throats and wide eyes, we sat silently, gazing outside at another world. I'd heard about the riots. And seen pictures on the *Detroit Free Press* front page. But it was another thing to witness the real thing. Driving down battered streets, me and my Kalamazoo buddies just sat in a state of semi-shock. Broken, burned down, remains of buildings sat next door to boarded-up places. Glass splattered the sidewalks. Windows were gone, in pieces below, shattered, we were all sure, by .44 Magnums. Little sidewalk shops were enclosed with iron gates. That was to keep out criminals who combed the streets. For 20 minutes a car that had for three hours bulged with 11-year-old noise fell dead quiet. We just sat while our imaginations raced. . . . That is until we saw the stadium. Then it was instantly all forgotten.

To first glance at Tiger Stadium was one of my all-time favorite thrills. The place glowed. Especially on the heels of our ghetto cruise. Perched up over the highway, its light standards thrust high above like castle towers, it was a palace amid the rubble of the city.

While we were "Wowing" out the window at the stadium, coach'd search out a parking place. Usually it was some old black fellow's front lawn. Front dirt seemed like a better description. Grass never grew on 'em, just rusting cars for three hours at a shot. I was amazed at how many could be stuffed into it. And always wondered how somebody who made so much money parking cars could be so poor. It was just a passing thought though. The car, and what was left of it when we got back, was coach's problem. I was concerned with other, more important matters.

Wired for baseball, we broke in a pack for the stadium. From every direction folks jammed toward the gates. Sights and sounds were a jumble. Honking cars, folks yelling, cops blowing their whistles to let us cross the busy streets. Each year I'd swear I'd never seen so many folks in a single place. Especially so many wearing something with an Olde English D on it. Once in a while we'd see guys from another team, but coach would stop us from doing much more than yelling their way. He kept a pretty good lasso on us. Usually none of us disappeared, which for a four-and-a-half-foot-tall kid, stumbling about in a daze in a strange place, would've seemed the norm. I'm sure Mom appreciated it.

At the gates Tiger Stadium turned its charm on full-force. Old silver-haired salesmen called out, "Scorecard, get your scorecard." Hot-dog smells whooshed through the aisleways. My mouth watered just taking a whiff of the place. Coach'd hand us our tickets. I'd give mine to the gate man, push through the turnstile, and be in. The stub I'd tuck away in a safe place to save forever. About then my stomach would be swarming with butterflies. As excited as rushing downstairs to greet that flood of presents under the Christmas tree, pushing through the Tiger turnstile was my summertime Christmas Eve.

No other ballpark was better. Partially because it was a beaut. Partially because it was all mine. Whichever, everything about Tiger Stadium was the best. The hot dogs were the tastiest, and so was the giant-size Coca-Cola. Peanuts, popcorn, caramel corn all were fantastic. Souvenirs were baseball's neatest. And always inscribed with that Olde English D. The rich green grass and bright blue Detroit sky, even the rickety wooden chairs, were special. Everybody and everything about Tiger Stadium was wonderful.

And the Tigers...they were gods. Usually we all parked out in lower left field. The sunshine'd sneak into the front rows, while back under the overhang shadows cooled. It seemed we always sat right where the two came together. Kids by the thousands, from all over Michigan, all in uniform, all cheering for anything, swarmed the place. In front of us was Willie "the Wonder" Horton, a home-run hero for every kid who followed the Tigers. For three hours those left-field seats rocked to "Willie-Willie-Willie." Once in a while he'd turn and wink, and we'd just go crazy.

Besides Willie there were others just as great. All of 'em were clean cut, all of 'em were superstars. At least to us, who knew their life history, they were. Al Kaline, Mickey Stanley, Jim Northrup, the Tigers really were a team to look up to. And for that one day a summer I got to worship 'em in person...my transistor radio tuned to Ray Lane and Ernie Harwell. Scoring it, like I did almost all the other games back in Kazoo, was more exciting at the ballpark. I had a real Tiger scorebook instead of just notebook paper. And an official orange foot-long souvenir Tiger pencil to write with. Best of all, the ball game was alive in front of me. The world's greatest food, the world's greatest team, in baseball's neatest park, and me sitting there with my Little League buddies. That's why Tiger Stadium, as Tony the Tiger would always say, was... "Gggrreat!"

Time changes things though... both little boys and ball players. Athletes become real people with real faults. And little boys grow up to read past stats on baseball cards. The new '84 World Champion Tigers, although they put on the same uni as my old guys, were different. Gone were Al Kaline and Mickey Stanley, guys who I knew played just because they loved the game. Instead the new breed of Tiger was bold and brash. Typified by stars like Kirk Gibson and Jack Morris, cockiness rather than loyalty dominated the '84 team. Instead of a wink to the crowd, Gibson would offer a finger. And Morris devoted the whole summer to blaming teammates for his mistakes. Willie never ripped the guys. Or did he? I wasn't sure if it was me growing up and watching reality unfold or if I was just witnessing a different breed of athletes where real heroes are few and far between.

One thing was certain—Detroit fans were sure different. All around Tiger Stadium, Detroit had crumbled through the sixties. Somehow, though, the ballpark and the folks who filled it hadn't. Like a rock, they endured. And as a result, helped Detroit to.

But things had changed. It wasn't race riots that reached Seattle's six o'clock news. It was that drunken, destructive World Championship celebration. It hurt to see Detroit in such pain. For all its problems, the city always had been a true-blue sports town. Folks were loyal. Good or bad seasons, they showed up and backed the Tigers. I'd been proud to be a Tiger fan. But now it seemed to swim in the same element that long ago I'd locked the car doors to get away from.

What of the ballpark itself? I wondered if it had crumbled along with the reputation of its fans and team. I wondered if the sanctuary had turned into a prison, if it wasn't something for kids to fear instead of worship. God, I hoped not! It'd been awhile since I'd last visited, and seemed like a lifetime since as an 11-year-old I lived for that summer trip. I prayed that I'd find the ballpark I loved so as a kid... at least a piece of the dream that I grew up with.

LAYOUT AND UPKEEP: GRADE B

Tiger Stadium is the essence of city baseball. Perched on the southwest side of downtown Detroit, it's surrounded by the same tired neighborhood that it was when I was a kid. Sidewalks and streets are still broken. Houses are as run down. And only a few have real yards. For the most part Mother Nature hides. An occasional maple tree breathes in the car-exhaust-fumed air. But its roots just add to the already cracking sidewalks. Even so, that first sight of the stadium is still as breathtaking... especially at night. Old-styled towers, topped with huge squares of lights, perch on the stadium roof. The bulbs burst with a bright fluorescent light. Early, before the game, they knife through the twilight. Later, in the black of night, they glow like a halo. They provide the grandest of invitations.

Outside its gates Tiger Stadium keeps up with the times. Sort of... you can at least guess the decade. Not by the neighborhood, which'll always be tired. Or by the shops and taverns close by. They still look about the same as they did 15 years ago. Colors don't reveal much either. Everybody's dressed in orange or dark blue. But there are ways to tell the sixties from the seventies or eighties. Michigan cars rust faster than any others on earth. Within ten years from birth, they die. Usually the ones swarming the ballpark are close to death. Orange and peeling wheel wells and rocker panels drop a clue. To figure the year all you've got to do is look at the cars, then add ten. Clothes styles change by the decade too. And the names of rock groups on the kids' T-shirts or which sex is wearing the earring also help out. While it might be tough, a time-machine drop outside on the stadium porch and you'd probably be able to come close to figuring the year.

Inside, forget it! A 1920s technology reappears. Thick steel girders, which hold the place up, grow out of the concrete and through the roof. Crowds already bottlenecked by the skinny ramps that serve the place back up even more. Chain-link fences break the levels into separate sections. They keep folks from wandering anywhere they please and aim them in the right direction. As for the walk, you just flow along with the tide. If you wanna turn around and go the other way, and it's about a half hour before game time on a sunny Sunday afternoon... good luck! It's like bucking a raging river current.

Almost everything about searching out a Tiger stadium seat is special. That first glimpse of the stadium is spectacular. Getting close enough to park, and parking, while a little scary, adds to the excitement. Swarming with all the folks outside the gates, then trudging elbow to elbow up the awkward ramps forces folks closer together. Baseball talk is everywhere. By the time I reach the right section, I'm usually bursting with anticipation. But it's that last 30 feet that thrills me most. One of my most favorite memories of Tiger Stadium is that walk out to an upper-deck seat. The stroll is baseball's grandest.

The upper deck aisleways are different from anywhere else on earth... except maybe in the movies. They remind me of those old saggy foot bridges in the Tarzan movies. The ones made of planks and rope that spanned huge gorges, that'd sway in even the slightest of jungle breezes, and to cross 'em was a 20-minute adventure.

The ones in Tiger Stadium don't extend out over gorges. And can't be hacked off with a machete. They aren't made of planks and ropes; concrete and steel are much steadier. Even so, they're nearly as exciting to walk. About 30 feet long, and only wide enough for two-at-a-time traffic, they lead from the hallways out to hidden upper-deck seats. An usher-guarded archway ends each one. White spindly iron support legs spring from their frame and fasten on the ceiling above. Attached along each side is a tough wire-mesh fence. About waist high, it keeps folks from falling overboard, but not from looking...all night long heads pop over the rail and scope the place. Voices call out for recognition, but usually lose themselves in echoes. Below, sloping gradually up as they move back from the field, are the lower-level seats. Some are 40 feet down; an empty peanut package tossed over the edge takes some flutter time to reach them. Hugging close above is the floor of the upper level. From nowhere on the aisle can you see the ball field—just people and seats and steel.

Everywhere else inside, stadium ramps and walkways are crammed with bodies. At all other places you walk on heels and are stabbed by elbows. But here, for about 30 feet in a stadium of 52,000, the stroll is solo. Leaving the cavern behind, the narrow bridge focuses on the open arch in front. The archway almost glows. Through it a Sunday afternoon reveals a bright blue sky, a weeknight game—blackness. Below, people buzz; behind, vendors bark; in front awaits baseball.

While I tingle all the way down it, it's that final stride that's most exciting. The aisle's flat most of the way, then it rises up. So at the end you step up, then look back down into the stadium. You're barraged by all kind of sights and sounds, and even smells. Crack of the batting-practice bats teams with soft organ music. In unison cheers arise and die back down. More hot dog, popcorn, and peanut smells float up from below. The greatest gift, though, is to the eyes. Colors explode. Spattering the stands, people's clothes brighten in the sunlight. If the welcome is at night, the scene is even more powerful. Bright lights above shower the green field. It glows with excitement. Standing there alone, I always feel as if the stadium is embracing me. Its spirit enters me. Walking down the aisle, it's my marriage with Tiger Stadium. Although the ceremony lasts only for a few precious moments, its memories linger for a lifetime.

BALL FIELD: GRADE A

Tiger Stadium and Comiskey, Chicago's old South Side ballpark, are a lot alike. Both have been around for years and sit in tired neighborhoods. Each oppose the new, clean, efficient multipurpose stadium standards and are neither clean nor efficient. Fat, obnoxious iron beams hold 'em both up. And at the same time get in everybody's way. Most important, though, each features a beautiful ball field. Set inside the concrete confines of a big city, both ballparks are centered by a lovely stretch of green.

Tiger Stadium is submerged in gray. Outside, cracked sidewalks and streets choke it. In the nearby neighborhoods, dirt covers broken front lawns. Through the gates and around the stadium, walkways are laid in concrete, asphalt, and steel. Other than blue sky, and a couple of ragged trees on the way in, nature abandons the place. With the stroll out onto the upper-deck porch, she reappears. All at once the splash of green is breathtaking. It reaffirms that even in Detroit, Mother Nature's in control.

Michigan summers are harsh. With hot humid weather, an occasional drenching by flooding thundershowers, green things don't always stay that way. They either turn brown or float away. You'd never know it by the Detroit turf. Aside from Baltimore's beauty, and the near-perfect sod in Anaheim, Tiger grass is probably the AL's finest. Lines stretching into the outfield are pronounced. Neat and clean, the cut reveals a tender care. A pureness radiates about the place. A pureness that allows only traditional touches to on-deck circles and coaching boxes. No ornaments are added, no fancy markings, no special additions, nothing but the greenest grass and richest earth. And wherever the two meet, the mesh is always sharp.

Like Comiskey's "Pride of the South Side," the Tiger garden is Detroit's brief fling with nature. In a city almost void of natural beauty, the ball field is a breath of fresh air. At a place where the nearby Detroit River runs thick with pollutants and city air is filled with car exhaust, it's fitting that downtown's most elegant lawn lies surrounded by six-lane streets and broken sidewalks on the corner of Michigan and Trumbull.

SEATING: GRADE D

Being the old park that it is, Tiger Stadium suffers from old-park diseases. Aisles aren't exceptionally roomy. Seats are sometimes cramped. And sight lines have to vie with all sorts of obstructions. Still the ancients offer a certain individuality that three plastic levels around cannot. Every seat, regardless of whether it's a good or bad one, is something special.

Two levels reach around the ballpark. Most lower-level seats are covered by the upper-deck overhang. The upper deck, in turn, is shadowed by the stadium roof. Since the park doesn't feature much foul ground, and both levels rise almost straight up, front-row views are great. At ground level they thrust you into the action, and make the game much more real, while upstairs, in certain places, seats actually hang out over the ball field.

Pushing back, though, is a whole different story. When the stadium went up in 1913, architects had different building ideas than they do today. Then it was sound practice to run iron roof supports through the middle of each seating section. If your chair is plopped behind one of the beams, you've got problems. Watching the game takes on a whole new meaning—baseball, hide-and-seek style. The whole night's spent leaning from left to right and back to the left again, just trying to follow the ball. Not only do supports pop up all over, but chairs back near the rear of each section have additional problems. From them anything other than a groundout or line-shot single to left takes off from the bat like it's gonna leave the park. It's funny to be sitting in the upper deck and hear the place roar on every measly pop-out to short.

Although only hundreds of views are totally destroyed by the obstructions, thousands are hindered. Buying at the gate on a crowded day can end up backfiring. And dealing with a scalper trying to unload a pair is just asking for trouble.

No posts in the bleachers, just a whole lot of distance. High above center field sit the majors' only real upper-deck benches. And while they could probably reveal some great stories if they could talk, watching baseball from 'em isn't always easy. The distance alone is a strain; the strike zone just a blur. Overhanging center field, you can only guess at what's going on directly below, and the seats are awfully uncomfortable. By game's end your butt's about had it.

Even so, they provide a special atmosphere. Crowds that live in 'em aren't just concerned with baseball, especially when it's hot out. Sometimes sunshine and beer gulping get the better part of valor. After a couple of hours of each, things can get a little crazy. I know back in college I soaked a few rays and drafts up there in the outer limits myself. Then, though, things were under control. Folks got rowdy, but never ruthless. In '84 bleacher life soured. Groups of idiots, posing as fans, spent home stands dreaming up vulgar cheers. They got enough folks following in unison to echo through the stadium...so loud that on Saturday's *Game of the Week* you could hear 'em in the background. Not only that, fights started breaking out, more often than in Fenway with the Yanks in town. Management was forced to get tough, removed the beer, and even closed 'em down a few times. With the brew gone, the language cleaned up, boxing gloves were put away and people went back to watching baseball. The beer ban remains. Too bad such a sweet flavor had to be spoiled. A sunny Sunday afternoon in Tiger Stadium bleachers without beer somehow doesn't seem truly American.

SCOREBOARD: GRADE C

A large scoreboard sits high atop the center-field bleachers. Its attitude to keeping score is basic. Its work ethic is impressive. It quietly covers everything a baseball park scoreboard should cover. In another place the setup might be considered great, but in Tiger Stadium something about it just doesn't fit.

In other ballparks the low-profile approach works fine. Wrigley and Fenway, both about the same age as the Tiger Park, have quiet scoreboards...white numerals on green rectangles pop up in a hole in the wall. At each the arrangement stands silent most of the game. If seen, it's only because it's looked for. If heard, it's only because somebody's listening for it. Rather than taking over, each just goes quietly about its business and lets baseball play center stage.

The Tiger display is simple too. All information is handled by the single electronic center-field unit and follows in the traditional mode. Updates are constant and visible. Ball-game coverage is basic. Even instant replay is low-keyed. A black-and-white matrix screen handles the chore as quietly as the rest of the stuff is covered. Only once in a while does it get carried away. Like at Fenway and Wrigley, any "charges" that come to the crowd do so for the most part without the help of the scoreboard.

Ideally the thought to stay traditional is a good one. But the Tiger screen can't pull it off. First, the traditional approach with new equipment is a strange mix. It's like computer colorizing old black-and-white movies. Plus, hanging up above center field, in the glaring sunshine, the scoreboard's a long ways away from most folks. That hominess that the other two ballparks get from their system is lost somewhere in Detroit's upper stratosphere. Finally, the replay board on a sunny day is nearly worthless. It glares so bad, it's more frustrating than enjoyable. Consequently, the whole system just sits there loaded with updated equipment used to half potential. Neither traditional nor modern, it never really finds a theme.

In almost everything else, including its floating organ music, the spirit of the park is antique. For the scoreboard to fit in, management would do best to pull the plug and let it fall back 40 years. Either that or tack up a bigger screen alongside it. Fringing each with exploding pinwheels and rocket launchers, they could copy the crazy one in Comiskey. Whichever direction would be better than the wishy-washy one they've got now.

FOOD: GRADE B

Selection: Fair   Accessibility: Very Good

Taste: Excellent   Cost: 25th

Mustard on a stick—it's the only way the stuff was meant to be spread. When I went as a kid that's the way they covered hot dogs at Tiger games. And those were the greatest ballpark dogs in the world. In fact, all the Tiger food was terrific. Today it's just as tasty. And that famous ballpark frank covered with stick-spread mustard is still in itself reason enough to enjoy a ball game in Detroit.

Not the same with beer, unfortunately. That championship season of vulgar drunken bleacherites forced management to lay down the law in '85. In an attempt to clean up its tarnished reputation, the park killed the sale of normal beer. Instead they turned to nine-ounce cups and a complete tap of low-alcohol brew. Consequently, prices rose (accounts for "Cost: 25th"), sales dropped, and in '85 fans behaved. But drinking L.A. beer out of a nine-ounce cup is like sipping warm tap water from a shot glass. The effect, especially on a hot Sunday afternoon, just isn't there.

With the craving for a ballpark beer cured, you're left with eating. In that category the old park still excels. While other places may offer more to choose from, nobody does more with what they have. Hot dogs and knockwurst are still cooked up on old black grills under the stands. Booths are out in the open; glass windows front the wieners. Rolling around on the hot slabs, they fill the hallways with tasty smells. The lingering aroma captures willing folks and holds them in line. Specialty stands pop up about the place. Italian sausages sizzle, buried under mounds of onions and green peppers. And they, too, provide almost as tasty a treat to the nose as to the tummy.

It's in the stands, though, where the stadium best struts its stuff. "Hey, hot dog" called out under a Tiger-blue summer sky is more than just a call for a mid-game snack. It's an experience that captures the essence of baseball, hot dogs, and history. A special presentation, it serves to link today with a simpler, more rewarding time.

First the "hot-dog guy" must be found. At Tiger Stadium he's a popular fella, always surrounded by hungry folks. It might take an inning or two, but he'll make it around. After that it's up to you to get his attention. Piece of cake! It doesn't matter how packed the place is, or how loud everybody's screaming, even three sections away, he reads you like an auctioneer. A raised hand or a "Hey, hot dog," no matter the situation, he stops, turns, and nods. And pretty soon is on the way.

With him is a special treat. Not just some prepackaged wiener wrapped in foil, his is baseball's best. And he even carries the kitchen along with him. Strapped over his shoulder is a huge stainless-steel box. It looks like those old things that bicycle-ice-cream boys used to pedal around. Compartments with lids and other little doors cover its bulky body. On the side in bold red-and-white letters reads, "BALLPARK DOGS."

The case is heavy. For the project to begin he has to set it down in the aisle. A few fans' views are blocked, some have to walk around to get to their seats, but it doesn't matter. Most enjoy watching the creation.

"How many?" is his greeting. It takes the place of "Hello."

When the total is settled on, work begins. First, he reaches for one of the lids. As it opens steam rushes out, revealing the still "hot" dogs within. Tongs, sitting in another of the doorless compartments, exist for just such an occasion. With them he reaches through the steam and clamps onto a dog. Out come the tongs, and he transfers wiener to bun... not just any wiener to any bun. At Tiger Stadium each is only the best. Hygrades Beef Franks, the kind that "plumped when you cooked 'em," were the choice when I was a kid. They're still the choice today. And they still plump. And the bun is carried fresh in its 12-pack plastic packaging. Always soft and never soggy.

With the perfect match complete, he issues his only request: "Mustard?" To which, whether you like the stuff or not, you have to answer "Please." If for no other reason than to watch it splashed on.

Back on the kitchen top is a bright red Coca-Cola cup filled with mustard. Stuck inside it is a flat wooden stick—like a Popsicle stick, only wider. After replacing the tongs on their proper hanger, he reaches for the yellow-covered stick. He stirs once, pulls it out, and slaps it on the still-steaming dog. Like a thick coat of varnish on an old oak table, the dog glistens. He shoves the completed project into a wax paper sleeve. And for only a buck and a quarter, passes it down the line.

No better hot dog exists. With it, a Coke in hand, a ball game in front, and blue skies overhead, nothing beats being a kid at Tiger Stadium... whatever your age.

BALLPARK EMPLOYEES: GRADE A

Much of what made those good ole Tiger days so special were the folks about the place. Stately old gentlemen ran the show. They gave the place a good heart. Whether it was scorecards or hot dogs that they sold, there was a real pride among them. To wear the colors and to serve the ancient ballyard wasn't a job. It was a privilege. It showed best in their warm smiles.

Problems of the eighties—the language, the fights, and drunken bleacherites—must be tough to deal with, even for employees who weathered the sixties. With all the crap going on nowadays, it'd be easy to pull back the welcome mat. To be short-tempered and not put up with anything. For survival's sake alone, stadium workers could easily play the heavy. They could even justify acting like—heaven forbid—native New Yorkers. I expected it! I figured the good-natured gents that helped me love the '68 team so would be gone. In their place I'd find a work force as nasty as the group they were trying to control.

Not true! Good folks still work the aisles. Usually willing to help out, most will gab a little too. If time permits, and in the beer lines now it does, '68 reminiscing is even allowed. I spent one inning visiting with an old guy who was forced into living off of the sales of low-alcohol beer. Financially, he revealed, things could be a lot better. But it didn't affect his memory. We spent most of the conversation thinking back to '68. Comparing the boys of '68 with the '84 team, we decided Kaline's Tigers would've eaten 'em up. If nothing else, 'cause they had more heart.

Most other workers were friendly too. Concessionaires didn't mind answering my "what-kind-of-sausages-are-those" questions. Gate guards, if approached right, were flexible. Even though my ticket wouldn't allow for it, I was able to roam around the stadium. All it took was a "Please." And ushers are still the majors' toughest ticket checkers. In pairs, at the mouth of each narrow walkway, like always, they're almost impossible to sneak past.

Only the younger employees lack that Tiger dedication. To most of them their ballpark job is just another nine-to-fiver. They lack a binding loyalty that only time can create. Unfortunately, they'll probably never find it. Times aren't like they used to be. Jobs are temporary now. Dedication is to one's self rather than a ballpark. And satisfaction is more concerned with a wage than pride in the workplace.

Nevertheless, the old folks carry on as always. In a city where you're not always made to feel welcomed, the Tiger ballpark still rolls out its carpet with a smile.

FACILITIES: GRADE D−

If ever there should be a trial case for moving all baseball parks out to the suburbs, Tiger Stadium's parking problems will be exhibit 1A for the prosecution.

The adventure is almost frightening. As a kid not knowing what a car payment was, I used to love the search. I was amazed at some of the places coach'd pay to leave his car. It was actually fun to watch how close he could pull the new station wagon up over the curb to the front porch. Better yet was seeing it swallowed up on all four sides by other cars. It made even getting out of the car exciting. Once we parked we'd scramble out the doors. If we weren't fast enough, we might be trapped inside all afternoon. A quarter-inch clearance on each side doesn't leave a lot of room for squeezing through.

Today, not a thing has changed. With almost no stadium lots, or decent mass transit, driving and parking near Tiger Stadium is still an odyssey. Front lawns of houses, drugstore alleyways, church sidewalks all turn into three-hour parking lots. Good spots are only up and over a single curb. Others take a mastery of looking into the rearview mirror and inching along in first gear. Home-stand businessmen rent out any patch of ground that a car can squeeze into. Then, like newspapers crammed into a bundle, they pack another 15 around it.

And everybody gets in on the act. Kids with cheap orange flashlights wave signs and blow whistles. They work the early birds. A few old folks sit in lawn chairs alongside the street. Signs in their laps tell cost and direction. For them the low-keyed approach works better. No use raising the blood pressure, yelling for the early cars. After the kids' lots fill up they'll get the rest. Fans got no place else to put 'em.

Inside, rest rooms are better than when I was a kid. All the bubonic plague has been moved out. Then they were scary. Now they border on normal. Even though small and simple, they serve the stadium well enough.

ATMOSPHERE: GRADE A+

On game day the old ballpark is nearly impossible to reach. Parking outside of it has life-threatening implications, for car and for driver. And the rest rooms for the longest time weren't fit for man or beast. But at heart, the park's a classic beauty. Entering through its gates, you make a special pact with baseball. The graceful spirit of Tiger Stadium makes up for all the frustrations along the way.

I came to town confused. I knew Detroit had its problems. That it'd earned a reputation only a native could, or would even want to, defend. That crime was an accepted social event. That racial unrest will always be in the time-bomb stage. All that I could accept. Having grown up in Michigan, I knew it as part of the Detroit facts-of-life. It was the darker side I wasn't sure how to handle. The fear that baseball had been infected too. That Tiger Stadium, a sanctuary from the violence in years past, had gone the way of the ghetto. I was afraid the ballpark wouldn't be special anymore. That instead of stately old gentlemen in Tiger ball caps and anxious Little Leaguers looking for heroes, I'd find drunken rowdies everywhere. Vulgar, violent bleacherites would dominate the place and spoil what was once a very sweet flavor.

What I found instead was refreshing. In the newspapers and on television Tiger Stadium may have spoiled. But those horrors have been dealt with. I guess I should've given it a little more credit. If it could make it through the turbulent sixties, a few drunken lamebrains would be easy pickin's. While the rest of the world may see only World Series reruns, regulars know the real truth. They know that at heart the old park's as stately as it was when Kaline roamed in right.

Oh sure... it still has problems. Anything 75 years old will struggle with the 1980s. But its problems are the same ones that it suffered from, and overcame, 20 years ago. And probably 20 years before that. And although they cause inconveniences that suburban America will never have to fight, they provide Tiger Stadium with a special flavor.

Parking borders on a real-life Saturday-night horror picture show. But it drives away "fair-weather fans." Those that go do so because they love the game—at least more than they do their cars. As a result the place is still filled with good loyal people... some of baseball's most sincere. Tiger fans possess a baseball allegiance that, instead of being judged by a single night in October of '84, ought to take into account what they put on the line each time they leave their cars outside the stadium.

Inside, ancient construction still causes all sorts of headaches. Narrow, inefficient walkways turn stringy groups into cluttered bunches. Heels and toes and elbows are traded in an uncomfortable tour. But those same aisles also provide some very special moments. Even the big dumb iron posts that get in the way have a good side to 'em. They make you just a little more picky when buying a ticket. A bit more skeptical when that outside scalper tells you "Great seats, not a single obstruction." Just being choosy and finding something that's really good can make you pretty proud, and a hero on family night.

Things that were always all right still are. And not much different than 15 years ago. Folks working the place are still friendly. And as dedicated to the ballyard as they were when I was a kid. Buried in a neighborhood of concrete and car exhaust, the ball field still shines as radiantly as ever. That first look is just as breathtaking. Even the food is as tasty. The luscious aromas still float you around the place by sense of smell alone.

Contrary to popular belief, the Detroit ballpark's still a beauty. In what can be an awfully painful world, burdened with riots, crime, and untamed emotions, Tiger Stadium remains a rock. It retains simple pleasures for a simple game and makes life more livable in a tough town. In a baseball era where requests for a hot dog are answered with a wet bun, a cold dog, and a plastic packet of mustard, inside the home on the corner of Michigan and Trumbull it's a slice of history. A ballpark frank with a little mustard on the stick is a dream fulfilled. And proof that worthy experiences never die in the tradition of a fine baseball park.

17

EXHIBITION STADIUM, *TORONTO BLUE JAYS*

First and Ten...Do It Again

REPORT CARD	*Exhibition Stadium*
	BASEBALL PARK
July 23, 85 vs Mariners	*Toronto Blue Jays*
GAME	BASEBALL CLUB

CATEGORY	GRADE	POINTS
Layout and Upkeep	*C*	*75*
Ball Field	*D-*	*60*
Seating	*D-*	*60*
Scoreboard	*D-*	*60*
Food	*D-*	*60*
Ballpark Employees	*C*	*75*
Facilities	*B*	*85*
Atmosphere	*D-*	*60*
Total Points		*535*
Average		*67*

D+

FINAL GRADE

26th

RANK

219

"A plastic baseball diamond literally rolled out onto a plastic football field, presenting a hollow, artificial atmosphere. ...Only the sea gulls don't seem to mind."

PREGAME THOUGHTS

Baseball is like Charlie Brown. Steady and reassuring, for all the weird things that come around in life, it stays pretty much the same. Watching a ball game now, on a warm July night, isn't a whole lot different than it was for me 15 years ago. Ball players dress and play about the same. Strategies haven't changed a lot. And I still spend as much time tracking down the hot-dog guy as I do watching the game. No, not a lot has changed... for baseball or for Charlie Brown. Charlie's always gonna get hammered on the mound. Every smash back up the middle is gonna send him and his clothes flying. He'll always mess up with the little red-haired girl. And every spring he's gonna be strangled and left hanging upside down, bound in his own string, by that dreaded kite-eating tree.

Football, on the other hand, is brash. It's loud and boastful. Sometimes I think its equipment and rules changes dictate modern thought rather than follow it. Highlight films of Dick Butkus smashing bodies, with neither his nor theirs breaking, must've done wonders for plastic stocks in the sixties. Comparing an old-timer's uniform—no face mask, a leather helmet, and wads of tissue paper for shoulder pads—with one of today's plastic-coated warriors, the two don't even look like they're from the same planet. The sport is anything but steady and reassuring. In the world of *Peanuts*, football, especially in the pros, is Lucy.

It's not that I dislike football. As a kid I was in love with it. Pickup games at the school-yard playground were a Labor Day-to-Christmas weekend must. They did all sorts of character building. High school football continued the construction and provided me a little scrapbook "ink." How could I complain? Plus it's kept all my competitive urges under control—as a kid and even now as a creaky old coach. I am able to live at least a seminormal 8:00 to 3:00 life, 'cause from 3:00 to 5:00 I relive past glory days out at the blocking sled. As for following it, while Brent and Jimmy the Greek bring on Pepto-Bismol attacks, the college game is still magic. Crisp autumn Saturday afternoons in Spartan Stadium, the fanfare, the colors and excitement, I think Big Ten football kept me enrolled. It had and still has a special romantic lure that'll always keep me dreaming of Michigan State Rosebowl.

But football belongs in its own separate world, far away from baseball, at a place the two don't have to share. For when they're forced together in the same place, football's brashness takes over. Kind of like when Lucy charges Charlie Brown for her little psychiatric talks. She does all the talking, gets all the "ink," and is paid five cents to boot. Chuck just sits quietly, unable to do much but fork over the nickel and sigh.

Pure baseball parks aren't built anymore. Wrigley Field, Fenway Park, even Dodger Stadium, good ones "for baseball only," will someday just be museum relics. Sure, once in a while an idea so perfect that it makes you wonder what was wrong with the architect comes around. The result's a beauty like Royals Stadium. But it's a shooting star. The idea splashes for a brief shining moment. People gaze in amazement at the product, they ooh and ahh, they say "It's great... it's wonderful!" Then they think about it sitting empty half the year, and it's back to concrete and plastic, three levels around.

Instead of baseball parks the rage is multipurpose stadiums. Fiscally profitable, they're built for every kind of ball game; football, soccer ball, tennis ball, basketball, and baseball—all in the same place, and if they wanted, probably all at the same time. All they really care about is who's got a buck.

Now multipurposeville works in the NFL. Football can exist anywhere a hundred yards of flat ground rests. At home on grass, plastic, or even asphalt, the game survives on toughness. Set in standard worldwide 100-yard rectangular proportions, it really doesn't matter if the Smashers are at home or away against the Crushers. To win they must move the ball ten yards in four tries, in a straight line parallel to the sidelines, perpendicular to the goal line, until they cross it. Then they go back and try again—over the same stretch of plastic, grass, dirt, or snow. Back and forth for the course of the game, a season, a lifetime. The field that happens to be in use really makes no difference. If Walter Payton can dance, spin, and squirm his way to eight yards and six points in Miami, he can do it just as easily in Chicago. If Kenny Easley can take some poor soul's head off in the Kingdome, there's absolutely no reason why he can't be as efficient in L.A.

For fans, too, each stadium is a clone of the next. Football fans only need seats up over each of the sidelines and in opposite end zones to watch "their guys" bash "those guys'" brains in. It really doesn't matter where they are. In fact "good seats" are 50 yards up and 50 yards out from everything that counts in the scoring column. While end zones seats, if at the wrong end of the field, might as well be in a different hemisphere. For Walter down on the field, or his screaming supporters upstairs, each surface, each seat, each stadium is as good or bad as the next.

Baseball parks, on the other hand, for players and followers, vary. Every line drive, each bunt or fly ball changes depending on where it comes off the bat. As a result each and every ballpark touches the game a little differently. A shot out of the stadium in North Side Chicago might just be a long lazy fly out on the city's South Side. A foul pop in Dodger Stadium makes it into a lap in the fifth row behind first base. Popcorn, pop, and mustard-covered Dodger dogs will go flying, but it'll give the hitter one more chance to win the game. That same batter hits that same pop-up in Oakland's Coliseum and he's out with 10 feet to spare. The ball game's over.

Ball players must constantly adjust. Eric Davis, who's practiced all season long grabbing carums off of Riverfront's perfectly symmetrical wall, could find himself in a league championship searching for that same hit in a glob of Wrigley ivy. While Harold Baines, if he's gonna make it through a weekend series in Kansas City, is gonna have to head out four hours early just to figure the bounce off the wall, the plastic grass, and get used to the sound of splashing water behind him. Meanwhile, Walter and the boys can practice anywhere trees aren't in the way.

Ballparks also vary for the baseball fan. Each section of seats offers an insight into the game that no other does. Boxes behind home plate allow a glimpse into a Fernando screwgie... and give real meaning to a tabletop drop. From them a good pitchers' duel is more exciting than that 9-to-8 extra-inning hit-a-thon. From behind first base the pivot on 4-6-3 twin killing is baseball's prettiest play. While sitting next to third, the hot corner really does sizzle. It makes you wonder if Brooks Robinson might've been a god. Even the cheap seats provide some pizzazz. Bleachers, although miles from the launching pad, are the destination for baseball's touchdown equal, a home run.

Simply put, baseball craves its own identity. Pro football does not. When the two come together in the same place, football survives. Baseball struggles. It becomes just another sport. A summer renter.

Both sports show their true colors come championship time. It's in that final moment of truth that real loyalties are revealed. Where Charlie's game shows just how important a home is, Lucy's proves it doesn't even need one. Every season pro football ends up somewhere warm, convenient, and balmy, at a neutral site. Someplace where two weeks of cameras and a five-hour Super Bowl pregame show have pleasant sunshiny scenery... and folks can carry on about everything but the game. While for six months and over 162 games, baseball teams scratch, claw, and fight to determine the site of that last game of the World Series, the final circumstance that might give them the World Championship—the home-field advantage.

LAYOUT AND UPKEEP: GRADE C

No major league ballpark enjoys a prettier setting. No other stroll from car to stadium is quite as inviting. Backed up against the bright blue waters of Lake Ontario, Exhibition Stadium, home of the Jays, sits surrounded by 300 acres of a tidy green Exhibition Park. A few miles away a tight Toronto skyline says "Hi." Everything and everybody are pleasant.

Exhibition Park is delightful. Narrow streets weave throughout its well-kept grounds. Cars cruising the scene take their time. Nothing's really in much of a rush. Sidewalks bordered by tidy shops and a few refreshment stands roll up to the stadium's front gates. By game time they flow thick with fans on their way to the ball game. Open grassy areas dotted with touch football and Frisbee toss mix in more friendly sights and sounds. Everywhere is a neat, scrubbed-clean freshness.

Surrounded on three sides by the park, the stadium's fourth view is its prettiest. Only a block from its front gates, close enough on a windy day to catch a mist, splashes Lake Ontario. Between the two is a small man-made island, an island only because a wisp of the lake sneaks between it and the park. A couple of footbridges lead from the stadium across the water to it. One of them empties at the front porch of Ontario Place, a huge, glass, futuristic-looking building propped up on stilts above the water. The other bridge leads down to the island. The island's as quaint as the rest of the park. Sturdy trees and well-trimmed grass give it a pretty green tint. A marina welcomes visiting boats. Beyond is the lake. Bright yellow and red sails dot the white-capped water. Fresh breezes roll in and cool off the shadows. Folks in friendly groups of twos and threes, families posing while Dad snaps off a few shots, meander about. Sea gulls cruise the scene, search for spilt popcorn, and screech their approval.

As well kept as the rest of the grounds, the stadium fits the park. Ticket windows sit politely back in a modern glass-and-concrete facade. The plaza in front is swept and litter-free. Its only trimmings are more landscaped patches of grass and trees. Security guards mingle, securing a place that seems to have no security problems.

Despite such a pleasant setting, something about the stadium was weird. No baseball vibrations buzzed from inside. No special smells or sounds, or even sights, hinted of the Jays. People quietly funneled inside, then vanished. I didn't see or hear from them again. Outside, peanut vendors circled but were politely quiet. Even that ballpark roar that all stadiums have was missing. It felt real strange, almost like I'd come on the wrong night, that the Blue Jays were out of town. That maybe instead of baseball I was on my way to a symphony concert...a very, very quiet one.

BALL FIELD: GRADE D−

After cruising through more clean, quiet, well-kept hallways inside, I entered up a ramp into the stadium. What I saw almost floored me. I knew instantly why the place was so quiet, why there was no buzzing, no roar of the crowd. Folks that crammed both sides of the place were too embarrassed to speak. About all I could do was stand there with my mouth hanging open. In front of me was the strangest-looking baseball field I'd ever seen.

The ballpark is a football stadium. It isn't multipurpose. It's not set up to play a bunch of sports, not really even two for that matter. As football dominated as Pasadena's flamboyant Rosebowl, or stately Soldier Field, Exhibition Stadium is home for Canadian football's Argonauts. It merely dresses up a few months out of the year to give the Blue Jays something that I guess is supposed to look a little like a baseball diamond to play on.

The ball field itself is one big rollaway turf. Warning track, infield–outfield plastic, squares of dirt around the bases, even the fence looks like a single connected section. It reminded me of those old pop-up, school-kid reader books where when you opened 'em the little houses inside rose out of the pages. Each April the field rolls out. Every fall it rolls back in again. For the six months in between what you've got is a perfectly symmetrical piece of plastic ...complete with warning track, white lines, and fences.

Problem is, the ball diamond doesn't cover the whole plastic rectangle. Beginning in the west end zone, it crosses midfield and pulls up at the right-field fence, along the 35-yard line. Beyond it, football markings, hidden underneath the outfield pop-up roll, take over. They run parallel with the fence all the way to the opposite end zone, every five yards, as clear and white as if they were gonna pull out the pigskin that inning.

Propped up all alone, fake warning track and plastic outfield in front of its, acres of plastic football field behind it, no fans anywhere near it, that right-field fence is eerie-looking. All night long I stared at it. It was like looking at a gross highway pile-up—I couldn't drag my eyes away. No matter what was going on with the Jays, I kept easing back to the fence and beyond. Finally I stopped trying to resist and reserved my stare time for between innings. That way I could at least get some of the ball game in. During inner-inning warm-ups I played a little game. Sitting about even with the fence, first I'd shut my right eye and size up the field. What'd I see? An ugly but normal-looking plastic baseball field. Then I'd switch and close my left. And baseball, being played right in front of me, would disappear altogether. All that was left, in the middle of July and a 12-game Blue Jay home stand, was the CFL.

In fact, it was so CFL-ish that if they'd wanted to the Argonauts could've probably carried on a normal practice on their half of the turf at the same time the Blue Jays played a game on theirs. If the football didn't get kicked over the fence, and George Bell promised not to blast any homers over the other way, neither team would've been bothered.

SEATING: GRADE D−

Football seats in a football stadium just don't work at a baseball game. While 50-yard-line tickets might be prime time for watching the Argonauts, to a Jays fan they only serve as pathetic general admission reminders that the rollaway ball field isn't Exhibition's only problem.

The stadium is one level. Most of the seats, a section along each sideline, rise straight up and back from the football field down in front. In the outfield it's plastic chairs. Folks fill them about as far out as the 50-yard line—which is way out behind the left center-field fence. After that chairs running farther out and away from the diamond are empty...even with the Yanks in town. In addition, none of the rows start until some 50 feet behind the left-field fence. It all adds up to the majors' worst general admission seats. The only good thing about 'em is that they're one of the few places where you actually face home plate.

Across on the first-base side of the ball field, also running from end zone to end zone, stares an uncovered football bleacher section. Cold aluminum benches, they make shorts and a chilly night a fatal combo for Blue Jay backers' butts. Like the general admission seats, folks fill 'em up even with the outfield fence. After that they're empty too. Thirty-five yards of empty aluminum bleachers stare across an empty football field at 50 yards of empty general admission chairs; it really makes for a strange, strange baseball feeling. As for watching baseball from them, good luck. Home plate's nowhere to be seen. In fact, they draw a bead on the center-field fence. Sitting down and looking straight ahead, unless you have fantastic peripheral vision, the only Blue Jays in sight are Barfield in right, Moseby in center, and an occasional feathered one flying overhead.

Only down the third-base line and around behind home plate, end-zone seats at the football game, is the situation decent. There chairs have backs, and some, unbelievably, face the pitcher's mound. For a few sections at least, the view's a normal one. Everywhere else baseball lies far off in the distance. For some the only hint that it's even happening are the hundreds of Blue Jay ball caps that have to be stared through just to find it.

SCOREBOARD: GRADE D−

With a hideous ball field to look at, and horrible seats to watch from, an equally pitiful scoreboard rounds out Exhibition's big three. It's a good thing for the Jays when starting out that I promised I wasn't gonna flunk anyone. Eighth graders assigned a last-minute, spring-break, ten-page Thomas Jefferson report would've had a better chance of passing.

The scoreboard's worst asset—or considering just how bad it is, maybe its best—is that it's too far away for anybody to read it. Perched out beyond the east end zone, a football field away from home plate, over 50 yards from the right-field fence and any living human being, the thing is barely in binocular range. It's so far away that I wondered if it wasn't working another Canadian ball game, maybe one in Montreal.

Plus it's way overworked. A single screen is all right for football games. First down and ten yards to go, ball on the 45-yard line, and a fourth-quarter clock are easy to take care of. But when it comes to batting averages, lineups, pitching changes, and major league updates all on one screen, it's just too much to handle. Consequently, the thing is flip-flopping back and forth between all sorts of info all night long. Fans sit like they're watching a tennis match, swinging their heads back and forth between home plate and scoreboard, over a hundred yards apart.

Music's not much better. Aside from a delightful seventh-inning theme song, quiet tapes snooze through the night. For the most part silent fans sit by while a silent P.A. system plays an even match to the silent scoreboard that frustratingly struggles somewhere off in the distance.

FOOD: GRADE D−

Selection: Poor   Accessibility: Fair
Taste: Poor   Cost: 9th

Even the sea gulls watch what they eat! Aside from a great assortment of cold Canadian beer, over 50 percent of it Labatts Blue, at all sorts of easy-to-get-to express locations, ballpark food rivals the stuff they serve in Texas as the majors' all-around worst. In fact, most of it's left half-eaten at the seats. First time by people, second time by the gulls.

Blue Jay food's consistent anyhow—all of it is lousy. Peanuts were stale. I didn't get halfway through the bag before I dropped 'em down under the seat. Hot dogs were even worse. Next to the Fenway Frank, baseball's most grotesque wiener files its way through the stands in plastic 24-quart coolers. The coolers do their job. By the time it reaches the seats the dog's good and cold. I was able to take one skeptical bite and drop it below with the nuts. Underneath at the concession booths things weren't much better. The only advantage there is that the dogs and grilled burgers, skinnier even than McDonald's singles, can be watched shrinking away on the grill before you fork over your cash.

Only the sea gulls win out...or do they? After the game they flood the place. From the fifth inning on Exhibition takes on an eerie, Alfred Hitchcock flair. Closer and closer, the birds work their way in for their free feast. When the game finishes and lights dim, they swarm the aisleways.

I asked an usher how long the birds stayed. "Three, sometimes four hours," he revealed. "They're here until almost everything is gone."

I wonder though. Does anybody ever really stay and watch them? Nobody, man or animal, could eat Exhibition Stadium food for four hours. I'll bet they've got everybody fooled. They're not munching down food. Ten-to-one they're just hanging around looking for money.

BALLPARK EMPLOYEES: GRADE C

As quiet and polite as the Toronto fans are, there isn't much need for a real aggressive stadium work force. The workers oblige; most are just as mellow. Actually, as simple and boring as the stadium is, it could probably work as well on autopilot.

"Food" vendors were superslow...and superquiet. All night long they just drifted through the stands, quietly made their sell, quietly made change, then quietly slid out of sight. All before a hungry fan bit into one of those cold, tasteless dogs and demanded his money back. Or a sea gull remembering a meal the night before, took a bead on the top of a vendor's head.

Meanwhile, the rest of the work force pretty much just stood around and did nothing. The place was crawling with ushers and security cops, milling around the walkways, leaning against the walls, and hanging out in the stands. Their record numbers, I guess, were to make sure no Blue Jay fan got too unruly. A job that couldn't take too much effort considering most folks rarely even raised their voices.

At such a mellow place, so many folks keeping the peace is a waste. Seems if Jays management really wanted to be efficient, they might lay off a few security guards and with the leftover bucks set up some aid stations. That or maybe send attendants trained in CPR and stomach pumping around with the vendors. That way if a fan too loaded on Labatts got the munchies and ate a whole Blue Jay wiener by mistake, they might be able to save him.

FACILITIES: GRADE B

My pregame stroll through tidy Exhibition Park told me, if nothing else, that Exhibition Stadium was gonna have clean bathrooms and be nice to cars. A place with such well-kept sidewalks wouldn't possibly let garbage pile up in the johns.

Parking for a Jays game is different... but pleasant. Aside from a couple of large stadium lots, most cars spend the evening at tiny lots dotting the park. Consequently, game night is kind of festive. Folks in orange reflective jackets waving cars into all sorts of cracks and crevices, cars creeping about looking for most anyplace to squeeze into—it might be Toronto's best baseball feeling. Although a little expensive, and a bit of a walk from the stadium, the cost was worth it. It forced me to browse around the grounds. Besides, the rest was good for my car. After a terrifying three-hour stay in Detroit, it needed something a bit more mellow.

Unfortunately, I wasn't able to try out one of the finest features of getting to a Jays game. Mass transit on the safe clean streets looked great. And a lot of folks were using it. Before the ball game city buses trucked in hundreds of fans. Then came back afterward and whisked them away. Final destination wasn't a problem either. Or so I was told. The buses dropped folks off at city subway stops, which were supposedly as spotless as the tidy park grounds. While all the reports might've just been proud Canadian boasting, I kind of doubt it. With everything else in town so safe and neat and clean, I guess subways could be too.

Inside facilities are also fine. Nothing to write home about, but in comparison with the rest of the place, the big bathrooms could be stadium-highlight-reel material. One thing's for sure—seats inside 'em are certainly a lot more comfortable than the ones up in the stands.

ATMOSPHERE: GRADE D−

Somehow, someway, baseball in Exhibition Stadium survives. On a silly-looking football field, surrounded by cold aluminum benches, the Blue Jays keep on winning. Blue Jay fans keep on coming. And the sea gulls keep on munching. All three should be awarded baseball's congressional medal of bravery—players and fans for an iron will in taking on such an ugly place, and the gulls for having iron stomachs.

Football totally dominates the place. Everything, everywhere, you can't help but feel it. If you listen real close, ghost calls of "first down and ten yards to go" can be heard over the distant speaker system. I kept watching and waiting for cheerleaders to run out and build a pyramid. Or for a marching band to take the field and spell out "Blue Jays" while they play a fight song. It wouldn't have surprised me in the least if, in the sixth, Jim Clancy had dropped back off the rubber, set up, and hit Barfield on a deep post route over the middle. Or Ernie Whitt had stepped in behind home plate decked out in shoulder pads and a football helmet instead of his catching gear.

In such a place only true baseball fans could exist. That or very sick people. I'm still not sure which they've got. Blue Jay fans are almost as strange as their park. Although friendly, and stuffed in by the thousands, in a baseball sense they're different. And quiet, almost Riverfront quiet. When somebody made a nice play they whispered and quietly clapped. When somebody screwed up they made faces, turned red, whispered, and quietly booed. The rest of the time they just whispered. A busload of drunken old ladies at Shea would make more noise and certainly feature a more colorful vocabulary than all of the Exhibitionites put together.

Jays fans do have a few specialties though. Although they didn't cheer much, each and every inning break folks stood up. Not just a couple here and there, or for a moment. All of 'em for the whole warm-up. As soon as the last out was made, everybody stood, stretched, and looked around. Then they just kept on standing and stretching till the ump was ready to go again. The only thing I could figure was that their butts were beat from being parked on aluminum benches all night. Or they were looking for the hot-dog guy, who had gotten away before that first bite.

Another tradition, which by the way also involves standing, is probably the ballpark's neatest feature. In the seventh, for the fourteenth time of the night, everybody stood. This time, though, they sang. Not "Take Me Out to the Ballgame"—the Jays have their own theme song. An adorable little upbeat number with a chorus that goes "Okay—okay, Blue Jays—Blue Jays. Let's play—let's play BALL!" Great for singing along to, it's actually the only time fans really let loose. When it was finished everybody quietly clapped, whispered, and looked around. Then sat back down for three more outs.

Although quiet, and a little offbeat, Jays fans are at least kind to birds...I think. Or maybe it's the birds that are kind to the fans. While folks suffered the whole game, sense of sight maimed by the ball field, hearing strained by the sorry sound system, and balance thrown off by standing and sitting over and over again, the taste buds got a bit of a break. At least the last few innings. Those screechy sea gulls swooping around the ball field all night long, by game's end moved in for the kill. Their objective: to gobble up all the leftover goodies. Feeling sorry for the birds, and sick to their stomachs already, Jays fans did their humanitarian duty of the day. They dropped their hot dogs a few bites sooner than they might've otherwise. They left a few extra stale peanuts in the plastic bag. Some, I think, even ripped the bag open so that the poor birds' bills wouldn't get caught inside.

It's a weird ritual in a weird place filled with 'em. With the absolute weirdest one... that neither birds nor fans seem to mind.

18

OLYMPIC STADIUM, *MONTREAL EXPOS*

A Day at the United Nations

| REPORT CARD | *Olympic Stadium* |
| | BASEBALL PARK |

| *July 24, 85* vs *Braves* | *Montreal Expos* |
| GAME | BASEBALL CLUB |

CATEGORY	GRADE	POINTS
Layout and Upkeep	*B*	*75*
Ball Field	*D-*	*60*
Seating	*D*	*65*
Scoreboard	*B*	*85*
Food	*C*	*75*
Ballpark Employees	*B*	*85*
Facilities	*A*	*95*
Atmosphere	*C*	*75*
Total Points		*625*
Average		*78*

| *C+* | *15 th* |
| FINAL GRADE | RANK |

"An eerie-looking stadium placed in a very tidy, quiet setting... Still, the chance to feel baseball bilingually is a treat."

PREGAME THOUGHTS

Once in a great while even eating McDonald's burgers can get old. Normally that takes some doing, but believe me I was there. My players'-strike switch had finally taken its toll. Six ballparks in the past eight days, over 2,200 miles darting all around the Midwest and Canada, had thrust me back into the real world. My body protested a return to endless hours in the car. My stomach wasn't real pleased either. A rerun assortment of ballpark dogs and Mcburgers in between 'em, it was wondering what'd happened to Mom's home cooking.

The past week, in terms of ballparks at least, had been a good one. It'd been like visiting old friends. County, Comiskey, and Tiger Stadium, three of my longtime buddies, were still as quaint. The others, Riverfront, Exhibition, and the Metrodome, although pure plastic, sat inside three charming cities. And I had company along the way. Picked up Drew in Chicago. Along with Amy, we had had a couple at McCuddy's before the White Sox game, then toured Chi-town afterward. Took him along with me to Riverfront and visited Tiger Stadium with my four teenaged cousins. Between the ballparks and family, the week had been like a reunion... a very hectic family reunion. By the time I'd left Toronto in search of Montreal, I was feeling it.

Biggest problem, I think, was that players' strike. Morally, it was such horse crap. Besides, it threw my schedule out of whack. Not that the whole thing was ruined, it just upset a pattern. For four months I'd lived with my schedule; I'd run it through my mind millions of times. Each day when springtime teenagers had gotten to me, I just looked to the wall where the schedule was taped up—and felt better. Each night I'd fallen asleep dreaming about it. And dreamed better. It was printed on the top of my brain. Now it was different. And all because $400,000 a year wasn't quite enough to play baseball.

Besides that, I'd gotten a little lazy. The Kazoo week off in luxury had softened me. Mom had gone on a cooking binge. Real meals, pork chops with mashed potatoes and gravy one night, burgers on the grill the next. A stock-piled fridge with leftovers and a microwave less than ten feet away, two kinds of ice cream and three toppings—my stomach was in ecstasy. The last thing it wanted was another month of hot dogs and peanuts in the shell.

Then there was the "ink." My head was still swelling. Getting in and out of the car without whacking it against the roof was a continual problem. If I had gotten sports-page headlines halfway through, I could only wonder what was in store for the finale... *Kalamazoo Gazette* front page. Who knew? Maybe even the six o'clock news. Either way, I was sure to be a celebrity. I was famous, fat, and rested. Taking off to live in the car for another month took unswerving dedication... or lunacy. There's a fine line between the two. When I pulled out of the drive for the All-Star game, I felt like I was walking it.

And that was before the mileage pileup. Cruising leisurely across the West, I'd tacked on some big miles. The Kingdome to Candlestick was 750 miles. Jack Murphy to Arlington almost 1,300 miles. And my longest overnight haul of all time those 800 back-road miles through the middle of Oklahoma on the way to watch the Royals. That stuff was easy. Relaxing for the most part. All I had to do was switch on the cruise control, adjust the air, tune in Frank, and find something to dream about for five hours at a time. But this Midwest binge had been like popping through a pinball machine at full speed. Six parks in eight days. Montreal'd be seven in ten. Big-city traffic at least once a day. Two long-haul cruises—one 585 miles to the Metrodome and a killer of a drive from my Saturday-night game in Riverfront to that Sunday afternoon in Detroit. By the time I took off from Exhibition Park for Montreal I was frazzled.

Now on paper the trip between the two Canadian stadiums looked simple. The journey isn't a particularly long one—344 miles. It was night, my favorite driving time. The car was running great. There's hardly a town between the two, so I couldn't get lost. I was coming off of my only real off-day in the last nine... an overnight stay in Detroit with my Aunt Sue and Uncle Greg. It should've been easy. It wasn't. Cram scheduling had finally caught up with me. Home for a week, out for a week, then in Detroit for two days had hammered me good. I felt like a yo-yo that had twanged one too many times. Disaster, or at least what looked to be disaster, struck about 100 miles outside Toronto. My tape deck blew a fuse. Without my music I was left to sleepy silence or Canadian talk shows from my cheapo transistor radio. Each equally exciting. At the time I also thought the deck was dead. No more Frank the rest of the trip horrified me. I blew a fuse too. Any cheeriness in my mood was drowned out by the breakdown.

Plus I was anxious for the East Coast. I wanted the Bosox, the O's, even the Yanks. I'd been waiting for real Eastern baseball. Montreal was not top-of-my-wish list. Worn out, a victim of a strike-induced killer week, I decided I'd just get to Montreal as soon as possible, see the Expos, cross 'em off my list, forget Canada, and get on to Fenway.

Things weren't quite that simple—344 miles is longer than it seems, particularly when it's constantly updated in kilometers, all 560 of 'em. To make matters worse, bull-headed me had to make it before I slept. You see, I'm what psychiatrists might describe as an "overly imbalanced nearly obsessive, goal-oriented" person. Each morning the first thing I do, even before putting together my peanut-butter toast, is make a list. The list consists of my "Things for the Day." Each thing has a little box in front of it. When I finish doing whatever it is, I "X" the box. I try like hell to have all of 'em "X'd" by the end of the day. If I do, I consider the day a success. If not, I am a failure. Consequently, each little stupid accomplishment becomes an obsession. Each is a character challenge.

Montreal by morning was my "Thing for the Day." Bouncing from coffee shop to coffee shop, I struggled closer toward it. Every exit that had a lit sign, I staggered in for another cup of coffee. And I left every one with a Styrofoam cupful for the road. By 3:00 A.M. I was beat; my post-All-Star game hangover throbbed. Still at each stop I'd pound another cup, stare blankly at the same news, in the same paper, and tell myself, "You're not a man if you don't make it." Then I'd pick up a couple of toothpicks, prop up my eyelids, splash a little Visine on my eyeballs, and hit the road again.

Once, in a tiny town about a hundred miles outside of Montreal, realizing I was probably going to end up in a ditch with the steering wheel wrapped around my neck, I gave up. I cruised around looking for a motel, found only "No Vacancy" signs, killed another cup of caffeine, and got back on the road. At another stop, some big-truck munch-and-run off the freeway, I tried to snooze. Pulled in and stopped the car, tilted back the seat, drew a blanket over me, and lay there for 20 minutes entranced with a rip in the roof's upholstery. Caffeine finally surged. High-intensity lights overhead zinged through the windows. I felt like a cadaver on display at the morgue. Without even a hint of sleep, I threw the blanket in the back, tilted up, headed out, and almost nodded off pulling out of the drive onto the freeway.

All told, Toronto to Montreal took in at least eight cups of coffee, three honey-glazed doughnuts, two filled with some kind of jelly stuff, a couple of Cokes, and a dill pickle. When I reached Montreal, sometime in the midst of an early-morning traffic rush, I was a mess. My tummy was crying. My eyes, the only part of my body immune to caffeine, were slits. The rest of me shook. About all I could do was stumble into some sleazy French motel room, take a shower, and collapse unconscious face-first into an unmade bed. If I was gonna stay sane before Fenway I needed help. Montreal was going to have to be better than what I'd seen so far. The Expos, more exciting than they were on the tube. For me to survive baseball in a country where most kids ice-skated to school, I needed a royal Canadian shot in the arm.

LAYOUT AND UPKEEP: GRADE B

Montreal was just the breath of fresh air I needed! After a nap and an afternoon crepe, I cruised into town looking for the Expos. I found more than just baseball. I found another world.

Toronto is Canadian. Montreal is French-Canadian. The difference is enormous. Except for being a little cleaner, a little quieter, and a lot safer than most major league cities, Toronto could just as easily be stamped "Made in the U.S.A." Its culture, while a foreign one, is red, white, and blue all about the edges. Montreal, on the other hand, not only resists any ties with the United States but with Canada as well. The city's almost its own separate little foreign country. As different as the two are, that nine-hour drive eastward from Exhibition Stadium could just as well have been by boat across the Atlantic. While I might have been a lot closer to Detroit than Europe, I could've sworn I was in Paris.

Olympic Stadium lies buried deep in the heart of the city's dominating French Quarter. Surrounded by gas stations, with attendants who can only point the way in English, it's a remnant of the '76 Olympic Games and part of enormous Olympic Park. The park's grand, but the stadium doesn't quite fit in. Instead of hosting baseball, it looks like it might provide a "Close Encounter of a Third Kind." Concrete walls, almost immediately above the ground, bow out, then back in. They give it a saucerlike appearance. Curving back in as they rise, the gray walls meet near the top and nearly enclose the place. But they don't connect. Instead they leave a small oval hole in the roof. Big enough to allow snow and rain inside to cancel games, about all the roof keeps out are sunsets and blue skies. Rising above the hole from the center-field end of the stadium, like a killer beast in *War of the Worlds,* is a hideous, alien-looking concrete neck. When finished it's supposed to drape a cover over the oval opening. With cover in place, apparently early- and late-season snow-outs will be prevented... and voyage to another world will at last be possible.

While it may be frightful to look at, the stadium is one of the majors' most efficient. Heavy doors lead from the outside into a huge, theaterlike lobby. The lobby separates ballpark from neighborhood. There, sheltered from the harsh Canadian weather, are all ticket booths, customer information, and souvenir stands. Wandering about the place is like walking through an international airport terminal. Announcements in both French and English ring out over the inside speaker system. Interesting people speaking different languages roam about. It's really quite refreshing. In fact, so much so that it's almost possible to forget you're at a ballpark uglier than the Kingdome.

BALL FIELD: GRADE D−

Olympic Stadium wasn't originally built for baseball. Its job was to take care of track and field events in the '76 Olympic Games.... Unfortunately for baseball fans, it looks like it'll handle 'em in '88 too.

Circling the green artificial turf is a brown all-weather tartan track. It runs around the entire outside edge of the playing field and separates synthetic turf from synthetic seats. Lane lines that served the Olympic dashes still cover its face. Great for running events, the lines on a baseball field's warning track look ridiculous.

So silly that part of me kept waiting for Tim Raines to trot out to his position with a set of starting blocks, plop 'em down on the rubber track, dig in, and challenge Dale Murphy to a 100-meter sprint. That or maybe take on the whole Braves team in a sixth-inning relay race. The Expos would've been unbeatable—Hubie Brooks, Herb Winningham, Mitch Webster, and Raines for an anchor.

SEATING: GRADE D

The lane-lined warning track isn't the only evidence that the stadium's first love was track and field—so are the lousy sight lines. Priorities for watching an 800-meter run are not quite the same as they are for catching a baseball game. Although front-row seats might have been right on top of the high-jump pit, they're miles from home plate. And even if a good chair in '76 was close enough to see the third baton hand-off of the 400-meter relay, you might as well forget a close call at second base. Distances between baseball and fans are just too much... in all three of the circling tiers.

Chairs themselves are strange too. They aren't uncomfortable, just a bit different. Actually, they do look like the type that a concrete spaceship might feature. Molded plastic in an array of pastelish colors, they resemble tiny separate captain's chairs. Instead of four legs like a normal chair, each is attached to the floor by one. Armrests are molded plastic that grow out of the seat. The whole thing is a single plastic form.

As weird-looking as they are, the chairs, like the weatherproofed lobby outside and clean hallways in the stadium, are nevertheless comfortable. In fact, comfort and neatness are an all-around Olympic Stadium priority. Too bad baseball isn't as well.

SCOREBOARD: GRADE B

Montreal poses a problem to baseball that no other major league city does: fans come in two languages. Turn to one radio station, the DJ is French, another and he's English. Driving down the road, you see some advertisements that covet the French franc, others go after the English pound. And ask directions from a cruising taxicab driver, you never know what to expect.

For the ballpark to serve both, I figured, would be a difficult task. Baseball's no more English than it is French-Canadian. A strike isn't thrown in a language. A home run isn't belted in a certain cultural style. Yet to work, Olympic would have to cater to both. And it does—both scoreboard and P.A. do a good job. For a purist, the setup's not all that great. It doesn't pay a lot of attention to basics. Nor does it do much with updates from around the league—it just doesn't have the spare time. Certain sacrifices must be made so that nobody watching is left tongue-tied.

Its first plus is its placement. A center-field panel is matched identically in shape, size, and information with one behind home plate. This allows fans in the cheap seats to get the same scoreboard goodies as those in the boxes. All 25 other ballparks have their biggie in the outfield. For bleacherites to enjoy, they have to turn around every other pitch. Then half the time the screen is either so close that it hurts to watch or so glaring that it isn't readable. The way it is in Expoville, everybody's happy.

As for appealing to French and English, the stadium handles that well too. Player introductions and fan messages are made in both languages over a booming public address system. A constant posting of the player at bat, balls, strikes, and outs is labeled on both big screens, above the numerals in French and below them in English. And instant replay doesn't need translation. Best of all, though, is the organist. Unlike the screens, which must split time between two languages, he can go merrily about his business. A constant barrage of snappy little numbers from "Hello, Dolly" to stuff made famous by the Tijuana Brass pick up the place. He's one of the majors' peppiest.

In fact, the whole audiovisual setup is full of spirit. Having to take on problems that no other ballpark is challenged with, Olympic Stadium handles the chore in first-class United Nations style.

FOOD: GRADE C

Selection: Poor   Accessibility: Fair
Taste: Fair   Cost: 1st

If the Canadian economy keeps on swirling, pretty soon people will be driving across the border just to eat at the ballpark. With a 25 percent U.S. dollar discount tacked on to already low prices, the menu is easily the major league's cheapest.

Too bad it's probably the skimpiest as well. Neat and clean concessions are made neater and cleaner by a lack of food to clutter 'em up. Other than basic hot-dog and peanut-type baseball eats, a couple of tiny pizza stands, and an always crowded *"la meat"* deli sandwich counter, food's not a biggie. Neither is beer. At least tapped beer. Nothing but soda and OJ come out of a tap once the game starts. As for bottled beer, it's hearty Canadian stock. Molson, Labatts, and O'Keefe are popped and poured at separate booths.

Up in the stands vendors roam about. Some advertise hot dogs and peanuts in French, some in English. Most all do so very quietly. The majors' most reserved sellers, they creep almost invisibly about the place. Unless seen, they won't be found. It's almost for sure that they'll never be heard. With such low prices, they're probably just too embarrassed to speak up.

BALLPARK EMPLOYEES: GRADE B

The classiest feature of the ballpark are its employees. That potential communication problem that the scoreboard handles so well with technology, folks in the aisles match with smiles.

Some of the employees speak French, some speak English. In key positions, like at the parking-garage entrance and stadium information booth, they know both. Either way, they aim to please. And if one can't help you, doesn't understand your question, or can't get you to understand their answer, they just direct you to a better match. The majors' most intelligent group, they make sure that every fan, regardless of nationality, has a great time.

Ushers are the highlight. They're everywhere. At the box seats down in front, they're beautiful too. For a romantic French touch, lower box seats are ushered by gorgeous women. Dressed in stylish peach blouses and long dark skirts, with just a little leg peeking through, the Expoettes gotta be the world's most beautiful seat finders. As good-looking as they are, I wouldn't doubt it if the job was a prerequisite for any Miss Canada running for Miss Universe. And if it was, I wouldn't doubt if a couple of 'em were winners. Not only are they gorgeous, they're also well mannered. And that soft, sexy French accent is luscious. While the game's going on they stand at attention at the top of the aisles. Between innings they saunter down to the front row, pause, and face up into the stands. If a lucky ticket holder should come around, they provide a pretty escort. Taking the ticket, they lead the fans to their seats, dust them off, then wish them good day. Baseball can't possibly have a better incentive for buying season tickets.

One black mark smudged an otherwise perfect employee report card. Security was pushy. As quiet and harmless as Canadian fans seemed, the guards didn't need to be aggressive. But the guys with the badges were a pain in the ass, particularly after the ball game. From the moment the last strike popped the catcher's mitt, they were pushing people out the door. Fans quietly sitting around visiting were literally picked up and pointed to the doorway. By squads of the roaming cops. Folks just lazily heading for the exits were commanded to pick up the pace. While people like me, still caught in a trance, dreaming of those great-looking ushers, were shaken and brought back to reality.

FACILITIES: GRADE A

Olympic Stadium weathered millions of spectators in the '76 Olympics. Consequently, puny Expo crowds of the eighties aren't even a challenge.

Inside, outside, and around, few stadiums are as organized. Getting to it, particularly by foot, is simple. One of the world's most efficient subway systems makes for a pleasant journey. By car things get a bit slower; not a whole lot of roads feed the place. But once arrived and parked, the cakewalk returns. Huge, tidy parking garages connect to the stadium and offer safe, easy access inside. Elevators to stairways, to snow- and sun-proof lobbies, everything is well marked. Directions are simple. You just follow the bilingual signs. While it might not be baseball's most exciting pregame walk, the short trip from car to ticket turnstile is probably the easiest.

Inside, the stadium's also tidy. Everything has its proper place and is probably aerodynamically polished. Just like any good concrete spaceship should be. Bathrooms are Olympic size and typically Montreal clean. Only hand blow dryers taint a perfect setup. In fact, other than the blowers, facilities are probably as good as the ones on the *Star Ship Enterprise*. Or better yet, Dodger Stadium.

ATMOSPHERE: GRADE C

I stumbled into Montreal needing a pick-me-up. I was burned out, about as down as I was gonna get my whole trip. I needed something different, something refreshing. I needed a little more pizzazz than a bag of peanuts, a cold hot dog, and a plastic ballpark in a normal town. I found it in Montreal. A timeless, charming city, Montreal exists in its own little world—while Olympic Stadium looks like it should be hovering somewhere else, in a different solar system. The two together, and folks inside 'em, perked me up. They gave me a second wind, a pat on the back, and put a whistle in my tune that sent me happily off to Fenway.

For a teacher I guess I am a misfit—I like American. I'd rather read through the Declaration of Independence than the Magna Charta. My favorite war is between Americans dressed in blue and gray uniforms; Winston Churchill or Adolf Hitler have nothing to do with it. And I am actually glad this country never has had any real "Dark Ages." The bubonic plague I can do without. For most of my colleagues, though, Europe is it! It's dreams of European voyages, traipsing around famous French art galleries and reliving World War I on the open field, not baseball park trips, that get most normal teachers through springtime. Each June I am told at least a dozen times, "If I was still single, boy I'd be on a plane as soon as the kids were out the door. You know you could be in London by Friday." That's great! But they play soccer in London. And my golf clubs would probably get lost in flight. An apple-pie-gobbling, red-white-and-blue American history teacher, I'd just as soon stay put. Spending all summer slicing out of bounds and sipping beer in the bleachers suits me fine.

After a day in Montreal, though, I can see the European appeal. The town is delightful. Old churches and museums, standing side by side with modern bank buildings. Streets lined with inns and shops that just as well could've sat across the ocean a century or two ago. And French and English sharing in every facet of the city. The place is refreshing—probably a lot like Europe.

Olympic Stadium is kind of neat too. Not in a baseball sense it isn't. Shaped like a spaceship, overhung by a death-ray concrete eye, surrounded inside by that silly-looking sprint-lined warning track, and filled with plastic seats and silent fans, in a strictly baseball sense... it's a disaster. Other factors are at work though. Attitudes and situations more akin to a day at the United Nations create a totally unique feeling. If nothing else, a night out with the Expos, like an afternoon in Montreal, is a refreshing date.

It's the language thing that gives the place its pizzazz. Signs and scoreboard info are a little more lively when given in two languages. The friendly bilingual employees keep things loose too. Not to mention the babes at the box seats down in front. The place also provides some off-the-wall fun, stuff that isn't normally offered at a baseball park. The duo scoreboard messages provide an ideal chance to do a little comparative linguistic research. French and English advertisements dot the stadium program. I had a great time paging through it, trying to make out the sales pitches. Best of all was tuning into the radio. French and English stations cover the Expos. Each is listed in the program and can be reached from inside the stadium. All night long I flip-flopped my transistor radio dial. Watching Tim Raines make a diving sliding catch in English, and listening to Monsieur Announcer "lose it" in French is an Olympic Stadium must.

Music joins with the little language combos to brighten up the place and give Expo fans the chance to all pull together. For no matter the tongue, ears hear the same melody. Hands, English and French ones, clap to the same beat. "Charge" is yelled at the end of the same intro. All night long organ tunes merrily break down the barriers and provide the place a special kind of charm.

Even the night's most magical moment was performed to music. "O Canada" officially begins Expo ball games. As a small traditional marching band assembled at home plate to play it, I wondered what would happen. In the United States "The Star-Spangled Banner" is a wonderful baseball tradition. In the States, though, everyone sings together. Every scoreboard highlights the same lyrics. Everybody in unison misses those same high notes. I wondered how such a proud people with mixed loyalties would react to a single anthem.

"O Canada" was announced. All quietly rose. The tiny band began its introduction. As the melody continued people all about me sang—some in French, some in English. Above, on the center-field scoreboard, verses alternated between the two languages. I joined them and relished the idea that major league baseball was fortunate enough to enjoy the flavor of Montreal . . . as only it could be, both in French and English.

19

FENWAY PARK, BOSTON RED SOX

Essence of Tradition

REPORT CARD

Fenway Park
BASEBALL PARK

July 26/27, 85 vs Mariners **Boston Red Sox**
GAME   BASEBALL CLUB

CATEGORY	GRADE	POINTS
Layout and Upkeep	B	85
Ball Field	A	95
Seating	A+	100
Scoreboard	A+	100
Food	D	65
Ballpark Employees	C	75
Facilities	D	65
Atmosphere	A+	100
Total Points		685
Average		86

B+
FINAL GRADE

5th
RANK

"An Old North Church-ish charm hangs like the scent of freshly baked bagels in the ballyard air.... The history of Boston and the magic of Fenway blend with that hard-core East Coast attitude to wield a captivating baseball spell."

PREGAME THOUGHTS

Memories... to be 21 again, 800 miles from home, munching bagels and guzzling beer on the broken concrete walk outside of Fenway. It was the middle of June of '78, and the Bosox were already in front by six and a half. Three straight over the Yankees would clinch the pennant. It'd be over before the All-Star break! Bouncing from Dunkin' Donuts to Dunkin' Donuts along U.S. 80, living on glazed buttermilk doughnut holes and Strohs from Michigan to Beantown, we arrived just in time for what would be the greatest three-game series of our lives.

Bob and I had made the trek once before, four years back, in '74. Those were the days when we were still part of the Kalamazoo Tiger clan—not diehard, but Tiger fans just the same. We drove to Fenway to see Detroit play the Sox. I was 17, just a junior in high school, and Bob was 22. We both returned from Boston that summer changed for all time. After peering into the heart of the "Green Monster," watching Captain Carl, and sampling the intensity of the bleacherites, we switched allegiance to the Red Sox. It was from that day on in July of '74 that I, a victim of Fenway's charm, became a "dyed in the wool" Sox fan.

While it was Fenway's seduction in '74 that made a convert out of me, it was the three-game set in '78 that made me a lifer. Since '74 the Sox had blossomed. That team that nearly derailed the "Big Red Machine" in the '75 Series had jelled into what looked to be one of the best of all time. Sox fans all over the world, not just in Boston, were comparing their lineup with some of the game's best. Youngsters Freddie Lynn and Jim Rice, and the veteran Fisk, could be talked about in the same conversations with Mantle, Maris, and Berra. Nobody laughed, not even fearful New Yorkers, who for a change were sizing 'em up from below. Loaded with power and oozing with confidence, Boston was on a roll. And Bob and I were back. This time to see 'em hammer on the Yanks.

Now to truly love the Sox, you must not only dream of Fenway and Rice tattooing the "Monster," but live to hate blue pinstripes. No rivalry in all of sports is so intense, no opposing team so hated as New York is by Bostonians.

While Yankee followers also despise New Englanders, it's not with such an obsession. Probably because everybody everywhere since the twenties has loathed the Yankees, they deal with the issue better. New Yorkers have adapted to being hated. And some, I'm sure, even relish it.

At Fenway though, the situation's not so simple. People's lives are altered by just the mention of the Yanks. It affects the way they live, particularly in the summer, but year-round as well. It alters their choice of food and how it settles in their guts. It probably has in some way affected monumental religious and political decisions. A fanatic obsession to say the very least. To claim allegiance to the Red Sox, in the same breath you must admit with every ounce of sinew to hold the Yankees in the very utmost contempt.

Of all New Yorkers, no single soul is more despised than George Steinbrenner. To Bostonians he is the Darth Vader of baseball. From the major league script he's removed poetry, leaving instead debits and credits. And a littered trail of overpriced free agents in his wake. Yet even as contemptuous as he is, for all nine innings Steinbrenner hides, protected up in his booth. Roaming mercenaries, a different set it seems each season, carry out his evil deeds. So for Sox fans, each visit, somebody else has to bear the brunt of all those frustrating seasons. In 1978 the load fell upon the ultimate mercenary, Mr. Reginald Jackson.

Reggie in '78 was everything that Boston hated. A filthy rich free agent, he was the cockiest ego on a team flooded with 'em. And a flip side to Fenway tradition. Sox stars played because they loved baseball. Not Reggie—he did it for the money. On top of that, he wasn't a complete player. Sure, he could hit. But unlike Dewey Evans, the Sox right-field golden glover, Reggie couldn't pick up a ball rolled dead, much less pluck one from the sky. Worst of all for Bostonians, more than the ego and the errors, or the pinstripes, as much as they hated to say it, "Mr. October" was one hell of a baseball player. Even better come crunch time. The center-stage spotlight or the glitter of the limelight, it didn't matter which, Reggie reveled in it. He was immune to pressure. Stationed in right field, out in front of the world's loudest and most frustrated bleacherites, it was predetermined that Reggie would draw all the wrath that Boston could muster.

It was into this setting—Yankee frustration and Sox arrogance, roles reversed for the first time in history—that Bob and I arrived. Everything was perfect. The weather was great, sunny and hot. The Sox were on fire, the Yanks swooning. Eighteen straight hours on the road, we pulled into Boston about 8:00 A.M. Sleep not being a priority, we showered, dodged the crazy city traffic, and reached the park by 9:00. Even ten hours from game time the place was alive. Those who'd settle for nothing but the bleacher's best had been in place since dawn. They waited, 15 to 20 strong, alongside Fenway on the old cracked Lansdowne Street sidewalk. The line began at the boarded-up bleacher ticket window and ended at the curb. It grew in spurts of twos and threes, and more as the day wore on. With each addition the electrical current that surrounded us buzzed a little stronger. It was there that we set a pattern that ran throughout the series. For three days, from breakfast till they opened the gates, we lived on the sidewalk.

Our Monday morning pregame was the best that any fan could hope for. Sitting in the hot sun for a number of hours, you become good friends, or at least drinking buddies, with your neighbors. So we partook. Equipped with a dozen freshly baked bagels for trading bait and the novelty of having come the farthest, we quenched our thirst with beer and munched down bagels with the locals. We became official Fenway sidewalk groupies. In fact, our only free time away from the ballpark was for bagel runs off to nearby Kenmore Square. And those we took, with the regulars, on a rotating basis.

Cards were played to pass the time. Jackson's own Reggie Bars substituted for poker chips. Chocolate-covered peanut globs, packed in bright orange wrappers, Reggie's picture graced the cover. One fella brought dozens. He passed 'em out, giving us all stakes to lose. Poker five-card draw was house game. Loser was forced to eat the grotesque caramel crunch. Then quickly wash it down with more beer. Meanwhile, winners would laugh and rag Reggie in the process. Not all of the candy was eaten though. The stakes manager had other uses for it, which we found out about later.

In addition to bagel munching and card playing, we talked baseball... with folks who lived baseball at Fenway each day. Every topic in the majors was fair game. And with varied opinions buzzing about, each got a good workout. While there were always the derogatory comments about Reggie's glove and the size of the hole in it, most discussions were good hard-core baseball ones. Many pitted Yanks against the Sox. We compared Red Sox past with Red Sox present, the current Yankees with the Bombers of years gone, Burleson's arm with Nettles' glove. We sized up Piniella versus Evans, who was better in the clutch, who had more power, more finesse. Answers were varied, talk interesting. Sox fans are as hard on their own as the others. But with Boston on a World Series roll, we all agreed on one thing—that red socks were much better than blue pinstripes.

The card games and Reggie bars, baseball talk and bright warm sunshine made the morning fly by. And turned Bob and me into celebrities. As the line grew word spread that we were in all the way from Michigan... just for the series. We became famous. In fact, aside from the Cambridge College pair, first in line at dawn, we were the most famous—modern-day Red Sox folk heroes. The *Boston Herald American* and some puny Rhode Island newspaper interviewed us. Asked us why we came, how we grew to be Sox fans. They even took our pictures—flashing Reggie Bars.

When the gates opened the party, conversations, baseball, all the excitement migrated inside. Friends on the walk outside remained friends for the series inside. All three nights in the bleachers we were known as "Hey, Kalamazoo." During warm-ups we'd move around the different groups, talk baseball, and plan the following day's sidewalk assault. When to show up, what to bring, where to go afterward. Tuesday's game, after the Sox pounded 'em 10-4 in the opener, a "Hey, Kalamazoo" during batting practice got our attention. A bagel-and-beer buddy from the day before showed us the Tuesday morning *Herald American*. Our names were in it, front page. He gave us his copy, we bought him a beer, and together we toasted the Sox.

While bleacher eating and drinking habits stayed about the same as on the sidewalk, ways to pass the time changed. Instead of card playing, we took part in what was called "The Jim Rice Show"—known at most major league parks as batting practice. At Fenway, batting practice is a festive event. With the big green wall tattooed on every other pitch, keeping track just of Rice was—and probably still is—a standard occupation.

In '78, Boston in first and New York in town, it was the main attraction. When the Sox hit, a bulging bleacher section would pick a batter. For ten solid minutes they'd adorn him with a rhythmic rendition of his name. "Dewey, Dewey, Dewey," announced Dwight Evans. "Louie, Louie, Louie" rang through the bleachers whenever Tiant tipped his cap. Since they were most fun to chant, Louie and Dewey were fan favorites. But it didn't matter—whoever was in the cage or near the right-field wall was everybody's idol.

With the Yanks going through warm-ups, language soured and the intensity of yelling increased. We watched that inner Red Sox frustration boil over. Only booing wasn't enough. Cussing, swearing, and imaginative obscenities, all directed at the nonchalant New Yorkers, who seemed to handle it admirably, peppered the place. Still the outbursts were isolated—just taunts here and there. That was until Reggie stepped into the cage.

Only then did the collectiveness that adorned the Sox return. In unison some 6,000 strong vented their wrath the whole series with their favorite slogan. Over and over again, starting in the Monday-night pregame cage, for three nights straight Fenway rocked to "Reggie Sucks." If Reggie K'd during the game, the chant continued until the Yanks were out of the inning. If Reggie errored, like he did twice in Game One, thunderous applause and "Reggie Sucks" in total bleacher harmony rang throughout the park. When the screen replayed his error, then left up a big E-9, all of New England drowned in a sea of "Reggie Sucks." Hundreds of orange-wrapped Reggie Bars flew out into right field. Time was called for the candy to be collected. Reggie stood unfazed.

Even going to the bathroom, the fans chanted. Closet-size bleacher rest rooms at Fenway take at least a couple of outs to wade through. Still, nobody missed a beat. While people peed they shouted. Stuffed bathrooms shook with chants of "Reggie Sucks." The place was a zoo! While the sidewalk stay was mellow and of cultural benefit, it was a madhouse in the bleachers.

Not only in the Barnum and Bailey bleacher presentation and on the dirty concrete walks outside was pennant fever rampant, neighborhood pubs and restaurants surrounding the park buzzed as well. Pre-bleacher-line breakfast across the street was eaten to the tune of baseball statistics and the Sox. After the game ballpark bars bulged at their seams with people spilling over from Fenway. Red Sox was the only allowed topic of conversation, and everybody spoke. Just a few leading words about Burleson's arm or Rice's bat was enough for anybody to yell "Give this guy a draft... on me!" It was June and the city was on fire. Never did I know baseball could get so intense. Never have I seen an entire tribe of people so concerned with a single common interest and so willing to share their thoughts, beer, bagels—whatever—as long as the recipe loved baseball and hated the Yankees.

It was during those three days in and about Fenway Park that I felt the real intensity of a town obsessed with a pennant chase. Emotions erupted—some sincere, some rude, some purely baseball, while some came just as a result of too many brews. The Sox and the Yanks in that June of '78 were as powerful as the game can get. Those memories, especially of our friendly sidewalk stays, will always linger. And turning over a three of clubs in search of a heart to complete a "Red" Sox flush, winning my first-ever Reggie Bar and being forced to eat it is a taste I'll never forget.

LAYOUT AND UPKEEP: GRADE B

From the concrete walks that surround it, Fenway today looks much like it did when I first visited in '74. And probably isn't a whole lot different than when it went up in 1912. The street outside is still littered, the sidewalk bleached white by the sun... and the Yawkey Way (used to be Jersey Street) entrance is still the most quaint in all of baseball. A two-story red brick facade is broken at ground level by a series of tiny archways. In twos and threes, folks enter through them into the stadium. On game night, crowds bottleneck the entrance. Baseball talk ripples in a pool of anxious bodies. Square white windowsills rise, split in pairs, then threes, above the arches and the people.

At the crest a simple stone marker states "Fenway Park." Only bulky air-conditioning units in each of the windows hint that today inside it's Boggs not Williams shooting for .400.

Kind of like Wrigley, Fenway makes no royal announcement. No seat or scoreboard peek is available from the outside. Giant parking lots are nowhere to be seen. Instead of dominating the worn urban neighborhood, the ballpark silently slips in alongside, doing as little as possible to upset what years have taken to shape. Consequently, she fits right in, a regular in the community, just like the delis and the taverns that hug the nearby sidewalks.

Inside, she's homey and convenient. While some of the other ancients, Comiskey and even Tiger Stadium, tend to lose themselves in confusing ramps that lead all about the place, Fenway's coziness allows only for efficiency. Simple concrete walkways need only concentrate on ushering around, since the park really has no up. Besides cozy, she's also surprisingly clean. When I had last visited in '78, the place was a pit. Papers littered the floor. Boxes and crates cluttered walkways. Now it's as though trivial matters like sweeping have finally entered onto the stadium's list of "do's." No Dodger Stadium by any means, still a newfound commitment to tidiness suits the Bostonian just fine. A discovery of the broom, the quaint two-story front, and a simple layout provide those entering with a pleasant homey welcome.

BALL FIELD: GRADE A

Despite the harshness of East Coast weather, Fenway's turf is handsome. Rolled out under the "Green Monster," it's one of the American League's finest.

I was scheduled for a two-game stay in Boston; the Mariners were in town. Unfortunately, monsoons joined us. While the rain probably made the M's feel at home, it only terrified me! Friday afternoon was nerve-racking. I spent it floating along the Freedom Trail, squinting through the raindrops, reading historical plaques. Saturday-morning breakfast played to the tune of cracking thunder. But each day a couple of hours before game time the monsoons stopped.

Even with the weather break, I half expected to find all three bases floating in a ballpark bathtub. Fenway, I was sure, would resemble a swimming pool. Instead, with the tarp rolled back and a few passes with the squeegee, the ball field looked almost Southern Californian...both days.

Besides fielding a classy green, Fenway sports a few options that add a little luster to it. Eyes at most stadiums spend a lot of their time between pitches roaming the field. If the turf's worn, by the third inning everybody in the place knows it. The scars almost scream for attention. Stadium peculiarities, by providing other scenery, take pressure off the field and give the turf a break. Wrigley's ivy has that power. Like a new summer dress, the vines add a special sparkle to an otherwise normal-looking gal and turn her into a stunner. So does Comiskey's exploding scoreboard. Just about the time you find a flaw, the giant screen goes bonkers. You have to look.

The Bostonian has a few specialties of its own. Climbing high into the left-field sky, a deep rich green, the "Monster" hovers over the field. It dominates everything—the ball game as well as the grass and the fans. It's so intimidating that instead of lazily rolling over the ball field, eyes always end up focused on the big green thing out in left.

Another ball-field helper is the shape of the park. Most stadiums nowadays, particularly the new plastic models, are perfectly symmetrical. They pick a distance from home plate to left and match it in right. Between the two is an arc. The boring layout puts a lot of pressure on the outfield grass. Fenway's shape is anything but symmetrical. Huge but close in left, the wall trickles down to a half-size "Baby Monster" in center. At the same time it pushes way back. While a check swing to left can lollipop a ball onto Lansdowne Street, it takes a missile shot to hit one out in center. As the wall swings around to right, it turns into a waist-level fence and circles right field in front of the bull pen and bleachers. Just before the foul pole, for not more than 15 feet or so, the short fence curls even closer than the big one does in left. And although it take the accuracy of a pool-cue shot to get it there, the porch is the majors' shortest.

The ins and outs, ups and downs bring new meaning to "home-field advantage." And they make the grounds a whole lot prettier. Without its quaint peculiarities, Fenway's "common" would be good-looking. With them, it's downright handsome.

SEATING: GRADE A+

Only in Wrigley are seats as close to the field. In Boston, as well as in Chicago, a hanging curve can actually be seen hanging. And if it comes in too fat, you can watch it riding high into the sky—at Fenway up and over the "Monster," at Wrigley bouncing up into the ivy.

Baseball in both is personal. In Fenway it's also comfortable—plastic has found a niche. Sporting the best of both worlds, the Boston ballpark has adapted to the benefits of modern technology better than Wrigley. Colors inside are still traditional—only orange and green. But those wooden chairs and bleacher benches, those that I lived on for three nights in '78 and whose splinters I picked out of my rear end, have vanished, to be replaced by comfortable plastic.

Even in plastic a quaint character remains. Fenway is still the majors' only real single-level ballpark. And at 33,000 capacity, easily the smallest. A tiny roof addition for corporation owners and their clients runs down both foul lines. For a normal fan, though, most seats are down below. Besides close, views are varied. Down in the left-field corner front-row seats rise above and hover over Mr. Rice. Only a foot or two from fair territory. You can actually reach over and chip a little in-play paint off of the "Monster." Behind the plate, boxes hug the field—at some spots closer to the batter than the dugout is. Like at Wrigley, you actually look up to the crest of the mound. Roger Clemens sizzles white blurs to the plate; Gedman's mitt pops with a slap. You wonder how on earth anybody can touch the guy. Sliding back and away, down the right-field foul line, more unique views. Jutting into fair territory, the short porch provides baseball's best chance to see the game up close and catch a homer at the same time.

From all the reserves, even those tucked up under the overhanging roof, you feel like you're really a part of the game. That if you scream just a little louder, Clemens will throw just a little harder. And the Sox will be just a little tougher. You really feel like you make the difference.

Beyond the bull pens in right field and peaking under the scoreboard in center sits a huge bleacher section. Wooden benches on my Yankee visit in '78, now they're all plastic chairs. North and South Side Chicago, Tiger Stadium, and old run-down Municipal in Cleveland still have wooden planks. They're the best. Baseball's magic seems to take its strongest hold when folks sit in the sunshine and share flat wooden benches. Even so, the Fenway bleachers are still filled with crazies. Folks like in '78, who'll share their beer and bagels and, most willingly, their opinions... just as long as you hate the Yankees.

SCOREBOARD: GRADE A+

Boston is a charming city. Churches built before the war (the one in 1776), rest in city squares hovered over by 60-story skyscrapers. The Old World and a new exciting age exist side by side, providing a flavor only a few special towns can claim. Fenway is the same. Traditional and at the same time modern—built in 1912, the eighties still have a place inside. Together the old and new give baseball a touch of Boston.

Nowhere else is the park's old and new mix more obvious than in the way it keeps score. Two boards do the job. Each is as different from the other as the Old North Church from the Prudential Building.

In left is the Colonial style. Like Wrigley, the Fenway panel is almost entirely hand-operated. Embedded into the base of the "Monster," dwarfed by the big green wall, the board looks even simpler than it is. An "American League" label runs across the top. Below, openings for inning-by-inning scores, runs, hits, and errors consume it. AL scores and pitching changes are also kept up to date. Tiny human beings hurry about inside the wall and fill the openings with green-squared white numerals. Only red and green light bulbs, reflecting balls, strikes, and outs, acknowledge that Sox baseball in '85 gets any different coverage than it did in '25.

In stark contrast to the classic left-field panel, above the bleachers, silhouetted by the city skyline, perches a modern matrix screen. It's not a grand setup like in Comiskey or at Jack Murphy. It doesn't explode on each Dewey Evans blast. Nor does it concern itself with "charges" or fancy slogans to work the fans into a frenzy. Instead it just quietly carries on. National League scores, and important messages that can't be spelled out in a little hole in the wall, show up on its giant computer face. And replays, although not the clearest, appear occasionally. While the giant computer could do it all if it really wanted to, it holds back. And the classic panel in left, besides being quaint, is useful too.

Simple and small in left, large and sophisticated in center, old alongside new, neither pulls from the other. Each serves to make its partner stronger. Together they are pure Boston.

FOOD: GRADE D

Selection: Fair   Accessibility: Poor
Taste: Poor   Cost: 19th

On my first two Bosox visits I couldn't figure out how such a wonderful place could have such horrible food. Not only were the concessions bad, but the folks that worked 'em were rude. And Fenway Franks... they were nauseating, to look at and to eat. I guess I grew up spoiled. At Tiger Stadium a ballpark dog was a work of art. A splash of mustard on that "plump when you cook 'em" wiener was baseball's best treat. And the cooks were artists—friendly old gentlemen "damn proud" of their work. Those first couple of Fenway comparisons were barely digestible.

Today the ballpark still charms. The concessions have added a few touches. Even the people serving are friendlier. The Fenway Frank, though, is still the absolute worst wiener known to man—at least the one served up in the stands is. Microwaved to shriveled perfection in its own little package, and garnished with two packets of mustard, just looking at it can send shivers down your spine... never mind taking a bite. Under a blue sunny sky with a brew at your side, and Bruce Hurst shooting BB's on the mound—at most places a ballpark dog is a must. At Fenway it only sours the scenery.

While those going into the stands are microwaved, at least the ones served underneath are steam-cooked. They are joined by a few newcomers—kielbasa, ham and cheese, and roast beef sandwiches. Although the selection is still no Denny's, at least it's past the 7-Eleven stage. Only beer is served in stop-and-go style. Probably to calm those hot-blooded New England fans, beer can only be bought from the tap under the stands. With the Yankees in town, probably not such a bad idea. But with the M's in... come on!

BALLPARK EMPLOYEES: GRADE C

If one thing about the ballpark has improved, it'd have to be the attitude of the folks serving it. Used to be in her aisles prowled some of the nastiest employees in the major leagues.

A rumor circulating the stands back in '78 was that the Sox imported Boston College linemen for the New York series. Their job—to pound on anybody who looked cross-eyed at a stadium official. No rumor at all—bouncers filled the stands. Only too big for Boston College. They looked more like New England Patriots. Regardless of the team, the series was a three-day brawl. Fistfights were an inning-by-inning occurrence, as many started by the stadium employees as the drunken bleacher bums. Then, as in '74, too many muscle men looking to flex roamed the place.

Nowadays bouncers still roam under the stands. Boston College probably still finds its linemen summer jobs tending Fenway's aisles. With each call for help the inspired studs still spring to assistance. However, there seems to be a change of attitude. No longer does the offensive line practice its wedge blocking on bleacherites' heads. In fact, the fine-looking gentlemen don't even drool anymore. Dressed respectably in shirt and tie, now they are pleasant and helpful.

Not only the bouncers, but ushers and concessionaires, too, seem much nicer than in the good ole bleacherite-bashing days. Box seat holders get a personalized escort to a dusted chair. And questions of baseball's most foul-tasting wieners are met with embarrassment instead of bitterness. While the attitude is a long way from that Midwest pat-on-the-back or old-home week on the West Coast, at least today a stadium jacket doesn't issue a license to pound face.

FACILITIES: GRADE D

Like most of its other Eastern park allies, Fenway isn't properly equipped to take on the masses. It suffers from all those problems that only age and urban life can bring.

Worse even than in Detroit or Chicago, parking next door to the ballpark is nearly impossible. It is bordered by only a few, very tiny, outrageously over-priced lots, and you're much better off leaving the car almost anywhere and finding another way to get there. A delightful alternative is the subway. For being American, and plopped in the middle of a big Eastern city, it's actually quite tidy. Stretching a few miles out into the western suburbs, the train picks up folks along the way and makes its Fenway stop only two blocks from the ballpark, at Kenmore Square.

The ride's exciting. Sandwiched in with all sorts of Sox caps and fans, it's a great way to get that pregame pump. And the stroll from Kenmore to Fenway is even better. The neighborhood comes alive as it prepares for baseball. Hot-pretzel carts and rolling Italian sausage grills, besides offering great food, cre-ate a friendly aroma. Streams of folks flood the sidewalks, cars plod by bumper to bumper. Doorways to the nearby taverns overflow with baseball-talking pa-trons. And good seats are available everywhere. Scalpers with fists full of tick-ets catch you at every corner. From the moment you leave the train, they work the turf: "Need a seat? Gotta great deal." They usually do. But if you hang around and wait till game time, the deal gets even "greater."

Inside, facilities are typically Eastern. Even so, Boston makes the best of a bad situation. Tiny rest rooms, with out-of-date accessories, are fairly well kept. At least taking a bathroom break, unlike at some other East Coasters, isn't life-threatening.

ATMOSPHERE: GRADE A+

It'd been eleven years since my first date with Fenway, and seven since I'd felt the heat of a Sox–Yankee pennant race inside her. In a decade the world's gone through a lot of changes. Most haven't been kind to baseball. A world of domes, plastic grass, and metal bats has taken its toll on tradition. I returned hopeful that the Boston park still lived by the old ways. Hopeful that inside time would take a vacation and that the Sox could still carry on in their own little world.

Only a few exist that can wield the sorcery that makes an afternoon of baseball a timeless experience. Besides Fenway, only the ancients—Chicago's Wrigley and Comiskey, and Tiger Stadium in Detroit—have that same magical appeal. Wrigley's a black-and-white photograph in an era of MTV color videos. Yellowing around the edges, like an old picture pasted in some worn scrapbook, it lies tucked away in its Wrigleyville attic. Cub fans and their home ignore the modern world. Comiskey has aged tremendously. Unlike Wrigley, the South Side Chicago stadium won't survive. Bulldozers and suburbs already call. Pressed up against the ghetto, it sits wrinkling away in its rocking chair, an exploding scoreboard proof of lingering senility. Rocking back 'n' forth, decaying but giggling in its South Side home. In Detroit baseball never changes. Like a rock, Tiger Stadium resists the troubled times that always seem to find the Motor City and offers a 1920s sanctuary to a battered, beaten, modern-day urban mess.

All three have weathered the modern plastic invasion. Comiskey and Tiger Stadium have borrowed a few items, then escaped back into a simpler time, while Wrigley refuses to admit that Thomas Edison has yet discovered electricity. I wondered how the past ten years had treated Fenway. I hoped that, like Wrigley, the old Bostonian would drink the poison hemlock before bowing down to technology. That would be the only way for it to survive—to resist and endure. Progress, I was sure, would only ruin her.

I was wrong. "Progress" has quietly crept inside the Lansdowne Street gates. In the past ten years Fenway has changed. Those old splintered bleachers are gone, replaced by comfortable plastic fold-up chairs. Unlike the Cubbie's faded sun-bleached scoreboard, a fresh coat of "Monster Green" covers the huge wall in left. Even a quiet computer screen perches high above the right-field bleachers.

But Fenway has survived. By choosing to be pampered, the old park's resisted those who'd just as soon bulldoze her. It's as though it knows that in this age of multipurpose stadiums, a 33,000-seater is no financial wonder. That Mr. Yawkey no longer holds the reins; instead it's bookkeepers and accountants. They now decide if she's maybe too much tradition and not enough profit. So she gives a little. Cracks the door open for progress—just enough to keep 'em happy. Then falls back into a simpler world of blue skies, real live green grass, and baseball. At heart still the same tough hard-core park as always, like the city of Boston, Fenway's a mix of the old and new. A bridge from baseball's past to its future.

First, Fenway is the neighborhood that surrounds it. A certain sincerity makes life about the ballpark special. Here is the city: milling people, street gutters, fire hydrants, the normalcy of urban Boston going about its daily routine. Streets are still narrow, concrete sidewalks bleached and cracked. Aside from an asphalt covering for a few of its crisscrossing streets, nothing is updated or improved. It offers that same flavorful invitation to the "Jim Rice Show" today that it did for years when Yaz hammered at the wall, and before when Williams roamed in left. From Fenway's porch, time stands still.

Loyal, if not always to the Red Sox, but to baseball itself, Sox fans are among the game's most intense. Whether to curse or cheer, Bostonians flaunt their right to each. Consequently, while following the Bosox's dead-end pennant drives might be frustrating, they're rarely dull. And with the Yanks in town, I'm sure they still border on lunacy. Sox fans bring to baseball a blue-collar, bottle-of-beer attitude in an age when wine sipping in the closed-circuit lounge is the trend. And an opinion... always an opinion.

Inside, along with Wrigley, Fenway remains the coziest. Even with the old splintered bleachers gone, the park is pure. And it still offers an intimate touch to the game. From the massive right-field bleachers to the chairs behind the on-deck circle, to the third-base box seats, fans are on top of, alongside, almost inside of the game.

Finally, Fenway is the "Monster." Like Wrigley's ivy, it just cannot be resisted. While the ivy charms one into a dream state, Boston's great green wall intimidates. Like a mountain range shadowing the short left field, the beast dominates the beauty of the park. Every play in some way is affected by it. Every pitcher throws with the wall in mind. Every batter swings with its presence felt. Every fan waits to see it ripped by a vicious line drive or its net creased by a soft, lazy fly ball. The "Monster" remains as dominating to the game today as it was when it first took its lair.

Boston's charming ballpark is surviving, and it does so without sacrificing integrity. Despite a little cosmetic primping, the very heart of the game, the people, and the park itself remain caught in time. Fenway today is baseball as it was in years past, and as pure as it will ever be again in the future. Time will never erode the "Green Monster," nor can it diminish the emotion that people have for the game. With America's most historic city looming overhead, the scent of fresh bagels and pretzels hanging in the air, with bright sunshine and green grass, sitting amid the flavor of Fenway you can't resist the feeling that time has stopped... or at least waited for a couple of hours until game's end.

20

VETERANS STADIUM, PHILADELPHIA PHILLIES

To Strike a Strike

REPORT CARD

Veterans Stadium
BASEBALL PARK

July 28, 85 vs Braves
GAME

Philadelphia Phillies
BASEBALL CLUB

CATEGORY	GRADE	POINTS
Layout and Upkeep	D	65
Ball Field	D-	60
Seating	D	65
Scoreboard	B	85
Food	B	85
Ballpark Employees	A	95
Facilities	C	75
Atmosphere	B	85
Total Points		615
Average		77

C+
FINAL GRADE

17th
RANK

"In spite of some rotten first impressions at a place obsessed with plastic... Philly tradition rallies a solid baseball atmosphere inside."

PREGAME THOUGHTS

A "Major League Baseball Fan Walkout" organized to protest the upcoming players' strike... what a wonderful idea! Baseball, America, and certainly I would never be quite the same!

Five days earlier up in Montreal, I'd read about it. A devout baseball fan, and a sportswriter on the side, was sick of what'd been going on. Unlike the rest of us, though, who just shared a beer and bitched about it, he decided to do something. He organized a series of nationwide fan boycotts—their goal to show the Players Association and the owners that the whole idea of a strike was horse crap. In the middle of the seventh, instead of just singing "Take Me Out to the Ballgame," folks were supposed to rise together and walk. For three outs they were gonna send a message to the world that baseball was their game. Don't anybody screw it up! God, I loved it!

The plan called for five boycotts. Target number one was the most important; if the idea was to catch on, it would surely have to work the first time. Well, target number one was Veterans Stadium, Philadelphia. And D Day was my Sunday afternoon in town. I was gonna get to be a part of it! In essence I was going to strike a strike.

This entire players' strike thing was sickening... if not ridiculous. Neither side was trustworthy. As usual, just self-centered. Through the worthless proposals and even more worthless counterproposals, nobody, not the players, not the owners, had even considered the very basis of the game—the fan. The simple guy with the transistor radio, a No. 2 pencil, and a scorebook. Without him attending, there'd be no negotiations, no arbitrations, no pension problems, no contract, no money, no game. If "Joe Fan" didn't leave Rover at home in the suburbs in the two-car garage, drive his wife and 2.3 kids in their Chevrolet station wagon to the ballpark on "Family Night," and spend $146 on tickets, hot dogs, peanuts, and pop, then ball clubs would lose money. Owners would get out. And players would have to go back to playing for the love of the game. It seemed like such a wonderful proposition, ball players out there for the love of the game.

From Fenway to Philly I lost myself in patriotic baseball dreams. I began to think of myself as part of "We—the fans." A solidarity arose in my brain.

We were "mad as hell and weren't going to take it anymore." No longer would we worry if poor Jack Morris had to retire at the age of 39 with only a $400,000-a-year pension. Tough, Jack—go out and get a part-time job selling used cars! Maybe it'd even lead to putting one of "us" on the arbitration panels. I could just see myself arbitrating for the Yankees: "Well, Mr. Winfield, I'm afraid that I'll have to rule in favor of the team proposal of $25 a game. However, since you love baseball so, it shouldn't matter too much. And by the way, George, now that you'll be saving so much cash on Dave, how 'bout cutting ticket prices in half and selling beer at cost?"

Sunday would mark the birth of major league baseball fan freedom. It'd be the day that the little guy stood up and spoke his mind. The spirit of the American Revolution would come alive again...in Philadelphia. The same place "we" decided to dump the British, "we" would wake up the majors. And those spirits that planted the seed of American independence could watch. Franklin, Jefferson, Washington—they'd have to be proud.

I got to Veterans early, a couple of hours before game time. It was a beautiful bright blue morning, perfect for a revolution. A fellow revolutionary was on the stadium sidewalk passing out walk-out flyers. The flyer stated our goals: "To show the players and owners our disgust with the pending strike." For all three outs in the bottom of the seventh, we'd walk. "The situation," it ended with, "is urgent. The time is critical." Short, sweet, and to the point. I liked it! There could be no confusion of what we wanted.

I turned to the fellow who was handing 'em out. "How many do you think will go?" I asked, positive the place would empty.

"Not sure. We're hoping at least a couple of thousand."

I figured he was just being modest. Folks were bound to race for the exits. Everyone, including me, would want to be first. It'd be like being the first signature on the Declaration of Independence. Maybe, I thought, we'd even join hands or sing together on the way out. Chills raced the goose bumps running down my spine. After tucking the flyer away in my back pocket, I left him with a "We'll give 'em a seventh-inning stretch to remember."

He nodded, thanked me, and offered up a "Hope so!"

Rest of the afternoon I spent on a cloud. Between cruising the stadium walkways, working up my Stadium Report Card, and kicking back in the sunshine watching baseball, I mulled the walkout over. Anybody I'd join in a casual baseball conversation with, I brought it up. "Well, you going?" was my favorite greeting. Most folks looked at me strangely. "Going where?" was a normal response. I was surprised so many didn't know about it. If they didn't, I'd get out my flyer and show 'em. After that they'd relax, let their kid move back in the seat next to me, and we'd talk "walk." A "Sure, I'll probably leave"

I took as a yes, considered myself a prophet of the word, and moved to another seat.

Unlike some of the fans, employees seemed to know all about the walkout. They were ready for it. One old fella who worked a lower-level gate thought it was a great idea. He'd been at Veterans for a number of years in a number of jobs. He'd "Seen 'em come and seen 'em go." He'd watched salaries (all except his, he told me) skyrocket, and ticket prices strive to keep up the pace. For the Sunday-afternoon boycott his job was to have the outfield gates open for folks to walk out. And to make sure they were able to get back in for the eighth. His was the gate I decided to walk from.

"What do you think about this walkout?" I asked him.

His eyes lit up. It was an issue he must've contemplated on many a drive home from the ballpark. "It's about damned time somebody did something. You know if I could, I'd go with you. You and I don't make that kind of money. And you don't see us striking."

I agreed wholeheartedly with him. And since he was on a roll, I just kicked back and listened. He brought up a line Bill Veeck used to preach: "It's not the high price of superstardom that bothers me, it's the high price of mediocrity." He gave Bill the credit and continued, "We're paying half a million a season to guys who hit .250. Hell, I could hit .250! Their average gets lower and their paycheck bigger. Something's just not right."

"And you know who pays the price? You know who?" He was talking to me, but didn't need an answer, so I didn't. "It's the fans! Families can't afford to come anymore!" he announced. "You know it costs a guy seventy-five bucks to bring the kids, park the car, buy tickets and a round of hot dogs. That's just not right! Maybe this will wake 'em up."

After nodding all through his lecture, I gave a good nod at the end. Kind of an exclamation mark. He was right. I told him so. And also let him know that his would be the gate I'd make my exit from. He was pleased and left me with a "Good luck." It was a sincere wish.

Report card completed, and exit mapped out, I headed back into my left-field seat. I sat in the sunshine, cracked a few more peanuts, and enjoyed the rest of a lovely afternoon. More important, though, I counted the outs till the seventh. Everything was set. If the old guy at the gate was for it, I figured fans certainly would be. Us walking would be like water swirling down a bathtub drain. Veterans Stadium would empty. The bat cracking would echo through it like a Sunday-morning batting-practice session. It'd be quieter than the Kingdome on a Tuesday night with the Indians in town. Players would be dumbfounded. Stunned, they'd probably just stand at their positions with their mouths agape, look up into the empty seats while their gloves slipped off to the ground. It could happen no other way. In fact, it's been a long time since I've been as confident of anything baseball-related. I think the last time was Game Seven of the '75 Series.

A zero popped up on the board for the Braves' half of the seventh. On cue, "we" arose. Not to sing, but to leave. The exodus began. Holding my head up high, I marched to my prearranged exit. One of the first ones there, I nodded to my gate-guard friend standing by and passed outside.

I'd done it! I'd struck the players' strike. A drop in the first wave of a moral flood that would sweep America. I stood at the cutting edge of history. Pumped up, I turned to greet the tide of my fellow striking revolutionaries. I half expected 'em to swallow me up. We'd all give high fives in the parking lot. Cheering, speech-making, self-congratulations, we'd carry on like congressmen on election night. And maybe if we were having a good enough time, even skip the eighth and ninth.

But as I turned I was stunned. Instead of a moral flood, barely even a trickle squeezed through the gate. It must be the wrong day, I figured. That, or the wrong inning, maybe the wrong ballpark. I fumbled for my instruction handout. Reread it. No, I was right! The date was right, so was the inning. Four or five folks were hanging around outside my gate. Not more than a hundred, that I could see, outside the park. It didn't make sense. But since my strike pamphlet called for a half-inning boycott, I decided to circle the stadium. Maybe, I hoped, I'd find the crowd. Maybe a walkout rally was taking place on the other side.

I searched, but sidewalks were empty. Some people hung around outside the exits. A few folks trickled into the parking lot. So few, though, that it could've just been the beat-the-traffic crowd. I couldn't believe what had happened. Or worse yet, what hadn't. I'd expected a mass movement, 1776 all over again. Instead, nothing.

I sat outside and waited my three outs. My spirit was broken. Philly was a good, honest sports town. Folks knew the issues, what was on the line. The walkout was safe, it didn't involve any risks. Hell, we could even go back inside and finish the ball game. And yet, no response. Nobody cared.

A fellow as confused as I stumbled up. He was a little tipsy and had snuck his draft outside with him.

"What happened?" he asked me.

"I dunno," I mumbled. "I thought the place would empty."

"Me too. Me too."

I offered him what was left of my bag of salted nuts. He accepted. He offered me a swig of beer. I passed. For three outs we talked about baseball. Not pennant races or World Series, we didn't even mention a single batting average. Instead we concentrated on the bad things, the slow erosion of the game's standards and how money dominated it today. We asked each other what had happened to American ideals. We talked about the sixties, when people were proud to protest. We even got into a little Vietnam. Most important, we congratulated one another for having such integrity, for seeing what the gate attendant saw so well.

Bag of peanuts finished, and the eighth inning begun, I left him with the same Bill Veeck quote that the gate attendant had hit me with. It just seemed to fit. And we headed back inside. Me to my upper-level, left-field sun seat. He to his first-base box. Both of us to watch the mercenaries finish out a single insignificant game. In a single insignificant season, in a pastime based on the very truest of principles, yet destined for another immoral strike.

LAYOUT AND UPKEEP: GRADE D

I was so pumped pulling into Philly, thinking strike and all, that it didn't even bother me that the ballpark looked like a hole. And it does!

The idea is great. Three arenas sit side by side by side. Basketball, football, and baseball all have separate stadiums. Unlike in Kansas City, though, where the same thought blooms into a ballpark masterpiece, the Philadelphia triplex is tacky. First off, none of the three arenas, JFK Football Stadium—which is hardly used for anything anymore, the Spectrum—a boxy little basketball hockey arena, or plain ole Veterans, is good-looking. They certainly don't complement one another like the bright red pair in Kansas City. And secondly, even though they've got three of 'em, baseball's Phils and football's Eagles share the same place. And guess who gets the better of the deal? A multidimensional circle stadium...a clone of Riverfront. Concrete and barren on the outside, plastic and barren on the inside. "The Vet" caters to anyone who's got a buck.

Layout, however, is not the ballpark's only problem. The place looks trashy. Acres of parking lots that surround it were splashed in the corners with broken bottles. A cold 12-foot-high, chain-link fence, tall enough to keep out the neighborhood but not its garbage, surrounds the cars.

Inside, stadium tackiness intensifies. Halls that circle the circle are painted a gaudy green and orange. Whoever interior-designed them should've been checked for color blindness. With Philly colors maroon and white, and the Eagles a bright green, I've no idea what he was thinking of. Maybe a medieval Halloween festival? Besides miscolored, they're also ill kempt. Pipes run exposed overhead. Annoying litter and piled-up junk mix to hang a stale smell over the place. A cruise from the filthy parking lot through the gates and filthy halls presents a perfectly awful intro to baseball. And a hint to horrors beyond.

BALL FIELD: GRADE D−

During my Sunday-afternoon stay in "the Vet" I moved around more than a Pentecostal minister filtering through the crowd on "healing day." While working up converts to the walk, I switched a lot of seats. About a dozen of 'em. So I got to see the ball field from all sorts of views. Each was nearly blinding.

Philly's fake grass rivals the floor of the Astrodome as baseball's ugliest. It has all sorts of problems. First is its color. One shade of green, even if it's plastic, is usually the best choice for a baseball field. Veterans, though, features all sorts of them. Aqua-green, bright green, lime-green, grass-green, Crayola Crayons Super School Starter 500 box doesn't offer as many choices. They break the ball field into separate sections, like a patchwork quilt. And also make whatever it was you had for lunch more difficult to digest.

Besides changing colors, the turf reflects light like an ocean beach on a hot August day. Sun rays bounce off of it so violently that management ought to consider handing out no-glare sunglasses with each ticket purchase.

If the assorted green glaring isn't enough to force you to cover your eyes between innings, the outfield seam will do it. Like a giant zipper, it runs through the middle of the quilt.

Finally, one last touch of ugly floods the thing. Faded into the face of the baseball diamond is a football rectangle. After leaving the lushness of Fenway grass, and plopping down in Veterans tacky plastic, I got to see one of the majors' best and worst turfs back-to-back. I now know what it's like if you're bad and die: they screw up and send you to heaven for a day, take back the offer, then kick you downstairs. Hell has gotta have carpeting that looks a little like the stuff in Philly.

SEATING: GRADE D

I sat just about everywhere there was to sit in "the Vet." My complimentary tickets down behind home plate were great for batting practice. A Coke, some bright warm sunshine, and Mike Schmidt cranking out moon shots only a few feet away. I could've stayed and the game would've been as good. But I was antsy; I needed to mosey around and "talk seventh-inning walkout." By the second I was moseying.

As for rating the seating, I really didn't even need to go inside. I could've just stayed in the car and reread my Cincinnati chapter. There's not a lot of difference. Like Cincy's concrete river bowl and St. Louis's, too, for that matter, "the Vet" is an enclosed circle of plastic seats. With field section topped by a few more tiers, it is not as perfectly round as Riverfront, but otherwise the two are pretty much the same. Like Reds fans, those in Philly get movie-theater comfort. Walkways between the sections are wide and plentiful. They're almost as wide between the aisles of seats. Sitting and standing is simple. So is the transition between the two.

Watching baseball, on the other hand, can be tough. Field seats down in front are good. Largest of the sections, however, is not down in front—it's way up in the sky. It is the majors' biggest upper level, and when the Phils pack 'em in most folks are about as far from the pitcher's mound as they are from their cars out in the parking lot. It's a shame that Pete Rose has spent most of a career in two ballparks where cheap-seat folks can barely make out his body let alone a number. To many, as a Red and as a Philly, Charley Hustle probably best resembles a common ordinary housefly.

SCOREBOARD: GRADE B

Philly is a good sports town. Its baseball fans are hard-core. Unfortunately, just not hard-core enough to take a half inning off to prove it. The scoreboard, too, like the folks that watch it, is all business.

Structurally the setup is state-of-the-art. Above the right-field fence, red and white lights cover the Phils and whoever's in town. The panel flashes individual stats of both teams. And also provides regular updates of all NL games. AL scores get playing time too—only just not as much.

Panasonic's Astro Vision, second half of the pair of scoreboards, hangs high above center field. Its clear picture is easy to see from almost anywhere inside...even on a sunny Sunday. Plus it gets good use. While some parks treat their giant movie screen like a ceremonial set of silverware that gets pulled out only at holiday time, in Philly it's usually on. And unlike other parks where I wondered if the screen had a cable hookup to MTV, the Philly one was all baseball. Both of the boards, the digital panel in right and the instant-replay screen in center, like the town itself, are good hard-core baseball.

More than what the scoreboard setup is...is really what it isn't. Trumpet "charges" are not a Veterans Stadium biggie. Fans are seldom asked to chant something. Catchy slogans, running quiz shows, or an obsession with "baseball's bloops and blunders" that dominate other scoreboards, particularly Diamond Vision ones, just aren't found in Philly. About as fancy as it gets is a simple big-screen, postgame highlight show. A good blue-collar job for a traditional blue-collar crowd. I just wish that when the bottom of the seventh had rolled around it'd commanded everyone to get up and leave... instead of calling for the ole traditional stretch.

FOOD: GRADE B

Selection: Excellent   Accessibility: Poor
Taste: Excellent   Cost: 14th

After leaving the broken-bottled parking lot and touring the plastic place inside, I wondered if I could work up much excitement for anything but my seventh-inning walkout. Needless to say, first impressions of "the Vet" are not the stuff dreams are made of... nightmares, maybe, but not dreams.

Ditto for the concessions. Closet-size souvenir stands were about as well stocked as a gas-station vending machine, while food stands, especially those under the outfield seats, were almost all closed. Worst of all was a grotesque little five-picnic-tabled beer garden in the lower level. Set up along the concrete hallway, bordered by a hideous scene of something painted in fluorescent colors, the concrete garden typifies the place—pure ugly. After passing it I seriously wondered if it'd be safe to eat any food that wasn't packaged and safety sealed.

But like the ballpark that slowly smooths out its jagged edges, food gets better as the game goes on. Most of the good stuff's in stands behind home plate. And since you're free to roam almost anywhere, even if you're sitting way up in left field, it's definitely worth the stroll. Then prepare—all of the food, particularly the specialty stuff, is great. Sandwiches galore, served in home-style portions, provide one of the majors' best neighborhood-deli impersonations. BBQ pork is tangy and dripping in extra sauce. Corned beef and baseball's best roast beef look like Dagwood Bumstead midnight snacks. And taste probably as good. Stuff's fried too—chicken, french fries, shrimp rolls pop up in a few of the stands. And the pizza, like everything else, is stacked—thick and cheesy.

The menu peaks, though, back up in the stands. Coming from Fenway and the world's worst in-stand wiener, I ran into one of the best in Philly. It's kind of like a flip-flop of the ball field. Like in Detroit, a Veterans ballpark wiener is a work of art. Instead of answering "Mustard, please" with a couple of packets, the hot-dog guy responds the old-fashioned way. He dips a flat wooden stick into a full cup of mustard, slaps on a thick yellow coat, shoves it in the wax paper, and sends it down the line from hands to hands to hands to mouth. Any place that still does that can't be all bad... even if it has a neon plastic field and broken-bottled parking lot.

BALLPARK EMPLOYEES: GRADE A

Despite its nickname, Philadelphia is not filled with "brotherly love." In fact, in spots it's kind of nasty. One of those nastier spots is "the Vet's" corner of town. The ballpark's misleading too. As part of a triplex, you'd expect efficiency to be the first order of business. Instead it's ugliness. Still, something makes the sorry-looking stadium plopped down in a sorry end of town special. I think it might be the folks who run it.

Ushers swarm the ballpark. Down close to the field they follow the Olympic Stadium tradition. Mostly teenaged girls, dressed in powder-blue Philly jerseys and matching shorts, work the lower boxes. The kids do a nice job. And seem to have a good time too. One that happily transfers over to the folks they seat. Other aisles around the place are also well ushered. Old fellas are helpful without being nosy. Since the stadium was less than packed, they didn't check every single ticket. And I was able to visit different seats and spread the "walkout gospel."

Like ushers, security guards, too, are all over the place. In some stadiums security people are as tough to find as late-night city cops tucked away in a Dunkin' Donuts caffeining themselves to death. At others they live to slap folks around. At "the Vet" it's neither. Security roams pretty much at will. But never was I hassled nor did I see a hassle taking place. In fact, about all I saw the badged men handing out were "Hellos." Besides roaming, the cops did a good job of softening up potential trouble spots. Each ramp landing had a cop perched on a chair. Not there to nag for ticket stubs, they just made sure anybody who wanted to was able to take a short, safe, between-inning stroll.

Rest rooms even get patrolled. At the more crowded sections a pair of employees sit in each of them, their job being to clean up while the game's going on. They also have a couple of other duties. By being there, the last of the stadium's potential trouble spots is safe. And at least one of them, outside section 220, is, as rest rooms go, also a happy place.

Nate runs it. And does so in his own peculiar way. While most attendants sit bored out of their minds for nine innings of ball, Nate has a little fun. And also picks up a few tips, which, by the way, is allowed. His folding chair, instead of sitting in an empty corner, was immersed in Sinatra. Pictures, posters, newspaper articles, all of Frank, flooded the wall behind him. Meanwhile, a Sinatra collection of tapes kicked out over the tape player. Nate danced around the room with a roll of paper towels in hand. If anybody needed to dry off washed hands, he was there to roll off the paper. If anybody needed the faucet held down, Nate was never above holding the lever. He kidded with the youngsters, was friendly with the old folks. As full of good cheer as a fake Santa Claus on Christmas Eve, Nate gave his little room a touch of unusual class and "the Vet" a little character.

In fact, good characters are the ballpark's strongest suit. Whether to usher, serve, or protect, those that bring Philly fans Philly baseball are all right. Even if the city isn't filled with it, at least for nine innings at a time "the Vet" tries to live up to its billing as the stadium in the City of Brotherly Love.

FACILITIES: GRADE C

Nate and his buddies keep the rest rooms habitable. They are regularly swept and polished, and while they're a long way from men's rooms at the Golden Arches, at least they're free from crime and disease.

The parking lot, however, is a different story. Although acres of it surround the three stadiums, it was a mess. First off, despite all the open spots, not enough roads lead from the highway to stadium gates. Although I was a couple of hours early for my Sunday-afternoon stay, and found an easy entrance, traffic jams look like they might be a regular problem. Secondly, most of the lot was unkempt. Unpaved in many places, littered with junk and chuckholes in others, it was about as neat and clean as the stadium walkways inside. Finally, there's that 12-foot chain-link fence. The last thing it does is ensure confidence in the neighborhood.

Even on a warm sunny Sunday, I just wasn't sure. Between the chuckholes, broken bottles, fencing, and city, my little car didn't seem safe. I figured if folks looked after cars as closely as they did the lot, mine probably would be history. But I didn't have much of a choice. So I got as close as possible to the front door, checked the locks four or five times, and zigzagged off between the bottles and chuckholes to the ball game.

ATMOSPHERE: GRADE B

If first impressions were all that mattered, "the Vet," like an old Western ghost town, would be best abandoned and left to wither away. That or blown up and put out of its misery. First impressions, however, don't include a look into the heart. And "the Vet" has a good one—not soft, but sincere. Baseball in Philadelphia, despite all its cosmetic faults, belongs.

No other major league stadium looks so barren. Surrounded by acres of broken concrete, and separated from a tired neighborhood by 12 feet of steel—rolling into "the Vet" has all the appeal of being processed into a World War II prisoner-of-war camp. Inside, things get worse! Those clean sterile hallways, which Riverfront proved go so well with plastic seats in a concrete circle, are absent in Philly. Instead they're filthy. Meanwhile, the plastic playing field is hideous—as ugly as Houston's, even worse on a sunny day. Sitting in the pit, covering my eyes from the reflecting plastic below, I wondered how baseball in such a rich East Coast city could be so lousy. It was about then that the Philly Phanatic sped out on his motor scooter.

The Phanatic is as sorry-looking as everything else. A pear-shaped, green-haired, elephant-nosed creature, he looks like a living defect caused from grazing off the stadium's plastic grass. For two hours of batting practice, the Phanatic motor-scooters, dances, runs, and cartwheels himself all over the ball field. I figured, "My God, when the game starts the big oaf will probably lead the wave from the third-base coaching box." I prayed that somebody would get out a net and carry him off to some loony bin.

Something happens, though, when the ball game starts. The moment that first pitch pops the catcher's mitt, "the Vet" reveals a hidden luster. A sincerity hidden under plastic, broken bottles, and a fluorescent-green, motor-scooter-riding creature emerges. And baseball, old-time, traditional-style flowers.

I'd heard that Philly fans were tough, cruel, almost New York Met-ish. As great as Mike Schmidt is, I read they'd hammered him his whole career. That they threw things at him and cursed him each time he didn't hit one out. I didn't see it! All I found were good baseball people. Folks who seemed to really know what was going on and paid attention too. And the scoreboard followed suit. Nothing to laugh at, sing along with, or contemplate, it was just plain baseball. "Guess the Attendance"—a celebration at almost all other major league parks—at "the Vet" slipped quietly by. The dreaded wave—absent in only two other major league cities (New York and Chicago)—on my visit to Philly had no takers. Fans didn't need hype. Or cutesy sideshows. Just baseball... and that's all they got. Simple and straightforward.

Even the Phanatic took a sedative once the game began. His antics during it were minimal, and really kind of fun. He spent an awful lot of time making the kids happy. All over the stadium I saw little guys tugging on their daddies' shirt sleeves and pointing at the ugly green thing.

The plastic palace itself also reveals a few hidden specialties. No other ballpark is so well patrolled, so concerned with safety. No other park features a rest room like Nate's. His Sinatra collection and dancing paper towels are classic. And only at Tiger Stadium is an in-stand hot dog as traditional.

It's at that section 220 rest room, on that mustard-coated wooden stick, and in the hard-core fans' love of the game where the real heart of "the Vet" beats. From its crippled artificial beginnings, baseball thrives. Despite an ugly ball field, housed by an ugly stadium, surrounded by an ugly parking lot, the game goes on... unfortunately even through the seventh inning. Although marred by the fact that hardly anybody got up and walked, I still found a rich spirit at "the Vet"... and, unbelievably, a good home for baseball.

21

MEMORIAL STADIUM,
BALTIMORE ORIOLES

Baseball's Best-kept Secret

REPORT CARD   *Memorial Stadium*

BASEBALL PARK

July 29/30, 85 vs Blue Jays   *Baltimore Orioles*

GAME   BASEBALL CLUB

CATEGORY	GRADE	POINTS
Layout and Upkeep	*B*	*85*
Ball Field	*A+*	*100*
Seating	*A*	*95*
Scoreboard	*A+*	*100*
Food	*B*	*85*
Ballpark Employees	*A*	*95*
Facilities	*D*	*65*
Atmosphere	*A+*	*100*
Total Points		*725*
Average		*91*

A−   *3rd*

FINAL GRADE   RANK

"What a pleasant surprise!...A delightful ballpark and friendly people meet at a quaint little nest in 'Birdland.'"

PREGAME THOUGHTS

Approaching Baltimore is a bit like entering into a free combat construction zone. The city's an endless series of detours from detours, set up and supposedly working throughout the night. Not since all those hours I spent in the sandbox as a kid have I seen more trucks in one place. And mine, at least, carried something. Still, without the construction problems, finding Memorial Stadium would have been a tough enough chore. The ballpark lies trapped between the city and its outskirts. Hardly a major street, let alone highway, runs into it. To make matters worse, I approached the mess from its messiest side. So to get within hiking distance of "Birdland," as the locals call it, I was treated to a not-so-scenic tour of town. Included for free was a stop and plea for help at every major gas station along the way and a brush with a real live hoodlum gang. But in the end my reward was a date with one of the majors' friendliest places.

Slowed considerably by all of the detours, starting time for the Blue Jays–Orioles game came and went, and still by the end of the first, instead of watching, I was listening. Normally tuning into a ball game mellows me out—not this time! As late as I was, it only made me more uptight. With every pitch my blood pressure pumped a few digits higher. Each inning change brought a renewed cussing outburst. Finally, by the bottom of the second, after four more gas-station stops and God knows how many traffic lights, I reached signs that stated "Memorial Stadium this way two miles." By the middle of the third, I cruised the park.

Late, I was nevertheless relieved. Thanks to Mobil, Chevron, and Shell, I'd conquered what looked to be a hopeless situation. I pulled up and stopped at a driveway across from the stadium. Still gloating, I failed to notice the small sign hanging on the weathered wooden sawhorse in the middle of the drive. It read "Lot Full." A crusty attendant standing nearby reminded me that meant I was too late to park there.

"Where do I go?" I asked.

"I dunno, parking isn't real good around these parts," he reassured me. "You should've gotten here sooner."

I'd have loved to stay and debate his city's road construction zoning laws, but the game was getting on. So I took what I thought was his "Probably your best bet is east of the stadium" advice, and headed on down the street. Now, other than left and right, forward and backward, myself and directions have never hit it off well. Familiar with maps, I have great difficulty in applying those same directions to the road. North is always up. South is down. West is left, which means east obviously is right. So I rolled on past the park and did what I was told to do. I took a right.

Bad choice! Crawling along the side of some broken street, I searched for an open spot. Not a thing. Driveways, small lots, back alleys every inch of concrete curb space had a tire pried in against it. Had the dirty front yards been filled as well, I'd have sworn that I was in Detroit. Meanwhile, the Orioles went down in order in the third. Besides striking out in the parking-lot department, I had other problems. I failed to notice the area I'd stumbled into was a rather nasty one. Quaint homes that graced the other side of the stadium had vanished. In their place stood cheap worn apartments and tired houses with dirt piles for front lawns. Garbage crowded up the curb lawns and squeezed between the parked cars. Still, I couldn't drum up eight feet of curb space anywhere.

And the ball game just kept moving on. Between the two, the game and the neighborhood—and no parking place—I was getting panicky. I needed help—anybody's help. So when a group of four teenagers, in search of lost frustrated fools like me, ran up and offered theirs, I could only oblige them. For five bucks the entrepreneurs promised to rescue me. They'd run me down deeper into Baltimore's seedy section, where the boss told me, "Ya, we've got good spot for you." I wasn't the first sucker to bite. This was a summer job— me merely another fish.

Creeping along behind the four jogging kids, I got the basic neighborhood tour—and what a lovely neighborhood it was. Battered houses, broken streets, everywhere were snarling Dobermans and cross-bred mongrels the size of water buffalo. And kids running around half dressed. I checked my locks, wondered what on earth I was getting into, but followed. Finally, we stopped at a scummy little post office. Its parking lot was nearly full; only my spot remained. The kids came to my window, I shelled out the five bucks, and crammed in along with the others who'd paid before me.

It was there in that parking lot that dedication to my summer's pilgrimage would show forth. And trust in the integrity of the human race would be put to the supreme test. Resting in my front seat, taking a deep breath, I took a good look around. A sandlot football game was going on in front of the post office, on the only patch of grass in the area. Groups of five and more, like the gentlemen who had so graciously parked me, roamed the streets. Houses that backed up to the drive were progressively worse than those I'd passed along the way. I figured that the community had a crime rate about 137 times the national average.

Even so, other cars surrounded me in the same predicament. And they must've been familiar with the local crime reports. So before giving up on the place, I decided to walk over and check 'em out. I eased out of my car and crept over. At a closer glance, most, there for the game like me, were a good match to the neighborhood. Many, if from a three-car family, had to be the third car. And some were even unlocked. I guess it made sense. If the roaming gangs wanted in, better to let 'em open the door than smash the windows.

I looked back at my brand-new Toyota. Like an overweight sheep lost in the middle of a hungry wolf pack, it sat waiting to be gobbled up. Clothes hung in the back seat, suitcases stacked up to the rod that held the hangers. Assorted junk was stuffed on top. If ever a car was ripe for the picking, it was mine. All I needed was for its out-of-state plates to flash in neon. They already glowed. A "Please Rip Me Off" sign plastered to the back window probably would've been appropriate. Still, I tried hard to convince myself that everything would be all right. The game was already in the fourth, it wouldn't last much more than another hour and a half. Darkness hadn't yet crept in. People would behave. Maybe I was wrong about the neighborhood. Maybe the teenage kids, walking about and drooling every time they looked my way, weren't sizing up their evening's take.

Right! I was dreaming! To leave it where it stood would be grounds for committal to some nut house. So everything of value—my camera, my tape recorder, my road atlas, and my favorite Sinatra tapes—I stuffed into the undersized backpack I was taking inside. All other objects I hid throughout the car. Like colored eggs around the house on Easter Sunday. Under the seat, up behind the dashboard, in the spare-tire rack—I emptied as much from sight as was humanly possible. And to the rest, I said good-bye. I knew by the time I was out of sight, everything, even the stuff in hiding, would be split up among my parking buddies. And probably sold that night somewhere in the neighborhood on the basic ball-game discount. Yet, for some pathetically unknown reason, I took one last look, sighed deeply, and walked off.

Radio in hand, I headed the few miles back toward the stadium. The game had just entered the fifth. Along the way I passed my personal parking-lot attendants. They watched me walk past. And nodded. That made it official— my car was history. Yet, obsessed, I continued on. I had to go to the game. I had to see Memorial Stadium. I had to do it that night. I felt like some brainless zombie from a horror picture. I just looked straight ahead and walked on.

About halfway to the stadium, near the point where front lawns turned from dirt piles back into grass and a resemblance to real houses began again, a lone city cop was stationed. Arms folded, he leaned against the hood of his parked squad car. Average cop height, average cop build, probably 35 or so, he'd have made a believable extra on *Hill Street Blues*. Relaxed, he seemed to be at ease with the nasty surroundings.

Timidly, I approached the Baltimore cop. "Hello," I said. Not real interested, he nodded back. Then I posed to Officer McCallister probably the most idiotic question he's ever been asked. I told him about my car; I wondered if he thought it'd be safe.

Still leaning against the hood, relaxed as he could be, McCallister busted out laughing. "You want me to tell you it's going to be okay?" Nervously I laughed along with him. It saved me from crying.

"Well, I ain't gonna," he added, after wiping his eyes and catching his breath.

My heart dropped. He was right. But I didn't know what to do. I was desperate! I needed help, advice, anything. I spilled my guts as fast as I could. Told him of my cross-country tour, about what had already happened in Williams, about my postal parking place and the kids who parked me. I even brought up that I taught junior high school. McCallister looked at me with an almost pathetic grin. He was amused. Patrols on game night didn't usually include such entertainment. Even so, something I said struck a chord. Without moving from his relaxed lean, he told me, "Go get your car. We'll see what we can do."

Elated, I sprinted back through the neighborhood, praying that I wasn't too late. I came up behind my attendants already preparing for the night's take. They looked at me, confused-like. I nodded and raced on. Down the block, around the corner, into the post-office parking lot. I stopped. There it sat. Washington plates sticking out like a sore thumb. Crammed full with all my hidden possessions, the doors seemed to almost bulge. I screamed in delight, jumped in the air, and slapped an imaginary high five to an invisible hand. I ran a quick circle-check around it. All four hubcaps were still intact, and the windows were in one piece. I popped in. First time, it started up. A couple of beeps on the horn just for celebration sake, I threw it into reverse and squeezed out the drive. My attendants, who'd followed, could only shake their heads and look on.

I was extra-special careful to remember the route back to McCallister. God knows I didn't want to search out another makeshift lot. There I found him in the same position, not a care in the world, leaning up against his squad car, that big grin still plastered on his face. Upon seeing me, he shook his head and laughed aloud. Slowly he eased into his car, then motioned for me to follow. I obeyed. We headed out, back toward the stadium. Over a curb, around another detour sign, past a "Lot Full" poster attached to a small wooden sawhorse, he stopped in a marked-out no-parking zone. Leaning out of his window, he called for me to, "Just leave it here."

Directly across the street from Memorial Stadium, the Lone Ranger himself couldn't have done better. Heck, my new spot was probably closer to the ticket gate than Cal Ripken's mom gets on game night. Somehow I had to show my appreciation. The old "If you're in Seattle sometime, drop in and give me a call, I'll buy you a beer" didn't seem quite enough. He deserved better. I knew what to do. I was great at writing letters when I didn't like something. For a change I'd write something positive. I'd crank out a letter to his superiors requesting that he receive a medal of honor. It'd be the best-written commendation Officer McCallister ever received—the best any officer of the law had ever gotten. First, though, I needed a name and badge number. I've watched enough cop shows to know that.

I got out and approached the squad car. McCallister was still sitting inside, still smirking. After thanking him for the twelfth time, I asked for a name and number. He pulled out his own piece of paper and handed it to me. Already jotted down were his name and badge number.

"You're writing a book, aren't you?" He had guessed. "Nobody else would go to 'em all. Well, buddy, I want some ink."

It was my turn to bust out laughing. "How many chapters?" I asked.

"One will be enough. Just make sure you get that right. It's M-c-C-a-l-l-i-s-t-e-r!"

LAYOUT AND UPKEEP: GRADE B

The neighborhood west of Memorial Stadium, at least in the daylight, is a decent one. Grass instead of dirt covers front yards. People walk about with small dogs on leashes. Although not as quaint, it reminded me a bit of Chicago's Wrigleyville. As for Officer McCallister's beat, Chicago's Comiskey side is a fair description. With normal streets to the west, broken ones to the southeast, decent homes standing on one side of the stadium and seedy versions on the other, baseball in Baltimore lies on the fringe.

As for the stadium...it's not really much to look at. Plain tan brick walls nearly enclose the semicircular building. From the outside it's neither intimidating, like Royals or Dodger Stadium, nor does it offer a Fenway-type quaintness. Baseball doesn't even look like it's a primary concern. Aside from a good-size Oriole insignia blazed into the grassy bank across the street, everybody walking about dressed in orange and black, and lights looming overhead, the ballpark looks more like a disguised government building or a large school, especially if you read the stadium's welcome. Across the three-story brick facade, etched in white stone, is a dedication to all veterans.

Inside, Memorial is convenient. Not spotlessly clean, but considering the neighborhood, not bad either. In a simple layout, ramps extend regularly from the inner-stadium walkways into the stands. Getting around is easy. All in all, the stadium looks to be a decent place to meet for a good time, unless, of course, you've left your car in a tiny post-office parking lot down the wrong street.

BALL FIELD: GRADE A+

Sandwiched in on my trip between Fenway and Yankee Stadium, I never expected Baltimore to house the AL's most beautiful turf. That, I was sure, would be the claim of one of the two more famous parks.

Well, maybe it's Memorial's quaint size that gives the turf its pizzazz. Or it could be that it resists its seedy neighborhood so well. It might even be those tomato vines climbing the wall down the third-base line; they add a delightful touch. Whatever the case, the playing field's gorgeous. Only San Diego's, with its never-ending sunshine, looks as handsome.

Trimmed in three distinct patterns, it's unique from almost every other ball field save Candlestick's. The infield edge ripples its contour across the outfield all the way to the wall and is trimmed as smoothly as the checkerboard infield. While the same effect in Frisco is strange, at Memorial it's marvelous. The biggest difference is the depth of the cut. At "the Stick" deep wide tracks give the ball field an interstate highway appearance. In Baltimore they're much softer. Instead of screaming for attention, the cuts just quietly show off.

From the upper deck looking down across the green, the view is wonderful—the sod glows in the stadium lights. Looking out from the lower boxes, a fresh grassy scent rises up and adds to the delight. But from the pitcher's mound the sight must be truly grand. Perched on the rubber and surveying such a domain has to be inspiring. Palmer, Cuellar, McNally—the ball field must've had something to do with all those wins. One thing's for sure... they didn't have to worry about anything hit down the third-base line. With Robinson covering the corner, an absolutely flawless grass carpet in front of him, and baseballs bouncing perfectly true, 5–3 in the Weaver glory years was as automatic as baseball can get.

SEATING: GRADE A

Like Milwaukee's County Stadium, Memorial is a middle-ager. Rebuilt for baseball in 1953, its technology is up to date enough to be comfortable. But not so updated that it's a three-level plastic clone. Getting the best of both worlds, within its tight friendly confines, the mix is a healthy one.

Three levels swing in a semicircle from foul pole around to foul pole. Aside from a few support posts, the view down across the grass is pretty much unobstructed. The lower-level ceiling is high—even pop-ups can be followed to their peak. And the steep rise way up top keeps third-level fans in touch with the game. Only too much foul territory in front of the dugouts causes much of a problem. But there's really nothing to complain about. Box seats to watch Cal Ripken and Eddie Murray crank 'em out are as good as they were when the Robinsons did the cranking.

Where the dingers land ain't bad either. Beyond the bull pens in left and right fields, bleachers are inviting. Bench seats with backs cover each of the two separate sections. Besides being fairly close to the action, they feature a special option. In a lot of stadiums, particularly the newer ones, bleacherites don't benefit from the scoreboard. Either too far under or over it, the ballpark's front page is hidden from view. At Memorial it's pushed back and up enough to allow everyone a look. Which is a must, considering how much fun the setup is to watch.

SCOREBOARD: GRADE A+

It's one of baseball's best. Diamond Vision's imaginative. Music's snappy. By taking advantage of modern technology, without losing touch with the old traditions, together the two really rock to baseball.

Two large screens stand behind the outfield bull pens. One, a digital electronic panel in left field, shows the basic baseball stuff. And all of it on the same screen. Which is nice. At some parks players' stats and ball-game info are divided between two screens. You spend the night bouncing back and forth between the two, like it's Connors and McEnroe dueling instead of Murray and Jimmy Key. In right is Memorial's other board—one of the majors' best-used Diamond Vision screens. Besides a regular grinding out of scores, the screen pumps out some neat baseball videos.

A central theme ran through Baltimore's use of Diamond Vision. That theme was the O's. One gigantic Oriole advertisement set to music—the Birds got rave reviews. First the screen highlighted the visiting team and some of their stars. The number was short but sweet, and the few Jays fans at the game seemed to get a kick out of it. Next came the main feature. And it always began with the same shot—Fred Lynn making a grab while smashing into the center-field wall. Fans waited for the Lynn catch, then roared their approval. Music picked up and the Orioles' stars shone. Hitting home runs at every at-bat, making a myriad of diving catches, throwing strikeout after strikeout, it made me begin to wonder if an Oriole player ever made a routine play.

In addition to hot videos, musical selections are also great. Tunes crank out in high-fidelity style on a sound system nearly as good as the one in Oakland. The fan favorite is Memorial Stadium's famous (at least in Baltimore it's famous) bugle charge. Instead of pushing a few keys on some synthesizer, a clear, crisp blast on the bugle rings through the place. Fans love it. No major league park provides a better reason to yell "Charge." In fact, not a better job is done in all of baseball to get people as excited with the hometown team.

FOOD: GRADE B

Selection: Very Good   Accessibility: Fair
Taste: Very Good   Cost: 5th

Good inexpensive food gives folks just one more reason to keep on coming back. From the presence of the little things, like mustard and ketchup squirt bottles in the stands to cold beer at great prices, Baltimore's ballpark serves up another fine dish:

It's the cheapest beer per ounce in the East, and also some of the lowest priced in the majors! Matched with America's least expensive hot dog, Bird food is quality food with "I'll take a couple instead of just one" prices. Selection's good too. Ice cream, peanuts, and popcorn get spiced up with added favorites—an Italian kitchen highlighting zesty pizza, a decent Mexican food booth, and the local favorite, fresh crab cakes, are best of the rest.

Only one problem taints the menu—booths are awkwardly set up. In the hallways under the stadium, food's tough to get at. The weird arrangements make for slow, cluttered lines. It's one of the few stadium things that isn't as good as it could be.

But back up in the stands, it's back to normal. Roaming vendors, besides pounding their beats at a quick pace, carry around a little option that makes eating more fun. Mustard packets are illegal. Rather than struggling to find

out which end of the packet has those little lines that say "Tear Here" and
wondering if it really matters, you need only answer to "Mustard or ketchup?"
and the fellow walking the dogs will squirt it on free of charge. Just another
pleasing touch at a friendly place full of 'em.

BALLPARK EMPLOYEES: GRADE A

From McCallister's rescue of my Japanese import to a cordial escort back
through detour city U.S.A. by a stadium employee, I found Oriole folks, fans
and employees alike, to be some of the majors' nicest.

Ushers at nearly every aisle are eager to please. Plenty of vendors with
good food roam the stands at a fast pace. Even bathroom attendants, an Eastern city custom, appear content with their lot. But it was a little thoughtfulness thrown my way by an Oriole employee on my leaving Baltimore that
confirmed what I found out inside. Those paid to serve "Birdland" are a
class act.

If the ballpark was a big enough mess to get into in daylight, I figured
getting out at night would be suicidal. So before leaving after my second night
in town, I looked around for help. No gas stations were close by, and the cops
were busy directing traffic. Besides, I'd already promised the force its "ink." I
found instead an orange-clad Oriole employee and asked him how to reach
the highway. Foolishly I hoped for a "go up two blocks, turn right, you can't
miss it." Instead I found getting out of Baltimore was gonna make coming in
seem like a cakewalk. The old fellow noticed the panic on my face. He looked
at my out-of-state plates, shook his head, and gave a good summation of the
city's roadway system.

"Hell," he said, "with as many detours as they've got out there, I get lost
going home. And I've been doing it for 15 years. It's not that far out of my
way, just stick close and I'll get you there."

Such a gracious invitation I had to accept. Plus I was sure that at night the
city streets would swallow me up. So I trailed his bright Oriole-orange van—
simple as following the bouncing orange ball. And we dodged the steady flow
of detour signs in nothing flat. Before leaving me at my exit, he pulled over
and rolled down his window, offered up a few more final instructions, and
wished me well. A couple of friendly beeps on the orange steering wheel and
he headed home. As for me, after such a cordial escort from "Birdland," I hit
the road for gracious New York City. From there I hoped just to return alive.

FACILITIES: GRADE D

Providing parking spots is not Memorial's forte. Rest rooms aren't much of a priority either. In short, the only real drawbacks surrounding baseball in Baltimore are, as I found out the hard way, facilities that bring on memories of Chicago and Detroit.

At one point in my vain search for a safe parking spot within hiking distance of the stadium, a "regular" mentioned something about bus shuttles and a giant parking lot somewhere in "that general direction." It was a place, he said, where cars were safe and even watched in well-lit lots by honest men. I never found that lot off in the distance. Maybe it was real, maybe just somewhere over the rainbow. For the sake of car owners who don't wish their cars to be picked through by bands of teenagers with nothing better to do, I hope that it exists. Otherwise, Oriole baseball, as fun as it is, on a regular basis could get to be a very trying and expensive experience.

Inside, things aren't much better. Rest rooms are tiny and cluttered. And like the rest of the place, could use a once-more-over with the broom. But just as the Baltimore police force didn't abandon me and my car to the horrors of Oriole parking, neither are those who have to use the rest rooms left entirely on their own. Bathroom attendants make sure that while the seats might not be as luxurious as those at the Chevron station down the block, at least they're as safe.

ATMOSPHERE: GRADE A+

Eastern baseball lies at the very heart of the major league game. In the East, tradition hangs in the air, like sweltering humidity on a hot August night. It's where the memory of immortalized players lives on within the confines of their old, still-standing ballparks, where the game is never over till the final out... and fans actually stay to prove it.

The legacy of that tradition, of the folks who flock to watch, blooms most brilliantly in two places. Two parks we all know about. Under the shadow of the "Monster" and up among the monuments in Yankee Stadium, baseball and tradition fuse. Blue pinstripes and red socks have a history all their own. Baltimore's ballpark home for the Weaver teams, some of the seventies' most powerful powerhouses, goes relatively unnoticed. Yet within its very normal walls is an atmosphere that breathes the essence of Eastern ball.

Memorial Stadium doesn't come packaged in the most elegant of wrapping paper. On the outside it's plain. Only that dedication to United States veterans serves any notice of the sincerity that awaits within. Through the gates and about the stadium walkways, simplicity continues. No lovely view to mountains beyond brightens the not-so-kept hallways. A giant monument doesn't arise to remind you where in the world you are. There isn't even a city skyline hovering on the horizon. Until you enter up and into the stands, Memorial does a good job of concealing its charm. But once you gaze down upon the ball field, as polished as any in the game today, it's apparent that a night out with the Orioles will be more than just a casual date.

Memorial's refreshing. And filled with those simple little things that make a house a home. A ground crew that does such a fine job coddling the turf also makes sure that tomato plants down the left-field line get cared for. The tiny garden, its leafy vines climbing up the green wall, add a pleasing touch. The Oriole MTV videos bring back memories of some great Bird teams. And do a pretty good job of glamorizing Birds of the eighties too. Best of all is "Birdland's" rendition of the national anthem. Like in every other ballpark, some folks sing along. Others stand silently by and listen. In Baltimore everybody sings—at least for one syllable. When that line "O say, does that star-spangled banner yet wave" is finally reached, and that last "O say" rolls around, on cue everybody shouts out "O." A tribute to their O's, it's a grand way to start the celebration of another night of Oriole baseball.

Then let the festivities begin. Good folks have a great time. With baseball and one another. One late start in the boxes behind home plate, another in the bleachers surrounded by happy, helpful people, convinced me the East Coast can be neighborly. If it really tries. Intense but not suicidally fanatical, fans love their little traditions. Proud of their bugle call, as well as their very own "Star-Spangled Banner," they don't mind boasting just a bit about either one. And there's always a stray conversation circulating about the good ole days—back when Palmer paraded around on the mound instead of on billboards in his underwear and the O's ruled the AL roost.

Baseball in Baltimore is fun. A solid tradition, enjoyed by nice people, both sitting and serving, the game gets the sincerity it deserves. Overshadowed by richer legacies up in New York and Boston, Memorial Stadium nevertheless covers all the basics with a homey touch. And continues on very quietly among the giants as "Baseball's Best-kept Secret."

22

SHEA STADIUM,
NEW YORK METS

Pardon Me if I Smile

REPORT CARD		**Shea Stadium**
		BASEBALL PARK
July 31, 85 vs Expos		**New York Mets**
GAME		BASEBALL CLUB

CATEGORY	GRADE	POINTS
Layout and Upkeep	C	75
Ball Field	B	85
Seating	C	75
Scoreboard	A	95
Food	D	65
Ballpark Employees	D-	60
Facilities	C	75
Atmosphere	D	65
Total Points		595
Average		74

C	19th
FINAL GRADE	RANK

"A terrorizing ride to a depressing park. Rude employees, rude fans, even rude food. Not exactly a Disneyland production."

PREGAME THOUGHTS

New York City traffic—just the thought terrified me. I wouldn't, I couldn't under any circumstances face it. Before I left Seattle I'd promised my new Toyota one thing: "We will not drive in New York City!"

I didn't care how dirty, smelly, or dangerous the subways were—I'd use 'em. And somehow survive. It wasn't like I didn't know what I was getting into. I'd seen Charles Bronson in action plenty of times. *People* magazine told all there was to tell about Bernhard Goetz. *The French Connection* is one of my favorite movies. I knew the real truth! New York City trains crawled with slime. They were a breeding ground for the New York State Penitentiary. Innocent folks (like me) were blown away by the bucketful—either by the slime or Popeye Doyles shooting at the slime. Less disciplined than a junior high classroom on substitute teacher day, they were the cesspool of the world. To want to ride 'em, agreed, was weird. I was just too much of a chicken to accept the alternative—to drive!

So, I'd been preparing myself. The closer I got to New York the more I'd thought about it. To ride the subway and live to tell the story had become an obsession. I asked myself, "If he were me what would Bronson do?" Easy, he'd kick some ass. Then so would I. I couldn't fit a shotgun in my backpack. Handguns were illegal. Instead, I'd bring along my hunting knife. For 9,000 miles it'd sat under the seat, a weapon if some loony messed with me on the road. It'd be my subway protection insurance. The plan I'd run through my head at least 62 times since Fenway. Rehearsed it over and over again. Pictured every possibility, mentally recorded every reaction. The script was set. I'd make eye contact with nobody. If I did, somebody'd get pissed off and slap me around. I couldn't look down, the hoods would know I was a chicken shit. When Bronson rode the train he just stared straight ahead—like he was in a trance. He never got messed with, so I'd do the same. I'd step in, find a corner seat, and stare straight ahead. Back to the wall, five-inch blade in front. I figured, barring an armed personal escort, it was about as safe as I could get.

I also had some help. A high school buddy, Sharon, had invited me to stay with her. She lived in a normal city, Red Bank, in a normal state, New Jersey, only 60 miles or so from New York City. Her place is where I'd launch my Shea Stadium attack from. The scenario was simple; Bronson would have been proud. I'd drive to the Red Bank train station, park my car in the safe, quiet New Jersey town, hop on a clean Amtrak train, and journey to New York's Penn Station. There I'd transfer to the death train, open my hunting knife, hide it under a *Wall Street Journal*, back into a corner, and hold my breath until I got to Shea. After the game I'd retrace my steps to the train, find another corner, and head back to Jersey. By 7:30 P.M. I'd be safe and sound in sweet little Red Bank. Shea would be behind me, and I'd be alive to tell the story. I was ready for New York and all its gracious offerings, just as long as my car could stay new in New Jersey.

In my perfectly planned itinerary, though, I made one major mistake. I'm not one to get to places on time. Normally, it's no big deal. It's cost me a few dates, a few scoldings in the principal's office both as a student and a teacher, and confusion at the movie theater, but I've survived. And haven't changed. This time it almost cost me my life.

Sharon drew me a cute little map. Arrows, highway markers complete with numbers, even a compass up in the corner. Her directions to town, a few miles away, were ungodly simple. They were so easy, I got a little lax. I left a little late. Probably didn't study them as closely as I should've. Consequently, my short 20-minute drive doubled. Alone, that wouldn't have bothered me. New Jersey's seaside scenery in early August is lovely. However, my schedule allowed only a half hour, and 40 minutes is more than 30. I screeched into the parking lot just in time to watch the train pull away.

For a moment I sat there in my front seat. Totally silent. Staring straight ahead. Praying the whole scene would flip into reverse. That the train would chug back into view and stop at the depot. A conductor would lean from the caboose and call to me, "Robert Wood, we're waiting for you. Come on, you don't want to be late." I waited and waited. Then blinked. And I gasped. Not since I laid eyes on the Kingdome have I felt so sick. My stomach gurgled. My fingers went numb, my throat dry. My greatest fear in the world had become reality. I was about to drive solo into the jaws of New York City.

I let out no screams. No tantrum. Void of any emotion, I just stared at the empty tracks, sighed deeply, and pulled out of the lot. It was as if I was in a trance. A twilight state of mind. The streets, the quaint Red Bank shops blended into the background as I groped my way toward the expressway.

By the time I'd reached the turnpike consciousness at least had returned. And as I tooled along it, even confidence. Despite stopping every 12 miles to be nickled and dimed to death, I was at least plodding along in the right general direction. Lines at the toll booths were only 10 to 12 cars deep. And in between them speeds pushed all the way up to 50. Actually, Jersey was easy.

When I passed a "New York City—36 Miles" sign, still an hour and a half from game time, things looked pretty good. I even felt a bit cocky. This, I thought, was gonna be okay.

That's when it hit. Panic rushed me again. For the past two months I'd lived life according to *Rand McNally*. It had directed me through L.A. freeways, across empty Arizona deserts, through Texas, Oklahoma, and Chicago. Over 9,000 miles under my belt, and thanks to that "Highway Bible" I had yet to get lost. But on the verge of my greatest test, the flash hit that it was sitting on the kitchen table back in Jersey. It couldn't be. I screamed and pounded the dash. I pulled over and stopped—even on a Wednesday, something not recommended on the turnpike. Ripping the entire car apart, I searched everywhere for it. The glove compartment, back seat, under the back seat, under the floor mats, in the back end, the wheel wells, everywhere. I emptied my two suitcases, throwing the stuff inside all about the back end. But to no avail. Back on the kitchen table, under the half-empty glass of juice, covered with peanut-butter-toast crumbs, in my most significant hour of need, *Rand McNally* was taking the day off.

Exhausted with fear and frustration, tears welling in my eyes and with a dry throat, I resigned myself to the fact that I truly was going solo. Without my maps, having no idea what Queens was, let alone where, I figured I'd just have to wish for the best and rely on the graciousness of New York's good people to pull me through. When I was a kid my grandpa set me straight on wishing. "Bobby," he'd say to me, "wish in one hand and poop in the other. Then see which gets filled the fastest." My grandpa, once upon a time, must've driven in New York City...without his *Rand McNally*.

My confidence was drained. I needed help, or at least reassurance that I was on the right track. So I decided to stop off at the next turnpike toll booth and plead a little. Maybe, I hoped, they'd have a map or at least some words of encouragement. Anything would help.

It was there in New Jersey that I got my first real taste of New York hospitality. Normal lost people aren't allowed to stop at the toll booths. Signs say so, but I was desperate. I pulled over into a no-parking zone and got out. A small office bordered the lot. I stumbled over to it. Voices mingled inside, probably a couple of employees on their break. Quietly, not sure if I was allowed, I opened the door, eased inside, and inched along the hallway in the direction of the voices...into a small lounge room.

"Excuse me?" I asked, clearing my throat. I surprised the three inside. Visitors obviously were not a regular occurrence. Before introductions could be made, questions asked, or "How do you do's" exchanged, I was bombarded.

"Whadda you want?" one of the three snapped.

At the same time his buddy demanded, "Who let you in here?" The third of the group just kept on reading the paper.

"Well, I am sort of lost. You see..." I continued dribbling about my missed train and lost atlas, Shea and how to find it. Looking up from his paper, the fellow who hadn't jumped me rolled his eyes and snickered.

Before my dribbling was finished the guy who'd asked what I wanted announced with a tenderness in his voice, "Just follow the damned tunnel."

The other, still upset that I'd made it in, repeated his earlier demand: "I asked once, what are you doing in here? This place is off limits!" Dazed from the barrage, I backed away. As I did I apologized—though I'm still not sure what exactly for—and stumbled back out to my car, got inside, and headed off...I guess to find the "damned tunnel."

The "damned tunnel," I found out later by way of highway directional signs, was actually the Holland Tunnel. It connects lovely Jersey City, New Jersey, to New York City. The former into the latter is like sitting in the frying pan before being tossed into the fire, or even more realistically to taking a good whiff of the sewer, then plunging in. Jersey City's a dump. Hideously filthy and dangerous-looking, I didn't have the nerve to get out of the car and ask for help. Even Chevron stations, an automatic for lost folks, looked spooky. I figured it'd be best to find the "damned tunnel" on my own. So I double-checked the locks, made sure the sun roof was latched, and, with my opened hunting knife on the passenger seat, toured town. Amid the dead ends, vacant walled-up business offices, and shady characters, somehow I stumbled onto the tunnel. Above it, out of the gray fog that had joined approaching thunderstorm clouds, New York City skyscrapers hovered. Shea, I guessed, couldn't be too far off.

But time was dwindling. Only 45 minutes were left till game time when I actually entered the tunnel's Jersey City side. The sign outside it read "New York City—2 Miles." It should have said "New York City—30 Minutes." My introduction to Big Apple traffic, one-tenth of one mile per hour, crammed me inside. And all the while, precious time ticked away. My blood pressure climbed. Nerve endings frazzled. Although I'm not normally claustrophobic, my car started to feel like a closet. It got smaller and smaller, then hot and cold. Air-conditioning had no effect. With the radio drowned out by static, I imagined innings flying by, the ball game finishing. I had to get out. I was losing it! Just before I snapped, a light shone ahead. At it, another toll, another booth, and another toll-booth employee. Some help!

I stopped at the booth. With the "damned tunnel" nearly behind me, all I needed were directions to the "damned ballpark." Certainly, I guessed, the young lady in the window would help. She had to. It was her job.

"Could you please tell me how to get to Shea?" I pleaded as I handed over the coins. I felt like I was buying the information.

"Here. Read this." She crammed a little booklet in my face. I opened it and took a quick glance. "Don't read it here!"

Behind me cars honked. People yelled. Like a spineless worm, I dropped the booklet, nodded my thanks, and lurched forward. I officially entered New York City and plodded into place. What a beauty! I rolled down my window and took a whiff. The sweet smell of 5 million idling automobiles, all going nowhere together, all impatient with the car in front, all blasting on their horns, all in an effort to push somebody up 12 more feet.

In the tunnel I'd lost touch with the game. Outside I found it. It wasn't over. In fact, it hadn't even started. The pregame show was still in progress. I opened my booklet to Shea and sized up the directions. "Take this road to that road, a few miles to the expressway and to the Shea exit." Things couldn't have been simpler. I was two blocks from an expressway that would zoom me off to Shea. The ballpark, a beer, a chance to relax, and all would be at peace. Once more I envisioned singing "The Star-Spangled Banner." Overhead the light turned green. Impatient horns blared. I sped ahead eight more feet.

I thought I was being realistic. Even on a Wednesday afternoon, traffic, I figured, would be thick. Until the expressway it was bound to be slow. So the ten-minute wait through two blocks and a half dozen light changes only made me a little nervous. I killed the time laughing at all the pissed-off people. When "The Star-Spangled Banner" played I stopped laughing and joined them—my first outburst since discovering that I had left my *Rand McNally* behind. Still, I stayed on course, confident that it couldn't be much longer.

At the express ramp my fantasy ruptured. I pulled up it and stopped, trapped behind eight other idling cars, all waiting to get onto what seemed more a parking lot than a highway. I screamed. My expressway wasn't expressing. It wasn't even moving. Two and a half miles earlier I'd entered the "damn tunnel." Almost an hour later, poised to express away all that lost time, I was trapped. I screamed again, beat the dash with my fist, and for some idiotic reason even laid on the horn.

I was terrified. I didn't know what to do. Panic plans surged through my brain. I thought about leaving my car on the ramp and running on car rooftops to the ballpark. It'd be faster, but I'd get towed and ticketed, if my car wasn't stolen first. Again I screamed, honked, and pounded the dash. But all the tirade did was wear me out. I was beaten. There was absolutely nothing I could do. Exhausted, with no alternative but to sit and wait out the slow death, I just turned off the radio and joined the molasses flow to Queens.

Slower and slower I eased up the ramp and onto the expressway. There things got worse. Other cars joining the mess thickened it. Speeds that seemed to begin as inches by the minute turned into half inches and quarter inches. At times the line sat totally still. Not disciplined enough to keep my hand off of the radio, I flicked it on. Mets went down in order in the first. Then the Expos in the second, the Mets in the second. With each rotation of my tires, and each out into the record book, I buried myself in self-pity. The worst would happen. I knew it. Five innings of no-hit ball would fly by. Black clouds would get blacker. The skies would open up. Just as I was leaving my car in Shea's parking lot, the game would be called. My trip would be ruined. . . . So would I.

Suddenly loud pounding sounds caught my attention. Wiping my eyes, I looked across to my right. Cracked concrete, pink pylons, flags, I recognized the sight from Baltimore. Finally jackhammers and hot filthy people running them. Road construction, that's what the holdup was. And I'd reached it! My 38-minute 46-second standstill—I'd kept track with my digital-watch lap counter. While it felt like four hours, I prayed to God it was over. I closed in on the noise. Large bearded men, sweaty and dirty, ran the equipment. A dumb-looking girl stood by holding a "Men at Work" sign. I smiled, glad it was them and not me. . . . In New York style, they scowled back.

I tuned into the game, by then creeping into the third. The flow started to thin from molasses to paint, to pea soup, all the way up to 30 mph. I passed a Queens sign and honked. My first honk for joy. A "Stadium This Way" sign got two more beeps. When Shea finally came into view a tingle shivered throughout my body. I might not make it back, but at least I knew I'd get in. A full 45 mph throttle, I wheeled down toward the parking lot. I was ecstatic! In front of me all I could see was that huge open stadium. And all I wanted was me inside of it. I parked the car. Not thinking to check the locks, something that I did four times around back in sweet little Red Bank, I slammed the door and headed for the game. Backpack in hand, I sang as I ran and jumped through the packed lot. Roars of cheering arose from inside the stadium. I'd been wrong about New York City, New York traffic, and even the people. The Big Apple was grand. Shea was beautiful. I was delirious.

Skipping up to the gate, I approached a gray-haired Mets employee. "Good afternoon, sir! How's it going?" I must've seemed at least a little fruity, happy as I was.

He looked at me, scowled, and blurted out, "Yeah, whadda you want?"

"Just to get into your beautiful ballpark. And me, I'm just wonderful today, thank you."

LAYOUT AND UPKEEP: GRADE C

I don't think I've ever been so happy to see a baseball park. Slow-motion love scenes where the gorgeous girl and studly guy glide through the meadow and embrace—this was my first touch with Shea. I was in love. For a while I was so pumped, it appeared as magnificent as Dodger Stadium.

Dancing to the front doors, as opposed to walking, must make the place look more grand than it really is. But I've a notion that even to a normal mind, it's pretty impressive. From the parking lot, it's the majors' closest to the palace in L.A. A gigantic open horseshoe, four stories of seats shoot up into the sky. The mood is festive. Fans crammed inside, their bright summer patterns blend into a colorful blur. Sounds volunteer a lively introduction; the place is a constant buzz. A collective roar raises and lowers with each crack of the bat. The deep booming voice of the public address adds to the anticipation. After what I'd just gotten through, I thought I was in heaven.

But at Dodger Stadium the inside is even better than the outside. Spotless hallways, warm employees, and an air of grandeur create a wonderful welcome. At Shea its best part is left in the lot. That rousing introduction is destroyed by cold steel.

It looks and feels like a prison. Twelve-foot chain-link fences are everywhere. They run alongside each of the concrete walkways, separate the different sections, and keep garbage from blowing all over the place. Guarded, roll-up gates connect the fences and open to the seats. At each a surly "no exceptions" attitude keeps the wrong tickets out and stadium social classes separated. Wandering about is prohibited.

Besides being broken up by all the fences, the walkways are dark and dingy. Lighting is awful, the mood depressing. It's also kind of scary. My day game seemed like night. I can only guess how gloomy the place is at night.

Because of the dark and the steel, and the New York City attitude, I was uneasy. I've never felt that way in a baseball park, not even in Detroit as a kid. For more than just curiosity's sake I found myself peering around corners before I walked past. In rest rooms I didn't stick around to dry my hands. I was careful where I went and how long I stayed. It's an eerie way to take on a baseball game, particularly a day game.

BALL FIELD: GRADE B

Shea is like a yo-yo. From the outside it's good-looking, inside it's a pit. Back through the aisles out into the stands, looking down on the field, I was dazzled again. The ball field's beautiful. I was confused.

Well kept, with a couple of Dodger-style luxuries, it doesn't look like it belongs in New York City. Grass is crisply trimmed, probably the only green version for blocks. A reddish-brown warning track borders the entire field. It, too, is neat. Where the two meet the mesh is sharp—no splotches, no wear. It doesn't hint that every playoff victory the place is ripped to shreds. Or that daily all sorts of crud is tossed out of the stands at whoever happens to be in town.

Those little things that made Dodger Stadium so pleasant touch Shea as well. Colorful mats cover each team's on-deck circle, identify both teams, and provide the fans another target to chuck stuff at. They also give the ball field that finely tuned West Coast flare. Bordering the bright green outfield is a blue wall. Covered with each of the twelve National League teams' pennants, it provides a simple and sharp contrast with the green. A traditional handsome ball field—too bad it's stuck inside a jail.

SEATING: GRADE C

The seating also has that California feeling. Three tiers of comfortable, fold-up, plastic seats stretch between the foul poles. A fourth, press-box level stuffed in between 'em pushes those above it even higher. Space down in front, between the four-level rise and the grass, is filled by a field section. Like in L.A., fans hover above the action.

What hit me most about Shea was its height. All three fan-filled tiers, particularly the top one, climb nearly straight up. That's why from the outside it can wield a Dodger Stadium-type spell. To get to the top row of the top level from below, it looks like you'd have to climb on hands and knees. Heading carelessly back down looks fatal. A trip and a stumble down the steps would sail you out over the field to end with a splat at Mr. Gooden's feet. Standing in the upper decks, they aren't quite that steep. Actually, they're exciting. I was very careful, however, not to trip.

The high rise does have a few problems though. So that fans toward the rear of each level can see the game, all seats are pushed farther away from the field. Although the view might be a clear one, it's bound to be a long ways away. Vertical obstruction's bad too. Back up and under in the lower levels, because of the low ceiling clearance, views are frustrating. They cause a lot of folks to rely on the judgment of those down in front, or way up on top, to tell if Strawberry's smash is a dinger or just a pop-out.

Even with the problems, though, seats are comfy. Leg and arm room is good. The steep rise doesn't make people's heads in front a pain. Aisles are frequently placed, particularly down in the field section. Getting in and out is almost hassle-free. Just like in California.

SCOREBOARD: GRADE A

Shea really tries to be traditional. Like its view from the parking lot to the inside and the good-looking grass; its scoreboard's also impressive (even though buried within mounds of advertisements).

Actually the setup is separated into two major scoreboards. The one in right field is huge, nearly as big as San Diego's monster. Five separate smaller screens combine to form one. With no seats behind it, the combo dominates the open space. Two small rectangular panels top it off and spend the game rotating American and National League scores. Running down each side, below the updates, are the day's lineups, batting order, number, and positions. At the base a fifth screen line-scores the ball game. Together the five are impressive. They cover the traditional stuff about as well as it can be covered. Their only problem, a big "This Bud's for You" sits right smack-dab in the middle and takes a little luster off an otherwise neat arrangement.

The second half of the setup is Diamond Vision. Placed back behind the left-field fence, it's as effective as its right-field partner. Always up to the task of making fans more unruly than they already are, the giant screen replays everything, no matter how controversial.

Plus it provides other entertainment. Good shorts run between innings—baseball and non-baseball stuff. A Three Stooges video, while "the Curly Shuffle" kicked out over stadium speakers, was the best. And a real crowd favorite. In fact, I'd bet it got a better ovation than the Mets.

FOOD: GRADE D

Selection: Poor   Accessibility: Poor
Taste: Fair   Cost: 24th

Thanks to the New York stadium practice of barring every section of the stands with chain-link prison gates, my roaming food-rating process was limited. Eventually, I worked my way into a few sections that I probably shouldn't have and at least got a decent feeling for the eats. What I found was boring and expensive.

On the East Coast only the Yanks serve as expensive beer. And nobody east of the Mississippi tacks a higher price tag on its hot dogs. However, high prices don't always equate with quality. If they did, multiyear, multiproblem, multimillion-dollar free agents would lead the league in every category. Not just contract clauses. Well, Mets food follows the free-agent route. While the wieners aren't bad, they're certainly not, as cost might indicate, the best this side of St. Louis. And the beer, even though almost the most per ounce anywhere, is just plain old Bud. A Wally Backman taste...the food's all right. Just not at Gary Carter prices.

BALLPARK EMPLOYEES: GRADE D—

Working at a baseball park should be fun. I used to dream about it. One summer I even wrote a letter to Fenway, asked if they needed ushers, and announced my availability. It was already June when I sent the letter. I was only 17 at the time, and they didn't reply, but all summer long I fantasized myself tearing tickets under the "Green Monster."

A lot of folks don't see ballpark work that way. Rather than a privilege, it's nine-to-five time. Other than almost all Californians, the 16-year-old Lady Rangers in Arlington, Milwaukee's old gents, and a spattering here and there throughout the East, stadium employees carry on like they've got just another job. At Shea most act like they're doing community-service time for breaking probation.

A middle-of-the-week afternoon game, and Gooden in the dugout, the place wasn't really packed. A lot of open cheap seats spattered the upper level. Fortunately the cheap seats accessed the same gate as my much better complimentary ticket. I was allowed in and found my way up to 'em. Third-base side, a long ways up, they were nevertheless just what the doctor ordered. Two chairs in front of me were open, so I filled 'em with my feet. A couple of seats to my right were also vacant. The backpack went there. Sipping on a cold beer I had bought on the way, I kicked back and relaxed. And tried to put the years back on my life that I'd lost on the expressway.

No sooner had I sat down than Mets security made their move. TJ Hooker himself came strolling up, ready to do battle.

"Let me see your ticket." The tone of his snarl told me the guy was not trained in Anaheim. I held it out. He snatched it up.

"Hey, man, you're in the wrong seat." I nodded that I knew, and added that I didn't see any harm in it. It was the fifth inning, the section was almost empty, and my complimentary seat was a lot better than the one I was in.

TJ wasn't swayed. The mismatch bothered him. That I could handle. It was his job to make sure dangerous people like me weren't allowed to sit in lousy seats. But when he noticed the freebie part, that really torked him off.

"Who'd you beg these from?" Such a clever line for a stadium rep, I couldn't believe he even asked it.

I tried to be polite, explained my letter to the Mets, their answer, that this was my only visit over to Shea. I told him about my three-hour ordeal on the expressway and how I almost died just getting to the place. He couldn't have cared less. He jumped on the anti-free-ticket bandwagon and ripped into me. He went wild, almost started foaming at the mouth. The only thing I can figure is that he asked for freebies once and they said no.

After finishing with his seizure he told me, "Get the hell out!"

By then I'd figured the key to Big Apple survival is to be as sour as everybody else. So I was. And came back with a few goodies of my own. I told him I didn't have to put up with his crap and capped it off by calling him a "fake cop." The "fake" part infuriated him. He got glassy-eyed and strangely quiet.

"This...," he said convincingly, "is nothing compared to what I can do if I really want to." A Charles Bronson movie flashback hit me. Hoods weren't the only ones who roughed you up in New York. After going through hell to get there, I wasn't about to be tossed out into the gutter after a 15-minute stay. So I backed off. A couple of parting shots, a badge number, and I left.

Intent on seeing justice served, I searched for a TJ supervisor. Since ushers usually know everything about a ballpark, including where security supervisors hang out, I looked for one. None were nearby. So I went to more of the "fake cops." "Where can I find a security supervisor?" I asked around. "Why?" was the only answer I could get. When I explained the situation they pretty much clammed up. I'd get worthless directions, but only to get me someplace else.

After wandering for a half inning, I stumbled into an usher. The fellow surprised me. He was concerned. I could tell that, unlike the cops, he enjoyed his job, as well as the ballpark, and he went out of his way to help me out.

Eventually we found a guy in charge. I even got the satisfaction of reporting TJ. The supervisor echoed the usher's sentiments and reassured me that things weren't always so bad. "A lot of the guys that work night games have other jobs during the day." Weekdays, he hinted, were overseen by the bottom of the employee barrel.

I didn't bother to tell him that the rest of security, those guys who probably work the nightshift, too, were about as helpful as TJ. Too bad Anaheim doesn't export...fake cops at least!

FACILITIES: GRADE C

Shea's yo-yo twangs again. For being stuffed inside New York City, facilities are decent. While it might be hell to get to, the parking lot, considering normal Queens parking, isn't bad. And rest rooms, in comparison to what they could be, are glamorous.

Subways stop right outside of Shea's door, almost within spitting distance of the ballpark. While traveling by subway is a lot less frustrating than going by car, unless one is properly armed, the trip could be fatal. That leaves driving as a fan's only choice—not much of an alternative. A short happy spin to Shea, as I found out, is neither short nor happy. It's a multihour blood-pressure raiser. Between the cross-cultural journey by train, which no parents would put their kid through if they really loved him, and the cross-country trek by auto, which no kid would put his parents through if he really loved them, the ballpark probably doesn't get a lot of wholesome family company.

For those who do make it, as long as kids aren't involved, facilities are all right. Parking's not bad. The lot around the stadium is good-sized. Overlooked by roaming officers, it provides a fairly safe stay for all the frightened autos, none of which, by the way, are station wagons. Rest rooms, graced with individual attendants, are safe. But not clean. Still, in a city not known for much in the way of white-glove standards, in this department Shea's probably the pride of the neighborhood.

ATMOSPHERE: GRADE D

Shea's a strange place. It tries to be traditional, and even succeeds on a few counts. Its welcome is Dodger Stadium-ish, the ball field immaculate. And bull pens, barely visible out beyond the fences, reminded me of the good old days.

In fact, the pens house Shea's most charming feature. Ballparks today, if they drive relief pitchers to the mound, do it in a brand-new Firebird or a Celica. Besides a waxy shine, the car's usually covered with advertisements. It gives the place one last place to pick up a buck. Shea, however, brings 'em out in the old-fashioned way—with jazzed-up golf carts. Giant ball caps, reproduced in all the NL logos, attach to the cart's roof and change with every home stand. It's the classiest ride in the majors, and a feel for the good side of the stadium.

It's funny...at times Shea really looks like a 2.3 kids-in-the-back-of-the-station-wagon outing, not a place for Charles Bronson target practice. But it isn't! It just doesn't have a heart. At least not a good one! What the Queens park fails to do, and what Yankee Stadium, in a much nastier section of town, does so well, is leave New York's ill feelings on the outside streets. Shea's not immune to the problems of the world, it's immersed in them. Just walking through the dark, guarded, fenced-in corridors under the stadium hint that horrors await.

Good quality heckling is an art, as important to a ballpark's character as peanuts, popcorn, and Cracker Jacks. In order to carry a voice above the buzzing of thousands, it doesn't need to be vulgar, only imaginative. Not everybody can do it. Those who can't sometimes come across as idiots. There's a fine line between a good heckler and a jerk. At Shea too many don't bother to walk the line. As impatient with the Mets as everything else on the field, fans let 'er rip. For almost any reason, at any time, no matter who's around—kids included—everything from the first-base umpire to first base itself is a target. Add that to the surly security force and you've got a potential for all kinds of problems.

Meanwhile, every half inning supersonic jets buzz the place, break the sound barrier, and remind you that outside the gates is a real world...uglier even than the one inside.

Shea doesn't provide that friendly baseball welcome or the good feeling the game can offer. It's definitely not a place for children or small pets. I'm sure there are good baseball folks submerged within. You can't fill up a ballpark as often as the Mets do and not run into a good side. But the feeling that floods the place is that New York survivalist attitude. A spirit that fares well out on the city streets, but one that fails miserably in the confines of a baseball park, a place that's supposed to provide an escape from it all.

23

YANKEE STADIUM,
NEW YORK YANKEES

The Great Escape

REPORT CARD	**Yankee Stadium**
	BASEBALL PARK
August 1, 85 vs White Sox	**New York Yankees**
GAME	BASEBALL CLUB

CATEGORY	GRADE	POINTS
Layout and Upkeep	*B*	*85*
Ball Field	*B*	*85*
Seating	*A*	*95*
Scoreboard	*A*	*95*
Food	*D-*	*60*
Ballpark Employees	*C*	*75*
Facilities	*D*	*65*
Atmosphere	*A*	*95*
Total Points		*655*
Average		*82*

B-
FINAL GRADE

13th
RANK

"Stationed in a filthy, broken section of the city. Blue pinstripes and monuments—that rich Yankee tradition—manages to escape the elements...and provide a fairy-tale
feeling to a nightmarish neighborhood."

PREGAME THOUGHTS

I'd made it! I'd driven to Shea and lived! Shaken but in one piece, back at Sharon's in sweet little Red Bank, I had an off day to recoup. Lying in the sunshine
at the beach, watching a little daytime tube, and finding my peanut-butter-
crumb-covered *Rand McNally*, I'd fully recovered. The Mets, TJ Hooker,
New York, and New York City traffic seemed a million miles away. Trip number two to the Apple, a Friday-night Yankee–White Sox game, was gonna be
a whole lot easier. Sharon would drive. My Toyota could hide in Red Bank.
Me, I was gonna lean back and relax in air-conditioned comfort and watch
everybody else lose it.

Sharon has it made. She works for Pepsi and, although she denies it, makes
a mint. She's got a company car and refrigerator full of Pepsi stuff. Best of all,
she can get box seats to any Yankee game she wants. Since I was poor, and a
guest, and she was loaded, she'd take care of everything. The driving, directions, parking, even the tolls. All I had to supply were the dogs and beer at the
ballpark. As a result...things couldn't have gone smoother! Getting to the
Bronx, even at 6:00 P.M. on a Friday night, beat the hell out of my Shea
Stadium disaster. Luxury riding, luxury parking, baseline boxes, my pregame
to Yankee Stadium was too good to be true. Afterward, on the "Great Post-
card Hunt," is where we almost died. So in this one case only, just to relive
the real flavor of the Bronx, pregame thoughts come after the game.

"The Great Postcard Hunt"

Seattle has got to be the flip side to New York City. The very absolute, complete black-to-white opposite. As safe as River City, Iowa, surrounded by green-
sloped mountains instead of gobs of pollution, no other American-made town
has a lovelier setting. Spit-shiny clean compared to the Big Apple, Seattle's
almost National Park material. Heck, if it wasn't filled with salt, you could
probably drink Puget Sound water. In New York you're better off with the
pre-bottled stuff.

As for sports fans, comparisons intensify. No place on earth has harder-core fans than New York City. Not only would they die for their team, they'd probably kill for 'em too. In fact, I'm sure some have. Seattle, on the other hand, is filled with fair-weatherers. When it comes to sports, it's the legitimate home of Casper Milquetoast. Sure it has all the biggies... pro football, pro basketball, pro baseball, and the U of W Huskies. But aside from the Hawks, or unless a team's undefeated halfway through the season, nobody really cares. Of them all, baseball gets the least respect. Talk shows, newspapers, six o'clock sports reports, all ignore it. It's alive for at most three months a year. From April to the end of June, when Seahawk talk starts back up again and the M's fold, are the game's few piddly moments.

Northwest TV sports announcers are just normal Pacific Northwest people. They follow the lead of the populace—baseball's not a biggie. Even so, one of them, Tony Ventrela, is great. Tony's not your classic sports announcer. Sure he follows the M's, reports their scores and talks about 'em during baseball season. But since his viewers don't care to hear about baseball, he doesn't saturate the airwaves with it. Instead Tony's prime items are a little more entertaining. He finds weird places to run his sports report from. Weird things to feature. His Wednesday night "Big-time Wrestling Hold of the Week" is a Seattle happening. Tony's style is a lotta fun! And definitely the best of the Northwest.

A week before I took off on my trip I was at the doc's loading up on drugs. Penicillin and whatnot. I had it stored up just in case I caught trichinosis from living on hot dogs for two months. I told him where I was going; the whole office thought it a grand idea. Barb, his nurse, suggested I get ahold of Tony. She thought it'd be right up his alley. So I did! And Tony loved it. He taped me cruising into the Kingdome for my first game and did an interview with me the night before I left. I was supposed to send him postcards from each ballpark. He promised to air 'em on his sports show and follow me around the majors. A great deal. I'd become a celebrity and Seattleites could see that baseball really was an American game. I also put together a built-in extra-credit assignment for the summer. Any kid who videotaped the segments would get an automatic "A" next fall.

At first I figured I'd just pick up cards when I got the chance. I wasn't gonna bust my butt trying to find ones that didn't exist. I had enough to do. But after a taste of California, things looked easy. The state is one giant post-card. Unlike the rest of the world, it doesn't have to wait for just the right day to shoot the scenes. Every day is postcard day. California drugstores devote half their shelf space to 'em. And why not? Babes in bikinis at the beach. Babes in bikinis at Disneyland. Babes in bikinis just standing around. With such good stuff to pick from, ballpark cards fill up the idle racks. So I bought at least two of every stadium, one for me and one for Tony, sent one north and kept the other—for creation of the all-time greatest scrapbook.

From San Diego I called friends back in Seattle. I wanted to see if Tony was keeping his end of the bargain. He was...and even reading them too! That made it official. I was determined. All 26! I had to get all 26! It became an obsession. Like collecting the 68 Tiger baseball cards all over again. Not only would I see every ballpark, taste a wiener at each, but I'd end up with at least 26 decent souvenirs, one good shot of each stadium.

In most of the early part of the trip, finding the cards wasn't a problem. Nearby KOAs and neighborhood drugstores in the stadium suburb world got me through K.C. Midwest city ballparks took a little more work but I found them too. Heading east, the challenge grew. Postcards are an American-made wonder. Other nationalities don't hold as much store in tacky plastic things as we do. Finding them in Canada was a royal pain. Both Toronto and Montreal took heavy digging. But each is safe. Their bad parts of town are better than most American city's good parts. The search wasn't scary, only time-consuming. Back in the States, things got easier. Fenway cards were a cinch. As historic as the Old North Church, almost every tourist shop carried 'em. The Phillies and the O's took more time, but after a little legwork were findable. Even Shea was easy compared to what it could've been. A few times I'd temporarily stumbled, but like the '68 Tigers, I was so-far so-good—22 for 22!

Yankee Stadium wasn't gonna be so simple. Even with Sharon's perfect Pepsi parking, the perfect tickets, and on a perfect warm summer night, we were in for problems. We got to the ballpark a little late to postcard-search in daylight. So afterward I decided we'd look.

"Not in my car!" Sharon wasn't real thrilled about the idea. She didn't want to spend Friday night searching the Bronx for postcards. She couldn't see why it was so important that I have a picture of a place I'd just taken two dozen of. Needless to say, Sharon's not a baseball fan. But she's nice. She partially agreed to my pleading...with restrictions. "Only three tries! No more!" Also, I was to do the legwork. Under no circumstances was she getting out of the car. She'd pull up, I'd run in, check for cards, complete my set, and we'd be off.

The search was on.

The few blocks that border right on Yankee Stadium are okay. Their livable lining is a thin one though. It evaporates several blocks from the stadium. Still, it was our best bet. We cruised the stadium streets. It was dark, but enough ball-game traffic was roaming the sidewalks to make my joining them without my hunting knife worth the risk. We found a corner place open and another down in the middle of the block. Sharon pulled up and idled. I ran in, looked, found nothing, and asked. In each the guy behind the register asked, "Postcards?" like I was some kind of a weirdo...and I ran out. For being the weenie that I am, I wasn't all that frightened. I think it was the thrill of maybe finding one that drowned out the sound of my knees knocking. Nevertheless, I'd come up empty.

With only one shot left, I suggested we drive around awhile till we found the right place. The right place for me would've had a neon sign in front that read "Yankee Stadium Postcards Here—Three for a Buck." There was one somewhere nearby. I could sense it, and was willing to spend the rest of the night looking. Sharon wasn't as optimistic and felt a little uneasy. She read New York papers more than I. She knew that eleven o'clock tours through the Bronx were not healthy. But she had said three, and being a big businesswoman, she felt compelled to follow through.

With "safe" stadium streets dried up, we continued farther out, and left all traces of civilization in the rearview mirror.

Things drop off real fast outside Yankee Stadium. In the Pepsi-mobile, we inched down narrow streets. Outside was spooky; inside the car, silent. We were speechless...absolutely speechless.

London during the World War II blitz—it's all I could think of. Bombed, blown up and deserted, it had to be close to what we were in. Dark and very, very quiet, streets were empty. Warehouses abandoned. Broken buildings, none with glass, windows and doors all boarded up. Slivers of streetlight made it back into the desolate corners. Only God knows what was going on there. The place oozed with filth and crime and drugs. Rats must've lined the alleyways. An eerie kind of sickness hung over everything. My neck hairs bristled, my body chilled. I just sat and stared.

After creeping for a few blocks, I regained some composure. Absentmindedly, I mumbled, "Postcards?" I'd forgotten the mission. Sharon turned and stared at me. Her face turned pale. "You are out of your mind." She said it nice and slow so I'd hear every word. Then added: "There is NO way. I am stopping here!"

"Please, Sharon. You promised three." I sounded like a whining little eighth grader begging for an extra weekend on his Thomas Jefferson report. I must've made her sick enough to say yes. She agreed, but made it official that she wasn't responsible for my death. All I could think of was 23 of 23.

We drove on...till we found a street only half boarded up. Most everything that wasn't was closed. A few people were walking around, enough cars were passing by, but the street was too narrow for Sharon to park and wait.

"Okay, you got as much time as it takes me to circle the block! That's it! Then we get the hell out of here! NO EXCEPTIONS! Got it?"

"Got it!" I echoed her.

Backpack around my shoulder, in tennis shoes, shorts, and Michigan State T-shirt, I slid out the door. The automatic door locks popped shut. Through the window she mouthed to me, "LAST ONE," and drove off.

In front of me, beyond the cracked sidewalk, was a store. It sure didn't look like a "last best hope." A tiny nasty-looking place, it smelled foul. Like wine and garbage mixed together. Outside an overhead lamp flickered every time an insect splatted into it. Lights glared through the glass door and lit up the broken walk in front. I pressed my nose to the window and looked inside. The floor was dirtier than the concrete walk outside, and the light not much better than the street. Walls were haggard. Racks on one of them were flooded with sex books—titles I'd never heard of, covers I'd never dreamed of. Dust-covered canned goods with ketchup bottles and jars of mustard occupied the middle aisles. The rest of the place was half-empty coolers littered with beer and cheap wine.

Suddenly I felt real stupid. Like a lamb sneaking into a lion's den. I wondered what in the hell I was doing. And glanced to see if Sharon was back yet. She'd just headed around the corner, out of sight. As I turned back around to the door I heard a click. I screamed. The door bolt locked. "Sorry, We're Closed" was flipping around.

I backed off. Onto the sidewalk. Thump! I hit something, jumped, and spun around. Staring face-to-face with...a no-parking sign. A few people walked past. A drunk staggered toward me.

"Shit! Sharon, where are you?" I was petrified.

Up near the corner a car braked...I broke for it. Halfway there I realized it wasn't her. Jesus, I thought, she's dead! Worse yet, so was I! I stood in the middle of the road, where the streetlight shone its brightest.

"Sharon, hurry, please hurry!"

A horn blared...I screamed. It was her, she'd come up behind me. I sprinted to the car and dove in. Slid across the seat. The automatic locks plunked shut behind me.

"You all right? Did you get it?" she asked.

I sighed and slinked down into the seat as low as I could slink. "No!" I took a breath and raised up just enough to peek through the window without being seen. "Twenty-two of twenty-three's not bad.... May we please go now?"

LAYOUT AND UPKEEP: GRADE B

I thought I'd seen it all. At least in the baseball world, I thought I had. Comiskey's neighborhood is nasty, and at night it can be a little unnerving. If you need some excitement, Tiger Stadium has plenty of dangerous places nearby. And Oakland, around the Coliseum, is a dive. They all add an extra phase to baseball—fear. They settle the eternal argument, day or night ball, which is better. If living through the ball game is important, there's no decision. The Bronx, though, is worse. It's slime. South Side Chicago, downtown Detroit, anywhere in Oakland is condo property compared to what Yankee Stadium sits in.

Sharon and I got to the game in luxury. Pass parking, an elevator ride from the parking garage down to ground level, and we passed security guards all along the way. We saw the stadium from a plastic tube. God only knows what I'd have done on my own—probably fainted. I wanted to see what I might've had to face, so before we went in I convinced her to circle the place once on foot. What we found was impressive. In '74 the stadium was given a $100 million face-lift. At the time they also cleaned up the block that bordered it. Both came out great. A young whippersnapper again, it has the vibrant feel of a Busch or a Riverfront—a ballpark that lives in a livable city.

Fortunately face-lifts fix up, they don't start from scratch. Too much of the old Yankee Stadium is irreplaceable. Its facade is still one of baseball's best. Tall thin archways are evenly spaced across the concrete stadium walls. They give the place that classical feeling. Kind of how the Roman Colosseum must've looked when it was in its prime—tall, proud, and handsome. Besides sprucing up the old things, modern conveniences were also added. At one end a circular Jack Murphy-ish walkway sticks out and attaches to the inside. People travel up and in. Above in neon, or about as bright, "Yankee Stadium" boldly identifies the place.

Its borders are taken care of too. Well-lit concrete walks circle the park. At places where crowds gather, entrances and ticket windows, clean open plazas spread out. Plenty of room in and out, the setup is suburbanish. In front, under the "Yankee Stadium" sign and next to the circle ramp, is "the bat"—a giant Louisville slugger. Standing on end, the barrel as big around as a small ticket booth, its knob reaches up almost even with the sign. A great meeting place, it's something you'd expect to find in a place like Anaheim... never the Bronx.

While outside the stadium eases away the Bronx, inside it chokes it off altogether. Like a concrete circle stadium, the Yankee park is clean, convenient, and organized. Escalators provide a West Coast-ish ride to the upper deck. That or you can walk the giant concrete swirl. Not quite as spotless as a California ballpark, it certainly gets the "New York City Ballpark Mr. Clean" award.

BALL FIELD: GRADE B

As suburban as the place may look, Yankee tradition would never allow for a plastic field. That'd be worse than filling in the pinstripes.

I can't figure why the newer stadiums leave out grass. They sink hundreds of thousands of bucks into a facility. Some add stuff that baseball never ever even dreamed of: scoreboards the size of drive-in theater screens, underground pop-up roll-out tarps, even computerized fountains. Then they go and plant a plastic field. Although quiet, with grass Riverfront'd be a lovely place, as quaint as the riverboats chugging by. Busch already explodes inside and once had real grass. Those days before the switch must've really been wild. And Royals Stadium, it'd be perfect. It almost is already. Without real grass each lacks a little something.

When the Yankees switched everything else inside over to plastic, fortunately they stopped at the field. The garden is still green, still real, and, aside from just a few rough spots, still well kept. Together with its rich brown dirt and Yankee-blue outfield walls, they hint at how handsome suburban parks could look... if they really wanted to.

SEATING: GRADE A

New ballparks are loaded with creature comforts. So are most that, like Yankee Stadium, have been tuned up. Where before 12 or 15 chairs were stuffed into skinny rows, now there are eight, with arm, leg, even elbow room. Wooden slats that used to leave ridge implants in the rear have given way to human-butt-contoured plastic. Aisles are wider, rows farther apart. If nothing else, progress has made the game more comfortable.

The problem is, you never get something for nothing. At most stadiums the pain-free price is closeness. Row after expanded row has pushed farther and farther from the field. Instead of one or two levels of wood, now they're three tiers of plastic. Behind home plate, high rises have gone up. Shea, Dodger Stadium, and all the concrete circle stadiums have brought baseball nearer to God.

The Yankee Stadium face-lift made sacrifices to provide sitable seats. Fortunately, its cost was quantity, not quality. Close to 20,000 chairs were eliminated. Those that stayed were switched to plastic and widened. Pillars that took X-ray vision to see through were removed. Like the Dodger palace, it gets the best from both worlds—old-time traditions and modern technology. Beginning inside the foul poles, three levels of blue chairs reach around behind home plate. And views are good. It does a great job at getting the roofs up and out of the way without pushing that upper level too far back. Folks are neither squeezed together nor piled on top of one another. And yet plenty of seats still hang out over the field.

Best part of the setup is that it still has real bleachers. Plastic since the resurrection, but first-come, first-serve bench seats, they're bleachers just the same. More Hall of Famers have bounced shots onto Yankee outfield benches than anyplace else in the majors. Baseball's lucky that whoever performed the plastic surgery let the tradition continue.

SCOREBOARD: GRADE A

Like the playing field, the view, and the layout of the park, the scoreboard uses modern technology to produce an old-time feeling. It's got everything the new parks have: multi-scoreboards surrounded by mounds of advertisements, a great sound system, and Diamond Vision. Others, however, can't claim such a tradition. All night long, fans are reminded there's none richer than the Yanks'.

Much like at Arlington, four screens peppered with advertisements run along the back upper lip of the stadium. Working around from left, sandwiched between billboards, a small panel flashes updates of all the major league scores. Next, in left center, under Seiko's official digital time, is the Yankee line score. Continuing into right, there hangs a large combo screen. The top half keeps track of balls, strikes, and outs. The bottom, other assorted details. Finally in right, wedged between the Marlboro Man and "The King of Beers," is Diamond Vision.

Diamond Vision gets a good workout. Like at Shea, the Yanks don't shy away from replays. Most anything's fair game. Fans keep a close eye on it and get in their share of boos.

Besides modern-day baseball, it also shows black-'n'-white oldies. Actual footage of Gehrig, Ruth, DiMaggio, and Mantle—almost every other between-inning stretch features a different Hall of Famer. The Babe smashes one into the very seats fans are sitting in. DiMaggio roams the same outfield that Winfield stands in. The numbers link past with present. They take a history that no other franchise can claim and make it come alive. They remind folks that being a Yankee fan carries an aura with it. If anybody inside didn't already know, the place just drips with tradition.

The sound system is good too. Most of the night, organ music floats about. It isn't really crowd-carrying like Comiskey's Nancy Faust's, but melodies fill in empty spaces and create a happy feeling. Recorded music is also slipped in once in a while. Usually it has a specific purpose. Its finest hour is its last.

Every ball game I go to, every movie I attend, I like to be the last to leave. People don't do that enough—nobody even knows what a movie credit is anymore.

At the ballpark, instead of cramming up the aisles, racing to the car just to get caught in traffic, I'll watch 'em put the field to bed. Lights darken, sprinklers or tarp, depending on the forecast, come out. Home plate and pitcher's mound get their Band-Aids. I like it. Puts the game back in perspective, reminds me it's not like football. They play it every day. At Yankee Stadium it's even a little more special, a little more personal. Kicked back, thoroughly pleased with the night I'd had, I put my feet up and relaxed. Over the stadium speakers Sinatra rolled into "New York, New York"... a perfect way to cap a perfectly pleasant night.

FOOD: GRADE D−

Selection: Poor   Accessibility: Poor
Taste: Poor   Cost: 20th

Everything else inside the place escapes the Bronx. Not the food. It tastes like it came out of the street gutters.

While Fenway's Frank has no challenger for the worst vended hot dog, at least it comes with a bun. My Yankee wiener was not only colder than my warm beer, but the mangled bun covered only a quarter of the dog. That was up in the stands. Underneath, things got worse. With no separate beer lines, just a draft can cost a couple of innings. That or send you back into the arms of the vendors. And although the guys are fast enough, they're stocked with cold things that ought to be hot and warm things that ought to be cold.

One special item, however, saves the menu from total embarrassment. A knish; it's one of the tastiest little things I've ever eaten at a ballpark. And goes with a draft as good or better than a bag of salted peanuts in a shell. A small potato-type roll, a knish is about the size of a doughnut and sells for under a buck. Cooked specially at the ballpark and limited to a specified number so that they run out by the seventh, the little wonders almost melt in your mouth. With a cold Bud, if a cold Bud can be found, they can make you forget about the lousy hot dogs, the packaged mustard, and even the gruesome things that for the past two hours have been happening to your car outside in the parking lot.

BALLPARK EMPLOYEES: GRADE C

I was ready for the Yankee Stadium police force. This time, I promised myself, I'd fight back.

Three days of that "New York State of Mind" had hardened me. I was tired of watching people consistently act like they owned the sidewalks, the road, the world, then pass it off with that "Oh, you gotta be that way to survive in the Apple" attitude. Not true! Nothing says a New Yorker can't be a human being at the same time. I've taken a couple of physiology courses; in college I made anatomical dissections. There's no special organ in a New York cadaver that isn't in a Midwestern one. At least none yet discovered.

I also had a few problems of my own. Somehow I figured I'd let it slip that I was a Sox fan. In Yankee Stadium, even with Chicago in town, that'd be fatal. In '78 I'd watched and squirmed with delight as Fenway's security force pounded on Yankee fans... just because of the NY on the hat. Paybacks, particularly in such a surly place as New York, were bound to be ugly. Plus my little run-in with TJ and the boys over at Shea had convinced me that in the Bronx things could only get worse. I wasn't out looking for trouble. Somehow, though, I figured it'd find me.

I was shocked! Instead of Thugsville, U.S.A., Yankee Stadium is filled with normal people. Compared to Shea, workers look like those yellow "Have a nice day" smily buttons. Not California friendly by any means, not even as friendly as the Baltimore employees, they're at least as pleasant as the folks at Fenway. Ushers are easy to find, and when I spoke they smiled. Vendors carry on like they're doing a job, not hard time, make change without grumbling, and don't come unglued with a last-minute switch on the number of hot dogs. Concessionaires are pleasant too. I even found one who explained what exactly a knish was and just why it was so tasty. Most of all, security cops are decent. Instead of TJ Hooker, the fellas with the badges act like Barney Miller and the gang at the Twelfth Precinct.

Considering all I'd seen and expected, the folks that brought me Yankee Stadium were a treat. In comparison to the rest of the civilized world, they're just average... but for New York City they're wonderful. In fact, the ballpark might just be the friendliest place in town.

FACILITIES: GRADE D

Yankee Stadium provides some of the best bathrooms in the neighborhood. And its parking garages look safe...although they're probably not. For what it's got to work with, the place offers decent facilities.

If ever there was a "Car Hell," it'd probably be in New York City. And it'd be hottest somewhere close to Yankee Stadium. If your car isn't bashed in or ripped off, just the fright from endless traffic jams would be enough to kill it in its youth. Knowing this, the ballpark tries to be nice to cars. Special parking garages, for the special few, are closely watched over. If you get there five hours early, or, like Sharon, know the right people, everything that can isolate an auto from the Bronx is available.

Even then, though, some of the neighborhood filters through. Public streets, like public schools, don't get good just because the desks are new or the chalk boards clean. As long as the Yankees are surrounded by the Bronx, a car will never be totally safe. To arrive in one with anything less than a personal police escort is not enough. Which leaves the train ride. Worse than to Shea, subwaying it—even if joined by a dozen Guardian Angels, armed for a change—morning, noon, or night isn't recommended. Regardless of the route chosen, getting to the stadium could be a fan's greatest challenge.

Inside, things are a little better. Folks sharing the rest rooms aren't as shady as those scoping the parking lots. And roaming broom boys and broom girls keep things tidy. But just to be on the safe side, everything's unbreakable—even rest-room mirrors are stainless steel.

ATMOSPHERE: GRADE A

After holding my nose through a day at Shea, I wondered if baseball anywhere in New York City could be fun. That "chip on the shoulder" attitude that soured the "good side of town" stadium I figured would destroy it in the Bronx. Never did I expect to find a ballpark I'd enjoy. Particularly at a place that feasted on the woes of the Red Sox. But I did. By the seventh-inning stretch I'd forgotten that somewhere out in the parking lot, Sharon's poor car was alone and waiting, probably frightened out of its tires.

Yankee Stadium is a beauty, an oasis thriving in the ugliness of city slums, as well planned as any the burbs have. Everything that 1980s technology can provide to baseball the ballpark picked up when it was resurrected. Escalators, wide halls, circular walking ramps—it's simple to get around in. And oddly enough, filth and crime, the Bronx's two greatest diseases, vanish. At times I almost thought I was in Anaheim.

However, more important than a ballpark's body is its heart. Shea showed me what baseball is like without one. It flirts with being human. Parts are decent. It's even a little traditional at times. But its character is so nasty that baseball dies inside. Yankee Stadium has a good heart, a little coarse, but true. The New Yorkers inside of it are all right. Friendly employees, concessionaires, cops—most of all, fans—are human.

I was surprised. I've seen Yankee games on television. At Fenway I've met real Yankee fans. I've played softball and worked with some who claim allegiance to the pinstripes. Most are obnoxious. They probably deserve the hammering that the BC linemen handed out at Fenway in '78. For my one-night stay, though, they were nice.

So nice, I decided to try something I'd only fantasized. Nightmares of Bucky Dent's homer still haunt me. Since he hit it, I've been hard-pressed to ever pull for the Yanks. Even in the Series, with AL pride on the line. Often I've dreamed of the chance to sit in Yankee Stadium among those who hated the Sox and cheer for Boston. In a warped kind of way I actually admire those New Yorkers who came to Fenway in '78. They were *real* fans. Only by facing the wrath of the Yanks in their very lair could I claim total Red Sox loyalty. Well, this was my chance. Even if they were playing Chicago. Fisk was up for Chicago in the eighth. To me he'll always be a Bostonian. His greatest moment, Game Six of the '75 Series, will never be topped in a White Sox uniform. He'd do just fine. I took a swig of beer, stood up, cupped both my hands to my mouth, and yelled, "Let's go, Sox!"

People around me were only mildly annoyed. "Sit down you asshole!" "Tell someone who cares!" Nothing was thrown at me. Nobody threatened to pound my face in. Nobody even brought up '78 or Bucky Dent. I fooled 'em. They had no idea it was the Red Sox, not the White ones, I was cheering for.

Yankee Stadium has it all: sky, green grass, and good hard-core fans. Had it no history, I'd still have had a grand time. But the place adds something intangible, a spark that can't be bought by any ballpark. That great Yankee tradition hangs in the air. All night long the legacy returns. In things like Diamond Vision movies, the blue pinstripes, and the hanging white roof trim, memories are revived. Mattingly joins the same classical heritage as Gehrig—just by wearing the uniform. And because of the tradition, Yankee fans of the eighties claim the status that New York fans did in 1927—just by being Yankee fans.

More than anyplace else, though, the legacy lives in a tiny flower garden between the two bull pens. Above and behind it are the bleachers. In front, the outfield. Inside is a simple display dedicated to Yankee greats. Small monuments to Gehrig, Huggins, and Ruth. Plaques for over a dozen others. The setting isn't grand, it's quaint. The memorials aren't flashy; they're quiet. But an aura hangs amid the lovely little place. In it the very history of the game touches today. It convinced me that baseball can survive anywhere. Whether stuffed inside the filth of a New York City slum or the plastic nothingness of a California suburb, baseball offers to anyone the chance to escape... into a simpler, more satisfying world.

24

THREE RIVERS STADIUM, *PITTSBURGH PIRATES*

Is Anybody Out There?

REPORT CARD

Three Rivers Stadium
BASEBALL PARK

August 3, 85 vs Expos
GAME

Pittsburgh Pirates
BASEBALL CLUB

CATEGORY	GRADE	POINTS
Layout and Upkeep	B	85
Ball Field	D	65
Seating	C	75
Scoreboard	C	75
Food	B	85
Ballpark Employees	B	85
Facilities	C	75
Atmosphere	D	65
Total Points		610
Average		76

C+
FINAL GRADE

18th
RANK

"The town is simply charming. The ballpark, merely simple. A boring clone of Cincinnati's one river concrete bowl with an added feature of its own...empty seats."

PREGAME THOUGHTS

I was alive. My car was intact. Neither of us had been beaten, robbed, or molested. And New York City was in the rearview mirror. I figured either God had answered Mom's prayers or I was just a very lucky fellow. To have lived through a midnight postcard hunt in the Bronx, survived midday New York City traffic without the help of *Rand McNally*, and not been shot and killed by one of Shea's "fake cops," powers that be had to have been at work. I wasn't about to question what they were, I was just gonna enjoy and savor being back out on the road. A lovely drive through the rolling hills of Pennsylvania, on a bright August afternoon, it was one of those "God I'm happy to be alive" days. I was so caught up in the sunshine, and my successful New York escape, I'd nearly forgotten that the next stop was "Iron City," home of—GOD, NO!—the Pittsburgh Steelers.

I despised Pittsburgh, and I'd never even seen the place. Not even a picture of it. All I knew were the Steelers. But that was plenty.

One is not born hating a city for such trivial reasons as professional football. It's an obsession that's created by the repetition of some horrible real-life experience. A hammering for me that came at the hands of a college roommate. A roommate who lived for Sunday afternoons, just to watch Jack Lambert's toothless grin munch on quarterbacks. So even as thrilled as I was to be leaving New York, the thought of Terry Bradshaw-ville made me cringe. Whether or not it was fair to blame the city for its football team didn't much matter. I was too far gone...Pittsburgh Steeler disease consumed me.

For three years at Michigan State, where the only football that counts is on Saturday afternoons in Spartan Stadium, my roommate drooled for Sundays. And of course every Sunday the Steelers were on. And of course every Sunday they won. And I, praying for anybody to beat them, picked a new NFL team a week (whoever Pit was playing) and bet a six-pack on 'em. And of course every week I lost. Then for six days, until the next Steeler massacre, I'd be reminded with a "Wanna bet this week?"

Unfortunately, Sunday wasn't the only day I saw the Steelers. In our apartment, every day was Steeler Day. I never knew so many things could be poisoned with a team logo. A Pittsburgh Steeler football clock hung in the living room. Our cupboards were filled with Jack Hamm, Donnie Shell, and Lynn Swann mugs. Playing cards, bath towels, magazines, posters, even Iron City beer cans lay around. Everywhere a body walked in an otherwise elegantly green- and white-trimmed pad was Steeler black and yellow.

Of all of it, though, the worst was the Lambert photo hanging on the bedroom wall. You see, typical college-kid apartments are puny. Four of us in a five-room place meant we shared bedrooms. I shared with Mr. Steeler. And over his desk, staring straight at me, was Lambert and that hideous toothless grin—a constant reminder that pro football must've existed in prehistoric times. Each morning I'd awaken to the smile. At night it was the last face I'd see before drifting off to sleep. It hovered over and stared at me all night long. And I swear to God, on full moons it came to life and stole the beer money off my dresser.

So because of the Steelers, Lambert's grin, and my roommate's obsession with each, I despised the city of Pittsburgh. Because of them I'd created my own image of Steeler-ville. Giant factories belching smoke into the air. Ironworks cranking out more pollution than product. Rivers running white with sludge. Pittsburgh, I was sure, would make Gary, Indiana, out to be a tropical paradise.

If that was all, I could still sleep nights. But the disease had affected my subconscious as well. I've wished horrible things to befall Pittsburgh, and I don't often do that, to anyone or anything...aside from Bucky Dent. Whenever a news flash relates some disaster around the States, I wait and hope that Pittsburgh is the town involved. It happens at the strangest times. On gray and rainy January afternoons, while sitting inside, protected from Seattle monsoons, sometimes I'll catch the tail end of an Eastern weather report. If it claims a portion of the country has just been paralyzed by 25 feet of freezing snow, deep down I hope that it's covering Pittsburgh, Pennsylvania. Worse yet, at the cost of millions of poor souls' jobs, I've prayed for the day when the Japanese create some cheap soybean substitute for steel...the city goes broke and just withers away. Sick thoughts for sure, but I have no control over them. Until I die I'll be haunted by the ghost of Don Criqui's voice signaling another Franco Harris touchdown...and that awful toothless Lambert grin.

Well, for eight years I'd suffered. Finally my showdown was at hand! Approaching "the Pit" from the turnpike, my intro to it was as expected—jammed into bumper-to-bumper traffic. Not since Baltimore had I seen so many orange "Men at Work" signs. Not since New York had I seen such backups. It figured. No doubt a river was being rerouted so more sludge could be dumped into it. Still, duty called, and the Pirates, as bad as they were, were next on my list.

Something strange happened after that. As traffic thinned and I drew nearer to town, a weird realization overtook me—the beast was more a beauty. I rolled into a fairly normal-looking city. In fact, it was even kind of pleasant. Sharp-looking skyscrapers silhouetted a clear blue sky. Rivers flowed a normal color and were made of water not sludge. Smoke didn't squat on top of the town. Hell, I couldn't even find a smokestack. The place looked pollution-free. I rolled down the window and took a whiff. Fresh air! I was confused. For almost a decade I'd envisioned how hideous Pittsburgh would be. And it ends up as tidy as Cincinnati. I felt robbed!

With the sky and water blue, and the air fresh, all that I had left to downgrade were the people. And I was sure they were gonna be low-lifes. As obnoxious as hell, they'd exist on Steeler memories. They'd cover their cars with black-and-yellow bumper stickers. Every conversation would end with "Long live Steeler power." And I knew for a fact they'd all be missing those front pearly whites. I cruised across the Fort Duquesne Bridge, past the stadium, and into a nearly empty parking lot. I paid my $3.50 and pulled in alongside a couple of normal-looking Japanese imports. Still not sure what the hell was going on, I locked the car and started off to the ballpark.

But before I'd gotten out of the lot, the attendant called out to me, "Hey, bud."

At last! My confrontation was at hand. The city might be cute, the water clean, but the people were still Steeler fans. Adrenaline surged through my body. Some no-good obnoxious Steeler fan was going to hassle me for something stupid. Well, I was ready. He was gonna get the verbal lambasting of his life. Eight years of pent-up frustration would explode and Terry Bradshaw's private parking attendant was gonna feel the lash.

"Hey, bud," he said again, "you gave me twenty-five cents too much. Here you go, enjoy the game."

What? A quarter? My jaw dropped. It wasn't fair! Since college I'd lived with an image of Steeler-ville on my brain. It'd hounded my very existence. Bet after bet I'd lost. Many a night I'd waken in a cold sweat with visions of Lambert's toothless grin chasing me through my dreams. It'd made me embrace such prima donnas as Vince Ferragamo and Roger Staubach. Once, God forbid, I even led Super Bowl cheers for the Dallas Cowboys. And here some no-account bum was giving me back my quarter. My dreams of personal Steeler conquest were dashed. I was even sure I'd end up pulling for the Pirates. It was too much. I just took my quarter, blindly thanked the fellow, and stumbled off toward the stadium... lost in what *Rand McNally* claimed was Pittsburgh, Pennsylvania, but I figured had to be *The Twilight Zone.*

LAYOUT AND UPKEEP: GRADE B

If I didn't know better, I'd have sworn I was back in Cincinnati. It's amazing how much the two towns look, act, and even house baseball alike.

Neither one's exactly what would pop into your head if you were reviewing neat-and-fun spots to visit in the good ole U.S.A. They should be though. Each is pleasant, nicer than a lot of places that get more "ink." Each has a colorful downtown skyline. Each has safe clean city streets and pleasant folks. And although Pittsburgh's got Cincy outnumbered in them three to one, they're both perched on rivers. The two towns look so much alike, all I can figure is that back in the pioneer days, Cincy and Pittsburgh settlement planners must've been related. They must've had a dream. Shared the same building plans, even the same river, and built twin cities—they just didn't put 'em in the same states.

As for the ballparks, they're more clonish than the towns. Concrete, round and filled with plastic, each is multipurpose. Each lie sandwiched between downtown and the water. Each opened their doors to baseball in 1970. Even their names are similar. Riverfront in Cincy and Three Rivers in Pit. Both sit on the bank of the same Ohio River. It's almost kind of spooky—like those settlement planners came back to life just long enough to match stadiums. That or their grand-great-grandkids fulfilled gramp's greatest wish and carried on the tradition.... Either way, the stadiums match.

Located a short bridge drive from downtown, Three Rivers Stadium sits where the Allegheny and the Monongahela flow into the Ohio. Like in Cincy, nearby skyscrapers hovering over the park look bigger than they are. They energize the place. Almost directly across from the stadium, steep hills shadow the Monongahela. Incline cars spend summer nights running folks up and down the hills to shuttle buses below. With the water, bright city lights, and the quaint cable cars plodding their way up the inclines, the setting is a pleasant one. For me, though, it was even better. A huge "Riverfest" summer celebration was in town and covered the riverbank with people. The music booming up from the river below and all the crowds added a little more color to the park. And made it all the more impossible for me to recall just how much I despised the Steelers.

The stadium is as well kept as the town. Acres of white concrete plaza engulf the place. Scrubbed and swept clean, no broken glass, no haggard shrubs or cracked sidewalks, not even much in the way of fans walking around, it provides a safe, secure feeling. Inside, safety, convenience, and Riverfront cleanliness continue. The resemblances are just remarkable. No two major league ballparks look so much alike. In fact, Cincy fans over for a Reds–Pirates series could tour the place blindfolded, and odds are by night's end they wouldn't bump into a wall or a person. For me, not as practiced in walking about Ohio River stadiums, I had to keep my eyes open and just spend the night suffering from déjà vu attacks.

BALL FIELD: GRADE D

Pennsylvania was one of the prettiest states on my cross-country tour—soft rolling hills, farmland bursting with golds and greens and broken by sturdy oak and maple trees. The drive over from Jersey was gorgeous. I even snuck off the turnpike a few times and moseyed along the back roads. You'd think that a state where Mother Nature does such nice work would be picky as to what kind of grass it allows baseball on. It isn't!

Each of its ballparks feature gross-looking ball fields. "The Vet's" multi-colored-glare turf is probably Pennsylvania's greatest eyesore. On a sunny day it's even dangerous to look at. Three Rivers plastic is, on the other hand, closer to tacky-ugly. Rather than a spectrum of assorted greens like in Philly, the Pirate park picked just two. Two totally different shades. And although it doesn't glare as bad, you're smart to shade your eyes between innings.

The two shades of green don't look right. Like separate patches just randomly plopped down, there's really no rhyme or reason to where one leaves off and the other picks up. Nothing as organized as the outfield one shade and the infield another. Instead it looks like when they laid the thing, they just ran out of plastic, then made the mistake of buying the rest by catalog from a color-blind salesman.

He probably told 'em, "Green's green, don't worry about it. You know that turf over in Philly—they had the same problem. I took care of them, and they've got a beaut!" Unfortunately, Three Rivers' management must've believed him.

SEATING: GRADE C

Since I've become a Mariners regular, I've had this thing for checking ballgame attendances in the box scores. One point I've noticed is that on a regular basis the M's actually do outdraw one major league team—the Pirates. Oddly enough, it's the only team that usually has a lousier record. Geez, I wonder if there's a correlation there somewhere?

Too bad for Pittsburgh. Or is it? For good baseball fans who don't mind moving to seats that don't really belong to them, it provides a little inexpensive luxury. By the third inning, baseline boxes are open for the taking. For general admission prices you can actually see the ball players. And while the Pirates might not be worth it, to watch Gooden singe the bat of each new Pittsburgh hitter or see Andre Dawson hammer on Pirate pitching from the front row for the cost of back row is a great deal.... A deal that in the American League only the Kingdome can promise, and one that for the last five years I've thoroughly enjoyed.

As for the seating layout, it's back to Cincy again: plastic chairs, aisle space, a field section, and three levels up and around with the biggest one on top. Probably even down to the angle of the fold of the chairs, the two river stadiums are almost identical.

In fact, if you fell into a deep sleep sitting in a Three Rivers chair, were quietly shipped to Riverfront and sat in the same seat, when you woke up you probably wouldn't know you'd moved. At least not until you left the game. And even then, looking at the cities, it'd be tough. About the only way to be certain would be by checking out the stadium wave... Reds fans are obsessed with it. In Pittsburgh there are usually not enough folks around to even start one up.

SCOREBOARD: GRADE C

In the seventies, when the "family" was swinging on the Three Rivers turf, when Parker and Stargell and the rest of the clan were popping the bleachers with a load full of dingers, I am sure the scoreboard was rockin' right along with 'em. But nowadays, like the rest of the place and the Pirates themselves, the scoreboard's a bore.

Like Cincy's system, it hangs miles from the field in the upper part of the upper level. And although a lot more technologically gifted than Riverfront's, it's got the same problem. It's just too far away from most human life to get the place going. Two big screens, up above center field, run most of the show. One of them, a simple electrical light panel, concentrates on the Pirates game. The rest is taken care of by Diamond Vision. Highlights and replays are crisp; players' stats are easy to see. It's a dandy... when it's turned on. Problem is, most of the night it's not. Unlike in Baltimore and Oakland, where the ball clubs get round-the-clock movie-screen advertising, the Three Rivers one ignores the Pirates. It'd probably rather not remind folks that they usually end up in last place.

Instead of present-day Pirates, the big screen's best feature is an airing of heroes of the past. A barrage of Pirates trivia questions and highlights of better days play all night long. Flashes of running, diving Clemente catches. Of "the Candy man" dishing out his own batch of sweets. A Willie Stargell facts-and-figure-a-thon fill the idle moments and remind folks that once upon a time the team actually won more than it lost. For a town with not much recent baseball to cheer about, the idea's a good one. If nothing else, fans will always have the Mazeroski shot.

FOOD: GRADE B

Selection: Very Good   Accessibility: Fair
Taste: Very Good   Cost: 13th

While a Pirates game might not conjure up all the images that singing "Take Me Out to the Ballgame" promises, at least it tastes the part.

The ballpark's filled with good things to eat—normal baseball peanuts, popcorn, Cracker Jack-type stuff, as well as all sorts of specialties. Pizza's pretty good, better than at most stadiums. While the plastic cheese spread nachos, the kind that have migrated from 7-Elevens around the world, are extra-loaded with both chips and cheese. And oddly enough they're even edible. Burgers, polish sausage with kraut, and fish and chips are tacked onto the regular menu and give it just a little more pizzazz.

Then beer takes over. And it comes out of all sorts of Pennsylvania-type taps. Rolling Rock, Iron City, and Iron City Light team up with the old blue-collar standbys—Bud, Strohs, and Miller. They provide folks that home-state flavor and gave me flashbacks to Sunday afternoons at State.

The place also provides a West Coast-style luxury. Behind a screened-in wall down in the left-field corner, so that you can kick back, munch out, and watch the ball game all at the same time, sits The Bullpen Cafe. The cafe features an exotic menu (at least by Eastern stadium standards) and looks kind of like a lounge you might find at the Big A in Anaheim. Roast beef, chicken breast, and meatball-type stuff all simmer in trayfuls of thick juicy sauces and come with a freshly tossed salad. It was a refreshing change of pace for me ...something green and healthy that wasn't shoved in a bun or trapped in a peanut shell. And with the clipped-away wall I got a little luxury without having to catch the ball game in California style, on a big-screen color-television set.

BALLPARK EMPLOYEES: GRADE B

Although Three Rivers might be dull, at least it's friendly. Gracious and professional, folks that work the place are all right. In fact, before I got inside I'd already met two fellas more hospitable than anybody I found in all of New York City.

It started at the parking lot. Getting that quarter refunded from the attendant was strange. At the main gate, though, things got even stranger. I was talked to like a human being by a stadium security guard. Fresh from my run-in with TJ Hooker, it's the last thing I expected.

Today, policy around the majors is to check fans' backpacks on the way into the stadium. On the constant lookout for bottles and other potential weapons, the policy is a sound one. Crazies turn up everywhere nowadays, even in baseball parks. However, the request to take a look, usually handled by stadium security, isn't always real neighborly. It goes from the standard "You wanna open your pack, please" to "You wanna open your pack, NOW!" Sometimes if you look at the guy strangely enough, and he's having a bad enough day, or if it's taking place at Shea, the search intensifies: "Get your hands against the wall. Feet back and spread 'em."

Pittsburgh's too mellow for such things. An empty ballpark on a pleasant night, me moseying in by myself in the bottom of the second didn't seem too awfully dangerous a situation. At least not to the security guard at the front gate. He stopped me just outside. Three times while looking through my pack he apologized for the search.

"Sorry I've gotta do this. It's stadium policy, ya know," he explained, then re-explained, then echoed it once more to himself.

All three times I nodded and said, "No problem." The last time I added, "You know, I actually think it's a good idea. Some places can get pretty scary."

On "scary" we stopped, kind of looked at each other, and at the same time said, "New York City!"

Nice folks aren't limited to outside the gates. Inside they're pleasant too. Concessionaire and souvenir-shop employees, probably 'cause they're so lonely, are more than happy to chitchat. Vendors up in the stands push their wares hard enough...at least hard enough to keep all 12,000 folks satisfied. And ushers dressed in boldly printed "STAFF" shirts stand in pairs at the top of nearly every aisle. Besides answering any stadium questions, the staffers lead folks to their seats and dust off the chairs. Because of them, and since the city's such a mellow place, and the ballpark's usually more empty than full, security guards aren't really needed. Actually, their only real challenge is backpack-checking.

FACILITIES: GRADE C

You'd expect a three-ring multipurpose stadium filled with plastic and built in the seventies to have top-notch facilities. Riverfront does! It only figures that its clone should too. Not so! Tough to get to, surrounded by only a few meager parking lots, and filled with rather plain rest rooms, in the facility department Three Rivers is average.

Stadium parking and parking for Pirates games take on two entirely different meanings. Lots immediately around the stadium are hardly major league size. But because the Bucs are so bad, and so many people treat them like a plague, those who do go get a reprieve. Parking's a snap. In fact, city parking meters could probably handle the puny baseball crowds. Like Seahawk Sunday in Seattle, Steeler Sunday in Pittsburgh is the only time stadium lots get a good workout.

Inside, facilities are just okay. I expected better. Water fountains, telephones, and rest rooms are accessible, although not as accessible as in Cincy. Still, like the rest of the place, they're kept tidy. Other than that they're just basically, boringly complete. Quiet, clean, and empty—about as exciting as the rest of the place.

ATMOSPHERE: GRADE D

Coming in, as far as I was concerned, Three Rivers Stadium had just one thing going for it—the Pirates followed the Yankees. After two games in New York, anything had to be an improvement... anywhere but Steeler-ville. Those four years of Steeler mania had warped me. From its sure-to-be smog-filled skies to polluted rivers and lousy ballpark, I was ready for a dive. A place that really did deserve to be the stop sandwiched in between New York and Cleveland.

Was I off base! Pittsburgh's the best thing Three Rivers has got going for it. In fact, about the only thing. Just another three-level plastic clone, this one with a lousy team and hardly any fans around to watch 'em lose, the spirit inside Three Rivers challenges the Kingdome as baseball's biggest bore. But Pittsburgh... now that's a different story.

Rand McNally's most livable city of 1985, I enjoyed Pit in its finest dress. Catching the Pirates at home on the eve of their biggest summer river festival was a treat. Instead of an industrial hole, I found a vibrant, progressive city. Quaint, yet at the same time exciting, it's a place that major league baseball is lucky to savor. All night long the town's charm rubbed off on me. On my drive in it destroyed false images and showed a pleasant side. At the ball game it showed me good people. By game's end, back out at my car, it even offered up a fond farewell. Like it was happy it'd won over another Steeler hater.

While the ballpark emptied, to the glow of Three Rivers' fading lights, the city exploded in color. Music from riverfront park, a few blocks down below, drifted up to the stadium. Cheers rose and died as fireworks burst overhead. Their reflection off the PPG Building, hovering behind the stadium, brightened the darkness with more blues and greens and reds. Dads pulled lawn chairs out of their car trunks; kids, still in their Pirates caps and carrying their ball gloves, laid their blankets out on the curb and sat. Everybody stopped and watched, then "ohhed" and "ahhed" at the celebration. Quietly, across the river, the Duquesne incline cars just kept chugging up the hillside. Ah, yes... just goes to prove that *Rand McNally's* always right.

As for me, I am nearly cured. Black and yellow together still make me oozy. Like the bell in Pavlov's doghouse, every time I see the combination I've got to fight off nausea. I still pull for the Bengals to hammer on the Steelers. And once in a while, usually Super Bowl week, my Lambert nightmares recur. Now, though, after Pittsburgh, my mind is no longer warped. I now know how charming a town it really is. And that it houses normal people with normal dreams... and, best of all, normal teeth.

25

MUNICIPAL STADIUM, CLEVELAND INDIANS

The Sound of Distant Drum

REPORT CARD		
Municipal Stadium		
BASEBALL PARK		
August 4, 85 vs Orioles		
GAME		
Cleveland Indians		
BASEBALL CLUB		

CATEGORY	GRADE	POINTS
Layout and Upkeep	C	75
Ball Field	D	65
Seating	C	75
Scoreboard	D-	60
Food	C	75
Ballpark Employees	D	65
Facilities	D	65
Atmosphere	B	85
Total Points		565
Average		70

FINAL GRADE	RANK
C-	22nd

"Old, empty, and run down. Still there is something lovable about the place. . . . Maybe it's the lone fan pounding on his big bass drum out there in the bleachers."

PREGAME THOUGHTS

Bad reputations are a hard thing to shake. Trusting to stories, and somebody else's prejudices, we form warped ideas about people who we find out later aren't so warped. It's just our brains that are. By jumping on the bandwagon and throwing in our two cents' worth, we help create a monster out of a mouse. Take away all the made-up crap, and usually there's a normal human underneath.

Places aren't any different. We've all seen at least one town get hammered on *Sixty Minutes*. Watched Mike Wallace and the boys methodically take it apart. Spiraling crime rates, swirling economy, gobs of pollution, lewd and immoral governmental practices—by the time they're done the place looks like hell. And we suck it all in. Partially because it's got some truth to it, partially because ole Mike would never lie to us. If it's not *Sixty Minutes*, then it's the six o'clock news or a front-page headline. And what do we do? We watch. . . a little longer if the scenes are gory enough. We read. . . a little farther if the pictures are gross enough. We laugh a little, shake our heads that people can't act more civilized. Then pray to God we never get transferred there.

Well, Cleveland, Ohio, is such a place. Deserved or not, it's got probably the crummiest big-city reputation in the United States. A punch line to all sorts of rotten-city jokes, it's hammered on by every form of the media. Then added to by us. . . who haven't got a clue as to what it's really like. We just enjoy the gossip. For many Americans it's the city at the bottom of the barrel. A focus for even Detroiters to look down on. A place where only mothers-in-law, probation violators, and the Yankees belong. Cleveland is the Rodney Dangerfield city of all time.

And how do we know? Because we've been there, right? Wrong—because we saw a picture in *Time* magazine that showed Lake Erie spouting a chemical fire. We watched a segment on *Sixty Minutes* that said the city's electricity was gonna be turned off. We read somewhere that some dumb poll said it was the most unlivable place in the United States.

Well, I am a normal human. I've accumulated my share of the Cleveland media blitz. TV shows and magazines did a good job on me. I had a perfect picture of Cleveland in my brain. The electric bill hadn't been paid, so the plug had been pulled. Or it would be when I got there. The crime rate and the unemployment rate would be racing to see which could reach triple figures first. Both were close. Factories would cover the place. Not tidy Milwaukee ones that made everything neat like beer. Cleveland's only product would be pollution. It'd be Gary, Indiana, on a super scale—only worse. Most things would be shut down. Warehouses, stores, broken buildings—all would be boarded up. While bums who were once respectable nine-to-fivers would line the streets begging for quarters.

Not only was the city dead, but so were the Indians. I watched the box scores, checked the attendances, studied the standings. Cleveland never won... except in September when they played the Sox. Then they never lost. Either way, nobody ever went. Crowds of 8,000 in a stadium that holds 80,000. I figured they had to be the lousiest sports fans in the world.

But worst of all in my Cleveland portfolio was what it'd done to the lake. Cleveland sits on the shores of Lake Erie. Back in '69 newspaper headlines and magazine covers flashed "Erie Catches Fire." It wasn't the *National Enquirer* reporting. *Time* and *Newsweek* ran the stories—it had to be true. It didn't matter when I found out later that it wasn't really Erie but the Cuyahoga River that flowed into it that was torched. I didn't care. All I knew was that one of the Great Lakes was a burning mass of stinking chemicals. Cleveland was the cause. And I was sick about it.

You see the Great Lakes are special to me. As a kid I spent summers frying in the South Haven sunshine at Lake Michigan. Lying on the hot white sand, I'd bake while the whitecaps crashed to shore. The smell was fresh, the sounds and sights wonderful. Baseball was always on the radio, something cool to drink in the cooler. I loved those days at the lake.

And I loved getting there. The whole drive over I spent anticipating that first sight of the water. It was like getting to the ballpark and seeing the grass for the first time—it always took my breath away. The drive was slow. Single-lane M-43 almost turtled us over. If it was hot, traffic would thicken and lines would be slower. In town it'd bottleneck even more. And at the channel bridge that hung over the sailboats heading out to the lake, on a real busy day traffic would stop. We'd inch forward, just like at the ballpark. The closer to the stands, the more crowded it would become; the closer to the lake, the slower the lines of cars. At each I could only wait and be dragged along by the tide. Then finally that explosion of color—green at the ballpark, blue at the lake. Bright, bright blue, the water dotted with whitecaps glistening in the sunshine, rising up until it evaporated into the blue horizon. God, it was beautiful.

It was gonna hurt to see Lake Erie. I know they're all being poisoned. The factory crud has to go somewhere. At least Lake Michigan hides it—it'll last till I am gone. But to catch fire, I figured Cleveland had to be a sewer of pollution. Erie, just a hole filled with white sludge. A dead Great Lake— another nail in the Cleveland coffin. Had I been able to shut my eyes and pass it by, I would have, but Municipal Stadium sits on the water's shore. To visit number 25 I was gonna have to face the lake.

It was almost noon Sunday morning when I headed into town, about the same time we used to get to South Haven. The Cleveland drive wasn't nearly as pleasant though. Instead of passing through small towns and tidy farmlands like on my summer trips to the beach, I-77, Cleveland's driveway, is battered. A worn industrial section lines it. Old, beaten-up, and soot-covered factories run back off the road. They're tired. So is the road. Cracked and pitted concrete, and littered with men at work signs, like a drain into a sewer, the highway empties into Cleveland.

I flowed along, bouncing on the torn concrete, dodging the construction projects, finally swirling smack-dab into...a ghost town. Downtown was strange and very, very quiet. Buildings were old and decrepit, many of 'em closed or boarded up. Streets were empty of people and cars. An eerie kind of feeling hung over the place. Like everybody just gave up and decided to leave town together. I slipped through in search of the ballpark. Over some tracks, through a couple of empty intersections, toward the stadium and the water.

Almost simultaneously I saw them both—the big hulking stadium and the Great Lake that it sat on. Perched up over Municipal was the smiling Indian mascot. He welcomed me to number 25. But it was out behind him where my eyes were fixed. Erie, the dead sludge pit that I dreaded, at least there under the home of the Indians, was as blue as the sky that it was joined to. Maybe not chemically, but at least in color, she was gorgeous. Just like her four sisters, she still splashed lazily against the shore, whitecaps dotted her, and those nasty-tempered sea gulls still screeched overhead. I looked back at the ballpark. It wasn't pretty, actually kind of haggard. But I figured baseball inside would be better than I'd expected.

How could it not be? Behind it, sparkling as blue as a robin's egg, was a reminder that reputations, deserved or not, are a hard thing to shake.

LAYOUT AND UPKEEP: GRADE C

It's called the "Mistake by the Lake." I wondered though. I'd made the mistake. The lake was beautiful. With Erie's image shattered, I decided I'd be fairer with "the Mistake." Actually, I was excited to get inside.

The place is ungodly huge. Only Dodger Stadium looks as big, and it's grand. It glistens in the sun. And climbs five levels up into the heavens. Municipal, on the other hand, looks clumsy. It's a huge open semicircle of seats. Two levels supported by sturdy steel beams peek out from inside. A white brick facade covers the outer shell. At three places on its parking-lot side the shell turns into small buildings. Each look like old downtown post offices and double as ticket booths. On top of one of the corner buildings, flashing his big toothy grin, is a giant billboard cutout of baseball's best mascot. Bat cocked back, Chief Wahoo smiles out at the parking lot, ready to hammer one into the lake. He's a great doorman to the wandering few coming in off the streets.

Folks forget that Municipal is so old. Built in 1932, age-wise it's in the same class with the classics—Fenway, Tiger Stadium, and the two in Chicago. You'd never know it though. Nobody in Boston, Detroit, or Chicago'll ever admit it. Their parks are a part of history, stadiums that should live forever. Municipal?. . . It's just out of date. Maybe it is, but it also has the sincerity of the other four. It's got that good feeling that can only come from sticking around so long.

Old things make the place homey. Ticket windows and gates inside are old style. Not built for quick funneling, instead they bottleneck fans waiting to get in. That's if there are any. Inside, like Comiskey, it's ready for retirement. Cracked and worn walkways lead endlessly back and forth and up, seemingly forever, but to nowhere. Walking up them I saw signs of the South Side Chicago park all around. Wires globbed over by tape and paint hung from the iron posts. Floors were clean but cluttered. Unhidden boxes with nothing in them sat unstacked in corners. Empty kegs waited to be filled up again. It was like a basement or an attic crammed with things that had no useful purpose but nobody really knew what to do with.

Tired and out of date, Municipal's looked after but not really cared for. Like a big old sad-eyed dog, it gets fed, but nobody gives it any good loving. It just lies around and watches the days slip by. I felt kind of sorry for it.

BALL FIELD: GRADE D

The ball field fits the place. It's huge! And, like the cluttered hallways and ancient steel girders that surround it, worn. Not particularly well cared for, patchy and littered with age spots, anything else would seem out of place.

Beyond the grass, between the outfield wall and bleacher seats, is an open area about 60 feet deep all the way around. It has two functions. One is to push the bleachers back almost out into the lake. Secondly, it serves as a picnic area for pregame parties. Like Comiskey's inside field-level picnic area, the setup is dumb-looking...but, like in Chicago, it fits. Problem is, the wooden tables sit in grass and the other side of the cheap outfield wall is a dirt warning track. Grass sneaks through the cracks and grows in the dirt. It looks tacky. But also at home inside Municipal.

From the track on in, the outfield is sharp. A huge unbroken pasture of cross-cut green, it's everywhere. Little Brett Butler standing in center field gets swallowed up in the stuff. Near the infield the grass loses its edge. It's splotchy and worn. All around home plate, the pitcher's mound, and down both baselines, wherever dirt and turf meet, it's patchy. The blend's haggard.

Yet, as sorry-looking as the ball field is, Municipal wouldn't seem right dressed in anything else. Some folks just look good in Salvation Army clothes.

SEATING: GRADE C

The best Sunday-afternoon deal in all of major league baseball—a $2.00 bleacher ticket and an empty stadium of 80,000 seats to roam around in. It leaves lots of room in the wallet for buying hot dogs.

I watched the Indians from more views than NBC could get on a Saturday *Game of the Week*—upper deck, lower level, down each baseline, behind the plate. I watched from behind posts, in front of them, even leaning up against them. I sat in different quality seats—front-row boxes, the best in the house, and out in the bleachers, miles from any moving objects. The place is so big and was so empty, I even experienced different climates. In the bright sunshine it was hot; back in the shade a tad chilly. Down in the left-field corner I caught an inning and a half of both at the same time. Best of all, at each seat I sat in pure luxury. With less than 20,000 in a place that holds over 80,000, I was able to relax. My backpack could take a seat, either left or right. Both were usually free. My legs went up and over the chair in front of me. And nobody's head was anywhere in sight.

The park's setup is about as simple as they come. Two levels stretch in a semicircle behind home plate. Each curls around the foul pole and is set back off the field. Views aren't particularly close. Neither are they clear; steel posts pop up all over. Also, most of the chairs are wooden. Beyond the center-field fence, cosmetically at least, things get worse. Out there, open only on the weekends, 500 feet from the batter, are some of baseball's most worn bleachers. They're as far as a major league fan can get from home plate and still be in the ballpark.

Comfortable, close, and convenient, Municipal seats are not. That is if the place is packed. Most every night, though, at least 50,000 seats are empty. With no ushers around to tell you differently, and no guilt from seat-hopping, all three C's get easily covered. Plus one is added...cheap: $2.00 for a baseline box, and still able to stretch all the way out, I could sit on those old wooden chairs all season long.

SCOREBOARD: GRADE D−

Some of Municipal's crummy offerings are forgivable. They add a little character to the place. The grass, although it looks like a weed patch, fits the stadium. Despite being obstructed by hundreds of poles and in some places hundreds of yards, seats are too easy to switch to complain about. Even the old building itself, although ready for retirement, is simply charming. The scoreboard, however, stinks. Neither cute, classic, nor informative, it's almost totally worthless.

It sits too far away from everything—a single screen way out on the top of the bleacher section. For folks behind home plate it's almost in a different county. And it's way overworked for what it's able to put out—keeping track of all those Tribe losses is not as easy as it seems. Actually, it pretty much matches the Indians themselves. Probably not so bad back when Tiant and Sudden Sam McDowell were throwin' for the Tribe. In a modern Diamond Vision movie-screen world, it has all the flair of a nine-inch black-'n'-white television set...without the cable hookup.

A system doesn't have to have Diamond Vision to be good. Plenty of simple electronic panels do decent work. They just have to try a little harder. By splitting their faces into sections they're able to handle updates, messages, score the ball game, and even flash an occasional replay. Milwaukee's does it. So does Detroit's. Not Cleveland's. It plods along covering one thing at a time, each in Neanderthal fashion. Obviously Indians games get first priority. So most of the game the screen sits there with a dumb line-score look on its face. When it's not line-scoring it's usually flashing information on the batter. Problem is, they both use the same space. Flip-flopping back and forth between the two is a pain. It seemed like whenever I wanted to see the score, somebody's .243 average was posted. If I was looking for an average, the line score was up. It's a lot less frustrating when you know where to look for what.

Meanwhile, updates of other games are practically ignored. Occasionally they'll sneak on between innings or during a pitching change. The pattern is so awkward, though, that it's not worth the search. Only the organist is decent. Imaginative and lively, he tries to breathe a little life into the place. But it's just not enough. If he really wanted to help, he'd learn Morse code. Since the scoreboard doesn't show scores, maybe he could play 'em.

FOOD: GRADE C

Selection: Fair   Accessibility: Fair

Taste: Fair   Cost: 7th

The food's about as exciting as the Indians. It's got the basics covered, but not much more.

Prices are good. They should be, because nothing's worth a whole lot of money. Except maybe the pizza, which is cheesier than most. Or the mustard, which is some of the league's best. Otherwise, it's standard stuff: standard beer—Bud; standard peanuts—salted and in the shell; and standard dogs—ballpark ones in a bun.

About the best thing going for the food is the booths it comes out of. Like the empty chairs out in the stands, nobody's around to clutter 'em up. The wait's a short one. Not the best for a wining-and-dining experience, or much of a match to the West Coast liquor lounges. For a lazy sunny Sunday Oriole–Indian game, however, it did just fine. Plus, after forking out only two bucks to get in, I had all that leftover moola for food.

BALLPARK EMPLOYEES: GRADE D

Major league baseball's most boring job must be selling anything at Municipal Stadium. With so few folks in the stands, underneath, where pennants and buttons, hot dogs and peanuts go out, it's lifeless.

Up and in, employee-wise it's almost as empty.... Ushers are impossible to find, but that's all right, nobody's around to stop you from seat-hopping. Security officers are about as visible as ushers... and needed about as badly. The place is so huge and seems so harmless, the few that hang around might just as well go home. Only vendors pushing food around the place are available, and a reminder that the stadium isn't on automatic pilot.

I really couldn't blame folks for not busting tail. Municipal just doesn't have that bust-tail atmosphere. The Indians aren't famous for on-the-edge-of-the-seat seasons. There's no reason to get all hot and bothered if service is a little slow. So I didn't. I just waited the extra couple of minutes while the hot dog guy, as he wiped the sleep from his eyes, asked me how many more innings till it was all over.

FACILITIES: GRADE D

Cleveland's not a facility city. Not like Kansas City or Cincinnati. The minute I saw Kansas City I knew the ballpark bathrooms would sparkle, the parking lot would be immaculate. At Cincy it was even more obvious. A town as tidy would never allow filthy stadium rest rooms. Cleveland's more like Chicago: a bathroom is a bathroom, and don't spend a lot of time making it more than that. A parking lot is a place to put the car—nothing more, nothing less. Find a flat stretch of ground, charge three bucks a shot, then abandon it. And that's just about how the facilities came out—basic and pretty much left alone.

Surrounding the giant stadium, big enough to handle Indian crowds, is something that I think is supposed to be a parking lot. Unpaved and scarred with chuckholes, some so deep I thought my car was being swallowed whole, it's dangerous for any vehicle without the ground clearance of a standard army jeep. While it may be a pit, at least it's easy to get in and out of. Sandwiched between town and the ballpark is the expressway. Zooming off the ramp and down to the lot is simple. While the prize, a parking spot, may be no world-beater, at least it's available, which for a city stadium is saying something. Actually, if somebody would clear out a few of the boulders and fill in the holes, it wouldn't be half bad.

As for the rest rooms, they're like Cleveland... old and worn and empty.

ATMOSPHERE: GRADE B

It's not a pretty park. It's not in a pretty town. The Indians, it seems, beat only the Red Sox... and then only to benefit the Yankees or the Tigers. They're usually out of it by June. But something inside is good. Something not seen by *Sixty Minutes* or not told by *Newsweek* drew me to Municipal Stadium. Something said that, even though I was sitting nearly alone in an out-of-date ballpark, alongside a lake known best for catching on fire, in a town known for nothing good, baseball inside would be special. To the few who go, the awkward old place makes Indian games, as bad as they might be, just a little better.

Physically the place is worn. Most buildings its age, at least those with people roaming around inside, are on schedule to be leveled. Or they just store stuff now. Things inside are tired too. The ball field's a mess. Its warning track is nearly as grassy as parts of the infield, the infield as splotchy as the rock-covered parking lot. Seats are uncomfortable. Most are wooden, many have posts plopped in front of them, while some, like the bleachers, are nearly a half mile from home plate. And the scoreboard... they might as well pull the plug and save the electricity.

Yet, even with all the drawbacks, a good feeling floats about the place. Municipal is a living example that the sum parts of an object don't always equal up to the whole. Part of the reason is that the stadium, as tired as it is, is actually lovable. The other is the folks who go there.

I sat almost everywhere there was to sit in Municipal. And almost everywhere folks were into the game. They didn't come 'cause there was nothing else going on. Or because it was the social thing to do. Or even because of the free Tribe visors at the gate. They were there to watch baseball. With boisterous cheering and good crisp booing, they broke up the emptiness. Cowbells clanged everywhere inside. So many people had 'em, I wondered if they came on a coupon with a hot dog. With the noise of fans scattered in small groups, the clanging bells, the rise and fall of the cheering, Municipal reminded me of sitting in the stands at a high school football game. And high school football stands are filled with heart.

Besides rounds of applause for good things, and hisses for the bad, Indian fans are baseball's best hecklers. Insults to both teams echo like voices calling out at night through an empty warehouse. Not just in a couple of places—like the cowbells, they pop up everywhere. All afternoon long I found myself listening, smirking, and turning to see where the voice was coming from. Somewhere up in the dark shadows of the empty seats. Usually I missed the mouth, but I'd hear the voice a little later.

Besides being doused with good hecklers, Municipal itself is great heckler territory. Ballparks crammed with tens of thousands of people are a continual buzz. Single voices drown in a constant rise and fall of noise and excitement. But inside Municipal one voice is able to rise up and pierce the empty quiet. It gives the mouth an audience. And once in the limelight, whether it be a player's turned head or a group of fans laughing, it's set for the night. No wonder every season come crunch time, the Sox can't win in Cleveland. They're too busy listening to the shadows.

Indian fans, however, are not an unorganized hit-and-miss spattering. They have a leader... a very special leader. He's not some guy dressed up like a bird who runs around sticking babies' heads in his mouth. He's not a green Phanatic who rides a motor scooter all over the field. Nor is he a chief who war-chants around his teepee every time the Indians jack one out. He doesn't even have anything to do with the organization—in fact, he's unpaid. He's just a normal guy, a normal baseball fan with a big bass drum.

I'd seen John Adams on TV a few times. About five summers ago, I remember watching the Sox in Cleveland on *Game of the Week*. Out in the bleachers was this big guy pounding on a drum. Seemed rather strange, but I didn't really think much of it at the time. Hell, it was Cleveland, and I knew all about Cleveland. A couple of years later Seattle was playing in Municipal. I saw him again. Dave Niehaus, the M's announcer, commented about him always being there. Then whenever the Indians were on I started watching for him. I listened in the background of Mariner games, straining to hear the drum. Niehaus was right, the guy really was there all the time.

I wanted to meet him. For the first six innings I wandered as the drumbeat echoed across the field, the drummer and his drum just a spot way out in the center-field seats. In the seventh I headed out to meet him. There in the very back row of an almost empty bleacher section, 513 feet from home plate, sat John. Big and burly, about 225 pounds, 35 or so, he was dressed in a red T-shirt and jeans. Next to him sat his wife, Kathleen. In front of them, lying on the bench, was a big old wooden bass drum. It looked about as worn as the stadium.

I introduced myself, explained why I was visiting Cleveland, what I was doing, and that I'd seen him play before on TV.

John lit up! For the last three innings of the game, and an hour and a half afterward, he told me everything there was to know about Cleveland.

"I love this place," he told me. "All of it, the city, the ballpark, the Indians." Most of all, I could tell he loved baseball.

"Haven't missed a game in 13 years." Kathleen reminded him there were a few he didn't get to. "Oh yeah, a couple of early season day games, when I couldn't get off work. Not many, though, only nine or ten."

John has another more respectable but less important job. He data-processes something for the telephone company. But the ballpark is his life. He's the pulse of the fans. His drumbeat is the stadium heartbeat. Each Indian rally, he pounds the old drum. Every Indian home run he salutes with a thunderous ovation. Sitting next to him, the sound was deafening; it echoed through the stadium. Folks in the bleachers joined him. Those miles away behind home plate cheered to the beat. Down in the corners they clapped along and clanged their cowbells. Folks depended on him. If he missed a hit, they let him know. We were talking as Brett Butler slapped a single to right. John wasn't paying attention.

A small group sat ten empty rows in front of us. A couple of fellas turned. "Hey, the drum!"

"Sorry," he yelled back. Excusing himself to me, John hammered away. The group below clapped a little, a girl turned around and thanked him. John loved it.

"Want to give it a try?" he asked me. "Here, gimme your camera and I'll take a picture." I was honored. Positioning myself behind his big drum, my free Tribe visor in place, I grabbed ahold of the drum sticks. Just then Joe Carter drilled a double up the gap in left. I pounded away. People clapped.

"You're better luck than I am." He laughed. I felt like the cowardly lion when the Wizard of Oz gave him back his courage. Shucks, I was speechless.

With John back in the saddle the rally fizzled. He pounded all the way to the last fly out though. Looked like it was gonna drop in. Between batters he just kept on talking. He went on about Cleveland and how he loved it. His bleacher job and how he loved that. He was proud of his accomplishments.

"Yaz hated me," he boasted. "Once the Sox came to town, and the paper quoted Yaz as saying he hated this place. Every time we're here, all I hear is that damned pounding drum. Since then, when Boston's in I play a little louder." Now I know for sure why the Sox fold in Cleveland.

Even more than the city or the Indians or his drum job, John loves baseball. "This is a fantasy world," he told me. "It's a magic land, a place where I can escape. I don't want to hear about strikes, about how much somebody is or isn't getting paid. People don't go to Disneyland to hear how much the help makes. They go to leave it all behind. That's why I am here. If I didn't have this thing"—he pointed to his drum—"I'd still come."

He was right. Baseball is fantasyland. Even in old run-down Municipal Stadium. Beauty really is in the eye of the beholder, not because of a magazine article or some dumb poll. The spirit of a place, a town or a ballpark, lies in the people. Those I met in Cleveland were good people. Municipal, abused by those who'd rather spend summers lounging in the plastic of an artificial stadium, is an honest park. Cleveland's tired, but not dead like I'd thought. And the big lake's a beauty. A sunny afternoon in August on the eve of another strike, I became a convert of John Adams. Baseball anywhere can be beautiful, even in a clumsy-looking, empty warehouse on the shores of lake Erie. Because at Municipal baseball's the only thing special inside. No fancy scoreboards, or flashy food, or even a good team to lure the nonbeliever. Just an honest, unpaid drummer and a lot of seats to choose from. For folks to go they gotta have heart. In Cleveland they do.

26

FULTON COUNTY STADIUM, ATLANTA BRAVES

The End

REPORT CARD

Fulton County Stadium
BASEBALL PARK

August 5,85 vs Dodgers
GAME

Atlanta Braves
BASEBALL CLUB

CATEGORY	GRADE	POINTS
Layout and Upkeep	D	65
Ball Field	C	75
Seating	C	75
Scoreboard	C	75
Food	B	85
Ballpark Employees	D-	60
Facilities	C	75
Atmosphere	D	65
Total Points		575
Average		72

C-
FINAL GRADE

21st
RANK

"Trashy and ill kempt by chain-smoking employees...
Dixie's only real representative is a reminder that the South
has yet to rise again."

PREGAME THOUGHTS

I walked John and Kathleen out to their car. We wished each other well and
said our good-byes. I thanked John again for letting me bang the drum and
asked if he'd please go easy on the Bosox in September—they had enough
problems. He agreed to at least think about it. And with that we maneuvered
our ways out of the boulder-covered lot. I pulled over at the end of the drive,
took one more look at the lake, just to make sure I wasn't dreaming, and hit
the road for Atlanta. On the way to number 26, my last park.

God, I'd been lucky. The strike had held off just long enough. No rain-
outs or sun-outs, although Arlington's 100-pluser was a close call. I hadn't
gotten a speeding ticket anywhere along the way. My butt was even saved once
by a Baltimore cop. I'd driven in midday Queens traffic and postcard-hunted
at midnight in the Bronx. And lived to tell both stories. My round-the-world
KOA reservations had all held up. Gas prices had stayed reasonable, and
McDonald's were everywhere. My Japanese import, its engine, its air conditioner, and, most important, its tape deck were still running smoothly. Things
had gone pretty well. Although not everything had come up roses, it seemed
I remembered only the good stuff. It filed through my mind, ballpark by
ballpark, as I headed for "The End." I daydreamed: if somebody were to follow my lead, become a teacher, see them all, then retire, what things were
musts? What would make the show complete? *Rand McNally* has the perfect
highway guide. I figured I'd create the perfect ballpark guide. To each his
own, but to everybody the following thoughts:

Quick Ballpark Review

Kingdome

Buy a ticket, step inside, then leave. The place is depressing. Instead, hop a
ride on a Washington State Ferry, tune Dave Niehaus and Rick Rizzs in on
the radio, and listen to the M's. If the sun's out while you're in town... say a
prayer of thanks, to whatever god it is you pray to.

Candlestick Park

Bring along an umbrella. And a raincoat. Galoshes, shorts, a tank top, and even some Coppertone. Only God knows how the weather'll turn out. If you watched *Ironsides* when you were a kid, or are a big Dirty Harry fan, prepare for the worst. Beautiful Coit Tower is not the ballpark's press box.

Oakland Coliseum

Get there early. Find the A's Swingers and request "Oh! Susanna." They play it great. If you've a little something to nip on, better bring along five extra glasses. Raise a toast to green and gold. Then prepare to rock 'n' roll the night away. If you like MTV and baseball, you'll love the way they go together in the Coliseum.

Dodger Stadium

Have somebody blindfold you, lead you into the parking lot, and point you toward the ballpark. Take off the blindfold and look up. The view'll take your breath away. Inside, try a couple of tests. One: drop a hot-dog wrapper and see if it's swept up before it hits the ground. Bet it is! Two: keep track on a piece of paper of how many movie stars you see. Better write small.

Anaheim Stadium

Get a good photo of the Big A scoreboard. Make sure it's taken from the back side of the empty third level. Tell the sweet old guy at the gate that you're not gonna mess with anything, you just want a picture. He'll guide you to the best shot in the house... 'cause he's got a soft spot in his heart for that Big A too.

Jack Murphy Stadium

Save that money you were gonna spend flying to Hawaii. The beaches are whiter and the sunshine brighter in San Diego. And the scenery, particularly out at Black's Beach, is eyeball-popping. As for baseball, if Fernando's in town and throwing, go. It'll be festive! If he's not, go anyway. Just remember to bring plenty of coconut oil.

Arlington Stadium

Say "Hi" to any employee—the kids selling stuff at the ballpark or the nice folks at the offices down the street, even one of the security cops lounging around the stadium. Odds are they all will kick back and have a good long chat with you. Also tip the Lady Rangers. They're so cute... and they make only minimum wage.

Astrodome

If you must go, make sure to see somebody hit a home run. Then watch the scoreboard go bonkers. You'll better appreciate life's simpler things.

Royals Stadium

Make sure to bring a couple of extra rolls of film... talk about a photogenic baseball park. From the ridge outside overlooking it, get a few shots of the Royal-emblemed scoreboard and the sea of red plastic seats. Inside, catch the center-field fountains in one of their entertaining salutes to baseball. But whatever you do, don't miss the ground crew's pregame show. Find your seat, relax, and watch the American workers perform like they were trained in Japan ... on plastic even!

Busch Memorial Stadium

Look up at the Arch from inside the ballpark. Look down at the ballpark from inside the Arch. Each is a grand sight. And so you fit in, don't forget to wear something red!

Wrigley Field

First off, plan a home stand, not just a game. Beg, cheat, lie, steal, but see at least one inning from a rooftop out behind the bleachers. You'll think you've died and gone to heaven. Get to the ballpark a couple of hours early and watch it wake up. Bring a ball glove if you want to fight for souvenirs on Waveland, a pin to poke the voodoo doll if the Padres are in town, and a light heart to join with Harry in baseball's best seventh-inning sing-a-long.... Oh, and please don't forget to buy three bags of peanuts from Charley. It'll cost you only a buck.

Kalamazoo, Michigan

Stop in at Paul's Pantry. Welsh a bag of chips and a pop. If Bob's working, be prepared to talk a little Bosox or some Notre Dame football. But please, for decency's sake, don't bring up Bucky Dent.

Metrodome

Ask somebody how much it cost to put the bubble-thing up. Odds are you'll get a half-hour lecture on how public buildings can come in under budget. It may be boring, but listen. The person explaining is probably sincere.

County Stadium

Bring along a hibachi and some charcoal, a few pounds of burger, and an ice chest filled with Old Style. Get to the ballpark at least a couple of hours early and plop down in the middle of the world's greatest open-pit barbecue. Make sure not to get too filled up though. Sausages on the inside are great. . . . If you don't believe me, just ask one of the cooks. He'll give you the most in-depth sausage seminar of all time.

Comiskey Park

Take the El, get there early, and have at least one at McCuddy's. At the ball game be prepared for anything. Stuff your face. Roam around under the stands and check out all the strange sights. Stop out in left field, sit on a picnic table, and razz the other team's outfielder. Then head back up and in and play name-that-tune with Nancy. If the Chisox rally, bang your old wooden chair up and down. Have a great time! And pray that the Sox poke at least one dinger. Then watch all of the South Side light up like it's the Fourth of July.

Riverfront Stadium

Walk around the outer walkway of the upper level. Check out the plodding riverboats below, the bright lights of Cincinnati across the way. Order up the majors' coldest beer, go inside and have a nice, quiet, polite time. If you like the wave, you'll love baseball on the riverfront.

Tiger Stadium

If you have an adventuring spirit. . . drive to the ballpark, pay $5.00, abandon your car in some front yard, and pray that most of it's still there when you return. If you like simple pleasures, get a seat in the upper deck. Stroll out from under the stadium, down your single-file walkway, and be dazzled by the green. Then sit down and order up a ballpark dog from one of the vendors. Make sure to get it with mustard. . . if for no other reason than to watch him slap it on.

Exhibition Stadium

Don't eat anything and you'll probably be okay. Try not to be too hard on the fans for the ugly football field—it's not their fault. And when the "Okay Blue Jays" seventh-inning theme song is played, stand up and sing along. It's kind of cute.

Olympic Stadium

Bring along a transistor radio. If you're English, tune into a French station. If you're French, listen in in English. Or just flip-flop back and forth. Regardless of which station you choose, make sure to buy a lower-box-seat ticket... you'll get major league baseball's prettiest escort.

Fenway Park

Take the subway in, then walk from Kenmore Square. You'll probably be offered a hundred great deals along the way—everything from Italian sausages to pretzels to "a price you can't refuse" on a couple of great box seats. When you reach the park don't go right in—savor the place. Visit the delis and pubs that cover the blocks around it. Find somebody and just talk baseball. Like at Wrigley, stay awhile. And under no circumstances hint that you're a Yankee fan.

Veterans Stadium

Say "Hi" to Nate in the rest room outside section 220. Let him turn on the faucet for you, pull off a paper towel, and dance about. Leave a tip and compliment him on a great Sinatra collection.

Memorial Stadium

If you're late getting there, whatever you do, don't turn right after passing the stadium. Instead look for Officer McCallister. See if he can find you a place to park... the cost will only be "some ink." At the ball game have fun with a very friendly place. Don't miss "The Star-Spangled Banner." And on the way in better practice shouting "O."

Shea Stadium

First off, try to get out of going. If that's not possible, take a course in karate from Chuck Norris. You'll need it just to fight off Shea's "fake cops." Finally, take a helicopter to the game. The drive's too frustrating, the subway ride too scary. If you do get there alive, check out the ball-cap-covered golf carts. They provide the pitcher with the classiest bull-pen ride in all of baseball.

Yankee Stadium

Stand in the memorial garden, behind the center-field wall. Soak in baseball's greatest tradition. Before that, if you dare, tour the Bronx. It'll prove that baseball can survive any element. Just don't bother looking for Yankee Stadium postcards. Believe me, nobody sells 'em!

Three Rivers Stadium

You might want to skip the game. Besides a boring stadium, the Pirates nowadays aren't so great. But Pittsburgh is charming. Spend time roaming about town... you won't find a single steel mill. Just a pleasant city, with pleasant folks... most all of 'em by the way with all of their teeth!

Municipal Stadium

Take a good long look at Lake Erie. Then try to remember that bad reputations don't always tell the real story. At the game try all the seats and stretch out in each. Make sure, though, you end up in the bleachers. Sit with John Adams. Ask him what he thinks about the city of Cleveland and Municipal Stadium. In between drum pounding, he'll let you know that each has an awful lot of heart.

Next stop... Fulton County Stadium

On the drive down think about all the great things that happened to you in the past two months. Put a little Frank and Billy May on the tape player. Maybe "Come Fly With Me." Pop a cold soda, open a bag of Doritos, and tell yourself, "It just don't get no better than this."

And after 11,636 miles, after 30 ball games in 25 ballparks in 51 days, finally, park number 26:

LAYOUT AND UPKEEP: GRADE D

'Bout the only pictures I've ever seen of Atlanta are in history textbooks and were taken back in '64—1864 that is. It didn't look so good. Sherman was on his way through and everything was in flames.

It's my job, teaching ninth-grade American history, to know about the Civil War. Plus it was my favorite subject in college. Sherman, however, was not my favorite general. In fact, he wasn't even on my favorite team. A Confederate at heart, my guys were Jackson, Lee, and Longstreet. So I headed into Dixie pulling for Atlanta. For some reason I felt sorry for it. I assumed it'd still be suffering.

It's not. Atlanta is healthy. It's modern. It's progressive. It has skyscrapers like L.A.'s and a subway cleaner than Boston's. It even has two newspapers, and one in the morning. It's beaten back General Sherman's crunch... and then some. With Fulton County Stadium, a concrete bowl just outside of town, Atlanta has all the good looks of Cincinnati or Pittsburgh.

Shadowed by the Atlanta skyline, and crisscrossed by all sorts of expressways, the ballpark is last in the line of concrete river bowls. The only basic difference between it, Busch, Riverfront, and Three Rivers is that, like Veterans Stadium in Philly, roads instead of water flow by. Everything else is about the same. It's round; not real baseballish-looking. It's enclosed, so that nobody can look in or see out. And it's the home for anybody who wants it to be—baseball, football, soccer, or polo. All the way around the outside it's clean, convenient, and concrete. Seemed like a pretty typical place for me to finish up. At least, unlike my start, I'd end up in a place with stars overhead instead of a ceiling.

An inside priority of the round river stadiums is tidiness. At least at most of 'em. Riverfront and Three Rivers are immaculate. Busch and Veterans, not bad for the tough towns they live in. Fulton County, however, was a dump. An absolute crud-filled pit. Papers littered the aisleways. Junk piled in the corners was begging for a broom. And rest rooms overflowed with garbage. Maybe it was because the players' strike was scheduled to begin after the game. Management might not have wanted to waste manpower sweeping if they thought fans were gonna riot. Maybe Fulton County doesn't have a fire marshall or a health inspector. Or they were on vacation when I was in town. Whatever the case, not since touring the Bronx streets postcard-hunting had I seen such filth. And in the Bronx the Yankees had sense enough to lock it out instead of growing it on the inside.

BALL FIELD: GRADE C

The city of Atlanta was a complete surprise. Not charred and battered like in history texts, it's modern and cosmopolitan. The weather was strange too. I'd expected unbearable heat, but it was really rather pleasant. Even flags on the post offices caught me off guard. They had thirteen stripes and fifty stars. I thought I'd see that big red Southern Cross. But my biggest shock came at the ballpark.

Fulton County Stadium has a grass field! I couldn't believe it. I just assumed its floor would be plastic. Riverfront, Three Rivers, Busch, and Veterans, its four clones, do. Not Atlanta... it's grass!

Not only is the grass real, but the dirt is different too—sweet red Georgia clay. A deep red-brown, it gives the park a little individuality. On the warning track, in fair and foul territory, all around the infield, the dirt almost glows. Its rich color is an eye-catcher.

It's got to be. The rest of the place looks like a goat pasture. Grass pretty much grows where it wants to. Grainy and riddled with pockmarks, its texture's worse than even Cleveland's. And its color is like a tablecloth splattered with spilt mustard, faded between green and yellow-green. Wherever red Georgia clay met green Georgia grass—along the infield edge, at the mound, around home plate, and on the warning track—red got the better of the deal.

It's too bad ballpark grass doesn't grow right in Fulton County. Its combination with the red clay would be striking. It'd give the stadium something other than junky aisles to be remembered by. Best of all, it'd provide Dale Murphy the chance to win a couple of gold gloves to go along with all those gold bats. As patchy as it is now, he'd need a bushel basket to play the hops off that outfield turf.

SEATING: GRADE C

While the grass was surprising, seating was not. As expected, three levels of plastic seats circle the place. As expected, a lot of foul territory pushes even the boxes too far back. As expected, while a body can relax, for most folks the eyes have to strain.

Fulton County is pretty typical of the newer stadiums. Closeness has been traded for comfort. Most seats are way up high in the stadium's third tier, where it's tough to make out much more than uniform numbers. Even at ground level, though, there are problems. Foul territory is everywhere. Since the place is a circle and baseball's played on a diamond, there's a lot of room between field and fans. Close seats are just too far away from fair territory. Heck, so are the dugouts.

The stadium's best seat feature is that it pretty much kills vertical obstruction. The lip of the roof is small and angles up and away from the top of the stands. The lower level is an open porch and juts out to the field. And outfield fences are close. Tickets to their front row are a great deal. In fact, if you like to watch fly balls, the whole ballpark's a pretty good deal. Fulton County skies are usually clear, nothing hangs in the way, and the place serves up its share of homers. Grounders, on the other hand, who knows where they'll end up? A two-hop shot back up the middle and into the pasture might just hit a clump of something and bounce into the right-field stands. Either way, folks get a lot of souvenirs.

SCOREBOARD: GRADE C

While the ball field has all the lush green softness of a suburban mall parking lot, the park itself sounds like a mall music store. Plastic organ music, the kind that salesmen in polyester suits use to lure unsuspecting mall walkers inside their organ shops, dominates the place. Trashy enough in a mall, fake oboes, fake chimes, and fake horns in a baseball park sound ridiculous.

Although earplugs might be necessary for a Braves game, fortunately blinders aren't as well. The scoreboard, despite an awkward placement, is a good one. Half of it's set up normally and for everybody to see. Above the top level in dead center field a giant matrix screen rotates replays and messages. The rest of the stuff, Braves line scores and continual updates from around the majors, gets taken care of below and doesn't have such a normal setup. Panels are attached to the base of the outfield wall below the outfield fans. Only they aren't in play. A chain-link outfield fence sits in front of them. A little awkward to see through, but for the folks in foul territory it works fine.

As for those poor devils in the outfield...well, they have the biggie behind 'em to help with replays. And they can bring along a radio and tune into the game to catch the other scores. Unfortunately there's not a thing they can do about the noise. That 99-instrument calliope just keeps on banging away all night long.

FOOD: GRADE B

Selection: Very Good   Accessibility: Fair
Taste: Very Good   Cost: 4th

After wading through the mess surrounding the concessions—the napkins, the boxes, and piles of crud all over the floor—I guess I just expected that the food would be garbage too. But aside from the intensity of the folks passing it out, it's probably the stadium's finest asset.

Basic baseball eats are decent and cheap. Along with reasonably priced beer and good fresh peanuts, there's enough there to keep you in hot dogs, peanuts, popcorn, and Cracker Jacks all night long. However, if you like things a little more extravagant, that's possible too. The stadium features all sorts of extras that go nicely with a baseball game: chicken fillets, juicy barbecue pork sandwiches, big fat french fries, a few polish sausages, and an abundance of beer. Separate beer express stands pop up all over the place and are as stocked as the food booths.

The concessions' only real drawback is the concessionaires. Slow and uninspired, they seemed a better match to the struggling Braves ball club than the tasty food they were passing out.

BALLPARK EMPLOYEES: GRADE D–

Maybe it was the weather. Maybe the boss was out of town. Maybe in Dixie folks are just too laid back to get into hard work. Regardless, not since Houston's reproduction of *Night of the Living Dead* did I find so many people doing nothing. *Dawn of the Dead*, second in the zombie series, took place in a shopping mall. With the tacky organ music and its employee zombies, the Braves' stadium could've been the location for filming of the sequel.

About halfway through the game I finally figured out why the place was such a pit. Nobody did any cleaning. I felt like Mom must've when I was a kid and she'd stumble into my bedroom. She'd push through the door and I'd hear it: "Robert, you're not going anywhere until this room gets cleaned." Then I'd grumble a little, stuff everything in the closet, and sneak out the back door. After wading through the Braves' stadium walkways, I can see where Mom was coming from. I wanted to scream at somebody to grab a broom and a dustpan, or even a shovel and a barrel, and just make a dent in it. But nobody cared. Like me in my room, workers just plodded around the crap like it wasn't even there.

Not only were employees lethargic, but they smoked like fiends. Everywhere I roamed I saw 'em—along the garbage-covered walkways, up in the stands, even making food in the concessions, employees were lighting up. No other stadium in the majors, not even Houston's, had so many chain-smokers. In fact, most didn't have any. I've got to give 'em credit though. If you're going to have a cig, you might as well enjoy it. They did. Instead of breaking standing up, most were sitting down.

Even ushers puffed away. Stadium ushers are a ball club's real public relations people. They underline the class of a place. And a lot of times represent a cross section of the city's populace. In Milwaukee I decided folks were pleasant because all the ballpark ushers were. At Anaheim orange-and-blue clad ladies and gents were laid back and friendly. So were folks in the stands. Dodger Stadium is pure class. Those that donned the blue at the top of each aisle were a big reason why. In Atlanta they also typify the stadium's work ethic... or lack of one. I needed an usher to point me in the right direction. At the top of a center-field aisle I found one. But he was busy. Kicked back in a chair at the top of his section, he was watching the ball game while he enjoyed a smoke.

The situation is critical. The time is now. It looks like the only way to resurrect Fulton County's work force would be by offering a positive-image lecture-seminar series. The surgeon general could come in and give a talk on the evils of smoking. The fire marshall and health inspector could review all city safety codes. Somebody might also invite over a Dodger Stadium usher to cover the American work ethic.

FACILITIES: GRADE C

For being as close to town as it is, stadium facilities aren't bad. In fact, along with the food and Dale Murphy's home run to at-bat ratio, they're probably one of the few highlights good enough for a Braves media guide.

Expressways crisscross the quarter-mile between the stadium and town. Ballpark access is good. Finding a place to leave the car is also easy. Well-organized parking lots surround the stadium. The lots are well lit and looked after, and most cars are probably safe. Even if they weren't, it'd still be simple getting to a ball game. The subway's immaculate. A five-minute ride from downtown Atlanta, it's one of the majors' tidiest city trains. And probably on game night your last chance to sit in a clean seat.

On the inside, like at all of the concrete bowls, facilities are well built—it almost offsets their lousy care. Rest rooms are easier to find than they are to get around in. Things suspended up off the floor, things that don't need to be swept up after, things like drinking fountains and telephones work fine.

Actually most of the stadium plans have probably been followed through quite well. Only the self-cleaning system, installed to make up for a lazy work force, doesn't work. And as a result the garbage just keeps piling up.

ATMOSPHERE: GRADE D

That first look inside is wonderful! White, circular, and concrete, from the outside Fulton County Stadium looked like all her river-city-park cousins.

Since I'd seen the other four in the past month, I knew what to expect. Wide, efficient concrete walkways, comfortable seats with plenty of space between them, and down in front—plastic grass. When I walked up that typical concrete ramp, under the typical three tiers of plastic chairs, and looked out over the diamond, I was ready for fake grass to glare up at me. I could almost smell it.

Instead it wasn't even green but red that stared back. Deep rich red, and real grass. I was thrilled. It was like driving to the dump, getting out of the car, and being barraged by the scent of fresh lilacs. It didn't matter that the turf had all the lushness of an Iowa cornfield. Or that the green spit and struggled all over the place. The red was gorgeous, absolutely wonderful. Fulton County Stadium's greatest feeling comes, as silly as it may seen, from the very ground it rests on.

After the dirt, though, the place deteriorates and its charm evaporates, drowned out in a circus of garbage and smoke. Well-planned walkways fill up with crap; well-ordered rest rooms ooze with wastepaper. Chain-smoking employees plod about like the junk isn't even there. Meanwhile, circus music fills the air. Clanging away, turned to only God knows what fake instrument, the organist's preludes seemed more in tune to high-wire trapeze acts than a baseball game. And the fans, they just quietly sat around like they didn't know the difference.

Worst, though, the most unbaseballish of all of the stadium character, was its mascot, Chief Nac-a-homa. Or better yet how he was abused. The chief's wigwam sat on a small stand that jutted out above the left-field stands. Just enough room for him, his teepee, and a small walk around it. The chief sat inside, probably cross-legged smoking a peace pipe. At least until a Brave belted a homer. Then he war-danced, hooted, and hollered while he circled his house. I guess the idea was that he please the gods and ask for more. If more came, though, they'd been best to hit 'em in the first three innings. Through the middle innings Nac-a-homa didn't have the room to boogie. Fans waiting for autographs crammed up into his teepee. The line stretched back under the stands, nearly 20 minutes long. In assembly-line fashion, the chief pumped out signatures. At the end of the seventh, doors closed, lines evaporated, and he disappeared. So did his teepee. His only reminder, a message on the scoreboard that he'd be back again next Braves home game.

All this at a place where Henry Aaron broke the game's most renowned record! It's just not baseball. I tried hard to figure out where Nac-a-homa fit in. Why the stadium had such a feature. Why they flooded him with people. Why a kid would spend three innings of a ball game in line for a fake chief's autograph and why a parent would let him. If the Chicken wants to strut out and to the roar of the crowd kick dirt on the umpire's shoes, that's okay. He's funny, he doesn't keep anybody from the game, and he only downgrades chickens. I can even handle the Phillies Phanatic riding his motor scooter all over left field before the game. Just as long as he disappears when it starts. But to watch Nac-a-homa sign autographs for four innings to massive lines of people on a regular Tuesday night game told me folks in the stands didn't have a clue. As apathetic to traditional baseball as the employees were to cleaning up the garbage. Atlanta might just as well bag the Braves and bring in a couple more teepees. Then autographs could be pumped out all night long instead of for just four innings. And Fulton County Stadium might attract more than a few thousand fans a night.

Well, I guess I can only pray that the Nac-a-homa trend doesn't catch on. That Wrigley never cages a real Chicago Cubby and hangs it out over the bleacher bums in center field. Or that the folks in Detroit never decide to leash up a Bengal tiger and train him to jump through flaming hoops. Or—God forbid—that one day somebody in Boston dresses up as a big red sock and leads the Fenway wave. 'Cause if that day should ever come, it'd be time for me to drop baseball and find something with a little more tradition—maybe professional wrestling. My old cronies in Detroit, Chicago, and Boston... they could sign up and join the circus down South.

A FINAL NOTE...

The major league parks are not exactly the same as when I sojourned through them in 1985. In such a technologically dominated world even baseball has trouble resisting change. Huge movie screens, like the one in the Kingdome, have continued to pop up. As of the last pitch in '87, according to *Electronic Display News*, another Diamond Vision in Atlanta and Sony JumboTRONs at Candlestick and Riverfront had been installed. No doubt more are on the way. Menus, too, are in continual flux. Plastic grass gets replaced by newer, but just as plastic, grass—and potholes in parking lots eventually get filled. Even some mascots get their walking papers. For his sake, '85 was Nac-a-homa's last year. And always there's dollars and cents. Food and souvenirs, ticket prices and parking costs, just keep climbing.

At heart, though, the game, the ballparks, and the fans who fill the ballparks aren't really much different today than they were in 1937 when ivy came to Wrigley Field.